PLA...

CRICK...

1978

31st edition

EDITED BY GORDON ROSS

Statistics by Michael Fordham and Geoffrey Saulez

Front cover: Mike Brearley in India. Photo: Patrick Eagar

GILLETTE 'PICK-A-TEAM' COMPETITION
£500 TO BE WON

Prizes 1st: £200   2nd: £100   3rd: £50   4th: £25
Twenty-five runners-up: £5 each.

Plus A selection of Gillette products from the range advertised in this Annual

How to enter: Pick the **Best Gillette Cup Team** from the 40 English and England Test cricketers shown below who have appeared in the Gillette Cup in England, assuming them all to be at the top of their form. Then write in 20 words why you think the Gillette Cup has improved English cricket.

Write the names on the entry form on the opposite page with your name and address and post to the address shown.

Your Choice

Dennis Amiss, Geoff Arnold, Trevor Bailey, Bob Barber, Ken Barrington, Geoff Boycott, Mike Brearley, Tony Buss, Bob Cottam, Brian Close, Colin Cowdrey, Mike Denness, Ted Dexter, Basil D'Oliveira, Bill Edrich, John Edrich, John Flavell, Keith Fletcher, Tom Graveney, Tony Greig, Ray Illingworth, Alan Knott, John Lever, Peter Lever, Tony Lock, Brian Luckhurst, Colin Milburn, J. T. Murray, Chris Old, Jim Parks, John Price, M. J. K. Smith, John Snow, Brian Statham, Fred Titmus, Fred Trueman, Derek Underwood, Bob Willis, Barry Wood, Bob Woolmer.

Rules

Judging: Each entry will be considered by a panel of cricket experts and the entry which, in the opinion of the judges, constitutes the best Gillette Cup Team will be adjudged the winner. The decision of the judges is final and binding; no correspondence will be entered into. Employees of Gillette and Macdonald and Jane's and their families are not eligible to compete.

Proof of Entry: All entries must be on the entry form provided. Proof of posting is not proof of entry.

ISBN 0354 09031 3
© Queen Anne Press
Division of Macdonald and Jane's
(Publishers) Ltd, Paulton House,
8 Shepherdess Walk, London N1.
Printed by C. Nicholls & Company Ltd
The Philips Park Press, Manchester

ENTRY FORM

Your team in batting order, with a captain:

1

2

3

4

5

6

7

8

9

10

11

If you think the Gillette Cup has improved English Cricket, state why, in no more than 20 words.

Closing date: 12.00 noon Wednesday, 6 September 1978

Your name and address:

....

....

....

Post to Gillette Industries Limited
Cricket Competition
Great West Road,
Isleworth, Middlesex.

SUMMER OF DISCONTENT
by Gordon Ross

The summer of 1977 in England was overshadowed by the news during May, that an Australian businessman had signed up 35 of the world's top cricketers to play a series in Australia in the coming winter. That was the beginning of the long-drawn-out Packer Saga which ended in the High Court but with repercussions which will reverberate for months and perhaps years to come. To deal with the developments fully (and they will still be happening after this annual has long since gone to press) would require a dozen or so pages – and these cannot be spared if this annual is to fulfil the function that it has in the thirty previous issues: to record facts and figures of events past on the cricket field. It is sufficient to say that the 35 players swelled to over 50; that it became clear the idea stemmed principally from Mr Packer's anger at not being given rights for his television company from the Australian Board of Control, and that a High Court judge found in his favour when the Test and County Cricket Board took action to ban all his players from appearing in county cricket in England. But no High Court judge could interfere with Test selection, and Australia were swift to act in this direction. Pakistan followed suit, if only under pressure, but perhaps the salient feature of the whole situation was the very poor crowds who watched the Packer matches. This seemed to prove that sport in the late seventies is based, more and more, on partisanship, and that a collection of players, however great their skill in a team game, means very little to a sporting public bred on Australia beating England or Arsenal beating Manchester United. Mr Packer, apparently, is not the man to admit failure. He would rather lose money than pride and it may well be that he will have to accept this option.

Having watched the Australian team in England during the summer there were many cynics who suggested that Mr Packer was welcome to what was generally agreed to be the poorest Australian team ever to come to these shores, and even the most staunch Australian supporter would be hard put to it to deny this opinion. The score was England 3, Australia 0, with two drawn, and the size of England's three victories tells the true story: nine wickets at Old Trafford; seven wickets at Trent Bridge; an innings and 85 runs at Headingley. On the evidence of these five Test matches only Greg Chappell looked a world-class player, and even he showed signs of the strain of carrying Australia's brittle batting almost single-handed. But whatever the strength of the opposition, matches still have to be won, and full credit to England in a series which heralded the triumphant return to Test cricket of Geoff Boycott. He came back at Trent Bridge with 107 and 80 not out, and then at Headingley, before his own folk, he scored an amazing 191, which just happened to be his one hundredth century in first-class cricket, the eighteenth player in the history of cricket to achieve this. This match was also the first time that England had won three successive Tests against Australia this century – the feat was last accomplished in 1886. Boycott had been beaten a little earlier to one hundred centuries by John Edrich, who scored a century in each innings against Kent at the Oval on 27, 28 and 29 July. Boycott's hundred was scored on 11 August. With the limitation of the number of matches played these days in the County Championship (one-day games are still considered not to be first-class) it is unlikely that any player in the future will ever score a hundred hundreds. To those who consider that not to include one-day games in first-class cricket is wrong, it should be mentioned that with bowlers only allowed to bowl a prescribed number of overs, to some extent batting figures are false, and there are also many instances in one-day cricket when wickets have to be sacrificed in the helter-skelter for runs. In Sunday games averages are not a fair picture for bowlers who are restricted in their run-up, which must reduce their efficiency.

With the absence of the Packer players there were new faces in the England party to tour Pakistan and New Zealand and they did at least as well as most sides going to Pakistan where, on the wickets provided, a finish to a match is something of a cricketing event. The unfortunate injury to Brearley opened up the England captaincy for Boycott, a position which, in his heart of hearts, he has always wanted, and which he will take very seriously indeed.

On the domestic front in 1977, the County Championship was shared between Kent and Middlesex, although one event which affected the outcome has led to a change in regulations for 1978. The Middlesex v Somerset Gillette Cup semi-final at Lord's could not be played in the three days allocated, and a Middlesex County Championship match was cancelled the following week to allow another attempt to be made to finish the Gillette game. After three more days of bad weather the Gillette game was played over only 15 overs on the Friday. Kent were kept in the pavilion at Colchester without a ball being bowled in the three days, and had Middlesex fulfilled their Championship fixture over the same period, the same would have happened to them, and Kent would thus have won the Championship. The result is that in the future, Benson & Hedges and Gillette games not finished in the prescribed three days, will be decided on the toss of a coin, and not by a rearranged match.

A feature of the Gillette Cup was the enormous enthusiasm generated in Wales by the great advance into the final made by Glamorgan, whose record in the competition previously was a modest one; they had never before reached a semi-final. As the underdogs they had a lot of neutral support in the final, but Middlesex knew a little too much about Gillette cricket for them. Their efforts must have done a lot for cricket in Wales, and having had the taste of success, they could be back again.

Leicestershire, old hands at this sort of thing, won the John Player League from Essex (always so near yet so far), Gloucestershire, whose previous one-day success had been in the Gillette Cup final, added the Benson & Hedges Trophy to their list of achievements. They beat Kent in the final when Kent had clearly been the favourites, but had never looked like it on the day at 65 for five, in reply to Gloucestershire's 237 for six. Gloucestershire won in the end by 64 runs. Yet the match of the season in the Benson & Hedges was surely Gloucester's semi-final against Hampshire at Southampton when Gloucestershire were 121 for one, but all out for 180, and Hampshire were 18 for four (all four to Procter) and somehow recovered remarkably to get within eight runs of victory – a match only for the stoutest hearts. So in the two semi-finals, Gloucester won by seven runs and Kent by five – a dozen runs in a day when 770 runs were scored in the two games.

Australia v England, 1976-77

CENTENARY TEST MATCH

PLAYED AT MELBOURNE, 12, 13, 14, 16, 17 MARCH
AUSTRALIA WON BY 45 RUNS

AUSTRALIA

I. C. Davis lbw b Lever	5		c Knott b Greig	68
R. B. McCosker b Willis	4		c Greig b Old	25
G. J. Cosier c Fletcher b Lever	10		c Knott b Lever	4
†G. S. Chappell b Underwood	40		b Old	2
D. W. Hookes c Greig b Old	17		c Fletcher b Underwood	56
K. D. Walters c Greig b Willis	4		c Knott b Greig	66
‡R. W. Marsh c Knott b Old	28		not out	110
G. J. Gilmour c Greig b Old	4		b Lever	16
K. J. O'Keeffe c Brearley b Underwood	0		c Willis b Old	14
D. K. Lillee not out	10		c Amiss b Old	25
M. H. N. Walker b Underwood	2		not out	8
Extras (B4, LB2, NB8)	14		(LB10, NB15)	25
Total	**138**		**(9 wkts dec)**	**419**

ENGLAND

R. A. Woolmer c Chappell b Lillee	9		lbw b Walker	12
J. M. Brearley c Hookes b Lillee	12		lbw b Lillee	43
D. L. Underwood c Chappell b Walker	7		b Lillee	7
D. W. Randall c Marsh b Lillee	4		c Cosier b O'Keeffe	174
D. L. Amiss c O'Keeffe b Walker	4		b Chappell	64
K. W. R. Fletcher c Marsh b Walker	4		c Marsh b Lillee	1
†A. W. Greig b Walker	18		c Cosier b O'Keeffe	41
‡A. P. E. Knott lbw b Lillee	15		lbw b Lillee	42
C. M. Old c Marsh b Lillee	3		c Chappell b Lillee	2
J. K. Lever c Marsh b Lillee	11		lbw b O'Keeffe	4
R. G. D. Willis not out	1		not out	5
Extras (B2, LB2, W1, NB2)	7		(B8, LB4, W3, NB7)	22
Total	**95**			**417**

BOWLING

ENGLAND	O	M	R	W		O	M	R	W
Lever	12	1	36	2	...	21	1	95	2
Willis	8	0	33	2	...	22	0	91	0
Old	12	4	39	3	...	27.6	2	104	4
Underwood	11.6	2	16	3	...	12	2	38	1
Greig					...	14	3	66	2
AUSTRALIA									
Lillee	13.3	2	26	6	...	34.4	7	139	5
Walker	15	3	54	4	...	22	4	83	1
O'Keeffe	1	0	4	0	...	33	6	108	3
Gilmour	5	3	4	0	...	4	0	29	0
Chappell					...	16	7	29	1
Walters					...	3	2	7	0

FALL OF WICKETS

	A	E	A	E
	1st	1st	2nd	2nd
1st	11	19	33	28
2nd	13	30	40	113
3rd	23	34	53	279
4th	45	40	132	290
5th	51	40	187	346
6th	102	61	244	369
7th	114	65	277	380
8th	117	78	353	385
9th	136	86	407	410
10th	138	95	—	417

ENGLAND'S ASHES

England regained the Ashes – there is always joy in that, but other events of the summer took some of the thrill out of it. The Packer affair which resulted immediately in the dropping of Greig as England's captain, controversy over whether or not the three 'Packer men', Greig, Knott and Underwood, should even be selected for the Tests, and the belief that it must have had some unspecified psychological and detrimental affect on the play of the Australians, all contrived to take the gilt off the gingerbread. Whether without the Packer affair this Australian side would have done any better is a moot point because with one or two exceptions this was a team of very moderate cricketers, and probably the poorest Australian team ever to come here. Even Greg Chappell, who carried the batting almost single-handed, showed the strain later in the tour and his performance suffered accordingly; although he still managed to finish with a batting average in the Tests of 41. Admittedly, O'Keeffe headed the Test batting averages, but in a rather false position, since he had four not outs in six innings. Whilst he deserves full marks for standing firm this does show the unrealistic aspect of averages.

You have only to look at the Test averages of Australia's accredited batsmen to glean the full story – Hookes 31, McCosker 28, Walters 24, Serjeant 21, Robinson 16. Walters is the great enigma of Test cricket; a prolific run-getter in Test cricket in every country except England, his consistent failures here are hard to explain. His scores in this series in nine innings were: 53, 10, 88, 10, 11, 28, 4, 15, and 4; and the failure of a batsman of his undoubted class must have had an unsettling effect on the younger players trying desperately to establish themselves.

The bowling lacked the fire and pace of Lillee, and well as Thomson bowled he would undoubtedly have bowled that much better had Lillee been at the other end; most fast bowlers have hunted in pairs – Miller and Lindwall, Statham and Trueman – so that opening batsmen have no respite from sheer pace. Pascoe looked good at times, but Max Walker's 14 Test wickets cost him 40 apiece. There was precious little worthwhile spin; Bright taking only 5 Test wickets, and O'Keeffe toiling for 3 wickets which cost him over a hundred each. Marsh, a great wicket-keeper, failed to live up to his flamboyant reputation with the bat.

The first Test at Lord's was more a tale of all-round failures than successes and centred on the batting of Woolmer and Greig, of Chappell and Serjeant, and on the bowling of Willis and Thomson.

Willis bowled magnificently after England's main batting had broken down – Amiss 4, Brearley 9, Greig 5, Barlow 1 and Knott 8 – taking 7 for 78, and enabling England to restrict Australia's lead to 80. Whilst sections of the English batting were in tatters in the second innings (Amiss 0, Randall 0, Barlow 5, Knott 8) his bowling enabled Woolmer and Greig to take England away from possible defeat and to look the better side in the end. This view was amply confirmed at Old Trafford where England won comfortably by nine wickets. Woolmer showed his emergence as a Test batsman with 137 following his 79 and 120 at Lord's. Having dismissed Australia for 297, England built up a huge score of 437 and left Greg Chappell to battle alone for survival; he made more than half of Australia's second innings score of 218. Amiss and Brearley cruised towards victory, Brearley getting out just before it was accomplished.

The decisive Test was the third at Trent Bridge which England won and with two up and two to play could not possibly lose the series, and a win at either Headingley or the Oval would bring the Ashes back home again. The story of Trent Bridge was the return to Test cricket of Geoff Boycott on the highest possible note – 107 and 80 not out. It was just as well. After England had bowled Australia out for 243, England were 82–5 when Alan Knott joined Boycott. Their partnership was the most memorable of the summer – 82–5 rose to 297 for 6 and a final total of 364, Knott making 135. Australia topped 300 in the second innings, relying almost entirely on McCosker's 107, but an opening partnership of 154 by Boycott and Brearley gave England victory.

So to Headingley and Boycott to contend with and the result was a magnificent marathon innings of 191 and an England score of 436. Australia's batting wilted in the face of it and they were shot out for the paltry score of 103 by Hendrick (4 for 41) and Botham (5 for 21), the latter playing in his first Test match. The Australians followed on 333 runs behind and were saved from a heavier defeat only by an innings of 63 by Marsh.

It was now all over. The Oval was academic.

England v. Australia, 1977

FIRST TEST MATCH

PLAYED AT LORD'S, 16, 17, 18, 20, 21 JUNE
MATCH DRAWN

ENGLAND

D. L. Amiss b Thomson	4	b Thomson			0
†J. M. Brearley c Robinson b Thomson	9	c Robinson b O'Keeffe			49
R. A. Woolmer run out	79	c Chappell b Pascoe			120
D. W. Randall c Chappell b Walker	53	c McCosker b Thomson			0
A. W. Greig b Pascoe	5	c O'Keeffe b Pascoe			91
G. D. Barlow c McCosker b Walker	1	lbw b Pascoe			5
‡A. P. E. Knott c Walters b Thomson	8	c Walters b Walker			8
C. M. Old c Marsh b Walker	9	c Walters b Walker			0
J. K. Lever c Pascoe	8	b Marsh b Thomson			3
D. L. Underwood not out	11	not out			12
R. G. D. Willis b Thomson	17	c Marsh b Thomson			0
Extras (B1, LB3, W1, NB7)	12	(B5, LB9, W1, NB2)			17
Total	**216**				**305**

AUSTRALIA

R. D. Robinson b Lever	11	c Woolmer b Old	4
R. B. McCosker b Old	23	b Willis	1
†G. S. Chappell c Old b Willis	66	c Lever b Old	24
C. S. Serjeant c Knott b Willis	81	c Amiss b Underwood	3
K. D. Walters c Brearley b Willis	53	c sub (Ealham) b Underwood	10
D. W. Hookes c Brearley b Old	11	c & b Willis	50
‡R. W. Marsh lbw b Willis	1	not out	6
K. J. O'Keeffe c sub (Ealham) b Willis	12	not out	8
M. H. N. Walker b Willis	4		
J. R. Thomson b Willis	6		
L. S. Pascoe not out	3		
Extras (LB7, W1, NB17)	25	(NB8)	8
Total	**296**	**(6 wkts)**	**114**

BOWLING

AUSTRALIA	O	M	R	W	O	M	R	W
Thomson	20.5	5	41	4	24.4	3	86	4
Pascoe	23	7	53	2	26	2	96	3
Walker	30	6	66	3	35	13	56	2
O'Keeffe	10	3	32	0	15	7	26	1
Chappell	3	0	12	0	2	2	24	0
ENGLAND								
Willis	30.1	7	78	7	10	1	40	2
Lever	19	5	61	1	5	2	40	0
Underwood	25	6	42	0	10	3	16	2
Old	35	10	70	2	14	0	42	2
Woolmer	5	1	20	0				

FALL OF WICKETS

	E	A	E	A
	1st	1st	2nd	2nd
1st	12	25	0	5
2nd	13	51	132	5
3rd	111	135	224	48
4th	121	238	263	64
5th	134	256	286	71
6th	155	264	286	102
7th	165	286	—	—
8th	183	284	286	—
9th	188	290	305	—
10th	216	296	305	—

SECOND TEST MATCH

PLAYED AT OLD TRAFFORD, 7, 8, 9, 11, 12 JULY
ENGLAND WON BY 9 WICKETS

AUSTRALIA

R. B. McCosker c Old b Willis	2	c Underwood b Willis	0
I. C. Davis c Knott b Old	34	c Lever b Willis	12
†G. S. Chappell c Knott b Greig	44	b Underwood	112
C. S. Serjeant lbw b Lever	14	c Woolmer b Underwood	8
K. D. Walters c Greig b Miller	88	lbw b Greig	10
D. W. Hookes c Knott b Lever	5	c Brearley b Miller	28
‡R. W. Marsh c Amiss b Miller	36	c Randall b Underwood	1
R. J. Bright c Greig b Lever	12	& b Underwood	0
K. J. O'Keeffe c Knott b Willis	12	not out	24
M. H. N. Walker b Underwood	9	c Greig b Underwood	6
J. R. Thomson not out	14	c Randall b Underwood	1
Extras (LB15, NB12)	27	(LB1, W1, NB14)	16
Total	**297**		**218**

ENGLAND

D. L. Amiss c Chappell b Walker	11	not out	28
†J. M. Brearley c Chappell b Thomson	6	c Walters b O'Keeffe	44
R. A. Woolmer c Davis b O'Keeffe	137	not out	0
D. W. Randall lbw b Bright	79		
A. W. Greig c & b Walker	76		
‡A. P. E. Knott c O'Keeffe b Thomson	39		
G. Miller c Marsh b Thomson	6		
C. M. Old c Marsh b Walker	37		
J. K. Lever b Bright	10		
D. L. Underwood b Bright	10		
R. G. D. Willis not out	1		
Extras (B9, LB9, NB7)	25	(LB3, NB7)	10
Total	**437**	**(1 wkt)**	**82**

BOWLING

ENGLAND	O	M	R	W	O	M	R	W
Willis	21	8	45	2	16	2	56	2
Lever	25	8	60	3	4	1	11	0
Old	20	3	57	1	8	1	26	0
Underwood	20.2	5	53	1	32.5	13	66	6
Greig	13	4	37	1	12	6	19	1
Miller	10	3	18	2	9	2	24	1

AUSTRALIA	O	M	R	W	O	M	R	W
Thomson	38	11	73	3	8	2	24	0
Walker	54	15	131	3	7	0	17	0
Bright	35.1	11	69	3	5	2	6	0
O'Keeffe	36	11	114	1	9.1	4	25	1
Chappell	6	1	25	0				

FALL OF WICKETS

	A 1st	E 1st	A 2nd	E 2nd
1st	4	19	0	75
2nd	80	23	30	—
3rd	96	165	74	—
4th	125	325	92	—
5th	140	348	146	—
6th	238	366	147	—
7th	246	377	147	—
8th	272	404	202	—
9th	272	435	212	—
10th	297	437	218	—

THIRD TEST MATCH

AUSTRALIA

R. B. McCosker c Brearley b Hendrick	51	c Brearley b Willis	107
I. C. Davis c Botham b Underwood	33	c Greig b Willis	9
†G. S. Chappell b Botham	19	b Hendrick	27
D. W. Hookes c Hendrick b Willis	17	lbw b Hendrick	42
K. D. Walters c Hendrick b Botham	11	c Randall b Greig	28
R. D. Robinson c Brearley b Greig	11	lbw b Underwood	34
‡R. W. Marsh lbw b Botham	0	c Greig b Willis	0
K. J. O'Keeffe not out	48	not out	21
M. H. N. Walker c Hendrick b Botham	0	b Willis	17
J. R. Thomson c Knott b Botham	21	b Willis	0
L. S. Pascoe c Greig b Hendrick	20	c Hendrick b Underwood	0
Extras (B4, LB2, NB6)	12	(B1, LB5, NB17)	24
Total	**243**		**309**

ENGLAND

†J. M. Brearley c Hookes b Pacoe	15	b Walker	81
G. Boycott c McCosker b Thomson	107	not out	80
R. A. Woolmer lbw b Pascoe	0		
D. W. Randall run out	13	not out	19
A. W. Greig b Thomson	11	b Walker	0
G. Miller c Robinson b Pascoe	13		
‡A. P. E. Knott c Davis b Thomson	135	c O'Keeffe b Walker	2
I. T. Botham b Walker	25		
D. L. Underwood b Pascoe	7		
M. Hendrick b Walker	1		
R. G. D. Willis not out	2		
Extras (B9, LB7, W3, NB16)	35	(B2, LB2, W1, NB2)	7
Total	**364**	**(3 wkts)**	**189**

BOWLING

ENGLAND	O	M	R	W		O	M	R	W
Willis	15	0	58	1	...	26	6	88	5
Hendrick	21.2	6	46	2	...	32	14	56	2
Botham	20	5	74	5	...	25	5	60	0
Greig	15	4	35	1	...	9	2	24	1
Underwood	11	5	18	1	...	27	15	49	2
Miller					...	5	2	5	0
Woolmer					...	3	0	3	0
AUSTRALIA									
Thomson	31	6	103	3	...	16	6	34	0
Pascoe	32	10	80	4	...	22	6	43	0
Walker	39.2	12	79	2	...	24	8	40	3
Chappell	8	0	19	0	...				
O'Keeffe	11	4	43	0	...	19.2	2	65	0
Walters	3	0	5	0	...				

FALL OF WICKETS

	A	E	A	E
	1st	1st	2nd	2nd
1st	79	34	18	154
2nd	101	34	60	156
3rd	131	52	154	158
4th	133	64	204	—
5th	153	82	240	—
6th	153	297	240	—
7th	153	326	270	—
8th	155	357	307	—
9th	196	357	308	—
10th	243	364	309	—

FOURTH TEST MATCH

PLAYED AT HEADINGLEY 11, 12, 13, 15 AUGUST
ENGLAND WIN BY AN INNINGS AND 85 RUNS

ENGLAND

†J. M. Brearley c Marsh b Thomson	0
G. Boycott c Chappell b Pascoe	191
R. A. Woolmer c Chappell b Thomson	37
D. W. Randall lbw b Pascoe	20
A. W. Greig b Thomson	43
G. R. J. Roope c Walters b Thomson	34
‡A. P. E. Knott lbw b Bright	57
I. T. Botham b Bright	0
D. L. Underwood c Bright b Pascoe	6
M. Hendrick b Robinson b Pascoe	4
R. G. D. Willis not out	5
Extras (B5, LB9, W3, NB22)	39
Total	**436**

AUSTRALIA

R. B. McCosker run out	27	c Knott b Greig	12
I. C. Davis lbw b Hendrick	0	c Knott b Greig	19
†G. S. Chappell c Brearley b Hendrick	4	c Greig b Willis	36
D. W. Hookes lbw b Botham	24	lbw b Hendrick	21
K. D. Walters c Hendrick b Botham	4	lbw b Woolmer	15
R. D. Robinson c Greig b Hendrick	20	b Hendrick	20
‡R. W. Marsh c Knott b Botham	2	c Randall b Hendrick	63
R. J. Bright not out	9	c Greig b Hendrick	5
M. H. N. Walker c Knott b Botham	7	b Willis	30
J. R. Thomson b Botham	0	b Willis	0
L. S. Pascoe b Hendrick	0	not out	0
Extras (LB3, W1, NB2)	6	(B1, LB4, W4, NB18)	27
Total	**103**		**248**

BOWLING

AUSTRALIA	O	M	R	W	O	M	R	W	FALL OF WICKETS		
									E	A	A
Thomson	34	7	113	4	...				1st	1st	2nd
Walker	48	21	97	0	...						
Pascoe	34.4	10	91	4	...			1st	0	8	31
Walters	3	1	5	0	...			2nd	82	26	35
Bright	26	9	66	2	...			3rd	105	52	63
Chappell	10	2	25	0	...			4th	201	57	97
								5th	275	66	130
ENGLAND								6th	398	77	167
Willis	5	0	35	0	14	7	32	3	7th	398	87	179
Hendrick	15.3	2	41	4	22.5	6	54	4	8th	412	100	244
Botham	11	3	21	5	17	3	47	0	9th	422	100	245
Greig					20	7	64	2	10th	436	103	248
Woolmer				...	8	4	8	1			
Underwood				...	8	3	16	0			

FIFTH TEST MATCH

PLAYED AT THE OVAL, 25, 26, 27, 29, 30 AUGUST
MATCH DRAWN

ENGLAND

†J. M. Brearley c Marsh b Malone	39	c Serjeant b Thomson	4
G. Boycott c Marsh b Malone	39	not out	25
R. A. Woolmer lbw b Thomson	15	c Marsh b Malone	6
D. W. Randall c Marsh b Malone	3	not out	20
A. W. Greig c Bright b Malone	0		
G. R. J. Roope b Thomson	38		
‡A. P. E. Knott c McCosker b Malone	6		
J. K. Lever lbw b Malone	3		
D. L. Underwood b Thomson	20		
M. Hendrick b Thomson	15		
R. G. D. Willis not out	24		
Extras (LB6, W1, NB5)	12	(W2)	2
Total	**214**	**(2 wkts)**	**57**

AUSTRALIA

C. S. Serjeant lbw b Willis	0
R. B. McCosker lbw b Willis	32
†G. S. Chappell c & b Underwood	39
K. J. Hughes c Willis b Hendrick	1
D. W. Hookes c Knott b Greig	85
K. D. Walters b Willis	4
‡R. W. Marsh lbw b Hendrick	57
R. J. Bright lbw b Willis	16
M. H. N. Walker not out	78
M. F. Malone b Lever	46
J. R. Thomson b Willis	17
Extras (B1, LB6, NB3)	10
Total	**385**

BOWLING

AUSTRALIA	O	M	R	W	O	M	R	W
Thomson	23.2	3	87	4	5	1	22	1
Malone	47	20	63	5	10	4	14	1
Walker	28	11	51	1	8	2	14	0
Bright	3	2	1	0	3	2	5	0

ENGLAND	O	M	R	W
Willis	29.3	5	102	5
Hendrick	37	5	93	2
Lever	22	6	61	1
Underwood	35	9	102	1
Greig	8	2	17	1

FALL OF WICKETS

	E	A	E
	1st	1st	2nd
1st	86	0	5
2nd	88	54	16
3rd	104	67	—
4th	104	84	—
5th	106	104	—
6th	122	184	—
7th	130	236	—
8th	169	252	—
9th	174	352	—
10th	214	385	—

15

TEST MATCH AVERAGES

ENGLAND—BATTING AND FIELDING

	M	I	NO	Runs	HS	Avge	100	50	Ct	St
G. Boycott	3	5	2	442	191	147.33	2	1	—	—
R. A. Woolmer	5	8	1	394	137	56.28	2	1	2	—
A. P. E. Knott	5	7	0	255	135	36.42	1	1	12	—
G. R. J. Roope	2	2	0	72	38	36.00	—	—	—	—
D. W. Randall	5	8	2	207	79	34.50	—	2	4	—
A. W. Greig	5	7	0	226	91	32.28	—	2	9	—
J. M. Brearley	5	9	0	247	81	27.44	—	1	7	—
R. G. D. Willis	5	6	4	49	24*	24.50	—	—	2	—
D. L. Underwood	5	6	2	66	20	16.50	—	—	3	—
C. M. Old	2	3	0	46	37	15.33	—	—	2	—
D. L. Amiss	2	4	1	43	28*	14.33	—	—	2	—
I. T. Botham	2	2	0	25	25	12.50	—	—	1	—
G. Miller	2	2	0	19	13	9.50	—	—	—	—
M. Hendrick	3	3	0	20	15	6.66	—	—	5	—
J. K. Lever	3	4	0	24	10	6.00	—	—	2	—

Played in one Test: G. D. Barlow 1, 5.

ENGLAND—BOWLING

	Overs	Mdns	Runs	Wkts	Avge	Best	5 wI	10 wM
R. G. D. Willis	166.4	36	534	27	19.77	7-78	3	—
I. T. Botham	73	16	202	10	20.20	5-21	2	—
M. Hendrick	128.4	33	290	14	20.71	4-41	—	—
D. L. Underwood	169.1	61	362	13	27.84	6-66	1	—
A. W. Greig	77	25	196	7	28.00	2-64	—	—
J. K. Lever	75	22	197	5	39.40	3-60	—	—
C. M. Old	77	14	199	5	39.80	2-46	—	—

Also bowled: G. Miller 24-7-47-3; R. A. Woolmer 16-5-31-1.

AUSTRALIA—BATTING AND FIELDING

	M	I	NO	Runs	HS	Avge	100	50	Ct	St
K. J. O'Keeffe	3	6	4	125	48*	62.50	—	—	3	—
G. S. Chappell	5	9	0	371	112	41.22	1	1	6	—
D. W. Hookes	5	9	0	283	85	31.44	—	2	1	—
R. B. McCosker	5	9	0	255	107	28.33	1	1	5	—
K. D. Walters	5	9	0	223	88	24.77	—	2	5	—
M. H. N. Walker	5	8	1	151	78*	21.57	—	1	1	—
C. S. Serjeant	3	5	0	106	81	21.20	—	1	1	—
R. W. Marsh	5	9	1	166	63	20.75	—	2	9	—
I. C. Davis	3	6	0	107	34	17.83	—	—	2	—
R. D. Robinson	3	6	0	100	34	16.66	—	—	4	—
R. J. Bright	3	5	1	42	16	10.50	—	—	1	—
J. R. Thomson	5	8	1	59	21	8.42	—	—	—	—
L. S. Pascoe	3	5	2	23	20	7.66	—	—	—	—

Played in one Test: K. J. Hughes 1, M. F. Malone 46.

AUSTRALIA—BOWLING

	Overs	Mdns	Runs	Wkts	Avge	Best	5 wI	10 wM
M. F. Malone	57	24	77	6	12.83	5-63	1	—
J. R. Thomson	200.5	44	583	23	25.34	4-41	—	—
L. S. Pascoe	137.4	35	363	13	27.92	4-80	—	—
R. J. Bright	72.1	27	147	5	29.40	3-69	—	—
M. H. N. Walker	273.2	88	551	14	39.35	3-40	—	—

Also bowled: G. S. Chappell 39-5-105-0; K. J. O'Keeffe 100.3-31-305-3; K. D. Walters 6-1-10-0.

TOUR AVERAGES

BATTING AND FIELDING

	M	I	NO	Runs	HS	Avge	100	50	Ct	St
G. S. Chappell	16	25	5	1182	161*	59.10	5	2	18	—
K. J. O'Keeffe	13	19	12	355	48*	50.71	—	—	5	—
R. D. Robinson	14	23	4	715	137*	37.63	1	4	31	—
C. S. Serjeant	15	22	2	663	159	33.15	1	6	2	—
D. W. Hookes	17	26	1	804	108	32.16	1	6	4	—
G. J. Cosier	12	20	1	587	100	30.89	1	4	7	—
I. C. Davis	13	20	0	608	83	30.40	—	5	5	—
K. J. Hughes	14	19	0	540	95	28.42	—	5	10	—
K. D. Walters	17	26	1	663	88	26.52	—	3	8	—
R. J. Bright	14	19	8	287	53*	26.09	—	1	5	—
R. B. McCosker	18	32	1	737	107	23.77	1	4	20	—
R. W. Marsh	17	24	2	477	124	21.68	1	2	30	2
M. H. N. Walker	15	17	2	250	78*	16.66	—	1	2	—
G. Dymock	10	6	5	16	8*	16.00	—	—	2	—
M. F. Malone	10	10	3	95	46	13.57	—	—	4	—
J. R. Thomson	16	17	1	130	25	8.12	—	—	3	—
L. S. Pascoe	11	9	3	44	20	7.33	—	—	—	—

BOWLING

	Overs	Mdns	Runs	Wkts	Avge	Best	5wI	10wM
R. J. Bright	333.5	114	794	39	20.35	5-67	2	—
L. S. Pascoe	323.4	79	893	41	21.78	6-68	1	—
M. H. N. Walker	514	154	1184	53	22.33	7-19	3	—
M. F. Malone	328	95	837	32	26.15	5-63	1	—
J. R. Thomson	385.2	84	1207	43	28.06	4-41	—	—
K. J. O'Keeffe	335.4	112	1035	36	28.75	4-21	—	—
G. Dymock	192	54	468	15	31.20	3-30	—	—
G. S. Chappell	106	28	304	6	50.66	3-45	—	—

Also bowled: G. J. Cosier 16-3-36-0; D. W. Hookes 4-0-18-1; R. B. McCosker 2-1-5-0; R. W. Marsh 1-0-6-0; K. D. Walters 17-5-30-0.

ENGLAND v AUSTRALIA

PRUDENTIAL TROPHY
ONE-DAY MATCHES

Old Trafford: England won by 2 wickets
Australia 169 (Underwood 3–29)
England 173–8 (Walker 3–20)
Man of the Match: R. W. Marsh
Adjudicator: G. Pullar

Edgbaston: England won by 101 runs
England 171 (Chappell 5–20, Cosier 5–18)
Australia 70 (Lever 4–29)
Man of the Match: J. K. Lever
Adjudicator: R. E. S. Wyatt

The Oval: Australia won by 2 wickets
England 242 (Amiss 108, Brearley 78)
Australia 246–8 (Chappell 125*, Robinson 70)
Man of the Match: G. S. Chappell
Adjudicator: P. B. H. May

India v New Zealand, 1976-77

FIRST TEST MATCH

PLAYED AT BOMBAY, 10, 11, 13, 14, 15 NOVEMBER
INDIA WON BY 162 RUNS

INDIA

S. M. Gavaskar c Cairns b Petherick	119	c Burgess b Hadlee	14
A. D. Gaekwad lbw b O'Sullivan	42		
M. Amarnath c O'Sullivan b Hadlee	45	c Roberts b Collinge	30
G. R. Viswanath b Petherick	10	st Lees b Petherick	39
B. P. Patel b Cairns	4	c sub b Collinge	82
A. V. Mankad c & b Hadlee	16	not out	27
S. Madanlal c M. Parker b Hadlee	8	not out	8
S. Venkataraghavan c Turner b Hadlee	3		
‡S. M. H. Kirmani c J. Parker b Petherick	88		
†B. S. Bedi c J. Parker b Cairns	36		
B. S. Chandrasekhar not out	20		
Extras (B2, LB1, NB5)	8	(LB1, NB1)	2
Total	399	(4 wkts dec)	202

NEW ZEALAND

†G. M. Turner c Amarnath b Venkataraghavan	65	c Gavaskar b Madan Lal	6
N. M. Parker c Kirmani b Chandrasekhar	9	c Amarnath b Chandrasekhar	14
J. M. Parker run out	104	b Bedi	7
M. G. Burgess c sub (Ghavri) b Bedi	42	c Gavaskar b Bedi	0
A. D. G. Roberts lbw b Chandrasekhar	2	c Mankad b Bedi	16
‡W. K. Lees c Kirmani b Chandrasekhar	7	b Venkataraghavan	42
R. J. Hadlee c Kirmani b Venkataraghavan	17	c Patel b Bedi	7
B. L. Cairns b Chandrasekhar	12	st Kirmani b Venkataraghavan	1
D. R. O'Sullivan c Venkataraghavan b Bedi	3	not out	7
R. O. Collinge c Kirmani b Venkataraghavan	26	c Madan Lal b Bedi	36
P. J. Petherick not out	0	c Amarnath b Chandrasekhar	1
Extras (B1, LB6, NB4)	11	(B4)	4
Total	298		141

BOWLING

N. ZEALAND	O	M	R	W	O	M	R	W
Collinge	15	5	41	0	...	12	2	45	2
Hadlee	25	5	95	4	...	16	0	76	1
Cairns	34	8	76	2				
Roberts	6	0	27	0	...	6	1	13	0
O'Sullivan	27	9	62	1	...	10	6	21	0
Petherick	31.5	6	90	3	...	16	1	45	1
INDIA								
Madanlal	9	2	27	0	...	6	0	13	1
Amarnath	13	3	33	0	...	3	0	9	0
Bedi	50.3	22	71	2	...	33	18	27	5
Chandrasekhar	44	13	77	4	...	19.2	5	59	2
Venkatarag'n	37	11	79	3	...	19	9	29	2

FALL OF WICKETS	I	NZ	I	NZ
	1st	1st	2nd	2nd
1st	120	37	24	6
2nd	188	143	63	25
3rd	218	220	118	27
4th	218	228	175	27
5th	239	238	—	50
6th	241	239	—	64
7th	247	267	—	67
8th	252	267	—	132
9th	357	298	—	136
10th	399	298	—	141

SECOND TEST MATCH

INDIA

S. M. Gavaskar b O'Sullivan	66	b Hadlee	15
A. D. Gaekwad c Lees b Hadlee	43	not out	77
M. Amarnath b O'Sullivan	70	c N. Parker b Hadlee	8
G. R. Viswanath lbw b Roberts	68	not out	103
B. P. Patel b Petherick	13		
A. V. Mankad lbw b Troup	50		
‡S. M. H. Kirmani c Turner b O'Sullivan	64		
K. Ghavri c Troup b Petherick	37		
S. Venkataraghavan c & b Petherick	27		
†B. S. Bedi not out	50		
B. S. Chandrasekhar not out	10		
Extras (B17, LB4, W1, MB4)	26	(LB4, NB1)	5
Total (9 wkts dec)	524	(2 wkts dec)	208

NEW ZEALAND

†G. M. Turner c Viswanath b Bedi	113	c Venkataraghavan b Bedi	35
G. P. Howarth c Kirmani b Ghavri	19	c Mankad b Venkataraghavan	4
J. M. Parker c Ghavri b Bedi	34	lbw b Bedi	17
M. G. Burgess c Ghavri b Bedi	54	lbw b Venkataraghavan	24
A. D. G. Roberts not out	84	c Mankad b Chandrasekhar	9
‡W. K. Lees b Chandrasekhar	3	not out	49
N. M. Parker b Venkataraghavan	6	lbw b Chandrasekhar	18
R. J. Hadlee b Chandrasekhar	0	c Venkataraghavan b Bedi	10
D. R. O'Sullivan c Chandrasekhar b Venkataraghavan	15	not out	23
G. N. Troup c Amarnath b Venkataraghavan	0		
P. J. Petherick c Kirmani b Chandrasekhar	13		
Extras (LB9)	9	(LB4)	4
Total	350	(7 wkts)	193

BOWLING

N. ZEALAND	O	M	R	W		O	M	R	W
Hadlee	29	2	121	1	...	15	1	56	2
Troup	20	3	69	1	...	10	0	47	0
Roberts	19	5	53	1	...				
Howarth	5	0	21	0	...				
Petherick	45	12	109	3	...	11	0	51	0
O'Sullivan	50	14	125	3	...	16	1	49	0
INDIA									
Ghavri	12	3	16	1	...	6	2	35	0
Amarnath	5	0	23	0	...	4	2	5	0
Bedi	41	12	80	3	...	40	23	42	3
Venkatarag'n	48	9	120	3	...	34	20	46	2
Chandrasekhar	36.5	6	102	3	...	33	15	61	2

FALL OF WICKETS

	I	NZ	I	NZ
	1st	1st	2nd	2nd
1st	79	54	23	43
2nd	193	118	45	59
3rd	196	224	—	86
4th	217	225	—	97
5th	312	241	—	110
6th	341	250	—	114
7th	413	250	—	134
8th	450	291	—	—
9th	493	298	—	—
10th	—	350	—	—

THIRD TEST MATCH

INDIA

S. M. Gavaskar b Cairns	2	st Lees, b O'Sullivan	43
A. D. Gaekwad c Parker b Cairns	0	b Hadlee	11
M. Amarnath c Petherick b Cairns	21	c Morrison b Hadlee	55
G. R. Viswanath st Lees b Hadlee	87	st Lees b O'Sullivan	17
B. P. Patel run out	33	not out	40
A. V. Mankad b Cairns	14	c Burgess b Petherick	21
‡S. M. H. Kirmani lbw b Petherick	44		
K. Ghavri c Petherick b Hadlee	8		
S. Venkataraghavan c sub (Collinge) b Cairns	64		
†B. S. Bedi c Cairns b Hadlee	5		
B. S. Chandrasekhar not out	1		
Extras (B7, LB8, W1, NB3)	19	(B11, LB2, NB1)	14
Total	**298**	**(5 wkts dec)**	**201**

NEW ZEALAND

†G. M. Turner c Kirmani b Chandrasekhar	37	c Amarnath b Chandrasekhar	5
J. F. M. Morrison c Kirmani b Ghavri	7	c Chandrasekhar b Ghavri	1
J. M. Parker c Patel b Ghavri	9	c Kirmani b Chandrasekhar	38
M. G. Burgess b Bedi	40	run out	15
A. D. G. Roberts c Venkataraghavan b Chandrasekhar	1	c Gavaskar b Bedi	0
G. P. Howarth c Venkataraghavan b Bedi	3	c Chandrasekhar b Bedi	18
‡W. K. Lees c Venkatarghavan b Bedi	9	c sub (Madanlal) b Bedi	21
R. J. Hadlee c Gaekwad b Bedi	21	c Amarnath b Bedi	5
B. L. Cairns c Mankad b Bedi	5	not out	8
D. R. O'Sullivan c Venkataraghavan b Chandrasekhar	0	c Patel b Chandrasekhar	21
P. J. Petherick not out	0	lbw b Venkataraghavan	1
Extras (B1, LB2, NB5)	8	(B7, LB1, NB2)	10
Total	**140**		**143**

BOWLING

N. ZEALAND	O	M	R	W	O	M	R	W
Hadlee	21	7	37	3	17	3	52	2
Cairns	33.1	11	55	5	16	2	49	0
Roberts	17	5	32	0	2	0	4	0
Petherick	25	5	77	1	6.5	0	12	1
O'Sullivan	34	9	69	0	20	3	70	2
Howarth	3	1	9	0				
INDIA								
Ghavri	13	3	32	2	8	4	14	1
Amarnath	8	3	17	0	3	1	6	0
Bedi	16.4	4	48	5	22	12	22	4
Chandrasekhar	15	5	28	3	20	4	64	3
Venkatarag'n	2	0	7	0	14	8	27	1

FALL OF WICKETS

	I	NZ	I	NZ
	1st	1st	2nd	2nd
1st	0	17	33	2
2nd	3	37	86	21
3rd	60	91	118	50
4th	137	99	142	53
5th	167	101	201	79
6th	167	103	—	85
7th	181	122	—	103
8th	258	133	—	114
9th	276	136	—	142
10th	298	140	—	143

New Zealand v Australia, 1976-77

FIRST TEST MATCH

PLAYED AT CHRISTCHURCH, 18, 19, 20, 22, 23 FEBRUARY
MATCH DRAWN

AUSTRALIA

A. Turner b Chatfield	3	lbw b D. Hadlee	20
I. C. Davis c G. Howarth b R. Hadlee	34	c Lees b R. Hadlee	22
R. B. McCosker c Parker b D. Hadlee	37	not out	77
†G. S. Chappell c Turner b R. Hadlee	44	c Parker b H. Howarth	0
G. J. Cosier c R. Hadlee	23	run out	2
K. D. Walters c H. Howarth b D. Hadlee	250	not out	20
‡R. W. Marsh c Parker b H. Howarth	2		
G. J. Gilmour b Chatfield	101		
K. J. O'Keeffe run out	8		
D. K. Lillee c R. Hadlee b Chatfield	19		
M. H. N. Walker not out	10		
Extras	21	(B10, NB3)	13
Total	**552**	**(4 wkts dec)**	**154**

NEW ZEALAND

†G. M. Turner c Turner b O'Keeffe	15	c & b O'Keeffe	36
G. P. Howarth c Marsh b O'Keeffe	42	c Marsh b Gilmour	28
B. E. Congdon c Gilmour b Walker	23	not out	107
J. M. Parker c Marsh b O'Keeffe	34	c McCosker b Walker	21
M. G. Burgess c Marsh b Walker	66	c McCosker b Walker	39
G. N. Edwards c Gilmour b O'Keeffe	34	c Marsh b Walker	15
‡W. K. Lees c Marsh b Lillee	14	c Marsh b Lillee	3
R. J. Hadlee c Marsh b O'Keeffe	3	c Cosier b Walker	15
H. J. Howarth b Walker	61	b Lillee	0
D. R. Hadlee not out	37	not out	8
E. J. Chatfield b Lillee	5		
Extras (LB9, W2, NB12)	23	(LB12, W1, NB8)	21
Total	**357**	**(8 wkts)**	**293**

BOWLING

N.ZEALAND	O	M	R	W	O	M	R	W
R. Hadlee	29	1	155	3	13	4	41	1
Chatfield	31	4	125	3	11	1	34	0
D. Hadlee	24.5	1	130	2	3	0	28	1
H. Howarth	19	2	94	1	10	0	37	1
Congdon	7	0	27	0	1	0	1	0
AUSTRALIA								
Lillee	31.2	6	119	2	18	1	70	2
Walker	26	7	66	3	25	6	65	4
Gilmour	10	0	48	0	10	0	48	1
O'Keeffe	28	5	101	5	20	4	56	1
Chappell					11	0	33	0

FALL OF WICKETS

	A	NZ	A	NZ
	1st	1st	2nd	2nd
1st	9	60	37	70
2nd	76	65	67	70
3rd	78	91	68	128
4th	112	189	82	218
5th	205	193	—	238
6th	208	220	—	245
7th	425	223	—	245
8th	454	265	—	260
9th	504	338	—	—
10th	552	357	—	—

SECOND TEST MATCH

PLAYED AT AUCKLAND, 25, 26, 27 FEBRUARY, 1 MARCH
AUSTRALIA WON BY 10 WICKETS

NEW ZEALAND

†G. M. Turner c Marsh b Walker	4	c Walters b Lillee	23
G. P. Howarth c McCosker b Lillee	59	c Turner b Lillee	2
B. E. Congdon c Marsh b Lillee	25	c McCosker b Lillee	1
J. M. Parker c Cosier b Lillee	20	c Turner b Walker	5
M. G. Burgess c Marsh b Walters	1	b Walker	38
‡G. N. Edwards c Lillee b Gilmour	51	c Marsh b Lillee	0
R. J. Hadlee c McCosker b Lillee	44	b Chappell	81
B. L. Cairns b Chappell	2	c Lillee b Walker	7
H. J. Howarth b Walker	4	lbw b Lillee	6
P. J. Petherick c Marsh b Lillee	4	b Lillee	1
E. J. Chatfield not out	0	not out	4
Extras (LB7, NB7)	14	(B4, LB2, NB1)	7
Total	**229**		**175**

AUSTRALIA

I. C. Davis b Chatfield	13	not out	6
A. Turner c Edwards b Cairns	30	not out	20
R. B. McCosker c Edwards b Cairns	84		
†G. S. Chappell run out	58		
G. J. Cosier c & b Cairns	21		
K. D. Walters c Hadlee b Chatfield	16		
‡R. W. Marsh lbw b Hadlee	4		
G. J. Gilmour b Chatfield	64		
K. J. O'Keeffe c Congdon b Hadlee	32		
D. K. Lillee not out	23		
M. H. N. Walker c Turner b Chatfield	9		
Extras (B9, LB9, NB5)	23	(LB1, NB1)	2
Total	**377**	**(0 wkt)**	**28**

BOWLING

AUSTRALIA	O	M	R	W		O	M	R	W
Lillee	17.3	4	51	5	...	16.7	2	72	6
Walker	24	6	60	2	...	17	4	70	3
Gilmour	7	0	56	1	...	1	0	11	0
Chappell	13	4	28	1	...	9	4	15	1
Walters	4	1	20	1	...				
O'Keeffe	1	1	0	0	...				
N. ZEALAND									
Hadlee	28	2	147	2	...	2	0	11	0
Chatfield	27.1	3	100	4	...	1.6	0	15	0
Cairns	28	9	69	3	...				
Congdon	5	1	8	0	...				
H. Howarth	5	1	16	0	...				
Petherick	4	2	14	0	...				

FALL OF WICKETS

	NZ 1st	A 1st	NZ 2nd	A 2nd
1st	6	31	10	—
2nd	63	56	12	—
3rd	112	171	23	—
4th	113	202	31	—
5th	121	217	31	—
6th	177	221	136	—
7th	202	245	162	—
8th	211	338	163	—
9th	228	364	169	—
10th	229	377	175	—

West Indies v Pakistan, 1976-77

FIRST TEST MATCH

**PLAYED AT BRIDGETOWN, 18, 19, 20, 22, 23 FEBRUARY
MATCH DRAWN**

PAKISTAN

Majid Khan b Garner	88	c Garner b Croft	28
Sadiq Mohammad c Croft b Garner	37	c Garner b Croft	9
Haroon Rashid c Kallicharran b Foster	33	b Roberts	39
†Mushtaq Mohammad c Murray b Croft	0	c Murray b Roberts	6
Asif Iqbal c Murray b Croft	36	b Croft	0
Javed Miandad lbw b Garner	2	c Greenidge b Croft	1
Wasim Raja not out	117	c Garner b Foster	71
Imran Khan c Garner b Roberts	20	c Fredericks b Garner	1
Salim Altaf lbw b Garner	19	b Garner	2
Sarfraz Nawaz c Kallicharran b Foster	38	c Murray b Roberts	6
‡Wasim Bari lbw b Croft	10	not out	60
Extras (B5, LB6, W1, NB23)	35	(B29, LB11, NB28)	68
Total	**435**		**291**

WEST INDIES

R. C. Fredericks c & b Sarfraz	24	b Sarfraz	52
C. G. Greenidge c Majid b Imran	47	c Raja b Sarfraz	2
I. V. A. Richards c Salim b Sarfraz	32	c Sadiq b Sarfraz	92
A. I. Kallicharran c Sarfraz b Imran	17	c Bari b Salim	9
†C. H. Lloyd c Sadiq b Salim	157	c Bari b Imran	11
M. L. C. Foster b Sarfraz	15	b Sarfraz	4
‡D. L. Murray c Mushtaq b Imran	52	c Bari b Salim	20
J. Garner b Javed	43	b Salim	0
A. M. E. Roberts c Bari b Salim	4	not out	9
C. Croft not out	1	not out	5
V. A. Holder absent hurt		b Imran	6
Extras (B2, LB6, NB21)	29	(B2, LB7, W1, NB31)	41
Total	**421**	(9 wkts)	**251**

BOWLING

W. INDIES	O	M	R	W	O	M	R	W
Roberts	30	3	124	1	... 25	5	66	3
Croft	31.4	6	85	3	... 15	3	47	4
Holder	4	0	13	0	...			
Garner	37	7	130	4	... 17	4	60	2
Foster	27	13	41	2	... 8	2	34	1
Richards	3	1	3	0	... 2	0	16	0
Fredericks	1	0	4	0	...			
PAKISTAN								
Imran	28	3	147	3	... 32	16	58	2
Sarfraz	29	3	125	3	... 34	10	79	4
Salim	21	3	70	2	... 21	7	33	3
Javed	10.4	3	22	1	... 11	4	31	0
Mushtaq	5	0	27	0	...			
Majid	1	0	1	0	... 1	0	1	0
Asif Iqbal					1	0	8	0

FALL OF WICKETS

	P	WI	P	WI
	1st	1st	2nd	2nd
1st	72	59	29	12
2nd	148	91	68	142
3rd	149	120	102	166
4th	186	134	103	179
5th	207	183	108	185
6th	233	334	113	206
7th	271	404	126	210
8th	355	418	146	217
9th	408	421	158	237
10th	435	—	291	—

SECOND TEST MATCH

PAKISTAN

Batsman	First innings		Second innings	
Majid Khan	lbw b Garner	47	c Kallicharran b Jumadeen	54
Sadiq Mohammad	c & b Croft	17	c Kallicharran b Garner	81
Haroon Rashid	c Lloyd b Croft	4	lbw b Fredericks	7
†Mushtaq Mohammad	c Richards b Croft	9	c Greenidge b Roberts	21
Asif Iqbal	c Murray b Croft	0	b Garner	12
Wasim Raja	b Croft	65	c Garner b Croft	84
Imran Khan	c Fredericks b Jumadeen	1	c Murray b Roberts	35
Intikhab Alam	b Croft	0	b Garner	12
‡Wasim Bari	c Murray b Croft	21	c Fredericks b Roberts	2
Salim Altaf	b Croft	1	not out	0
Iqbal Qasim	not out	0	b Roberts	4
Extras	(B3, LB3, NB9)	15	(B13, LB4, NB11)	28
Total		**180**		**340**

WEST INDIES

Batsman	First innings		Second innings	
R. C. Fredericks	c Sadiq b Mushtaq	120	c Asif b Raja	57
C. G. Greenidge	b Salim	5	c Bari b Imran	70
I. V. A. Richards	b Salim	4	b Imran	30
A. I. Kallicharran	c Bari b Intikhab	37	not out	11
I. T. Shillingford	lbw b Mushtaq	39	c Bari b Imran	2
†C. H. Lloyd	c Haroon b Intikhab	22	not out	23
‡D. L. Murray	b Mushtaq	10		
J. Garner	lbw b Imran	36		
A. M. E. Roberts	b Mushtaq	4		
C. Croft	not out	23		
R. R. Jumadeen	lbw b Imran	0		
Extras	(B5, LB11)	16	(B1, LB11, W1)	13
Total		**316**	**(4 wkts)**	**206**

BOWLING

W. INDIES	O	M	R	W	O	M	R	W
Roberts	17	2	34	0	26	4	85	4
Croft	18.5	7	29	8	25	3	66	1
Garner	16	1	47	1	20.1	6	48	3
Jumadeen	16	3	55	1	35	13	72	1
Fredericks					6	2	14	1
Richards					12	4	27	0
PAKISTAN								
Imran	21	5	50	2	24	8	59	3
Salim	18	3	44	2	21	3	58	0
Intikhab	29	6	90	2	2	1	6	0
Majid	8	3	9	0				
Qasim	10	2	26	0	13	6	30	0
Mushtaq	20	7	50	4	9	1	27	0
Raja	10	1	31	0	5	1	13	1

FALL OF WICKETS

	P	WI	P	WI
	1st	1st	2nd	2nd
1st	10	18	123	97
2nd	21	22	155	159
3rd	21	102	167	166
4th	103	183	181	170
5th	112	216	223	—
6th	150	243	239	—
7th	154	258	315	—
8th	159	270	334	—
9th	161	316	340	—
10th	180	316	340	—

Note: In Pakistan's first innings, Sadiq retired hurt at 6-0 and resumed at 112-5.

THIRD TEST MATCH

PLAYED AT GEORGETOWN, 18, 19, 20, 22 23 MARCH
MATCH DRAWN

PAKISTAN

Batsman	1st innings		2nd innings	
Majid Khan	c Murray b Roberts	23	c Greenidge b Roberts	167
Sadiq Mohammad	c Murray b Garner	12	lbw b Croft	48
Zaheer Abbas	b Garner	0	c Fredericks b Croft	80
Haroon Rashid	c Murray b Croft	32	c & b Garner	60
†Mushtaq Mohammad	c Murray b Julien	41	b Roberts	19
Asif Iqbal	c & b Croft	15	lbw b Garner	35
Wasim Raja	c & b Croft	5	b Garner	0
Imran Khan	c Shillingford b Roberts	47	lbw b Roberts	35
Sarfraz Nawaz	c Kallicharran b Garner	6	c Kallicharran b Fredericks	25
‡Wasim Bari	c Murray b Garner	1	not out	25
Salim Altaf	not out	0	lbw b Garner	6
Extras	(LB5, NB7)	12	(B13, LB7, W1, NB19)	40
Total		**194**		**540**

WEST INDIES

Batsman	1st innings		2nd innings	
R. C. Fredericks	c Majid b Sarfraz	5	not out	52
C. G. Greenidge	b Majid	91	c Haroon b Imran	96
I. V. A. Richards	lbw b Imran	50		
A. I. Kallicharran	lbw b Imran	72		
I. T. Shillingford	c Haroon b Sarfraz	120		
B. D. Julien	b Salim	5		
‡D. L. Murray	c Zaheer b Majid	42		
J. Garner	b Majid	4		
†C. H. Lloyd	c Imran b Majid	14		
A. M. E. Roberts	not out	20		
C. E. Croft	b Mushtaq	6		
Extras	(B1, LB9, W3, NB6)	19	(LB5, NB1)	6
Total		**448**	**(1 wkt)**	**154**

BOWLING

W. INDIES	O	M	R	W		O	M	R	W
Roberts	16.3	3	49	2	...	45	6	174	3
Croft	15	3	60	3	...	35	7	119	2
Garner	16	4	48	4	...	39	8	100	4
Julien	9	2	25	1	...	28	3	63	0
Richards					...	5	0	11	0
Fredericks					...	11.3	2	33	1
PAKISTAN									
Imran	31	6	119	2	...	12.5	0	79	1
Sarfraz	45	16	105	2	...	9	0	58	0
Salim	29	6	71	1					
Asif	4	1	15	0					
Mushtaq	29.3	9	74	1					
Majid	24	9	45	4	...	3	0	11	0

FALL OF WICKETS

	P	WI	P	WI
	1st	1st	2nd	2nd
1st	36	11	219	154
2nd	40	94	304	—
3rd	46	193	311	—
4th	96	244	381	—
5th	125	255	404	—
6th	133	378	417	—
7th	143	390	417	—
8th	174	422	471	—
9th	188	422	491	—
10th	194	448	540	—

FOURTH TEST MATCH

PLAYED AT PORT OF SPAIN, 1, 2, 3, 5, 6 APRIL
PAKISTAN WON BY 266 RUNS

PAKISTAN

Majid Khan c Murray b Croft	92	c Murray b Croft	16
Sadiq Mohammad c Lloyd b Roberts	0	b Inshan	24
Zaheer Abbas b Roberts	14	lbw b Garner	9
Haroon Rashid c Kallicharran b Inshan	11	lbw b Garner	9
†Mushtaq Mohammad c Greenidge b Richards	121	c Fredericks b Roberts	56
Asif Iqbal c Inshan b Roberts	11	c & b Inshan	10
Wasim Raja c & b Inshan	28	c Garner	70
Imran Khan c Greenidge b Inshan	1	c & b Croft	30
Sarfraz Nawaz c Richards b Croft	29	c Lloyd b Croft	51
‡Wasim Bari not out	5	not out	2
Iqbal Qasim b Richards	2		
Extras (B4, LB8, NB15)	27	(B8, LB11, NB3)	22
Total	**341**	**(9 wkts dec)**	**301**

WEST INDIES

R. C. Fredericks b Imran	41	c Majid b Qasim	17
C. G. Greenidge b Qasim	32	c Majid b Sarfraz	11
I. V. A. Richards b Imran	4	st Bari b Mushtaq	33
I. T. Shillingford st Bari b Mushtaq	15	c Qasim b Mushtaq	23
A. I. Kallicharran c Sarfraz b Mushtaq	11	c Asif b Mushtaq	45
J. Garner c Qasim b Mushtaq	0	b Sarfraz	0
†C. H. Lloyd lbw b Imran	22	b Sarfraz	17
‡D. L. Murray lbw b Imran	0	c Sadiq b Raja	30
A. M. E. Roberts c Qasim b Mushtaq	6	c Majid b Raja	35
Inshan Ali c Qasim b Mushtaq	4	c Sadiq b Raja	0
C. E. Croft not out	0	not out	0
Extras (B11, LB2, NB6)	19	(B7, LB1, NB3)	11
Total	**154**		**222**

BOWLING

W. INDIES	O	M	R	W		O	M	R	W
Roberts	25	0	82	3	...	20	2	56	1
Croft	21	4	56	2	...	22.5	6	79	3
Garner	24	6	55	0	...	23	4	71	3
Inshan	32	9	86	3	...	20	2	73	2
Richards	18.3	6	34	2	...				
Fredericks	1	0	1	0	...				
PAKISTAN									
Imran	21	6	64	4	...	21	5	46	0
Sarfraz	10	4	17	0	...	19	10	21	3
Qasim	13	6	26	1	...	20	6	50	1
Mushtaq	10.5	3	28	5	...	31	9	69	3
Raja	1	1	0	0	...	3.5	1	22	3
Majid					...	10	8	3	0

FALL OF WICKETS

	P	WI	P	WI
	1st	1st	2nd	2nd
1st	1	73	25	24
2nd	19	77	46	42
3rd	51	82	58	82
4th	159	106	74	126
5th	191	105	95	148
6th	246	122	211	154
7th	252	125	213	154
8th	320	144	286	196
9th	331	154	301	196
10th	341	154	—	222

FIFTH TEST MATCH

PLAYED AT KINGSTON, 16, 17, 18, 20, 21 APRIL
WEST INDIES WON BY 140 RUNS

WEST INDIES

R. C. Fredericks	c & b Imran	6	c Majid b Raja	83
C. G. Greenidge	c Bari b Sikander	100	c Majid b Sikander	82
I. V. A. Richards	c Bari b Imran	5	b Raja	7
†C. H. Lloyd	c Zaheer b Imran	22	c Asif b Raja	48
A. I. Kallicharran	c Bari b Imran	34	c Majid b Sikander	22
C. L. King	c Bari b Sikander	41	c Majid b Sikander	3
‡D. L. Murray	c Sikander b Imran	31	c Bari b Imran	33
D. A. J. Holford	c Majid b Imran	2	c Bari b Sarfraz	37
J. Garner	c Mushtaq b Sarfraz	9	c Sadiq b Imran	0
A. M. E. Roberts	b Sarfraz	7	c Bari b Sarfraz	2
C. E. Croft	not out	6	not out	12
Extras	(LB9, NB8)	17	(B13, LB7, NB10)	30
Total		**280**		**359**

PAKISTAN

Majid Khan	c Richards b Croft	11	c Fredericks b Croft	4
Sadiq Mohammad	b Roberts	3	c Greenidge b Croft	14
Zaheer Abbas	lbw b Roberts	28	c Richards b Croft	0
Haroon Rashid	c Greenidge b Croft	72	c Greenidge b Garner	31
†Mushtaq Mohammad	c Lloyd b Garner	24	b Garner	17
Asif Iqbal	c Kallicharran b Holford	5	st Murray b Holford	135
Wasim Raja	c King b Holford	13	c Fredericks b Holford	64
Imran Khan	c & b Croft	23	c Lloyd b Holford	22
Sarfraz Nawaz	c Holford b Croft	8	b Garner	9
‡Wasim Bari	returned hurt	0	run out	0
Sikander Bakht	not out	1	not out	0
Extras	(B1, NB9)	10	(B3, NB2)	5
Total		**198**		**301**

BOWLING

PAKISTAN	O	M	R	W	O	M	R	W
Imran	18	2	90	6	27.2	3	78	2
Sarfraz	24.3	5	81	2	27	6	93	2
Sikander	12	0	71	2	16	3	55	3
Asif	4	1	6	0				
Mushtaq	7	2	15	0	11	3	38	0
Raja					21	5	65	3
W. INDIES								
Roberts	14	4	36	2	18	6	57	0
Croft	13.3	1	49	4	20	5	86	3
Garner	9	1	57	1	18.2	0	72	3
Holford	16	3	40	2	18	3	69	3
King	4	2	6	0	3	0	12	0

FALL OF WICKETS

	WI	P	WI	P
	1st	1st	2nd	2nd
1st	6	11	182	5
2nd	22	26	182	9
3rd	56	47	193	32
4th	146	106	222	51
5th	200	122	260	138
6th	229	140	269	253
7th	252	174	335	289
8th	254	190	343	296
9th	268	198	345	301
10th	280	—	359	301

Pakistan v England 1977-78

FIRST TEST MATCH

PLAYED AT LAHORE, 14, 15, 16, 18, 19 DECEMBER
MATCH DRAWN

PAKISTAN

Mudassar Nazar c&b Miller	114	c Taylor b Willis	26
Sadiq Mohammad lbw b Miller	18	b Lever	1
Shafiq Ahmed c Rose b Old	0	lbw b Willis	7
Haroon Rashid c&b Lever	122	not out	45
Javed Miandad c Taylor b Lever	71	not out	19
Wasim Raja c Taylor b Cope	24		
Abdul Qadir lbw b Cope	11		
†‡Wasim Bari c Cope b Miller	17		
Sarfraz Nawaz b Cope	0		
Iqbal Qasim not out	8		
Liaqat Ali not out	0		
Extras (B1, LB4, NB17)	22	(NB8)	8
Total (9 wkts dec)	407	(3 wkts)	106

ENGLAND

G. Boycott b Qasim	63
†J. M. Brearley run out	23
B. C. Rose lbw b Sarfraz	1
D. W. Randall c Qasim b Liaqat	19
G. R. J. Roope b Qasim	19
G. Miller not out	98
C. M. Old c Mudassar b Qasim	2
‡R. W. Taylor b Sarfraz	32
G. A. Cope lbw b Sarfraz	0
J. K. Lever c Wasim Bari b Sarfraz	0
R. G. D. Willis c Qasim b Qadir	14
Extras (B2, LB8, NB7)	17
	288

BOWLING

ENGLAND	O	M	R	W		O	M	R	W	FALL OF WICKETS			
Willis	17	3	67	0	...	7	0	34	2		P	E	P
Lever	16	1	47	2	...	3	0	13	1		1st	1st	2nd
Old	21	7	63	1	...	4	0	18	0	1st	48	53	15
Miller	37	10	102	3	...	10	4	24	0	2nd	49	55	40
Cope	39	6	102	3	...	3	0	7	0	3rd	229	96	45
Boycott	3	0	4	0						4th	329	127	—
Randall						1	0	2	0	5th	356	148	—
PAKISTAN										6th	378	162	—
Sarfraz	34	11	68	4						7th	387	251	—
Liaqat	27	11	43	1						8th	387	251	—
Qadir	32.7	7	82	1						9th	403	253	—
Qasim	32	12	57	3						10th	—	288	—
Wasim Raja	10	2	21	0									

SECOND TEST MATCH

PLAYED AT HYDERABAD, 2, 3, 4, 6, 7 JANUARY
MATCH DRAWN

PAKISTAN

Mudassar Nazar c Edmonds b Cope	27	c Taylor b Willis	66
Sadiq Mohammad c Taylor b Willis	9	c Edmonds b Cope	22
Shafiq Ahmed c Miller b Edmonds	13	not out	27
Haroon Rashid c & b Edmonds	108	c Brearley b Cope	35
Javed Miandad not out	88	not out	61
Wasim Raja c Brearley b Edmonds	0	c Edmonds b Willis	24
Abdul Qadir c Brearley b Cope	4		
†‡Wasim Bari run out	10		
Iqbal Qasim c Roope b Willis	0		
Liaqat Ali c Edmonds b Lever	0		
Sikander Bakht run out	3		
Extras (B4, LB7, NB2)	13	(B13, LB11)	24
Total	**275**	**(4 wks dec)**	**259**

ENGLAND

G. Boycott run out	79	not out	100
†J. M. Brearley c Wasim Bari b Qasim	17	c sub (Hasan Jamil) b Wasim Raja	74
B. C. Rose b Qadir	27		
D. W. Randall c & b Qadir	7		
G. R. J. Roope c & b Qadir	1		
G. Miller c Wasim Bari b Qasim	5		
‡R. W. Taylor b Qadir	0		
P. H. Edmonds c Wasim Bari b Qadir	4		
G. A. Cope c Sadiq b Wasim Raja	22		
J. K. Lever b Qadir	4	not out	0
R. G. D. Willis not out	8		
Extras (B10, LB6, W1)	17	(B4, LB7, NB1)	12
Total	**191**	**(1 wkt)**	**186**

BOWLING

ENGLAND	O	M	R	W	O	M	R	W	FALL OF WICKETS
Willis	16	2	40	2	11	2	26	2					
Lever	16.6	7	41	1	20	2	62	0		1st	1st	2nd	2nd
Edmonds	24	2	75	3	30	6	95	0	1st	14	40	55	185
Cope	14	6	49	2	24	9	42	2	2nd	40	123	116	—
Miller	9	0	57	0	2	0	8	0	3rd	101	137	117	—
Roope					1	0	2	0	4th	213	139	189	—
PAKISTAN									5th	213	142	—	—
Sikander	16	4	35	0	10	3	22	0	6th	222	142	—	—
Liaqat	6	0	18	0	4	1	14	0	7th	247	146	—	—
Qasim	34	11	54	2	24.4	6	42	0	8th	248	152	—	—
Miandad	5	0	21	0	4	0	10	0	9th	249	157	—	—
Qadir	24	8	44	6	27	5	72	0	10th	275	191	—	—
Wasim Raja	1.6	0	2	1	12	5	14	1					

THIRD TEST MATCH

MATCH DRAWN

ENGLAND

†G. Boycott b Qasim	31	c Miandad b Sikander	56
B. C. Rose c Miandad b Sarfraz	10	c Haroon b Qadir	18
D. W. Randall lbw b Qasim	23	b Sikander	55
G. R. J. Roope lbw b Sikander	56	not out	33
M. W. Gatting lbw b Qadir	5	lbw b Qasim	6
G. Miller c Mudassar b Raja	11	c Bari b Qasim	3
‡R. W. Taylor lbw b Qadir	36	not out	18
P. H. Edmonds lbw b Qadir	6		
G. A. Cope b Qasim	18		
J. K. Lever not out	33		
R. G. D. Willis lbw b Qadir	5		
Extras (B3, LB21, NB8)	32	(B9, LB6, W3, NB15)	33
Total	216	(5 wkts)	222

PAKISTAN

Mudassar Nazar c sub (Botham) b Edmonds	76
Shafiq Ahmed c sub (Botham) b Willis	10
Mohsin Hasan Khan c Willis b Cope	44
Haroon Rashid c Taylor b Edmonds	27
Javed Miandad c Roope b Edmonds	23
Wasim Raja c Gatting b Edmonds	47
Abdul Qadir c Roope b Edmonds	21
†‡Wasim Bari lbw b Miller	6
Sarfraz Nawaz c Gatting b Edmonds	0
Iqbal Qasim b Edmonds	8
Sikander Bakht not out	7
Extras (B2, LB3, NB7)	12
Total	281

BOWLING

PAKISTAN	O	M	R	W	O	M	R	W	FALL OF WICKETS			
										E	P	E
Sarfraz	15	6	27	1	28	7	57	0		1st	1st	2nd
Sikander	15	4	39	1	17	4	40	2	1st	17	33	35
Qasim	40	20	56	3	29	11	51	2	2nd	69	121	125
Qadir	40.19		81	4	8	2	26	1	3rd	72	167	148
Raja	13	3	31	1					4th	85	170	162
Mudassar					1	0	1	0	5th	103	230	171
Miandad					2	0	5	0	6th	189	243	—
Shafiq					1	0	1	0	7th	197	263	—
Bari					1	0	2	0	8th	203	263	—
Haroon					1	0	3	0	9th	232	269	—
Mohsin					1	0	3	0	10th	266	281	—
ENGLAND												
Willis	8	1	23	1								
Lever	12	4	32	0								
Edmonds	33	7	66	7								
Cope	28	8	77	1								
Miller	14	0	71	1								

Australia v India 1977- 78
FIRST TEST MATCH
PLAYED AT BRISBANE, 2, 3, 4, 6 DECEMBER
AUSTRALIA WON BY 16 RUNS

AUSTRALIA

Batsman	1st	Dismissal (2nd)	2nd
P. A. Hibbert c Kirmani b Amarnath	13	lbw b Madan Lal	2
G. J. Cosier c Madan Lal b Amarnath	19	c Prasanna b Madan Lal	0
A. D. Ogilvie c Viswanath b Bedi	5	b Chandrasekhar	46
C. S. Serjeant c Gavaskar b Bedi	0	b Amarnath	0
†R. B. Simpson c Gavaskar b Bedi	7	c Viswanath b Amarnath	89
P. M. Toohey st Kirmani b Bedi	82	c Bedi b Chandrasekhar	57
A. L. Mann lbw b Madan Lal	19	c Amarnath b Madan Lal	29
‡S. J. Rixon c Amarnath b Bedi	9	c Kirmani b Madan Lal	6
W. M. Clark c Gavaskar b Chandrasekhar	4	b Madan Lal	12
J. R. Thomson b Chandrasekhar	3	not out	41
A. G. Hurst not out	0	run out	26
Extras (B3, LB1, W1)	5	(B6, LB11, NB2)	19
Total	**166**		**327**

INDIA

Batsman	1st	Dismissal (2nd)	2nd
S. M. Gavaskar c Cosier b Clark	3	c Rixon b Clark	113
D. B. Vengsarkar hit wkt b Thomson	48	b Clark	1
M. Amarnath lbw b Clark	0	c Rixon b Thomson	47
G. R. Viswanath c Hurst b Mann	45	c Ogilvie b Thomson	35
B. P. Patel c Serjeant b Clark	13	b Thomson	3
A. V. Mankad c Rixon b Thomson	0	b Hurst	21
S. Madan Lal b Clark	4	c Rixon b Clark	2
‡S. M. H. Kirmani c Ogilvie b Thomson	11	c Serjeant b Hurst	55
E. A. S. Prasanna c Thomson b Mann	23	c Hibbert b Clark	8
†B. S. Bedi not out	2	not out	26
B. S. Chandrasekhar lbw b Mann	0	c Rixon b Thomson	0
Extras (NB4)	4	(LB6, NB7)	13
Total	**153**		**324**

BOWLING

	O	M	R	W	O	M	R	W
Amarnath	13	4	43	2	8	1	24	2
Madan Lal	10	3	27	1	19	2	72	5
Bedi	13.7	3	55	5	18.5	2	71	0
Prasanna	4	2	2	0	4	0	59	0
Chandrasekhar	6	1	34	2	26	6	82	2
AUSTRALIA								
Thomson	16	1	54	3	19.7	1	76	4
Clark	18	5	46	4	26	1	101	4
Hurst	7	0	31	0	15	3	50	2
Cosier	3	1	6	0	15	1	10	0
Mann	6	0	12	3	13	0	52	0
Simpson					4	0	22	0

FALL OF WICKETS

	A 1st	I 1st	A 2nd	I 2nd
1st	24	11	0	7
2nd	33	15	6	88
3rd	33	90	7	147
4th	43	108	100	151
5th	49	110	184	196
6th	90	112	233	243
7th	107	119	237	251
8th	112	149	246	275
9th	132	151	277	318
10th	166	153	327	324

SECOND TEST MATCH

PLAYED AT PERTH 16, 17, 18, 20, 21 DECEMBER
AUSTRALIA WON BY 2 WICKETS

INDIA

S. M. Gavaskar c Rixon b Clark	4	b Clark	127
C. P. S. Chauhan c Gannon b Simpson	88	c Ogilvie b Thomson	32
M. Amarnath c Gannon b Thomson	90	c Rixon b Simpson	100
G. R. Viswanath b Thomson	38	c Rixon b Clark	1
D. B. Vengsarkar c Rixon b Clark	49	c Hughes b Gannon	9
B. P. Patel c Rixon b Thomson	3	b Gannon	27
†S. M. H. Kirmani c Rixon b Thomson	38	lbw b Gannon	2
S. Venkataraghavan c Simpson b Gannon	37	c Hughes b Gannon	14
S. Madan Lal b Gannon	43	b Thomson	3
†B. S. Bedi b Gannon	3	not out	0
B. S. Chandrasekhar not out	0	not out	0
Extras (B1, LB8)	9	(B1, LB4, NB10)	15
Total	**402**	**(9 wkts dec)**	**330**

AUSTRALIA

J. Dyson c Patel b Bedi	53	c Vengsarkar b Bedi	4
C. S. Serjeant c Kirmani b Madan Lal	13	c Kirmani b Madan Lal	12
A. D. Ogilvie b Bedi	27	b Bedi	47
P. M. Toohey st Kirmani b Bedi	0	c Amarnath b Bedi	83
†R. B. Simpson c Vengsarkar b Venkataraghavan	176	run out	39
‡S. J. Rixon c Kirmani b Amarnath	50	lbw b Bedi	23
K. J. Hughes c Patel b Bedi	28	lbw b Madan Lal	0
A. L. Mann c Vengsarkar b Bedi	7	c Kirmani b Bedi	105
W. M. Clark c Patel b Chandrasekhar	15	not out	5
J. R. Thomson c Amarnath b Venkataraghavan	0	not out	6
J. B. Gannon not out	0		
Extras (LB25)	25	(B8, LB10)	18
Total	**394**	**(8 wkts)**	**342**

BOWLING

AUSTRALIA	O	M	R	W		O	M	R	W
Thomson	24	0	101	4	...	21.5	3	65	2
Clark	17	0	95	2	...	18	1	83	2
Gannon	16.6	1	84	3	...	18	2	77	4
Mann	11	0	63	0	...	8	0	49	0
Simpson	11	0	50	1	...	8	2	41	1
INDIA									
Madan Lal	15	1	54	1	...	11	0	44	2
Amarnath	16	2	57	1	...	3	0	22	0
Chandrasekhar	33.6	2	114	1	...	15	0	87	0
Bedi	31	6	89	5	...	30.2	6	105	5
Venkataragh'n	23	4	55	2	...	28	9	86	0

FALL OF WICKETS

	I 1st	A 1st	I 2nd	A 2nd
1st	14	19	47	13
2nd	163	61	240	33
3rd	224	65	244	172
4th	229	149	283	195
5th	235	250	287	295
6th	311	321	289	296
7th	319	341	327	330
8th	383	388	328	330
9th	391	388	330	—
10th	402	394	—	—

THIRD TEST MATCH

PLAYED AT MELBOURNE, 30, 31 DECEMBER, 2, 3, 4 JANUARY
INDIA WON BY 222 RUNS

INDIA

S. M. Gavaskar c Rixon b Thomson	0	c Serjeant b Gannon	118
C. P. S. Chauhan c Mann b Clark	0	run out	20
M. Amarnath c Simpson b Clark	72	b Cosier	41
G. R. Viswanath c Rixon b Thomson	59	lbw b Clark	54
D. B. Vengsarkar c Simpson b Thomson	37	c Cosier b Clark	6
A. V. Mankad c Clark b Gannon	44	b Clark	38
‡S. M. H. Kirmani lbw b Simpson	29	c Thomson b Mann	29
K. D. Ghavri c Rixon b Gannon	6	c Simpson b Clark	6
E. A. S. Prasanna b Clark	0	c Rixon b Gannon	11
†B. S. Bedi not out	2	not out	12
B. S. Chandrasekhar b Clark	0	lbw b Cosier	0
Extras (LB3, NB4)	7	(LB1, NB7)	8
Total	**256**		**343**

AUSTRALIA

J. Dyson b Ghavri	0	lbw b Bedi	12
G. J. Cosier c Chauhan b Chandrasekhar	67	b Chandrasekhar	34
A. D. Ogilvie lbw b Ghavri	6	c Chauhan b Bedi	0
C. S. Serjeant b Chandrasekhar	85	b Chandrasekhar	17
†R. B. Simpson c Mankad b Chandrasekhar	2	lbw b Chandrasekhar	4
P. M. Toohey c Viswanath b Bedi	14	c Chauhan b Chandrasekhar	14
A. L. Mann c Gavaskar b Bedi	11	c Gavaskar b Chandrasekhar	18
‡S. J. Rixon lbw b Chandrasekhar	11	c&b Chandrasekhar	12
W. M. Clark lbw b Chandrasekhar	3	c Ghavri b Bedi	33
J. R. Thomson c Ghavri b Chandrasekhar	0	c&b Bedi	7
J. B. Gannon not out	0	not out	3
Extras (B6, LB7, NB1)	14	(B6, LB4)	10
Total	**213**		**164**

BOWLING

AUSTRALIA	O	M	R	W		O	M	R	W
Thomson	16	2	78	3	...	18	4	47	0
Clark	19.2	2	73	4	...	29	3	96	4
Gannon	14	2	47	2	...	22	5	88	2
Cosier	12	3	25	0	...	12.7	2	58	2
Simpson	3	1	11	1	...	3	0	22	0
Mann	5	1	15	0	...	4	0	24	1
INDIA									
Ghavri	9	0	37	2	...	4	0	29	0
Gavaskar	2	0	7	0	...				
Bedi	15	2	71	2	...	16.1	5	58	4
Chandrasekhar	14.1	2	52	6	...	20	3	52	6
Prasanna	10	1	32	0	...	8	4	5	0
Amarnath						3	0	10	0

FALL OF WICKETS

	I	A	I	A
	1st	1st	2nd	2nd
1st	0	0	40	42
2nd	0	18	89	42
3rd	105	122	187	52
4th	174	124	198	60
5th	180	166	265	77
6th	234	178	286	98
7th	254	202	294	115
8th	254	211	315	122
9th	256	211	343	151
10th	256	213	343	164

FOURTH TEST MATCH

PLAYED AT SYDNEY, 7, 8, 9, 11, 12 JANUARY
INDIA WON BY AN INNINGS AND 2 RUNS

AUSTRALIA

J. Dyson lbw b Chandrasekhar	26	c & b Chandrasekhar	6
G. J. Cosier b Amarnath	17	b Bedi	68
P. M. Toohey run out	4	c sub (Madan Lal) b Ghavri	85
C. S. Serjeant c Ghavri b Bedi	4	B Prasanna	1
†R. B. Simpson c Kirmani b Chandrasekhar	38	lbw b Prasanna	33
K. J. Hughes b Bedi	17	c Vengsarkar b Bedi	19
A. L. Mann b Bedi	0	c & b Prasanna	0
‡S. J. Rixon lbw b Chandrasekhar	17	c Viswanath b Chandrasekhar	11
W. M. Clark c Gavaskar b Chandrasekhar	0	b Prasanna	10
J. R. Thomson not out	1	b Ghavri	16
J. B. Gannon c Amarnath b Prasanna	0	not out	0
Extras (LB5, NB2)	7	(B5, LB6, NB3)	14
Total	**131**		**263**

INDIA

S. M. Gavaskar c Rixon b Thomson	49
C. P. S. Chauhan c Mann b Clark	42
M. Amarnath c Gannon b Clark	9
G. R. Viswanath b Thomson	79
D. B. Vengsarkar c Rixon b Cosier	48
A. V. Mankad b Thomson	16
‡S. M. H. Kirmani b Cosier	42
K. D. Ghavri c Serjeant b Thomson	64
E. A. S. Prasanna not out	25
†B. D. Bedi not out	1
B. S. Chandrasekhar did not bat	
Extras (LB9, NB12)	21
Total (8 wks dec)	**396**

BOWLING

INDIA	O	M	R	W	O	M	R	W	FALL OF WICKETS		
										A	I	A
Ghavri	7	1	25	0	12.7	3	42	2		1st	1st	2nd
Amarnath	7	4	6	1	5	3	9	0	1st	29	97	26
Chandrasekhar	15	3	30	4	24	8	85	2	2nd	34	102	87
Bedi	13	3	49	3	28	8	62	2	3rd	46	116	88
Prasanna	7.4	2	14	1	29	11	51	4	4th	61	241	106
AUSTRALIA									5th	84	261	171
Thomson	27	8	83	4					6th	84	263	171
Clark	21	3	66	2					7th	125	344	194
Gannon	20	4	65	0					8th	126	395	221
Mann	20	0	101	0					9th	131	—	257
Simpson	4	0	34	0					10th	131	—	263
Cosier	9	1	26	2								

FIFTH TEST MATCH

PLAYED AT ADELAIDE, 28, 29, 30 JANUARY, 1, 2, 3 FEBRUARY
AUSTRALIA WON BY 47 RUNS

AUSTRALIA

G. M. Wood st Kirmani b Chandrasekhar	39	c Vengsarkar b Bedi	8
W. M. Darling c Vengsarkar b Chandrasekhar	65	b Bedi	56
P. M. Toohey c Gavaskar b Chandrasekhar	60	c Kirmani b Prasanna	10
G. N. Yallop c Gavaskar b Amarnath	121	b Bedi	24
†R. B. Simpson c Viswanath b Ghavri	100	lbw b Ghavri	51
G. J. Cosier b Ghavri	1	st Kirmani b Bedi	34
‡S. J. Rixon b Bedi	32	run out	13
B. Yardley c and b Ghavri	22	c Vengsarkar b Ghavri	26
J. R. Thomson c Ghavri b Chandrasekhar	24	c Amarnath b Ghavri	3
W. M. Clark b Chandrasekhar	0	lbw b Ghavri	1
I. W. Callen not out	22	not out	4
Extras (B4, LB14, NB1)	19	(B5, LB15, W3, NB3)	26
Total	**505**		**256**

INDIA

S. M. Gavaskar c Toohey b Thomson	7	c Rixon b Callen	29
C. P. S. Chauhan c Cosier b Clark	15	c Wood b Yardley	32
M. Amarnath c Cosier b Thomson	0	c Callen b Yardley	86
G. R. Viswanath c Rixon b Callen	89	c Simpson b Clark	73
D. B. Vengsarkar c Rixon b Callen	44	c Toohey b Yardley	78
A. D. Gaekwad c Rixon b Callen	27	c and b Yardley	12
‡S. M. H. Kirmani run out	48	b Clark	51
K. D. Ghavri c Simpson b Clark	3	c sub (Hughes) b Callen	23
E. A. S. Prasanna not out	15	not out	10
†B. S. Bedi c sub b Clark	6	c Cosier b Callen	16
B. S. Chandrasekhar c and b Clark	2	c Rixon b Simpson	33
Extras (B4, LB1, NB8)	13	(B6, LB11, NB16)	33
Total	**269**		**445**

BOWLING

INDIA	O	M	R	W	O	M	R	W
Ghavri	22	2	93	3	10.5	2	45	4
Amarnath	12	0	45	1	4	0	12	0
Bedi	34	1	127	1	20	3	53	4
Prasanna	10	1	48	0	34	7	68	1
Chandrasekhar	29.4	0	136	5	14	0	52	0
Gaekwad	5	0	37	0				
AUSTRALIA								
Thomson	3.3	1	12	2				
Clark	20.7	6	62	4	29	6	79	2
Callen	22	0	83	3	33	5	108	5
Cosier	4	3	4	0	13	6	21	0
Yardley	23	6	62	0	43	6	134	4
Simpson	9	0	33	0	23.4	6	70	1

FALL OF WICKETS

	A	I	A	I
	1st	1st	2nd	2nd
1st	89	23	17	40
2nd	110	23	84	79
3rd	230	23	95	210
4th	334	159	107	256
5th	337	166	172	323
6th	406	216	210	348
7th	450	226	214	415
8th	457	249	240	417
9th	458	263	248	442
10th	505	269	256	445

Owing to injury, Thomson could not complete his 4th over.

ENGLAND v PAKISTAN
1954 TO 1974
SERIES BY SERIES

Season		Touring Team Captain	P	E W	P W	D
1954	In England	A. H. Kardar (P)	4	1	1	2
1961–62	In Pakistan	E. R. Dexter (E)	3	1	0	2
1962	In England	Javed Burki (P)	5	4	0	1
1967	In England	Hanif Mohammad (P)	3	2	0	1
1968–69	In Pakistan	M. C. Cowdrey (E)	3	0	0	3
1971	In England	Intikhab Alam (P)	3	1	0	2
1972–73	In Pakistan	A. R. Lewis (E)	3	0	0	3
1974	In England	Intikhab Alam (P)	3	0	0	3
	At Lord's		5	1	0	4
	At The Oval		4	2	1	1
	At Leeds		3	2	0	1
	At Manchester		1	0	0	1
	At Nottingham		3	2	0	1
	At Birmingham		2	1	0	1
	At Karachi		3	0	0	3
	At Lahore		3	1	0	2
	At Dacca		2	0	0	2
	At Hyderabad		1	0	0	1
	In England		18	8	1	9
	In Pakistan		9	1	0	8
	Total		27	9	1	17

HIGHEST INNINGS TOTALS

England

558–6d	at Nottingham	1954
545	at The Oval	1974
544–5d	at Birmingham	1962
507	at Karachi	1961–62
502–7	at Karachi	1968–69
487	at Hyderabad	1972–73
480–5d	at The Oval	1962
440	at The Oval	1967

Pakistan

608–7d	at Birmingham	1971
600–7d	at The Oval	1974
569–9d	at Hyderabad	1972–73
445–6d	at Karachi	1972–73
422	at Lahore	1972–73
404–8	at Karachi	1961–62

LOWEST INNINGS TOTALS

England

130	at The Oval (1st inns.)	1954
143	at The Oval (2nd inns.)	1954
183	at Leeds	1974

Pakistan

87	at Lord's	1954
90	at Manchester	1954
100	at Lord's	1962
114	at Nottingham	1967
131	at Leeds	1962

HIGHEST INDIVIDUAL INNINGS FOR ENGLAND

278	D. C. S. Compton	at Nottingham	1954
205	E. R. Dexter	at Karachi	1961–62
183	D. L. Amiss	at The Oval	1974
182	M. C. Cowdrey	at The Oval	1962
172	E. R. Dexter	at The Oval	1962
165	G. Pullar	at Dacca	1961–62
159	M. C. Cowdrey	at Birmingham	1962
158	D. L. Amiss	at Hyderabad	1972–73
153	T. W. Graveney	at Lord's	1962

A total of 29 centuries have been scored for England.

HIGHEST INDIVIDUAL INNINGS FOR PAKISTAN

274	Zaheer Abbas	at Birmingham	1971
240	Zaheer Abbas	at The Oval	1974
187*	Hanif Mohammad	at Lord's	1967
157	Mushtaq Mohammad	at Hyderabad	1972–73
146	Asif Iqbal	at The Oval	1967
140	Javed Burki	at Dacca	1961–62
138	Javed Burki	at Lahore	1961–62
138	Intikhab Alam	at Hyderabad	1972–73

A total of 18 centuries have been scored for Pakistan.

A CENTURY IN EACH INNINGS OF A MATCH

FOR ENGLAND
NIL

FOR PAKISTAN

111 & 104	Hanif Mohammad	at Dacca	1961–62

A CENTURY ON DEBUT IN ENGLAND v PAKISTAN TESTS

FOR ENGLAND

139	K. F. Barrington	at Lahore	1961–62
159	M. C. Cowdrey	at Birmingham	1962
108*	B. W. Luckhurst	at Birmingham	1971

FOR PAKISTAN

138	Javed Burki	at Lahore	1961–62
274	Zaheer Abbas	at Birmingham	1971

RECORD WICKET PARTNERSHIPS FOR ENGLAND

1st	198	G. Pullar & R. W. Barber at Dacca	1961–62
2nd	248	M. C. Cowdrey & E. R. Dexter at The Oval	1962
3rd	201	K. F. Barrington & T. W. Graveney a Lord's	1967
4th	188	E. R. Dexter & P. H. Parfitt at Karachi	1961–62
5th	192	D. C. S. Compton & T. E. Bailey at Nottingham	1954
6th	153*	P. H. Parfitt & D. A. Allen at Birmingham	1962
7th	159	A. P. E. Knott & P. Lever at Birmingham	1971
8th	99	P. H. Parfitt & D. A. Allen at Leeds	1962
9th	76	T. W. Graveney & F. S. Trueman at Lord's	1962
10th	55	D. L. Underwood & P. L. Pocock at Hyderabad	1972–73

RECORD WICKET PARTNERSHIPS FOR PAKISTAN

1st	122	Hanif Mohammad & Alim-ud-Din at Dacca	1961–62
2nd	291	Zaheer Abbas & Mushtaq Mohammad at Birmingham	1971
3rd	172	Zaheer Abbas & Mushtaq Mohammad at The Oval	1974
4th	153	Javed Burki & Mushtaq Mohammad at Lahore	1961–62
5th	197	Javed Burki & Nasim-ul-Ghani at Lord's	1962
6th	145	Mushtaq Mohammad & Intikhab Alam at Hyderabad	1972–73
7th	51	Saeed Ahmed & Nasim-ul-Ghani at Nottingham	1962
8th	130	Hanif Mohammad & Asif Iqbal at Lord's	1967
9th	190	Asif Iqbal & Intikhab Alam at The Oval	1967
10th	62	Sarfraz Nawaz & Asif Masood at Leeds	1974

HIGHEST RUN AGGREGATE IN A TEST RUBBER FOR:

England in England	453 (Av. 90.60)	D. C. S. Compton	1954
England in Pakistan	406 (Av. 81.20)	D. L. Amiss	1972–73
Pakistan in England	401 (Av. 44.55)	Mushtaq Mohammad	1962
Pakistan in Pakistan	407 (Av. 67.83)	Hanif Mohammad	1961–62

BEST INNINGS BOWLING FIGURES FOR:

England in England	8–51	D. L. Underwood at Lord's	1974
England in Pakistan	5–30	D. A. Allen at Dacca	1961–62
Pakistan in England	6–46	Fazal Mahmood at The Oval	1954
Pakistan in Pakistan	5–112	Antao D'Souza at Karachi	1961–62

TEN WICKETS OR MORE IN A MATCH FOR ENGLAND

13–71	D. L. Underwood at Lord's	1974

TEN WICKETS OR MORE IN A MATCH FOR PAKISTAN

12–99	Fazal Mahmood at The Oval	1954

HIGHEST WICKET AGGREGATE IN A TEST RUBBER FOR:

England in England	F. S. Trueman	22 (Av. 19.95)	1962
England in Pakistan	D. A. Allen	13 (Av. 25.69)	1961–62
Pakistan in England	Fazal Mahmood	20 (Av. 20.40)	1954
Pakistan in Pakistan	Intikhab Alam	15 (Av. 28.55)	1972–73

HIGHEST MATCH AGGREGATE: 1274–25 wkts at Hyderabad 1972–73

LOWEST MATCH AGGREGATE: 509–28 wkts at Nottingham 1967

ENGLAND v NEW ZEALAND
1929-30—1974-75

Season		Touring Team Captain	P	E. W	N.Z. W	D
1929–30	In New Zealand	A. H. H. Gilligan (E)	4	1	0	3
1931	In England	T. C. Lowry (NZ)	3	1	0	2
1932–33	In New Zealand	D. R. Jardine (E)	2	0	0	2
1937	In England	M. L. Page (NZ)	3	1	0	2
1946–47	In New Zealand	W. R. Hammond (E)	1	0	0	1
1949	In England	W. A. Hadlee (NZ)	4	0	0	4
1950–51	In New Zealand	F. R. Brown (E)	2	1	0	1
1954–55	In New Zealand	L. Hutton (E)	2	2	0	0
1958	In England	J. R. Reid (NZ)	5	4	0	1
1958–59	In New Zealand	P. B. H. May (E)	2	1	0	1
1962–63	In New Zealand	E. R. Dexter (E)	3	3	0	0
1965	In England	J. R. Reid (NZ)	3	3	0	0
1965–66	In New Zealand	M. J. K. Smith (E)	3	0	0	3
1969	In England	G. T. Dowling (NZ)	3	2	0	1
1970–71	In New Zealand	R. Illingworth (E)	2	1	0	1
1973	In England	B. E. Congdon (NZ)	3	2	0	1
1974–75	In New Zealand	M. H. Denness (E)	2	1	0	1
		At Lord's	7	3	0	4
		At The Oval	5	2	0	3
		At Manchester	4	2	0	2
		At Leeds	4	3	0	1
		At Birmingham	2	2	0	0
		At Nottingham	2	1	0	1
		At Christchurch	9	4	0	5
		At Auckland	9	3	0	6
		At Wellington	3	2	0	1
		At Dunedin	2	1	0	1
		In England	24	13	0	11
		In New Zealand	23	10	0	13
		Total	47	23	0	24

HIGHEST INNINGS TOTAL

England

593–6d	at Auckland	1974–75
562–7d	at Auckland	1962–63
560–8d	at Christchurch	1932–33
550	at Christchurch	1950–51
548–7d	at Auckland	1932–33
546–4d	at Leeds	1965
540	at Auckland	1929–30
482	at The Oval	1949
463–9	at Lord's	1973
454	at Lord's	1931
451–8d	at Nottingham	1969
440–9d	at Manchester	1949
435	at Birmingham	1965
428–8d	at Wellington	1962–63
424	at Lord's	1937
419	at Leeds	1973
416–4d	at The Oval	1931

New Zealand

551–9d	at Lord's	1973
484	at Lord's	1949
469–9d	at Lord's	1931
440	at Wellington	1929–30
440	at Nottingham	1973
417–8d	at Christchurch	1950–51
413	at Birmingham	1965

LOWEST INNINGS TOTAL

England

181	at Christchurch	1929–30
187	at Manchester	1937
190	at Lord's	1969
221	at Birmingham	1958
222	at Auckland	1965–66
227	at Wellington	1950–51
231	at Christchurch	1970–71
237	at Auckland	1970–71
242	at The Oval	1969
246	at Auckland	1954–55

New Zealand

26	at Auckland	1954–55
47	at Lord's	1958
65	at Christchurch	1970–71
67	at Leeds	1958
74	at Lord's	1958
85	at Manchester	1958
89	at Auckland	1962–63
94	at Birmingham	1958
97	at Nottingham	1973

HIGHEST INDIVIDUAL INNINGS FOR ENGLAND

336*	W. R. Hammond	at Auckland	1932–33
310*	J. H. Edrich	at Leeds	1965
227	W. R. Hammond	at Christchurch	1932–33
216	K. W. R. Fletcher	at Auckland	1974–75
206	L. Hutton	at The Oval	1949
196	G. B. Legge	at Auckland	1929–30
181	M. H. Denness	at Auckland	1974–75
178	K. W. R. Fletcher	at Lord's	1973
164*	D. L. Amiss	at Christchurch	1974–75
163	K. F. Barrington	at Leeds	1965
155	J. H. Edrich	at Nottingham	1959
141	E. R. Dexter	at Christchurch	1958–59
140	W. R. Hammond	at Lord's	1937

A total of 51 centuries have been scored for England.

HIGHEST INDIVIDUAL INNINGS FOR NEW ZEALAND

206	M. P. Donnelly	at Lord's	1949
176	B. E. Congdon	at Nottingham	1973
175	B. E. Congdon	at Lord's	1973
136	C. S. Dempster	at Wellington	1929–30
121	J. M. Parker	at Auckland	1974–75
120	C. S. Dempster	at Lord's	1931
117	J. W. E. Mills	at Wellington	1929–30
116	W. A. Hadlee	at Christchurch	1946–47
116	B. Sutcliffe	at Christchurch	1950–51
116	V. Pollard	at Nottingham	1973
114	B. W. Sinclair	at Auckland	1965–66

A total of 18 centuries have been scored for New Zealand.

A CENTURY ON DEBUT ENGLAND v NEW ZEALAND TESTS:
FOR ENGLAND

122	G. O. Allen	at Lord's	1931
137	L. E. G. Ames	at Lord's	1931
117	H. Sutcliffe	at The Oval	1931
114	J. Hardstaff, junior	at Lord's	1937
121	J. D. Robertson	at Lord's	1949
103	R. T. Simpson	at Manchester	1949
100	P. E. Richardson	at Birmingham	1958
104*	C. A. Milton	at Leeds	1958
126	K. F. Barrington	at Auckland	1962–63
131*	P. H. Parfitt	at Auckland	1962–63
125	B. R. Knight	at Auckland	1962–63
310*	J. H. Edrich	at Leeds	1965
138	D. L. Amiss	at Nottingham	1973
139	A. W. Greig	at Nottingham	1973

FOR NEW ZEALAND

117*	J. W. E. Mills	at Wellington	1929–30

* indicates debut in Test cricket.

RECORD WICKET PARTNERSHIPS FOR ENGLAND

1st	147	L. Hutton & R. T. Simpson at The Oval	1949
2nd	369	J. H. Edrich & K. F. Barrington at Leeds	1965
3rd	245	J. Hardstaff, jun., & W. R. Hammond at Lord's	1937
4th	266	M. H. Denness & K. W. R. Fletcher at Auckland	1974–75
5th	242	W. R. Hammond & L. E. G. Ames at Christchurch	1932–33
6th	240	P. H. Parfitt & B. R. Knight at Auckland	1962–63
7th	149	A. P. E. Knott & P. Lever at Auckland	1970–71
8th	246	L. E. G. Ames & G. O. Allen at Lord's	1931
9th	163*	M. C. Cowdrey & A. C. Smith at Wellington	1962–63
10th	59	A. P. E. Knott & N. Gifford at Nottingham	1973

RECORD WICKET PARTNERSHIPS FOR NEW ZEALAND

1st	276	C. S. Dempster & J. W. E. Mills at Wellington	1929–30
2nd	131	B. Sutcliffe & J. R. Reid at Christchurch	1950–51
3rd	190	B. E. Congdon & B. F. Hastings at Lord's	1973
4th	142	M. L. Page & R. C. Blunt at Lord's	1931
5th	177	B. E. Congdon & V. Pollard at Nottingham	1973
6th	117	M. G. Burgess & V. Pollard at Lord's	1973
7th	104	B. Sutcliffe & V. Pollard at Birmingham	1965
8th	104	D. A. R. Moloney & A. W. Roberts at Lord's	1937
9th	64	J. A. Cowie & T. B. Burtt at Christchurch	1946–47
10th	57	F. L. H. Mooney & J. A. Cowie at Leeds	1949

HIGHEST RUN AGGREGATE IN A TEST RUBBER:—

England in England	469 (Av. 78.16)	L. Hutton	1949
New Zealand in England	462 (Av. 77.00)	M. P. Donnelly	1949
England in New Zealand	563 (Av. 563.00)	W. R. Hammond	1932–33
New Zealand in New Zealand	341 (Av. 85.25)	C. S. Dempster	1929–30

BEST INNINGS BOWLING FIGURES FOR:—

England in England	7–32	D. L. Underwood (Lord's)	1969
New Zealand in England	6–67	J. A. Cowie (Manchester)	1937
England in New Zealand	7–75	F. S. Trueman (Christchurch)	1962–63
New Zealand in New Zealand	6–76	R. S. Cunis (Auckland)	1970–71

TEN WICKETS IN A MATCH FOR ENGLAND

12–97	D. L. Underwood at Christchurch	1970–71
12–101	D. L. Underwood at The Oval	1969
11–65	G. A. R. Lock at Leeds	1955
11–70	D. L. Underwood at Lord's	1969
11–84	G. A. R. Lock at Christchurch	1958–59
10–149	A. W. Greig at Auckland	1974–75

TEN WICKETS IN A MATCH FOR NEW ZEALAND

10–140	J. A. Cowie at Manchester	1937

HIGHEST WICKET AGGREGATE IN A TEST RUBBER

England in England	34 (Av. 7.47)	G. A. R. Lock	1958
New Zealand in England	20 (Av. 19.45)	A. R. MacGibbon	1958
England in New Zealand	17 (Av. 9.34)	K. Higgs	1965–66
	17 (Av. 12.05)	D. L. Underwood	1970–71
New Zealand in New Zealand	10 (Av. 15.10)	R. O. Collinge	1970–71
	10 (Av. 18.90)	R. S. Cunis	1970–71

HIGHEST MATCH AGGREGATE at Lord's, 1931, 1293–34 wkts.

LOWEST MATCH AGGREGATE at Lord's, 1958, 390–30 wkts.

John Edrich scored his 99th century in Surrey's penultimate match in 1976, but it was not until his 12th match and 21st innings in 1977, on July 12th, that he became the 17th batsman to score 100 centuries in first-class cricket. The other 16 batsmen were Bradman, Compton, Hutton, Hammond, Sutcliffe, Hendren, Hobbs, Sandham, Mead, Ames, E. Tyldesley, Graveney, Woolley, Cowdrey, Hayward and Grace. These players were soon to be joined by Geoffrey Boycott who reached his 100th hundred in an England v Australia Test match at Leeds, a ground on which Boycott scored 13 of his centuries.

Only one century was scored by a University player at Oxford and Cambridge during the 1977 season – 149 by Hignell, although four other Cambridge players reached the nineties, a feat altogether beyond Oxford.

MIDDLESEX
Achieve their first Gillette success

The Gillette Cup in 1977 will be remembered rather more for
the matches that were not played on schedule than for those
which were. New records of the wrong sort were set up with
the semi-finals at Swansea and Lord's. At Swansea, there
was no play on the first day and it took the other two days
for Glamorgan to beat Leicestershire. At Lord's, not a ball
was bowled during the three days allocated for the match;
neither was play possible on the first two days of a hurriedly
arranged match a week later, and on the final day, only a
fifteen-overs' match was played. The decision to play only
fifteen overs was strongly condemned in many quarters,
and whilst it is, in a competition of this nature, certainly a
totally unsatisfactory way of deciding on the entrant into the
final, the weather forecast was bad on that sixth day, and
although in the event the day turned out fine at Lord's, rain
was falling quite heavily as near to the ground as Kilburn
whilst play was actually in progress. The only possible
alternative would have been the toss of a coin which would
have been a travesty of a great competition. Overall, out
of the twenty-one Gillette Cup matches, eight were not
started and finished on their appointed day. In the previous
heat-wave summer not a moment was lost because of
weather in any of the twenty-one matches.

Controversy over the fifteen-overs' match should not be
allowed to detract from the performance of Middlesex,
although Somerset may well have every reason to argue to
the contrary. Middlesex were a finely balanced side in both
one-day and three-day competitions, and in the first round
of the Gillette Cup they had beaten Kent, who finally
shared the County Championship with them, at Canterbury; a creditable performance, especially as Shepherd
scored a hundred for Kent. After disposing of Warwickshire,
they then faced a total of 248 to win set them by Hampshire
– and they got the runs for the loss of only three wickets. In
the final there was rarely a minute's doubt that they would
beat Glamorgan.

Glamorgan, of course, were the big surprise of the competition. They had never before progressed beyond the
quarter-finals – and that not very often – and they did not

43

have, by any means, an easy path to the final, winning at Worcester, and then beating Surrey at Cardiff and Leicestershire at Swansea. They also contrived an historic moment in the final, when Mike Llewellyn hit a prodigious six, the ball striking the commentary box above the top balcony in the pavilion; few of the devotees among those sitting near could remember such a blow. It was a courageous innings by Llewellyn – if only he could have stayed a little longer who knows what might have happened.

Kent's defeat by Middlesex at Canterbury with only one ball still to be bowled was the only cliff-hanger of the first round. At Southampton, the complete reverse happened when Hampshire, set to make 216 by Nottinghamshire, got the runs without losing a single wicket with Greenidge 106 not out and Richards 101 not out.

The second round was the round for surprises: Derbyshire won by nine wickets at Hove; Surrey won by four wickets at Old Trafford where Lancashire had become almost invincible in Gillette Cup cricket; Glamorgan won at Worcester; and although Northants were the Gillette Cup holders at the time, when Gloucester scored 241–5 at Bristol they looked nearly home and dry – but they were not. It was hardly a surprise that Leicestershire won at Southend, as Essex have been one of the most disappointing sides in Gillette Cup cricket, but the same could be said, of course, of Leicestershire.

The quarter-finals could have gone either way and any result could have been expected – Hampshire might have won at Lord's; Derbyshire might have beaten Somerset at Ilkeston; Surrey might have won at Cardiff; the holders might have beaten Leicester at Northampton. But they all went the other way leaving Glamorgan, Leicestershire, Middlesex and Somerset for the ill-fated semi-finals.

Despite the unreliable weather, six centuries were scored, exactly the same number as in the fine summer of 1976. The 1977 centurians were: David Gower 117 not out for Leicester v Hertfordshire; Gordon Greenidge 106 not out and Barry Richards 101 not out for Hampshire against Notts; John Shepherd 101 for Kent against Middlesex; Mike Smith 123 for Middlesex against Hampshire and Brian Rose 128 for Somerset against Derbyshire. As for the bowlers, Wilkinson's 5 for 24 for Durham against the then holders, Northants at Northampton, was one of the best pieces of bowling of the Gillette summer.

THE GILLETTE CUP 1978

FIRST ROUND

Matches to be played on 5 July
Devon v Staffordshire at Torquay
Sussex v Suffolk at Hove
Yorkshire v Durham at Middlesbrough
Worcestershire v Derbyshire at Worcester
Somerset v Warwickshire at Taunton
Shropshire v Surrey at Wellington

SECOND ROUND

Matches to be played on 19 July
Devon or Staffordshire v Sussex or Suffolk
Northamptonshire v Kent at Northampton
Leicestershire v Hampshire at Leicester
Yorkshire or Durham v Nottinghamshire
Lancashire v Gloucestershire at Old Trafford
Glamorgan v Somerset or Warwickshire at Cardiff
Essex v Shropshire or Surrey at Colchester
Worcestershire or Derbyshire v Middlesex
Quarter-finals 2 August; semi-finals 16 August:
final at Lord's 2 September.

1977 RESULTS

Previous Man of the Match Awards are given in brackets where relevant.

FIRST ROUND—29 JUNE

Lancashire v Cornwall at Truro
Lancashire 180–8 in 60 overs (Wood 49, Toseland 3–27, Halfyard 3–30)
Cornwall 62 (Lee 4–7)
Result: Lancashire won by 118 runs.
Man of the Match: B. Wood (6)
Adjudicator: C. J. Barnett.

Bedfordshire v Northumberland at Luton
Bedfordshire 111 in 57.4 overs
Northumberland 112–1 in 36.3 overs (Woodford 56*)
Result: Northumberland won by 9 wickets.
Man of the Match: J. D. Woodford.
Adjudicator: W. J. Edrich.

Leicestershire v Hertfordshire at Leicester
Leicestershire 313–5 in 60 overs (Gower 117*)
Hertfordshire 159–9 in 60 overs (Osman 54, Ottley 54*, Balderstone 4–33)
Result: Leicestershire won by 154 runs.
Man of the Match: D. I. Gower.
Adjudicator: C. Washbrook.

Northamptonshire v Durham at Northampton
Durham 151 in 58.2 overs (Birtwistle 59, Sarfraz 3–27, Hodgson 3–18)
Northamptonshire 152–7 in 57.4 overs (Williams 51, Wilkinson 5–24)
Result: Northamptsonshire won by 3 wickets.
Man of the Match: J. S. Wilkinson.
Adjudicator: K. F. Barrington.

Hampshire v Nottinghamshire at Southampton

Nottinghamshire 215 in 58.4 overs (Hassan 79, Rice 4–37)
Hampshire 220–0 in 45.1 overs (Greenidge 106*, Richards 101*)
Result: Hampshire won by 10 wickets.
Man of the Match: C. G. Greenidge (2).
Adjudicator: Gordon Ross.

29, 30 JUNE

Kent v Middlesex at Canterbury

Kent 226 in 60 overs (Asif 59, Shepherd 101, Jones 5–23)
Middlesex 227–8 in 59.5 overs
Result: Middlesex won by 2 wickets.
Man of the Match: J. N. Shepherd.
Adjudicator: J. C. Laker.

SECOND ROUND—13 JULY

Essex v Leicestershire at Southend

Leicestershire 225–7 in 60 overs (Davison 99)
Essex 138 in 53.1 overs (Steele 5–19)
Result: Leicestershire won by 87 runs.
Man of the Match: J. F. Steele (2).
Adjudicator: W. J. Edrich.

Sussex v Derbyshire at Hove

Sussex 169–8 in 60 overs (Barlow 3–33)
Derbyshire 173–1 in 51.3 overs (Wright 87*, Barlow 70*).
Result: Derbyshire won by 9 wickets.
Man of the Match: E. J. Barlow (2).
Adjudicator: J. T. Murray.

Worcestershire v Glamorgan at Worcester

Worcestershire 213–9 in 60 overs (Humphries 58, Cordle 4–42)
Glamorgan 217–6 in 60 overs (Francis 62*, Llewellyn 52)
Result: Glamorgan won by 4 wickets.
Man of the Match: M. J. Llewellyn.
Adjudicator: C. Washbrook.

13, 14 JULY

Gloucestershire v Northamptonshire at Bristol

Gloucestershire 241–5 in 60 overs (Hignell 85*, Hodgson 3–48)
Northamptonshire 244–8 in 59.2 overs (Mushtaq 89, Steele 61, Procter 3–36)
Result: Northamptonshire won by 2 wickets.
Man of the Match: Mushtaq Mohammad (2).
Adjudicator: R. T. Simpson.

Middlesex v Warwickshire at Lord's

Middlesex 221–7 in 60 overs (Brearley 82)
Warwickshire 190 in 57.2 overs (Brown 41)
Result: Middlesex won by 31 runs.
Man of the Match: J. M. Brearley (2).
Adjudicator: K. F. Barrington.

Lancashire v Surrey at Old Trafford

Lancashire 193 in 60 overs (C. H. Lloyd 86)
Surrey 194–6 in 51.5 overs (Intikhab 42*)
Result: Surrey won by 4 wickets.
Man of the Match: C. H. Lloyd.
Adjudicator: J. C. Laker.

14 JULY

Hampshire v Yorkshire at Bournemouth

Hampshire 261 in 60 overs (Jesty 69, Greenidge 54)
Yorkshire 175 in 53.3 overs (Rice 5–35)
Result: Hampshire won by 86 runs.
Man of the Match: J. M. Rice.
Adjudicator: C. J. Barnett.

Somerset v Northumberland at Taunton

Northumberland 153–8 in 60 overs
Somerset 154–5 in 38.4 overs (Botham 91*)
Result: Somerset won by 5 wickets.
Man of the Match: I. T. Botham.
Adjudicator: T. W. Graveney.

QUARTER-FINALS—3 AUGUST

Middlesex v Hampshire at Lord's

Hampshire 247–7 in 60 overs (Jesty 54*, Rock 50)
Middlesex 248–3 in 55.5 overs (Smith 123, Radley 94)
Result: Middlesex won by 7 wickets.
Man of the Match: M. J. Smith (2).
Adjudicator: K. F. Barrington.

Derbyshire v Somerset at Ilkeston

Somerset 248–4 in 60 overs (Rose 128)
Derbyshire 189 8n 54.5 overs (Garner 5–30)
Result: Somerset won by 59 runs
Man of the Match: B. C. Rose.
Adjudicator: R. T. Simpson.

Glamorgan v Surrey at Cardiff

Surrey 199 in 59.2 overs (Edrich 53)
Glamorgan 200–6 in 56.2 overs (Jones 54, King 55)
Result: Glamorgan won by 4 wickets.
Man of the Match: A. Jones (2).
Adjudicator: C. J. Barnett.

Northamptonshire v Leicestershire at Northampton

Northanamptonshire 228–9 in 60 overs (Cook 95)
Leicestershire 231–5 in 57.3 overs (Davison 80, Balderstone 54)
Result: Leicestershire won by 5 wickets.
Man of the Match: G. Cook.
Adjudicator: J. D. Robertson.

SEMI-FINALS—18, 19 AUGUST

Glamorgan v Leicestershire at Swansea

Leicestershire 172–7 in 60 overs
Glamorgan 175–5 in 57.3 overs (Hopkins 63)
Result: Glamorgan won by 5 wickets.
Man of the Match: J. A. Hopkins.
Adjudicator: C. J. Barnett.

26 AUGUST

Somerset v Middlesex at Lords

Somerset 59 in 14.4 overs (Daniel 4–24, Selvey 3–32)
Middlesex 61–4 in 11.3 overs (Garner 4–27)
Result: Middlesex won a 15-over match by 6 wickets.
Man of the Match: W. W. Daniel.
Adjudicator: Gordon Ross.

THE GILLETTE CUP FINAL
MIDDLESEX V GLAMORGAN

Played at Lord's 3 September. Middlesex won by 5 wickets

GLAMORGAN

†A. Jones	lbw b Selvey	18
J. A. Hopkins	b Edmonds	47
C. L. King	c Barlow b Selvey	8
R. C. Ontong	c Gould b Gatting	0
M. J. Llewellyn	c Gatting b Featherstone	62
G. Richards	b Edmonds	3
‡E. W. Jones	run out	11
M. A. Nash	c Gatting b Featherstone	3
A. E. Cordle	not out	8
T. W. Cartwright	st Gould b Featherstone	3
A. H. Wilkins	did not bat	
Extras (B7, LB5, W2)		14
Total (60 overs) (9 wkts)		**177**

MIDDLESEX

†J. M. Brearley	c E. Jones b Nash	0
M. J. Smith	lbw b Cartwright	22
C. T. Radley	not out	85
M. W. Gatting	c Hopkins b King	15
G. D. Barlow	lbw b Richards	27
N. G. Featherstone	b Nash	3
P. H. Edmonds	not out	9
‡I. J. Gould		
J. E. Embury	} did not bat	
M. W. W. Selvey		
W. W. Daniel		
Extras (B6, LB11)		17
Total (55.4 overs) (5 wkts)		**178**

BOWLING

MIDDLESEX	O	M	R	W		FALL OF WICKETS	
						G	M
Daniel	11	0	41	0			
Selvey	12	4	22	2	1st	21	0
Gatting	7	1	28	1	2nd	47	45
Edmonds	12	3	23	2	3rd	50	72
Emburey	12	2	32	0	4th	115	146
Featherstone	6	0	17	3	5th	129	153
GLAMORGAN					6th	163	—
Nash	12	3	31	2	7th	163	—
Cordle	8.4	1	29	0	8th	171	—
Cartwright	12	2	32	1	9th	177	—
King	5	1	19	1	10th	—	—
Richards	12	2	23	1			
Wilkins	6	0	27	0			

Man of the Match: C. T. Radley (2).
Adjudicator: B. L. d'Oliveira

GILLETTE CUP
PRINCIPAL RECORDS

Highest innings total: 371–4 off 60 overs, Hampshire v Glamorgan (Southampton) 1975.

Highest innings total by a Minor County: 224–7 off 60 overs, Buckinghamshire v Cambridgeshire (Cambridge) 1972.

Highest innings total by a side batting second: 287–6 off 59 overs, Warwickshire v Glamorgan (Birmingham) 1976.

Highest innings total by a side batting first and losing: 283–3 off 60 overs, Glamorgan v Warwickshire (Birmingham) 1976.

Lowest innings total: 41 off 20 overs, Cambridgeshire v Buckinghamshire (Cambridge) 1972; 41 off 19.4 overs, Middlesex v Essex (Westcliff) 1972; 41 off 36.1 overs, Shropshire v Essex (Wellington) 1974.

Lowest innings total by a side batting first and winning: 98 off 56.2 overs, Worcestershire v Durham (Chester-le-Street) 1968.

Highest individual innings: 177 C. G. Greenidge, Hampshire v Glamorgan (Southampton) 1975.

Highest individual innings by a Minor County player: 132 G. Robinson, Lincolnshire v Northumberland (Jesmond) 1971.

Record Wicket Partnerships

1st	227	R. E. Marshall & B. L. Reed, Hampshire v Bedfordshire (Goldington)	1968
2nd	223	M. J. Smith & C. T. Radley, Middlesex v Hampshire (Lord's)	1977
3rd	160	B. Wood & F. C. Hayes, Lancashire v Warwickshire (Birmingham)	1976
4th	169	M. J. Harris & G. S. Sobers, Nottinghamshire v Somerset (Nottingham)	1970
5th	135	J. F. Harvey & I. R. Buxton, Derbyshire v Worcestershire (Derby)	1972
6th	105	G. S. Sobers & R. A. White, Nottinghamshire v Worcestershire (Worcester)	1974
7th	107	D. R. Shepherd & D. A. Graveney, Gloucestershire v Surrey (Bristol)	1973
8th	69	S. J. Rouse & D. J. Brown, Warwickshire v Middlesex (Lord's)	1977
9th	87	M. A. Nash & A. E. Cordle, Glamorgan v Lincolnshire (Swansea)	1974
10th	45	A. T. Castell & D. W. White, Hampshire v Lancashire (Manchester)	1970

Hat-tricks:	J. D. F. Larter, Northamptonshire v Sussex (Northampton)	1963
	D. A. D. Sydenham, Surrey v Cheshire (Hoylake)	1964
	R. N. S. Hobbs, Essex v Middlesex (Lord's)	1968
	N. M. McVicker, Warwickshire v Lincolnshire (Birmingham)	1971

Seven wickets in an innings: 7–15 A. L. Dixon, Kent v Surrey (The Oval) 1976

P. J. Sainsbury (Hampshire) 7–30 in 1965 and R. D. Jackman (Surrey) 7–33 in 1970 have also achieved this feat.

Most 'Man of the Match' awards: 6 B. L. D'Oliveira (Worcestershire), C. H. Lloyd (Lancashire) and B. Wood (Lancashire); 5 M. C. Cowdrey (Kent), A. W. Greig (Sussex).

73 centuries have been scored in the competition.

WINNERS OF THE 1977 GILLETTE 'PICK A TEAM' COMPETITION

Readers were asked to pick the best Gillette Cup team from a list of 40 overseas cricketers who have played in the competition, assuming them all to be at the top of their form. The winning selection was: Barry Richards (1), Gordon Greenidge (2), Rohan Kanhai (3), Clive Lloyd (4), Gary Sobers (5) (Captain), Viv Richards (6), Mike Procter (7), Farokh Engineer (8), Keith Boyce (9), Andy Roberts (10), Lance Gibbs (11). The batting order is in brackets.

1st Prize: £200 Neil Hargreaves, 19 Ditchling Crescent, Brighton BN1 8GD; Second Prize: £100 R. E. Bennett, 21 Wyndham Street, Riverside, Cardiff; Third Prize: £50 Miss G. E. Pearse, 6 Bramble Close, Kettering, Northants; Fourth Prize: £25 Paul Relf, 28 Haling Park Road, South Croydon, Surrey CR2 6NE; 25 Runners-up: £5 each Miss Meryl Davies, 46 Dagger Lane, West Bromwich, West Midlands; M. Campbell, Barrow Hill, Overton Lane, Arlingham, Gloucestershire; I. D. Haigh, 5 Strachan Gardens, Edinburgh EH4 3RY; David Collins, 249 Ilchester Crescent, Bedminster Down, Bristol; C. S. Adams, 4 Edmonton Way, Oakham, Rutland, Leicestershire LE15 6JE; Keith Bayley, 'Tynebank', 66 Sutton Avenue, Seaford, Sussex BN25 4LN; Dr John Hillier, Brierton School, Catcote Road, Hartlepool, Cleveland; Nigel Hughes, 165 The Greenway, Epsom, Surrey KT18 7JD; John Read, 'Mees', Seagrove Manor Road, Seaview, Isle of Wight PO34 5HW; N. P. Challis, 9 Downend Road, Fareham, Hants; Laurence Butcher, 15 Lucastes Avenue, Haywards Heath, Sussex; R. L. Collins, 26 Stangate Road, Strood, Kent ME2 2TU; M. R. Fenez, 6 Westpoint, 49 Putney Hill, SW15 6RU; D. P. Mayes, 20 Chestnut Drive, Leigh, Lancs; G. W. Jones, 29 Sidmonton Gardens, Off Convent Avenue, Bray, Co. Wicklow, Eire; H. Jones, Westfa, 8 Yniscedwyn Road, Ystradgynlais, Nr. Swansea SA9 1BE; K. McConnell, 21 Cranmore Gardens, Belfast BT9 6JL; Kenneth J. Hosking, 'Hambledon', 26 Kings Road, Binstead, Near Ryde, Isle of Wight; D. Plested, 7 Faulkner Way, Downley, High Wycombe, Bucks; A. G. Edwards, 26 Copley Lodge, Bishopston, Swansea; Brian Slough, 95 Beatrice Road, Kettering, Northants; M. M. Camp, 23 Headley Road, Billericay, Essex; Timothy Bellman, 24 Cranbrook Drive, Whitton, Twickenham TW2 6HN; Barry Lear, 2 Broad Green Avenue, Burgess Hill, W. Sussex RH15 0HA; M. H. Wheeler, 21 Little Breach, Chichester, Sussex PO19 4TY.

Each prize carries with it a selection of Gillette products.

GLOUCESTER WIN THE BENSON AND HEDGES

Gloucestershire, who had previously won the Gillette Cup on their first appearance in a final at Lord's, repeated the performance in this Benson and Hedges final against a much more experienced one-day side – Kent, who surprisingly were rarely given a look in. Gloucestershire – at one time, 144 for one wicket – perhaps didn't build the huge total which seemed quite likely, but the 237 they did score was far too much for Kent who, after a disastrous start, never looked even remotely likely to get near their target. Two wickets were down for 5, and 5 for 65, only Shepherd, coming in at number seven playing any sort of innings in support of Woolmer who had batted on despite the disasters all round him; Woolmer's 64 and Shepherd's 55 were virtually the sum total of Kent's batting in reply to a Gloucester score of 237. Stovold's innings of 71, with Zaheer's 70, laid the foundation for the match-winning score, and then Stovold snapped up three catches behind the wicket to round off an outstanding day which earned him the Gold Award.

The matches which really set the blood tingling in this competition were the two semi-finals; Kent scrambling home by five runs, and Gloucestershire by seven. Gloucester must have thought that their 180 at Southampton (they had been 106 for no wicket) would not have been nearly enough against Hampshire, with Richards and Greenidge in full cry, but a shattering piece of pace bowling by Procter ripped the heart out of the Hampshire innings; the first wicket fell at 13, and then three more went down at 18. Turner and Cowley fought bravely to recover to 127 for 5; now Hampshire were back in the hunt and they went down in the end only eight short of what would have been an outstanding victory. Conversely, Kent must have been reasonably satisfied with their total of 211 at Northampton, even more so when Northants were 39 for 3, but Steele, Larkins and Sarfraz accepted the challenge, and at 206 for 7 had run out of overs; it was as close as that. Procter's bowling at Southampton and Woolmer's batting at Northampton won them the Gold Awards.

Glamorgan and Middlesex who were later to meet in the Gillette final each headed their particular group.

BENSON & HEDGES CUP FINAL
GLOUCESTERSHIRE v KENT
PLAYED AT LORD'S 16 JULY
GLOUCESTERSHIRE WON BY 64 RUNS

GLOUCESTERSHIRE

Sadiq Mohammad	c Hills b Woolmer	24
‡A. W. Stovold	c Underwood b Shepherd	71
Zaheer Abbas	c Shepherd b Jarvis	70
†M. C. Procter	c Knott b Julien	25
J. C. Foat	not out	21
D. R. Shepherd	b Jarvis	9
D. A. Graveney	c Underwood b Julien	1
M. J. Vernon	not out	3
M. D. Partridge	} did not bat	
J. H. Shackleton		
B. M. Brain		
Extras (LB7, W2, NB4)		13
Total (55 overs) (6 wkts)		237

KENT

R. A. Woolmer	c Shackleton b Graveney	64
G. S. Clinton	b Brain	0
C. J. C. Rowe	c Stovold b Procter	0
†Asif Iqbal	c Stovold b Vernon	5
A. G. E. Ealham	c Stovold b Vernon	11
B. D. Julien	b Graveney	1
J. N. Shepherd	c Procter b Brain	55
‡A. P. E. Knott	c Zaheer b Partridge	14
R. W. Hills	c Procter b Shackleton	6
D. L. Underwood	b Brain	8
K. B. S. Jarvis	not out	0
Extras (LB7 NB2)		9
Total (47.3 overs)		173

Gold Award: A. W. Stovold (3)
Adjudicator: F. S. Trueman.

BOWLING					FALL OF WICKETS		
KENT	O	M	R	W		G	K
Jarvis	11	2	52	2		*1st*	*1st*
Julien	11	0	51	2	1st	79	4
Shepherd	11	0	47	1	2nd	144	5
Woolmer	11	0	42	1	3rd	191	24
Underwood	11	1	32	0	4th	204	64
GLOUCESTERSHIRE					5th	220	65
Procter	7	1	15	1	6th	223	100
Brain	7.3	5	9	3	7th	—	122
Vernon	11	1	52	2	8th	—	150
Shackleton	10	0	40	1	9th	—	166
Graveney	9	2	26	2	10th	—	173
Partridge	3	0	22	1			

BENSON & HEDGES CUP
PRINCIPAL RECORDS

Highest innings total: 327–4 off 55 overs, Leicestershire v Warwickshire (Coventry) 1972.

Highest innings total by a side batting second: 282 off 50.5 overs, Gloucestershire v Hampshire (Bristol) 1974.

Highest innings total by a side batting first and losing: 268–5 off 55 overs, Leicestershire v Worcestershire (Worcester) 1976.

Lowest completed innings total: 62 off 26.5 overs, Gloucestershire v Hampshire (Bristol) 1975.

Highest individual innings: 173* C. G. Greenidge, Hampshire v Minor Counties (South) (Amersham) 1973.

50 centuries have been scored in the competition.

Record Wicket Partnerships

1st	199	M. J. Harris & B. Hassan, Nottinghamshire v Yorkshire (Hull) 1973.
2nd	285*	C. G. Greenidge & D. R. Turner, Hampshire v Minor Counties (South) (Amersham) 1973.
3rd	227	M. E. J. C. Norman & B. F. Davison, Leicestershire v Warwickshire (Coventry) 1972.
	227	D. Lloyd & F. C. Hayes- Lancashire v Minor Counties (North) (Manchester) 1973.
4th	165*	Mushtaq Mohammad & W. Larkins, Northamptonshire v Essex (Chelmsford) 1977.
5th	134	M. Maslin & D. N. F. Slade, Minor Counties (East) v Nottinghamshire (Nottingham) 1976.
6th	114	M. J. Khan & G. P. Ellis, Glamorgan v Gloucestershire (Bristol) 1975.
7th	102	E. W. Jones & M. A. Nash, Glamorgan v Hampshire (Swansea) 1976.
8th	109	R. E. East & N. Smith, Essex v Northamptonshire (Chelmsford) 1977.
9th	81	J. N. Shepherd & D. L. Underwood, Kent v Middlesex (Lord's) 1975.
10th	61	J. M. Rice & A. M. E. Roberts, Hampshire v Gloucestershire (Bristol) 1975.

Note: A higher 1st wicket partnership of 224 occurred between Sadiq Mohammad, A. W. Stovold and Zaheer Abbas for Gloucestershire v Worcestershire (Worcester) 1975, Sadiq retiring hurt after 67 runs had been scored.

Hat-tricks: G. D. McKenzie, Leicestershire v Worcestershire (Worcester) 1972. K. Higgs, Leicestershire v Surrey (Lord's) 1974. A. A. Jones, Middlesex v Essex (Lord's) 1977, M. J. Procter, Gloucestershire v Hampshire (Southampton) 1977.

Six wickets in an innings: 6–13 M. J. Procter, Gloucestershire v Hampshire (Southampton) 1977, 6–27 A. G. Nicholson, Yorkshire v Minor Counties (North) (Middlesbrough) 1972.

Most 'Gold' awards: 8 B. Wood (Lancashire), 7 J. H. Edrich (Surrey).

BENSON & HEDGES CUP WINNERS	
1972 Leicestershire	1975 Leicestershire
1973 Kent	1976 Kent
1974 Surrey	1977 Gloucestershire

A young left-arm spinner named Hale,
Having bad luck with the tail
And was heard to say "Blow me!
I should have used *Foamy*—
The times that I've shaved that off
bail!"

Gillette· FOAMY (Regular and lemon-lime)
For a smooth shaving action.

LEICESTER WIN THE
JOHN PLAYER LEAGUE

Leicestershire won the John Player League for the second time, to join Lancashire, who have also won it twice, although both are behind Kent, three times winners.

It was very much touch and go, however, with Essex finishing with the same number of points – 52 (12 ahead of Middlesex in third place), and the issue not being finally decided until September 4, when had Leicester lost at home to a tired Glamorgan the day after the Gillette Final, Essex would have nosed in front at the post. As it happened, Leicester won comfortably by five wickets.

The result was merely a confirmation of the form in 1976 when both Leicester and Essex had finished immediately behind Kent, the 1976 winners. Perhaps the real surprise was that the bottom three counties should be Yorkshire, Lancashire and Northants – all one-day competition winners.

JOHN PLAYER LEAGUE
PRINCIPAL RECORDS

Highest innings total: 307–4 off 38 overs, Worcestershire v Derbyshire (Worcester) 1975.

Highest innings total by side batting second: 261–8 off 39.1 overs, Warwickshire v Nottinghamshire (Birmingham) 1976.

Highest innings total by side batting first and losing: 260–5 off 40 overs, Nottinghamshire v Warwickshire (Birmingham) 1976.

Lowest completed innings total: 23 off 19.4 overs, Middlesex v Yorkshire (Leeds) 1974.

Highest individual innings: 155* B. A. Richards, Hampshire v Yorkshire (Hull), 1970.
113 centuries have been scored in the League.

Record Wicket Partnerships
1st   218   A. R. Butcher & G. P. Howarth, Surrey v Gloucestershire (Oval) 1976.
2nd   179   B. W. Luckhurst & M. H. Denness, Kent v Somerset (Canterbury) 1973.
3rd   182   H. Pilling & C. H. Lloyd, Lancashire v Somerset (Manchester) 1970.
4th   175* M. J. K. Smith & D. L. Amiss, Warwickshire v Yorkshire (Birmingham) 1970.
5th   163   A. G. E. Ealham & B. D. Julien, Kent v Leicestershire (Leicester) 1977.

6th   121   C. P. Wilkins & A. J. Borrington, Derbyshire v Warwickshire (Chesterfield) 1972.

7th   96*   R. Illingworth & J. Birkenshaw, Leicestershire v Somerset (Leicester) 1971.

8th   95*   D. Breakwell & K. F. Jennings, Somerset v Nottinghamshire (Nottingham) 1976.

9th   86   D. P. Hughes & P. Lever, Lancashire v Essex (Leyton) 1973.

10th   57   D. A. Graveney & J. B. Mortimore, Gloucestershire v Lancashire (Tewkesbury) 1973.

Four wickets in four balls: A. Ward, Derbyshire v Sussex (Derby) 1970

Hat-tricks (excluding above): R. Palmer, Somerset v Gloucestershire (Bristol) 1970, K. D. Boyce, Essex v Somerset (Westcliff) 1971, G. D. McKenzie, Leicestershire v Essex (Leicester) 1972, R. G. D. Willis, Warwickshire v Yorkshire (Birmingham) 1973, W. Blenkiron, Warwickshire v Derbyshire (Buxton), 1974, A. Buss, Sussex v Worcestershire (Hastings) 1974, J. M. Rice, Hampshire v Northamptonshire (Southampton) 1975, M. A. Nash, Glamorgan v Worcestershire (Worcester) 1975, A. Hodgson, Northamptonshire v Sussex (Northampton) 1976.

Eight wickets in an innings: 8–26 K. D. Boyce, Essex v Lancashire (Manchester) 1971.

JOHN PLAYER LEAGUE CHAMPIONS

1969	Lancashire	1963	Kent
1970	Lancashire	1974	Leicestershire
1971	Worcestershire	1975	Hampshire
1972	Kent	1976	Kent
		1977	Leicestershire

JOHN PLAYER LEAGUE FINAL TABLE

		P	W	L	NR	Pts	Sixes	4 wkts
1	Leicestershire	16	13	3	0	52	18	5
2	Essex	16	12	2	2	52	21	2
3	Middlesex	16	9	5	2	40	21	2
4	Sussex	16	9	6	1	38	14	6
	Hampshire	16	8	5	3	38	39	4
6	Kent	16	7	6	3	34	19	2
	Gloucestershire	16	6	5	5	34	12	6
8	Glamorgan	16	7	7	2	32	35	4
9	Derbyshire	16	6	8	2	28	34	1
	Somerset	16	6	8	2	28	42	1
	Warwickshire	16	5	7	4	28	25	—
12	Nottinghamshire	16	6	9	1	26	27	2
13	Surrey	16	5	9	2	24	26	7
	Worcestershire	16	5	9	2	24	11	—
	Yorkshire	16	3	7	6	24	15	2
16	Lancashire	16	5	10	1	22	26	5
17	Northamptonshire	16	4	10	2	20	15	3
							400	52

MIDDLESEX AND KENT JOINT COUNTY CHAMPIONS

For only the third time this century, the County Champion-ship (now the Schweppes County Championship) has ended in a tied result, Middlesex and Kent becoming Joint-Champions. The previous ties were in 1949 and 1950 when first, Middlesex and Yorkshire, and then Lancashire and Surrey were the teams involved. It is unique to have as Joint-Champions two Southern counties. Both Middlesex and Kent were affected by the calls upon their players for Test cricket; Brearley and Barlow for Middlesex, and Wool-mer, Knott and Underwood for Kent – a substantial loss this one, and perhaps the difference between sharing a title and winning it outright. These three surely would have turned the scales had they not missed so much championship cricket. In fairness to Middlesex, however, it should be pointed out that Underwood, assessed by his own high standards, had a pretty moderate season taking only 33 wickets for Kent. The real surprise is that Woolmer should head the national bowling averages with 19 wickets at 15.21 apiece.

For Kent, even with their loss of players, the season was a considerable improvement on the previous one when they had finished only fourteenth. Kent apart, the top of the table was roughly consistent with the previous season, with Middle-sex, Gloucestershire, Somerset, Leicestershire and Essex all thereabouts. Northants had fallen from second place to ninth in a very indifferent season all round. Lancashire, very much in the doldrums, finished sixteenth again – their position in 1976 – sixteenth in the John Player League, knocked out the first time they met a first-class county in the Gillette Cup (and at Old Trafford, too) and third out of five in Group A of the Benson and Hedges tables. A dismal record indeed, which immediately provoked the Committee into announcing a change of captaincy as soon as the season was over. Frank Hayes is to replace David Hughes. The disappointment is highlighted by the fact that Lancashire once had three players in the England side – Hayes, Lloyd and Wood – all of whom failed to maintain their form and their position in the Test team. Their potential has never been realised at national level.

Whilst Brearley had a splendid season with the bat for Middlesex when he played, it was a triumvirate of bowlers who really sealed their success. Daniel bowling magnificently, took 71 wickets at 16.98 and he was well supported by Selvey with 72 at 19.61 and the spin of Emburey with 68 wickets at 20.25, two Surrey cricketers allowed to move on to other pastures. For Surrey, it was another nondescript season, worse, in fact, than 1976. They were joint-fourteenth instead of ninth. The same is true of Yorkshire about whom we were told that recovery was just around the corner, but they, of course, suffered from the absence of Old through injury, and subsequently Boycott to Test matches. Perhaps the bowling needs to be stronger if Yorkshire are to be back winning Championships again – they last won the County Championship in 1968, the Gillette in 1969, and have never won either the John Player or the Benson and Hedges. Tradition alone would indicate that they must be due to win a title soon.

SCHWEPPES COUNTY CHAMPIONSHIP
FINAL TABLE

		P	W	L	D	Bonus Pts Bt	Bonus Pts Bw	Pts
1	Kent (14)	22	9	2	11	54	65	227
	Middlesex (1)	22	9	5	8	43	76	227
3	Gloucestershire (3)	22	9	5	8	44	70	222
4	Somerset (7)	22	6	4	12	58	64	194
5	Leicestershire (4)	22	6	4	12	44	73	189
6	Essex (6)	22	7	5	10	38	65	187
7	Derbyshire (15)	22	7	3	12	38	64	186
8	Sussex (10)	22	6	5	11	52	60	184
9	Northamptonshire (2)	22	6	6	10	43	68	183
10	Warwickshire (5)	22	4	8	10	61	72	181
11	Hampshire (12)	22	6	5	11	53	54	179
12	Yorkshire (8)	22	6	5	11	36	63	171
13	Worcestershire (11)	22	5	10	7	29	55	144
14	Glamorgan (17)	22	3	7	12	36	60	132
	Surrey (9)	22	3	6	13	43	54	132
16	Lancashire (16)	22	2	4	16	36	57	117
17	Nottinghamshire (13)	22	1	11	10	34	52	98

1976 *positions in brackets*

COUNTY CHAMPIONS

1873	Nottinghamshire Gloucestershire	1901	Yorkshire	1939	Yorkshire
		1902	Yorkshire	1946	Yorkshire
1874	Derbyshire	1903	Middlesex	1947	Middlesex
1875	Nottinghamshire Lancashire Sussex	1904	Lancashire	1948	Glamorgan
		1905	Yorkshire	1949	Middlesex Yorkshire
		1906	Kent		
1876	Gloucestershire	1907	Nottinghamshire	1950	Lancashire Surrey
1877	Gloucestershire	1908	Yorkshire		
1878	Middlesex	1909	Kent	1951	Warwickshire
1879	Nottinghamshire Lancashire	1910	Kent	1952	Surrey
		1911	Warwickshire	1953	Surrey
1880	Nottinghamshire Gloucestershire	1912	Yorkshire	1954	Surrey
		1913	Kent	1955	Surrey
1881	Lancashire	1914	Surrey	1956	Surrey
1882	Lancashire Nottinghamshire	1919	Yorkshire	1957	Surrey
		1920	Middlesex	1958	Surrey
1883	Nottinghamshire	1921	Middlesex	1959	Yorkshire
1884	Nottinghamshire	1922	Yorkshire	1960	Yorkshire
1885	Nottinghamshire	1923	Yorkshire	1961	Hampshire
1886	Nottinghamshire	1924	Yorkshire	1962	Yorkshire
1877	Surrey	1925	Yorkshire	1962	Yorkshire
1888	Surrey	1926	Lancashire	1964	Worcestershire
1889	Nottinghamshire Lancashire Surrey	1927	Lancashire	1965	Worcestershire
		1928	Lancashire	1966	Yorkshire
		1929	Nottinghamshire	1967	Yorkshire
1890	Surrey	1930	Lancashire	1968	Yorkshire
1891	Surrey	1931	Yorkshire	1969	Glamorgan
1892	Surrey	1932	Yorkshire	1970	Kent
1893	Yorkshire	1933	Yorkshire	1971	Surrey
1894	Surrey	1934	Lancashire	1972	Warwickshire
1895	Surrey	1935	Yorkshire	1973	Hampshire
1896	Yorkshire	1936	Derbyshire	1974	Worcestershire
1897	Lancashire	1937	Yorkshire	1975	Leicestershire
1899	Surrey	1938	Yorkshire	1976	Middlesex
1900	Yorkshire			1977	Kent Middlesex

When C. G. Macartney scored 345 in a day for the Australians against Notts at Trent Bridge in 1921, he scored 231 in a single session of play – the afternoon session between lunch and tea. By tea the Australians had scored 484 for three, with Macartney 308 not out. No other cricketer in history has scored a triple century before tea in a first-class match on the first day.

One of the earliest references to 'cricket' in this country is to be found in Russell's history of Guildford, a document relating to a dispute in 1598 in respect of a plot of land at Guildford. 'When John Parvish was a scholler in the Free School of Guildford, he and several of his fellows did run and play there at "crickett" and other plaies.'

When the new batsman said "Two,"
The Umpire responded with "Pooh!
You haven't got set,
Yet you've started to sweat,
Gillette have the *Rightguard* for you."

THE COUNTIES AND
THEIR PLAYERS
Compiled by Michael Fordham

Abbreviations

B	Born	HSC	Highest score for County if different from highest first-class score
RHB	Right-hand bat		
LHB	Left-hand bat		
RF	Right-arm fast	HSGC	Highest score Gillette Cup
RFM	Right-arm fast medium	HSJPL	Highest score John Player League
RM	Right-arm medium		
LF	Left-arm fast	HSBH	Highest score Benson & Hedges Cup
LFM	Left-arm fast medium		
LM	Left-arm medium	BB	Best bowling figures
OB	Off-break	BBUK	Best bowling figures in this country
LB	Leg-break		
LBG	Leg-break and googly	BBTC	Best bowling figures in Test cricket if different from above
SLA	Slow left-arm orthodox		
SLC	Slow left-arm 'chinaman'		
WK	Wicket-keeper	BBC	Best bowling figures for County if different from above
*	Not out or unfinished stand		
HS	Highest score	BBGC	Best bowling figures Gillette Cup
HSUK	Highest score in this country		
		BBJPL	Best bowling figures John Player League
HSTC	Highest score in Test cricket if different from above	BBBH	Best bowling figures Benson & Hedges Cup

When a player is known by a name other than his first name, the name in question has been underlined.

All Test match appearances are complete to 30 September 1977.

'Debut' denotes 'first-class debut' and 'Cap' means '1st XI county cap'.

'*Wisden 1976*' indicates that a player was selected as one of *Wisden's* Five Cricketers of the Year for his achievements in 1976.

Owing to the increasing number of privately arranged overseas tours of short duration, only those which may be regarded as major tours have been included.

DERBYSHIRE

Formation of present club: 1870.
Colours: Chocolate, amber, and pale blue.
Badge: Rose and crown.
County Champions (2): 1874 and 1936.
Gillette Cup finalists: 1969.
Best final position in John Player League: 3rd in 1970.
Benson & Hedges Cup: Have never qualified for quarter-finals.
Gillette Man of the Match Awards: 13.
Benson & Hedges Gold Awards: 15.
Secretary: D. A. Harrison, County Cricket Ground, Nottingham Road, Derby, DE2 6DA.
Captain: E. J. Barlow.

DERBYSHIRE

Edgar John (Eddie) BARLOW (Pretoria Boys' High School) B Pretoria, South Africa 12/8/1940. RHB, RM. Debut for Transvaal 1959–60. Subsequently played for Eastern Province from 1964–65 and for Western Province from 1968–69 after returning to Transvaal for 1966–67 and 1967–68 seasons. Debut for county 1976. Appointed county captain during 1976 season. Tests: 30 for South Africa between 1961–62 and 1969–70. Played in 5 matches for Rest of World 1970. Tours: South Africa to Australia and New Zealand 1963–64, England 1965. 1,000 runs (2)— 1,162 runs (av. 29.05) in 1976 best. Scored 1,900 runs (av. 63,33) in Australia and New Zealand 1963–64. Hat-trick and 4 wkts in 5 balls, Rest of World v England (Leeds) 1970. Gillette Man of the Match Awards: 2. Benson & Hedges Gold Awards: 2. HS 217 v Surrey (Ilkeston) 1976. HSTC: 201 South Africa v Australia (Adelaide) 1963–64. HSGC: 70* v Sussex (Hove) 1977 (in South African competition – 186 Western Province v Eastern Province (Johannesburg) 1969–70). HSJPL: 88 v Yorks (Chesterfield) 1976. HSBH: 88 v Minor Counties (West) (Watford) 1977. BB: 7–24 Western Province v Natal (Durban) 1972–73. BBUK: 7–64 Rest of World v England (Leeds) 1970. BBC: 5–63 v Glamorgan (Burton-on-Trent) 1976. BBTC: 5–85 South Africa v Australia (Cape Town) 1966–67. BBGC: 4–51 v Hants (Southampton) 1976. BBJPL: 4–30 v Surrey (Chesterfield) 1977. BBBH: 3–37 v Glamorgan (Chesterfield) 1976.

Anthony John (Tony) BORRINGTON (Spondon Park GS) B Derby 8/12/1948. RHB, LB. Played for MCC Schools at Lord's in 1967. Played in one John Player League match in 1970. Debut 1971. Cap 1977. Benson & Hedges Gold awards: 2. HS: 115 v Notts (Ilkeston) 1977. HSGC: 28 v Hants (Southampton) 1976. HSJPL: 101 v Somerset (Taunton) 1977. HSBH: 81 v Notts (Nottingham) 1974. Trained as a teacher at Loughborough College of Education.

Harold CARTWRIGHT B Halfway (Derbyshire) 12/5/1951. RHB. Played in John Player and Gillette Cup matches in 1971 and 1972. Debut 1973. HS: 141* v Warwickshire (Chesterfield) 1977. HSGC: 36 v Somerset (Ilkeston) 1977. HSJPL: 76* v Middlesex (Chesterfield) 1973. HSBH: 45 v Minor Counties (West) (Watford) 1977.

James Martin Hilary GRAHAM-BROWN (Sevenoaks School) B Thetford (Norfolk) 11/7/1951. RHB, RM. Great-nephew of L. B. Blaxland, former Derbyshire player. Debut for Kent 1974. Left county after 1976 season and made debut for Derbyshire in 1977. HS: 29* Kent v Derbyshire (Folkestone) 1974. HSC: 5 v Leics (Burton-on-Trent) 1977. HSBH: 44 v Worcs (Chesterfield) 1977. BBJPL: 3–4 Kent v Lancs (Manchester) 1974. Obtained degree in English & American Literature at University of Kent.

Ashley John HARVEY-WALKER (Strathallan School) B East Ham 21/7/1944. RHB, OB. Debut 1971, scoring 16 and 110* v Oxford U (Burton-on-Trent) in debut match, the first player ever to do so for the county. Left staff after 1975 season but is still available if required. HS: 117 v Warwickshire (Birmingham) 1974. HSGC: 18 v Hants (Derby) 1974. HSJPL: 84 v Glos (Chesterfield) 1973. HSBH: 79 v Notts (Nottingham) 1972. BBBH: 4–37 v Minor Counties (North) (Derby) 1975.

Michael (Mike) HENDRICK B Darley Dale (Derbyshire) 22/10/1948. RHB, RFM. Debut 1969. Cap 1972. Elected Best Young Cricketer of the Year in 1973 by the Cricket Writers Club. Tests 13 between 1974 and 1977. Tours: West Indies 1973–74, Australia and New Zealand 1974–75, Pakistan and New Zealand 1977–78. Gillette Man of the Match awards: 1. Benson & Hedges Gold awards: 2. HS: 46 v Essex (Chelmsford) 1973. HSTC: 15 v Australia (Oval) 1977. HSGC: 11 v Sussex (Chesterfield) 1973. HSJPL: 21 v Warwickshire (Buxton) 1974. HSBH: 32 v Notts (Chesterfield) 1973. BB: 8–45 v Warwickshire (Chesterfield) 1973. BBTC: 4–28 v India (Birmingham) 1974. BBGC: 4–16 v Middlesex (Chesterfield) 1975. BBJPL: 6–7 v Notts (Nottingham) 1972. BBBH: 5–30 v Notts (Chesterfield) 1975 and 5–30 v Lancs (Southport) 1976.

Alan HILL (New Mills GS) B Buxworth (Derbyshire) 29/6/1950. RHB, OB. Joined staff 1970. Debut 1972. Cap 1976. Played for Orange Free State in 1976–77 Currie Cup competition. 1,000 runs (2)—1,303 runs (av 34.28) in 1976 best. HS: 160* v Warwickshire (Coventry) 1976. HSGC: 23 v Hants (Southampton) 1976. HSJPL: 120 v Northants (Buxton) 1976. HSBH: 21 v Notts (Nottingham) 1974. BB: 3–5 Orange Free State v Northern Transvaal (Pretoria) 1976–77.

Peter Noel KIRSTEN B Pietermaritzburg, Natal, South Africa 14/5/1955. RHB, OB. Debut for Western Province in Currie Cup 1973–74. Played for Sussex v Australians 1975 as well as playing for county 2nd XI. Played for Derbyshire 2nd XI in 1977 and has joined staff for 1978. Scored 4 centuries in 4 consecutive innings and 6 in 7 innings including two in match – 173* and 103 Western Province v Eastern Province (Cape Town) 1976–77. Scored 1,074 runs (av. 76.71) in 1976–77. HS: 173* Western Province v Eastern Province 1976–77. HSUK: 31 Sussex v Australians (Hove) 1975.

Geoffrey (Geoff) MILLER (Chesterfield GS) B Chesterfield 8/9/1952. RHB, OB. Toured India 1970–71 and West Indies 1972 with England Young Cricketers. Won Sir Frank Worrell Trophy as Outstanding Boy Cricketer of 1972. Debut 1973. Cap 1976. Elected Best Young Cricketer of the Year in 1976 by the Cricket Writers Club. Tests: 3 in 1976 and 1977. Tours: India, Sri Lanka and Australia 1976–77, Pakistan and New Zealand 1977–78. Benson & Hedges Gold awards: 1. HS: 98* England v Pakistan (Lahore) 1977–78. HSUK: 86* v Sussex (Hove) 1977. HSGC: 24 v Hants (Southampton) 1976. HSJPL: 44 v Kent (Chesterfield) 1973. HSBH: 75 v Warwickshire (Derby) 1977. BB: 7–54 v Sussex (Hove) 1977. BBJPL: 3–21 v Essex (Leyton) 1977.

Alan MORRIS B Staveley (Derbyshire) 23/8/1953. RHB, LB. Debut 1974. HS: 74 v Lancs (Manchester) 1976. HSJPL: 49 v Hants (Bournemouth) 1976. HSBH: 39 v Hants (Southampton) 1976.

Philip Edgar RUSSELL (Ilkeston GS) B Ilkeston 9/5/1944. RHB, RM/OB. Debut 1965. Not re-engaged after 1972 season, but rejoined staff in 1974 and is now county coach. Cap 1975. HS: 72 v Glamorgan (Swansea) 1970. HSJPL: 47* v Glamorgan (Buxton) 1975. HSBH: 22* v Lancs (Southport) 1976. BB: 7–46 v Yorks (Sheffield) 1976. BBGC: 3–44 v Somerset (Taunton) 1975. BBJPL: 6–10 v Northants (Buxton) 1976. BBBH: 3–43 v Minor Counties (Derby) 1972.

DERBYSHIRE

Frederick William (Fred) SWARBROOK B Derby 17/12/1950. LHB, SLA. Debut 1967 aged 16 years 6 months, youngest player ever to appear for county. Cap 1975. Played for Griqualand West between 1972–73 and 1976–77 in Currie Cup Competition. Gillette Man of the Match awards: 2. HS: 90 v Essex (Leyton) 1970. HSGC: 58* v Surrey (Ilkeston) 1976. HSJPL: 42* v Glamorgan (Ilkeston) 1977 and 42* v Notts (Ilkeston) 1977. HSBH: 20* v Hants (Southampton) 1976. BB: 9–20 (13–62 match) v Sussex (Hove) 1975. BBGC: 3–53 v Middlesex (Chesterfield) 1975. BBJPL: 4–15 v Glos (Bristol) 1976. BBBH: 3–29 v Minor Counties (West) (Watford) 1977. Soccer for Derby County Juniors.

Robert Stephen SWINDELL (Hallcroft Secondary, Ilkeston) B Derby 22/1/1950. RHB, OB. Joined staff 1970. Debut 1972. Left staff after 1974 season, but has re-appeared in one match in each season since. HS: 38 v Somerset (Chesterfield) 1972. BB: 6–79 v Oxford U. (Burton-on-Trent) 1975.

Robert William (Bob) TAYLOR B Stoke 17/7/1941. RHB, WK, RM. Played for Bignall End (N. Staffs and S. Cheshire League) when only 15 and for Staffordshire from 1958 to 1960. Debut 1960 for Minor Counties v South Africans (Stoke-on-Trent). Debut for county 1961. Cap 1962. Testimonial (£6,672) in 1973. Appointed county captain during 1975 season. Relinquished post during 1976 season. *Wisden* 1976. Tests: 1 v New Zealand 1970–71. Tours: Australia and New Zealand 1970–71, 1974–75, Australia with Rest of the World team 1971–72, West Indies 1973–74, Pakistan and New Zealand 1977–78. Withdrew from India, Sri Lanka, and Pakistan tour 1972–73. Dismissed 80 batsman (77 ct 3 st) in 1962, 83 batsmen (81 ct 2 st) in 1963, and 86 batsmen (79 ct 7 st) in 1965. Dismissed 10 batsmen in match, all caught v Hants (Chesterfield) 1963 and 7 in innings, all caught v Glamorgan (Derby) 1966. Gillette Man of Match awards: 1. Benson & Hedges Gold awards: 1. HS: 97 International Wanderers v South African Invitation XI (Johannesburg) 1975–76. HSUK: 74* v Glamorgan (Derby) 1971. HSTC: 4 v New Zealand (Christchurch) 1970–71. HSGC: 53* v Middlesex (Lord's) 1965. HSJPL: 43* v Glos (Burton-on-Trent) 1969. HSBH: 31* v Hants (Southampton) 1976.

Colin John TUNNICLIFFE B Derby 11/8/1951. RHB, LFM. Debut 1973. Left staff after 1974 season. Re-appeared in 1976. Cap 1977. HS: 82* v Middlesex (Ilkeston) 1977. HSGC: 13 v Somerset (Ilkeston) 1977. HSJPL: 30 v Sussex (Hastings) 1977. HSBH: 25* v Minor Counties (North) (Derby) 1974. BB: 4–22 v Middlesex (Ilkeston) 1977. BBJPL: 3–12 v Essex (Chesterfield) 1974.

John WALTERS B Brampton (Yorks) 7/8/1949. LHB, RFM. Has played in Huddersfield League. Debut 1977. HS: 28 v Leics (Leicester) 1977.

John Geoffrey WRIGHT (Christ's College, Christchurch and Otago University) B Darfield, New Zealand 5/7/1954. LHB, RM. Debut for Northern Districts in Shell Cup in 1975–76. Debut for county 1977. Cap

64

1977. Scored 1,080 runs (av 32.72) in 1977. Benson & Hedges Gold awards: 1. HS: 151 v Hants (Bournemouth) 1977. HSGC: 87* v Sussex (Hove) 1977. HSJPL: 75 v Glos (Heanor) 1977. HSBH: 102 v Worcs (Chesterfield) 1977.

NB The following players whose particulars appeared in the 1977 Annual have been omitted: R. G. A. Headley and C. Whyatt.

COUNTY AVERAGES

Schweppes County Championship: Played 21, won 7, drawn 11, lost 3, abandoned 1

All first-class matches: Played 22, won 7, drawn 12, lost 3, abandoned 1

BATTING AND FIELDING

Cap		M	I	NO	Runs	HS	Avge	100	50	Ct	St
1977	J. G. Wright	22	36	3	1080	151	32.72	1	4	18	—
1976	A. Hill	22	35	4	1014	90	32.70	—	9	4	—
1977	A. J. Borrington	22	33	8	806	115	32.24	1	4	11	—
1976	E. J. Barlow	21	33	4	886	88	30.55	—	7	34	—
1976	G. Miller	17	25	3	671	86*	30.50	—	5	10	—
—	H. Cartwright	22	30	6	626	141*	26.08	1	1	5	—
1975	F. W. Swarbrook	21	22	6	347	81	21.68	—	1	12	—
—	A. J. Harvey-Walker	7	11	2	189	101*	21.00	1	—	2	—
—	J. Walters	5	4	0	63	28	15.75	—	—	—	—
1962	R. W. Taylor	22	23	4	269	36	14.15	—	—	49	2
1977	C. J. Tunnicliffe	22	20	5	204	82*	13.60	—	1	11	—
—	K. Stevenson	8	8	5	25	9	8.33	—	—	5	—
—	A. Morris	7	8	1	53	16	7.57	—	—	3	—
1972	M. Hendrick	16	12	5	44	17	6.28	—	—	12	—
—	J. M. H. Graham-Brown	6	5	0	10	5	2.00	—	—	4	—

Played in one match: P. E. Russell 12*, 9; R. S. Swindell 1, 0.

BOWLING

	Type	O	M	R	W	Avge	Best	5 wI	10 wM
M. Hendrick	RFM	371	140	676	41	16.48	6–19	2	—
G. Miller	OB	570.4	196	1385	78	17.75	7–54	4	1
K. Stevenson	RFM	190.5	38	550	26	21.15	7–68	1	—
C. J. Tunnicliffe	LFM	544.1	142	1360	57	23.85	4–22	—	—
E. J. Barlow	RM	257.4	55	683	28	24.39	4–52	—	—
F. W. Swarbrook	SLA	548.5	214	1161	39	29.76	5–70	1	—
A. J. Harvey-Walker	OB	136.2	29	406	7	58.00	2–45	—	—

Also bowled: A. J. Borrington 0.4–0–4–0; H. Cartwright 5–2–10–0; J. M. H. Graham-Brown 27–3–119–2; A. Hill 3.2–0–14–0; A. Morris 5.3–0–43–0; P. E. Russell 18–8–15–1; R. S. Swindell 7–1–33–0; J. Walters 24–4–99–1.

County Records
First-class cricket

Highest innings totals:	For	645 v Hampshire (Derby)	1898
	Agst	662 by Yorkshire (Chesterfield)	1898
Lowest innings totals:	For	16 v Nottinghamshire (Nottingham)	1879
	Agst	23 by Hampshire (Burton-on-Trent)	1958
Highest individual innings:	For	274 G. Davidson v Lancashire (Manchester)	1896
	Agst	343* P. A. Perrin for Essex (Chesterfield)	1904
Best bowling in an innings:	For	10–40 W. Bestwick v Glamorgan (Cardiff)	1921
	Agst	10–47 T. F. Smailes for Yorkshire (Sheffield)	1939
Best bowling in a match:	For	16–84 C. Gladwin v Worcs (Stourbridge)	1952
	Agst	16–101 G. Giffen for Australians (Derby)	1886
Most runs in a season:		2165 (av 48.11) D. B. Carr	1959
runs in a career:		20516 (av 31.41) D. Smith	1927–1952
100s in a season:		6 by L. F. Townsend	1933
100s in a career:		30 by D. Smith	1927–1952
wickets in a season:		168 (av 19.55) T. B. Mitchell	1935
wickets in a career:		1670 (av 17.11) H. L. Jackson	1947–1963

RECORD WICKET STANDS

1st	322	H. Storer & J. Bowden v Essex (Derby)	1929
2nd	349	C. S. Elliott & J. D. Eggar v Notts (Nottingham)	1947
3rd	246	J. Kelly & D. B. Carr v Leicestershire (Chesterfield)	1957
4th	328	P. Vaulkhard & D. Smith v Notts (Nottingham)	1946
5th	203	C. P. Wilkins & I. R. Buxton v Lancashire (Manchester)	1971
6th	212	G. M. Lee & T. S. Worthington v Essex (Chesterfield)	1932
7th	241*	G. H. Pope & A. E. G. Rhodes v Hampshire (Portsmouth)	1948
8th	182	A. H. M. Jackson & W. Carter v Leicestershire (Leicester)	1922
9th	283	A. R. Warren & J. Chapman v Warwickshire (Blackwell)	1910
10th	93	J. Humphries & J. Horsley v Lancashire (Derby)	1914

One-day cricket

Highest innings totals:	Gillette Cup	250–9 v Hants (Bournemouth)	1963
	John Player League	260–6 v Glos (Derby)	1972
	Benson & Hedges Cup	225–6 v Notts (Nottingham)	1974
Lowest innings totals:	Gillette Cup	79 v Surrey (Oval)	1967
	John Player League	70 v Surrey (Derby)	1972
	Benson & Hedges Cup	102 v Yorks (Bradford)	1975
Highest individual innings:	Gillette Cup	87* J. G. Wright v Sussex (Hove)	1977
	John Player League	120 A. Hill v Northants (Buxton)	1976
	Benson & Hedges Cup	111* P. J. Sharpe v Glamorgan (Chesterfield)	1976
Best bowling figures:	Gillette Cup	6–18 T. J. P. Eyre v Sussex (Chesterfield)	1969
	John Player League	6–7 M. Hendrick v Notts (Nottingham)	1972
	Benson & Hedges Cup	5–30 M. Hendrick v Notts (Chesterfield)	1975
		5–30 M. Hendrick v Lancashire (Southport)	1976

ESSEX

Formation of present club: 1876.
Colours: Blue, gold, and red.
Badge: Three seaxes with word 'Essex' underneath.
Best final position in Championship: 3rd in 1897.
Gillette Cup third round (5): 1966, 1969, 1971,
    1972 and 1973.
John Player League runners-up: (3): 1971, 1976
    and 1977.
Benson & Hedges Cup semi-finalists: 1973.
Gillette Man of the Match awards: 11.
Benson & Hedges Gold awards: 15.

Secretary: S. R. Cox, The County Ground, New Writtle Street,
    Chelmsford CM2 0RW.
Captain: K. W. R. Fletcher.

David Laurence ACFIELD (Brentwood School & Cambridge) B
Chelmsford 24/7/1947. RHB, OB. Debut 1966. Blue 1967–68. Cap 1970.
HS: 42 Cambridge U v Leics (Leicester) 1967. BB: 7–36 v Sussex (Ilford)
1973. BBJPL: 5–14 v Northants (Northampton) 1970. Also obtained
Blue for fencing (sabre). Has appeared in internationals in this sport and
represented Great Britain in Olympic Games at Mexico City and Munich.

Michael Henry (Mike) DENNESS (Ayr Academy) B Bellshill (Lanark-
shire) 1/12/1940. RHB, RM/OB. Debut for Scotland 1959. Debut for
Kent 1962. Cap 1964. County captain from 1972 to 1976. Benefit (£19,219)
in 1974. Wisden 1974. Left county after 1976 season and made debut for
Essex in 1977. Cap 1977. Tests: 28 between 1969 and 1975, captaining
England in 19 Tests between 1973–74 and 1975. Played in one match
against Rest of the World in 1970. Tours: India, Sri Lanka, and Pakistan
1972–73 (vice-captain), West Indies 1973–74 (captain), Australia and New
Zealand 1974–75 (captain). Gillette Man of Match awards: 1 (for Kent).
Benson & Hedges Gold awards: 1 (for Kent). 1,000 runs (13)—1,606 runs
(av 31.49) in 1966 best. Scored 1,136 runs (av 54.09) in Australia and New
Zealand 1974–75. HS: 195 v Leics (Leicester) 1977. HSTC: 188 England v
Australia (Melbourne) 1974–75. HSGC: 85 Kent v Leics (Leicester) 1971.
HSJPL: 118* Kent v Yorks (Scarborough) 1976. HSBH: 112* Kent v
Surrey (Oval) 1973.

Raymond Eric (Ray) EAST B Manningtree (Essex) 20/6/1947. RHB,
SLA. Debut 1956. Cap 1967. Benefit in 1978. Hat-trick: The Rest v MCC
Tour XI (Hove) 1973. Benson & Hedges Gold awards: 3. HS: 113 v
Hants (Chelmsford) 1976. HSGC: 38* v Glos (Chelmsford) 1973. HSJPL:
25* v Glamorgan (Colchester) 1976. HSBH: 54 v Northants (Chelmsford)
1977. BB: 8–30 v Notts (Ilford) 1977. BBGC: 4–28 v Herts (Hitchin) 1976.
BBJPL: 6–18 v Yorks (Hull) 1969. BBBH: 5–33 v Kent (Chelmsford) 1975.

ESSEX

Keith William Robert **FLETCHER** B Worcester 20/5/1944. RHB, LB. Debut 1962. Cap 1963. Appointed county vice-captain in 1971 and county captain in 1974. Benefit (£13,000) in 1973. *Wisden* 1973. Tests: 52 between 1968 and 1976–77. Also played in 4 matches v Rest of the World in 1970. Tours: Pakistan 1966–67, Ceylon and Pakistan 1968–69, Australia and New Zealand, 1970–71, 1974–75, India, Sri Lanka and Pakistan 1972–73, West Indies 1973–74, India, Sri Lanka and Australia 1976–77. 1,000 runs (13)—1,890 runs (av 41.08) in 1968 best. Scored two centuries in match (111 and 102*) v Notts (Nottingham) 1976. Gillette Man of Match awards: 1. Benson & Hedges Gold awards: 1. HS: 228* v Sussex (Hastings) 1968. HSTC: 216 v New Zealand (Auckland) 1974–75. HSGC: 74 v Notts (Nottingham) 1969. HSJPL: 99* v Notts (Ilford) 1974. HSBH: 90 v Surrey (Oval) 1974. BB: 4–50 MCC under-25 v North Zone (Peshawar) 1966–67.

Matthew Kailey **FOSH** (Harrow School and Cambridge) B Epping 26/9/1957. LHB, RM. Scored 161* for Harrow v Eton 1975 – third highest score in history of fixture. Toured West Indies with England Young Cricketers 1976. Debut 1976. Blue 1977. HS: 94 Cambridge U v Sussex (Cambridge) 1977. HSC: 66 v Kent (Folkestone) 1977. HSJPL: 45 v Yorks (Scarborough) 1977. HSBH: 39 Combined Universities v Notts (Nottingham) 1977. Rugby Blue 1977.

Graham Alan **GOOCH** (Norlington Junior HS, Leyton) B Leytonstone 23/7/1953. Cousin of G. J. Saville, former Essex player and assistant secretary of club. RHB, RM. Toured West Indies with England Young Cricketers 1972. Debut 1973. Cap 1975. Tests: 2 in 1975. 1,000 runs (2) —1,273 runs (av 42.43) in 1976 best. Benson & Hedges Gold awards: 1. HS: 136 v Worcs (Westcliff) 1976. HSTC: 31 v Australia (Lord's) 1975. HSGC: 26 v Shropshire (Wellington) 1974 and 26 v Staffs (Stone) 1976. HSJPL: 84 v Yorks (Middlesbrough) 1975. HSBH: 89 v Surrey (Oval) 1976. BB: 5–40 v West Indians (Chelmsford) 1976. BBJPL: 3–22 v Northants (Chelmsford) 1976.

Brian Ross **HARDIE** (Larbert HS) B Stenhousemuir 14/1/1950. RHB, RM. Has played for Stenhousemuir in East of Scotland League. Debut for Scotland 1970. His father and elder brother K. M. Hardie have also played for Scotland. Debut for Essex by special registration in 1973. Cap 1974. 1,000 runs (2)—1,522 runs (av 43.48) in 1975 best. Scored two centuries in match for Scotland v MCC, Aberdeen 1971, a match not regarded as first-class. HS: 162 v Warwickshire (Birmingham) 1975. HSGC: 83 v Staffs (Stone) 1976. HSJPL: 94 v Northants (Northampton) 1973. HSBH: 42* v Cambridge U (Cambridge) 1974.

Patrick Anthony **HECTOR** (Warren Comprehensive School, Chadwell Heath) B Islington 29/7/1958. RHB, RM. Debut 1977 (three matches). HS: 40 v Cambridge U (Cambridge) 1977. BB: 3–56 v Leics (Leicester) 1977.

Reuben **HERBERT** (Barstaple Comprehensive School, Basildon) B Cape Town 1/12/1957. RHB, OB. Debut 1976. Played in only one match in 1977, v Cambridge U. HS: 12 v Cambridge U (Cambridge) 1977.

John Kenneth LEVER B Ilford 24/2/1949. RHB, LFM. Debut 1967. Cap 1970. Tests: 9 in 1976–77 and 1977. Tours: India, Sri Lanka and Australia 1976–77, Pakistan and New Zealand 1977–78. Gillette Man of Match awards: 2. Benson & Hedges Gold awards: 1. HS: 91 v Glamorgan (Cardiff) 1970. HSTC: 53 v India (Delhi) 1976–77 (on debut). HSJPL: 23 v Worcs (Worcester) 1974. HSBH: 12* v Warwickshire (Birmingham) 1975. BB: 8–127 v Glos (Cheltenham) 1976. BBTC: 7–46 v India (Delhi) 1976–77 (on debut). BBGC: 5–8 v Middlesex (Westcliff) 1972. BBJPL: 5–13 v Glamorgan (Ebbw Vale) 1975. BBBH: 5–16 v Middlesex (Chelmsford) 1976.

Michael Stephen Anthony McEVOY (Colchester RGS) B Jorhat, Assam, India 25/1/1956. RHB, RM. Debut 1976. HS: 67* v Yorks (Middlesbrough) 1977. Training as a teacher at Borough Road College of Education.

Kenneth Scott (Ken) McEWAN (Queen's College, Queenstown) B Bedford, Cape Province, South Africa 16/7/1952. RHB, OB. Debut for Eastern Province in 1972–73 Currie Cup competition. Played for T. N. Pearce's XI v West Indians (Scarborough) 1973. Debut for county and cap 1974. 1,000 runs (4)—1,821 runs (av 49.21) in 1976 best. Scored 4 consecutive centuries in 1977 including two centuries in match (102 and 116) v Warwickshire (Birmingham). Benson & Hedges Gold awards: 3. HS: 218 v Sussex (Chelmsford) 1977. HSGC: 63 v Somerset (Westcliff) 1974. HSJPL: 123 v Warwickshire (Ilford) 1976. HSBH: 116 v Minor Counties (East) (Norwich) 1976.

Keith Robert PONT B Wanstead 16/1/1953. RHB, RM. Debut 1970. Cap 1976. Benson & Hedges Gold awards: 1. HS: 113 v Warwickshire (Birmingham) 1973. HSGC: 10 v Kent (Leyton) 1972. HSJPL: 50* v Leics (Westcliff) 1976. HSBH: 60* v Notts (Ilford) 1976. BB: 4–100 v Middlesex (Southend) 1977.

Neil SMITH (Ossett GS) B Dewsbury 1/4/1949. RHB, WK. Debut for Yorks 1970. Debut for county by special registration in 1973. Cap 1975. HS: 126 v Somerset (Leyton) 1976. HSGC: 12 v Leics (Southend) 1977. HSJPL: 15 v Somerset (Chelmsford) 1975 and 16* v Glos (Cheltenham) 1975. HSBH: 61 v Northampton (Chelmsford) 1977.

Stuart TURNER B Chester 18/7/1943. RHB. RFM. Debut 1965. Cap 1970. Played for Natal in 1976–77 and 1977–78 Currie Cup competition. Hat-trick: v Surrey (Oval) 1971. HS: 121 v Somerset (Taunton) 1970. HSGC: 50 v Lancs (Chelmsford) 1971. HSJPL: 87 v Worcs (Chelmsford) 1975. HSBH: 41* v Minor Counties (East) (Chelmsford) 1977. BB: 6–26 v Northants (Northampton) 1977. BBGC: 3–16 v Glamorgan (Ilford) 1971. BBJPL: 4–14 v Hants (Portsmouth) 1969. BBBH: 4–22 v Minor Counties (South) (Bedford) 1975.

NB The following players whose particulars appeared in the 1977 Annual have been omitted: K. D. Boyce (retired), S. G. Plumb (not re-engaged). The career record of Boyce will be found elsewhere in this annual.

COUNTY AVERAGES

Schweppes County Championship: Played 21, won 7, drawn 9, lost 5, abandoned 1

All first-class matches: Played 23, won 7, drawn 11, lost 5, abandoned 1

BATTING AND FIELDING

Cap		M	I	NO	Runs	HS	Avge	100	50	Ct	St
1974	K. S. McEwan	23	37	4	1702	218	51.57	8	4	14	—
1963	K. W. R. Fletcher	22	37	6	1331	106*	42.93	3	7	27	—
1977	M. H. Denness	22	35	1	1343	195	39.50	3	7	13	—
1974	B. R. Hardie	16	27	3	661	118*	27.54	1	3	12	—
1975	G. A. Gooch	23	37	6	837	105*	27.00	1	5	11	—
1967	K. D. Boyce	7	7	1	139	69	23.16	—	1	5	—
—	M. K. Fosh	11	18	0	413	66	22.94	—	4	4	—
1970	S. Turner	22	28	5	504	73	21.91	—	1	14	—
1976	K. R. Pont	18	26	5	455	101*	21.66	1	1	9	—
1967	R. E. East	22	25	4	443	50*	21.09	—	1	11	—
—	P. A. Hector	3	5	1	75	40	18.75	—	—	—	—
1975	N. Smith	23	23	3	178	23	8.90	—	—	41	11
1970	D. L. Acfield	21	16	11	44	11*	8.80	—	—	6	—
1970	J. K. Lever	16	13	4	49	11	5.44	—	—	6	—

Played in two matches: M. S. A. McEvoy 2, 67*, 4 (1 ct).

Played in one match: R. Herbert 12 (2 ct); S. G. Plumb 20, 11.

BOWLING

	Type	O	M	R	W	Avge	Best	5 wI	10 wM
R. E. East	SLA	658.4	197	1477	73	20.23	8–30	6	2
J. K. Lever	LFM	429.4	101	1106	53	20.86	6–34	4	—
K. D. Boyce	RFM	189.4	45	496	23	21.56	4–48	—	—
S. Turner	RFM	718.4	187	1784	77	23.16	6–26	6	—
P. A. Hector	RM	56	7	190	7	27.14	3–56	—	—
D. L. Acfield	OB	669	174	1571	56	28.05	5–54	1	—
K. R. Pont	RM	186	27	599	20	29.95	4–100	—	—
G. A. Gooch	RM	109.3	26	345	8	43.12	4–60	—	—

Also bowled: M. H. Denness 1–1–0–0; K. W. R. Fletcher 8–0–76–0; B. R. Hardie 1–0–2–0; M. S. A. McEvoy 3–1–4–0; K. S. McEwan 3–1–8–0.

County Records

First-class cricket

Highest innings totals:	For .....692 v Somerset (Taunton)	1895
	Agst....803–4 by Kent (Brentwood)	1934
Lowest innings totals:	For .....30 v Yorkshire (Leyton)	1901
	Agst.....31 by Derbyshire (Derby) and by Yorkshire (Huddersfield)	1914 & 1935
Highest individual innings:	For .....343* P.A. Perrin v Derbyshire (Chesterfield)	1904
	Agst.....332 W. H. Ashdown for Kent (Brentwood)	1934
Best bowling in an innings:	For .....10–32 H. Pickett v Leicestershire (Leyton)	1895
	Agst.....10–40 G. Dennett for Gloucestershire (Bristol)	1906

Best bowling in a match:	For .....17–119 W. Mead v Hampshire (Southampton)	1895
	Agst.....17–56 C. W. L. Parker for Gloucestershire (Gloucester)	1925

Most runs in a season:	2308 (av 56.29) J. O'Connor	1934
runs in a career:	29162 (av 36.18) P. A. Perrin	1896–1928
100s in a season:	9 by J. O'Connor and D. J. Insole	1934 & 1955
100s in a career:	71 by J. O'Connor	1921–1939
wickets in a season:	172 (av 27.13) T. P. B. Smith	1947
wickets in a career:	1611 (av 26.26) T. P. B. Smith	1929–1951

RECORD WICKET STANDS

1st	270	A. V. Avery & T. C. Dodds v Surrey (The Oval)	1946
2nd	294	A. V. Avery & P. A. Gibb v Northampton (Northampton)	1952
3rd	343	P. A. Gibb & R. Horsfall v Kent (Blackheath)	1951
4th	298	A. V. Avery & R. Horsfall v Worcestershire (Clacton)	1948
5th	287	C. T. Ashton & J. O'Connor v Surrey (Brentwood)	1934
6th	206	J. W. H. T. Douglas & J. O'Connor v Gloucestershire (Cheltenham)	1923
		B. R. Knight & R. A. G. Luckin v Middlesex (Brentwood)	1962
7th	261	J. W. H. T. Douglas & J. Freeman v Lancashire (Leyton)	1914
8th	263	D. R. Wilcox & R. M. Taylor v Warwickshire (Southend)	1946
9th	251	J. W. H. T. Douglas & S. N. Hare v Derbyshire (Leyton)	1921
10th	218	F. H. Vigar & T. P. B. Smith v Derbyshire (Chesterfield)	1947

One-day cricket

Highest innings totals:	Gillette Cup	316–6 v Staffordshire (Stone)	1976
	John Player League	283–6 v Gloucestershire (Cheltenham)	1975
	Benson & Hedges Cup	294–4 v Minor Counties (East) (Norwich)	1976
Lowest innings totals:	Gillette Cup	100 v Derbyshire (Brentwood)	1965
	John Player League	69 v Derbyshire (Chesterfield)	1974
	Benson & Hedges Cup	123 v Kent (Canterbury)	1973
Highest individual innings:	Gillette Cup	101 B. Ward v Bedfordshire (Chelmsford)	1971
	John Player League	123 K. S. McEwan v Warwickshire (Ilford)	1976
	Benson & Hedges Cup	125* B. E. A. Edmeades v Minor Counties (East) (Norwich)	1976
Best bowling figures:	Gillette Cup	5–8 J. K. Lever v Middlesex (Westcliff)	1972
	John Player League:	8–26 K. D. Boyce v Lancs (Manchester)	1971
	Benson & Hedges Cup	5–16 J. K. Lever v Middlesex (Chelmsford)	1976

GLAMORGAN

Formation of present club: 1888.
Colours: Blue and gold.
Badge: Gold daffodil.
County Champions (2): 1948 and 1969.
Gillette Cup finalists: 1977.
Best final position in John Player League: 8th in 1977.
Benson & Hedges Cup quarter-finalists (3): 1972, 1973 and 1977.
Gillette Man of the Match awards: 13.
Benson & Hedges Gold awards: 13.

Secretary: P. B. Clift, 6 High Street, Cardiff, CF1 2PW.
Captain: A. Jones.

Thomas William (Tom) CARTWRIGHT (Foxford School, Coventry)
B Coventry 22/7/1935. RHB, RM. Debut for Warwickshire 1952, scoring
82 and 22* v Notts (Nottingham) in first match. Cap 1958. Benefit (£9,592)
in 1968. Left county staff after 1969 season to take post as coach at
Millfield School. Debut for Somerset by special registration and cap 1970.
Testimonial (£6,000) in 1975. Not re-engaged after 1976 season and made
debut for Glamorgan in 1977. Tests: 5 between 1964 and 1965. Bowled 77
and 62 overs in Australia's two completed innings in his two Tests in 1964.
Tour: South Africa 1964–65, 1,000 runs (3)—1,668 runs (av 30.88) in 1961
best. 100 wkts (8)—147 wkts (av 15.52) in 1967 best. Double in 1962.
Hat-trick Warwickshire v Somerset (Birmingham) 1969. Benson & Hedges
Gold awards: 4 (for Somerset). HS: 210 Warwickshire v Middlesex
(Nuneaton) 1962. HSTC: 9 v South Africa (Johannesburg) 1964–65.
HSC: 22* v Kent (Swansea) 1977. HSGC: 37 Warwickshire v Lancs
(Manchester) 1964. HSJPL: 61 Somerset v Middlesex (Lord's) 1972.
HSBH: 34 Somerset v Hants (Bournemouth) 1973. BB: 8–39 Warwick-
shire v Somerset (Weston-super-Mare) 1962. Had match analysis of
15–89 Warwickshire v Glamorgan (Swansea) 1967. BBTC: 6–94 v South
Africa (Nottingham) 1965. BBC: 4–46 v Yorks (Cardiff) 1977. BBGC:
3–16 Warwickshire v Worcs (Lord's) 1966. BBJPL: 4–7 Warwickshire v
Northants (Birmingham) 1969. BBBH: 4–13 Somerset v Glamorgan
(Taunton) 1975.

Anthony Elton (Tony) CORDLE B St Michael, Barbados 21/9/1940.
RHB, RFM. Debut 1963. Cap 1967. Benefit in 1977. HS: 81 v Cambridge
U (Swansea) 1972. HSGC: 36 v Lincs (Swansea) 1974. HSJPL: 87 v Notts
(Nottingham) 1971. HSBH: 27* v Hants (Swansea) 1976. BB: 9–49
(13–100 match) v Leics (Colwyn Bay) 1969. BBGC: 4–42 v Worcs
(Worcester) 1977. BBJPL: 4–16 v Somerset (Swansea) 1974. BBBH: 4–14
v Hants (Swansea) 1973.

Peter Gwynne CROWTHER B Neath 26/4/1952. RHB, OB. Debut
1977. HS: 99 v Cambridge U (Cambridge) 1977 (in debut match). Studied
at University College of Aberystwyth.

David Arthur FRANCIS (Cwmtawe Comprehensive School, Pontardawe) B Clydach (Glamorgan) 29/11/1953. RHB, OB. Debut 1973 after playing for 2nd XI in 1971 and 1972. HS: 110 v Warwickshire (Nuneaton) 1977. HSGC: 62* v Worcs (Worcester) 1977. HSJPL: 50 v Surrey (Byfleet) 1976. HSBH: 59 v Warwickshire (Birmingham) 1977.

Stuart Charles HARRISON (Abersychan GTS) B Cwmbran (Monmouthshire) 21/9/1951. RHB, RM. Debut 1971. Re-appeared in one championship match in 1977 – his first match since 1974. HS: 15 v Derbyshire (Derby) 1971. HSJPL: 20* v Middlesex (Cardiff) 1972. BB: 3–55 v Somerset (Cardiff) 1971. BBJPL: 3–47 v Derbyshire (Buxton) 1973. Trained as a teacher at Caerleon College of Education.

John Anthony HOPKINS B Maesteg 16/6/1953. Younger brother of J. D. Hopkins, formerly on staff and who has appeared for Middlesex. RHB, WK. Debut 1970. Cap 1977. Scored 1,357 runs (av 32.30) in 1977. Gillette Man of the Match awards: 1. Benson & Hedges Gold awards: 1. HS: 230 v Worcs (Worcester) 1977 – the fourth highest score for the county. HSGC: 63 v Leics (Swansea) 1977. HSJPL: 50 v Northants (Northampton) 1977. HSBH: 81 v Worcs (Swansea) 1977. Trained as a teacher at Trinity College of Education, Carmarthen.

Alan JONES B Swansea 4/11/1938. LHB, OB. Joined staff in 1955. Debut 1957. Cap 1962. Played for Western Australia in 1963–64, for Northern Transvaal in 1975–76 and for Natal in 1976–77. Benefit (£10,000) in 1972. Appointed county captain in 1976. Played one match v Rest of World 1970. 1,000 runs (17)—1,865 runs (av 34.53) in 1966 and 1,862 runs (av 38.00) in 1968 best. Scored two centuries in match (187* and 105*) v Somerset (Glastonbury) 1963 and (132 and 156*) v Yorks (Middlesbrough) 1976. Shared in record partnership for any wicket for county, 330 for 1st wkt with R. C. Fredericks v Northants (Swansea) 1972. Shared in 2nd wkt partnership record for county, 238 with A. R. Lewis v Sussex (Hastings) 1962. Has scored more runs and centuries for county than any other player. Gillette Man of the Match awards: 1. Benson & Hedges Gold awards: 1. HS: 187* v Somerset (Glastonbury) 1963. HSGC: 124* v Warwickshire (Birmingham) 1976. HSJPL: 90 v Derbyshire (Buxton) 1973. HSBH: 67 v Derbyshire (Cardiff) 1977.

Alan Lewis JONES (Ystalyfera GS and Cwmtawe Comprehensive School) B Alltwen (Glamorgan) 1/6/1957. No relation to A. and E. W. Jones. LHB. Played for 2nd XI in 1972. Debut 1973 at age of 16 years 3 months. Toured West Indies with England Young Cricketers 1976. HS: 57 v Oxford U (Oxford) 1976. HSGC: 11 v Hants (Southampton) 1975. HSJPL: 62 v Hants (Cardiff) 1975. HSBH: 30 v Glos (Bristol) 1975.

Eifion Wyn JONES B Velindre (Glamorgan) 25/6/1942. Brother of A. Jones. RHB, WK. Debut 1961. Cap 1967. Benefit (£17,000) in 1975. Dismissed 94 batsman (85 ct 9 st) in 1970. Dismissed 7 batsmen (6 ct 1 st) in innings v Cambridge U (Cambridge) 1970. Benson & Hedges Gold awards: 1. HS: 146* v Sussex (Hove) 1968. HSGC: 67* v Herts (Swansea) 1969. HSJPL: 48 v Hants (Cardiff) 1971. HSBH: 39* v Minor Counties (West) (Amersham) 1977.

GLAMORGAN

Michael John (Mike) LLEWELLYN B Clydach (Glamorgan) 27/11/1953. LHB, OB. Debut 1970. Cap 1977. Gillette Man of the Match awards: 1. Benson & Hedges Gold awards: 2. HS: 129* v Oxford U (Oxford) 1977. HSGC: 62 v Middlesex (Lord's) 1977. HSJPL: 79* v Glos (Bristol) 1977. HSBH: 63 v Hants (Swansea) 1973. BB: 4–35 v Oxford U (Oxford) 1970.

Barry John LLOYD B Neath 6/9/1953. RHB, OB. Formerly on MCC groundstaff. Debut 1972. HS: 45* v Hants (Portsmouth) 1973. HSJPL: 13 v Derbyshire (Swansea) 1976. BB: 4–49 v Hants (Portsmouth) 1973. Trained as a teacher at Bangor Normal College.

Kevin James LYONS (Lady Mary's Boys' High School, Cardiff) B Cardiff 18/12/1946. RHB, RM. Debut 1967. Appointed assistant coach after 1972 season. HS: 92 v Cambridge U (Cambridge) 1972. HSGC: 16 v Cornwall (Truro) 1970. HSJPL: 56 v Notts (Nottingham) 1969. HSBH: 40 v Somerset (Pontypridd) 1972. BBBH: 4–61 v Warwickshire (Birmingham) 1977.

Malcolm Andrew NASH (Wells Cathedral School) B Abergavenny (Monmouthshire) 9/5/1945. LHB, LM. Debut 1966. Cap 1969. Benefit in 1978. Benson & Hedges Gold awards: 2. Hat-trick in John Player League v Worcs (Worcester) 1975. HS: 130 v Surrey (Oval) 1976. HSGC: 51 v Lincs (Swansea) 1974. HSJPL: 68 v Essex (Purfleet) 1972. HSBH: 103* v Hants (Swansea) 1976. BB: 9–56 (14–137 match) v Hants (Basingstoke) 1975. BBGC: 3–14 v Staffs (Stoke) 1971. BBJPL: 6–29 v Worcs (Worcester) 1975. BBBH: 4–12 v Surrey (Cardiff) 1975.

Rodney Craig ONTONG (Selborne College, East London) B Johannesburg, South Africa 9/9/1955. RHB, RFM. Debut 1972–73 for Border in Currie Cup competition. Debut for county 1975 after being on MCC staff. Transferred to Transvaal for 1976–77 season. HS: 106 Border v Transvaal B (East London) 1974–75. HSUK: 62 v Hants (Cardiff) 1977. HSGC: 14 v Leics (Swansea) 1977. HSJPL: 47 v Surrey (Ebbw Vale) 1977. HSBH: 35* v Warwickshire (Birmingham) 1977. BB: 7–60 Border v Northern Transvaal (Pretoria) 1975–76. BBUK: 5–71 v Hants (Cardiff) 1977. BBJPL: 3–17 v Surrey (Ebbw Vale) 1977. BBBH: 3–12 v Minor Counties (West) (Amersham) 1977.

Gwyn RICHARDS B Maesteg 29/11/1951. RHB, OB. Formerly on MCC staff. Debut 1971. Cap 1976. Benson & Hedges Gold awards: 1. HS: 102* v Yorks (Middlesbrough) 1976. HSGC: 18 v Surrey (Cardiff) 1977. HSJPL: 39 v Surrey (Ebbw Vale) 1977. HSBH: 52 v Hants (Swansea) 1975. BB: 4–55 v Middlesex (Swansea) 1976. BBJPL: 5–29 v Lancs (Swansea) 1977.

Peter Douglas SWART (Jameson HS, Gatooma, Rhodesia) B Bulawayo, Rhodesia 27/4/1946. RHB, RM. Debut 1965–66 for Rhodesia in Currie Cup Competition. Subsequently played for Western Province from 1967–68. Played for International Cavaliers v Barbados (Scarborough) 1969 and for D. H. Robins' XI v Pakistanis (Eastbourne) 1974.

74

Professional for Accrington in 1969 and for Haslingden from 1974 to 1977 in Lancashire League. Has joined Glamorgan for 1978. HS: 109 Western Province v Orange Free State (Bloemfontein) 1968–69. HSUK: 19 International Cavaliers v Barbados (Scarborough) 1969. BB: 6–85 Western Province v Natal (Pietermaritzburg) 1971–72. BBUK: 4–74 International Cavaliers v Barbados (Scarborough) 1969.

Alan Haydn WILKINS (Whitchurch HS, Cardiff) B Cardiff 22/8/1953. RHB, LM. Played in two John Player League matches in 1975. Debut 1976. HS: 70 v Notts (Worksop) 1977. BB: 5–58 v Hants (Portsmouth) 1977. BBJPL: 5–32 v Notts (Nottingham) 1977. Trained as a teacher at Loughborough College of Education.

David Lawrence WILLIAMS (Neath CGS) B Tonna, Neath, 20/11/1946. LHB, RFM. Joined staff and made debut 1969 after playing for 2nd XI in 1967 and 1968. Cap 1971. Not re-engaged after 1976 season, but played in two one-day matches in 1977. Benson & Hedges Gold awards: 1. HS: 37* v Essex (Chelmsford) 1969. HSJPL: 10 v Kent (Swansea) 1973. BB: 7–60 v Lancs (Blackpool) 1970. BBGC: 3–15 v Essex (Ilford) 1971. BBJPL: 5–31 v Surrey (Byfleet) 1971. BBBH: 5–30 v Hants (Bournemouth) 1972. Rugby player.

NB The following players whose particulars appeared in the 1977 Annual have been omitted: A. W. Allin, G. D. Armstrong, G. P. Ellis, and C. L. King.

COUNTY AVERAGES

Schweppes County Championship: Played 21, won 3, drawn 11, lost 7, abandoned 1
All first-class matches: Played 24, won 4, drawn 13, lost 7, abandoned 1

BATTING AND FIELDING

Cap		M	I	NO	Runs	HS	Avge	100	50	Ct	St
—	B. J. Lloyd	7	7	6	54	13*	54.00	—	—	2	—
1962	A. Jones	21	35	1	1272	115	37.41	2	7	6	—
1977	J. A. Hopkins	24	43	1	1357	230	32.30	1	8	14	—
—	A. L. Jones	3	3	1	63	46	31.50	—	—	—	—
—	C. L. King	16	27	1	811	78	31.19	—	6	13	—
1977	M. J. Llewellyn	23	36	6	842	129*	28.06	1	4	12	—
—	D. A. Francis	21	35	3	738	110	23.06	1	1	10	—
—	K. J. Lyons	6	7	1	126	65*	21.00	—	1	—	—
—	P. G. Crowther	5	7	0	138	99	19.71	—	1	2	—
1976	G. Richards	24	37	5	621	74*	19.40	—	3	6	—
1969	M. A. Nash	22	31	6	477	56	19.08	—	2	6	—
—	R. C. Ontong	20	33	2	587	62	18.93	—	2	10	—
1967	A. E. Cordle	22	27	11	302	49	18.87	—	—	7	—
1967	E. W. Jones	24	31	5	481	51*	18.50	—	2	43	3
—	A. H. Wilkins	18	21	6	157	70	10.46	—	1	5	—
—	T. W. Cartwright	7	11	2	76	22*	8.44	—	—	2	—

Played in one match: S. C. Harrison 0, 4.

GLAMORGAN

BOWLING

	Type	O	M	R	W	Avge	Best	5 wI	10 wM
A. H. Wilkins	LM	356.1	73	1103	47	23.46	5-58	2	—
M. A. Nash	LM	646.3	176	1970	81	24.32	6-102	4	—
T. W. Cartwright	RM	131.3	52	258	10	25.80	4-46	—	—
A. E. Cordle	RFM	528	120	1612	55	29.30	6-13	3	—
R. C. Ontong	RFM	248.1	47	851	25	34.04	5-71	1	—
C. L. King	RM	259.1	58	730	20	36.50	4-31	—	—
B. J. Lloyd	OB	155	46	434	11	39.45	2-31	—	—
G. Richards	OB	288.2	52	927	10	92.70	2-18	—	—

Also bowled: P. G. Crowther 7-1-22-1; S. C. Harrison 20-6-59-1;
J. A. Hopkins 2-1-2-0; A. Jones 2.4-2-4-0; K. J. Lyons 12.1-3-47-1.

County Records

First-class cricket

Highest innings totals:	For .....587-8d v Derbyshire (Cardiff)	1951
	Agst.....653-6d by Gloucestershire (Bristol)	1928
Lowest innings totals:	For .....22 v Lancashire (Liverpool)	1924
	Agst.....33 by Leicestershire (Ebbw Vale)	1965
Highest individual innings:	For .....287* E. Davies v Gloucestershire (Newport)	1939
	Agst.....302* W. R. Hammond for Glos (Bristol)	1934
	302 W. R. Hammond for Glos (Newport)	1939
Best bowling in an innings:	For .....10–51 J. Mercer v Worcs (Worcester)	1936
	Agst.....10–18 G. Geary for Leics (Pontypridd)	1929
Best bowling in a match:	For ...17-212 J. C. Clay v Worcs (Swansea)	1937
	Agst.....16–96 G. Geary for Leics (Pontypridd)	1929
Most runs in a season:	2071 (av 49.30) W. G. A. Parkhouse	1959
runs in a career:	26590 (av 32.74) A. Jones	1957–1977
100s in a season:	7 by W. G. A. Parkhouse	1950
100s in a career:	39 by A. Jones	1957–1977
wickets in a season:	176 (av 17.34) J. C. Clay	1937
wickets in a career:	2174 (av 20.95) D. J. Shepherd	1950–1972

RECORD WICKET STANDS

1st	330	A. Jones & R.C.Fredericks v Northamptonshire (Swansea)	1972
2nd	238	A. Jones & A. R. Lewis v Sussex (Hastings)	1962
3rd	313	E. Davies & W. E. Jones v Essex (Brentwood)	1948
4th	263	G. Lavis & C. Smart v Worcestershire (Cardiff)	1934
5th	264	M. Robinson & S. W. Montgomery v Hampshire (Bournemouth)	1949
6th	230	W. E. Jones & B. L. Muncer v Worcestershire (Worcester)	1953
7th	195*	W. Wooller & W. E. Jones v Lancashire (Liverpool)	1947
8th	202	D. Davies & J. J. Hills v Sussex (Eastbourne)	1928
9th	203*	J. J. Hills & J. C. Clay v Worcestershire (Swansea)	1929
10th	131*	C. Smart & W. D. Hughes v South Africans (Cardiff)	1935

76

One-day cricket

Highest innings totals:	Gillette Cup	283–3 v Warwickshire (Birmingham)	1976
	John Player League	266–6 v Northants (Wellingborough)	1975
	Benson & Hedges Cup	245–7 v Hampshire (Swansea)	1976
Lowest innings totals:	Gillette Cup	76 v Northants (Northampton)	1968
	John Player League	65 v Surrey (Oval)	1969
	Benson & Hedges Cup	68 v Lancs (Manchester)	1973
Highest individual innings:	Gillette Cup	124* A. Jones v Warwickshire (Birmingham)	1976
	John Player League:	97* G. Ellis v Yorks (Leeds)	1976
	Benson & Hedges Cup	103* M. A. Nash v Hants (Swansea)	1976
Best bowling figures:	Gillette Cup	5–21 P. M. Walker v Cornwall (Truro)	1970
	John Player League	6–29 M. A. Nash v Worcs (Worcester)	1975
	Benson & Hedges Cup	5–30 D. L. Williams v Hants (Bournemouth)	1972

GLOUCESTERSHIRE

Formation of present club: 1871.
Colours: Blue, gold, brown, sky-blue, green, and red.
Badge: Coat of Arms of the City and County of Bristol.
County Champions (2): 1876 and 1877.
Joint Champions (2): 1873 and 1880.
Gillette Cup Winners: 1973.
Best Position in John Player League: 6th in 1969, 1973 and 1977.
Benson & Hedges Cup Winners: 1977.
Gillette Man of the Match awards: 17.
Benson & Hedges Gold awards: 16.

Secretary: A. S. Brown, County Ground, Nevil Road, Bristol, BS7 9EJ.
Captain: M. J. Procter.

Philip BAINBRIDGE (Hanley HS and Stoke-on-Trent Sixth Form College) B Stoke-on-Trent 16/4/1958. RHB, RM. Played for four 2nd XI's in 1976 – Derbyshire, Glos, Northants and Warwickshire. Debut 1977. HS: 49 v Hants (Southampton) 1977. Trained as a teacher at Borough Road College of Education.

Allan Robert BORDER (North Sydney Boys' High School) B Sydney 27/7/1955. LHB, LM/SLA. Debut 1976–77 for New South Wales. Debut for county 1977. One match v Oxford U (Oxford). HS: 68 New South Wales v Western Australia (Perth) 1976–77. HSUK: 15* v Oxford U (Oxford) 1977.

Brian Maurice **BRAIN** (King's School, Worcester) B Worcester 13/9/1940. RHB, RFM. Debut for Worcs 1959. Left staff in 1960. Rejoined staff in 1963 and reappeared in 1964. Cap 1966. Left staff in 1971, but rejoined in 1973. Not re-engaged after 1975 season and joined Glos in 1976. Cap 1977. Gillette Man of the Match awards: 1 (for Worcs). HS: 57 v Essex (Cheltenham) 1976. HSGC: 21* Worcs v Sussex (Worcester) 1967. HSJPL: 15 Worcs v Hants (Northampton) 1974. HSBH: 12 Worcs v Lancs (Manchester) 1973. BB: 8–55 Worcs v Essex (Worcester) 1975. BBC: 7–51 v Australians (Bristol) 1977. BBGC: 4–13 Worcs v Durham (Chester-le-Street) 1968. BBJPL: 4–27 Worcs v Somerset (Taunton) 1970. BBBH: 4–30 v Somerset (Bristol) 1977.

Andrew James (Andy) **BRASSINGTON** B Bagnall (Staffordshire) 9/8/1954. RHB, WK. Debut 1974. HS: 28 v Glamorgan (Cardiff) 1975. Plays soccer as a goalkeeper.

John Henry **CHILDS** B Plymouth 15/8/1951. LHB, SLA. Played for Devon 1973–74. Debut 1975. Cap 1977. HS: 12 v Derbyshire (Ilkeston) 1977. HSJPL: 11* v Essex (Cheltenham) 1975. BB: 5–39 v Hants (Bristol) 1976. BBJPL: 4–15 v Northants (Northampton) 1976.

Nicholas Henry Charles (Nick) **COOPER** (St Brendan's College, Bristol) B Bristol 14/10/1953. LHB. Debut 1975. HS: 106 v Oxford U (Oxford) 1976. HSJPL: 12 v Essex (Cheltenham) 1975 and 106 v Glamorgan (Cardiff) 1976. Studied at University of East Anglia.

Ian Cunningham **CRAWFORD** (Colston's School, Bristol) B Bristol 13/9/1954. RHB, OB. Debut 1975. Did not play in 1976 or 1977. HS: 12 v Notts (Nottingham) 1975. Studied at University College, Swansea.

Jack **DAVEY** (Tavistock GS) B Tavistock (Devon) 4/9/1944. LHB LFM. Played for Devonshire in 1964 and 1965. Debut 1966. Cap 1971. Joint benefit in 1978 with D. R. Shepherd. Hat-trick v Oxford U (Oxford) 1976. HS: 53* v Glamorgan (Bristol) 1977. HSBH: 16 v Somerset (Street) 1975. BB: 6–95 v Notts (Gloucester) 1967. BBGC: 4–35 v Essex (Chelmsford) 1973. BBJPL: 4–11 v Glamorgan (Lydney) 1975. BBBH: 3–26 v Somerset (Taunton) 1972.

Nicholas Hugh (Nick) **FINAN** (St Brendan's College, Bristol) B Knowle, Bristol 3/7/1954. 6ft 3in tall. RHB, RM. Debut 1975. HS: 18 v Worcs (Worcester) 1977. HSJPL: 11 v Essex (Cheltenham) 1975.

James Clive (Jim) **FOAT** (Millfield School) B Salford Priors (Warwickshire) 21/11/1952. RHB, RM. Debut 1972. Benson & Hedges Gold awards: 1. HS: 116 v Glamorgan (Bristol) 1975. HSGC: 49* v Northants (Bristol) 1977. HSJPL: 60 v Glamorgan (Bristol) 1973. HSBH: 73* v Somerset (Street) 1975.

David Anthony **GRAVENEY** (Millfield School) B Bristol 21/1/1953. Son of J. K. R. Graveney, RHB, SLA. Debut 1972. Cap 1976. HS: 62 v Glamorgan (Bristol) 1975. HSGC: 44 v Surrey (Bristol) 1973. HSJPL:

44 v Essex (Cheltenham) 1975. HSBH: 21 v Somerset (Street) 1975. BB: 8–85 v Notts (Cheltenham) 1974. BBGC: 3–67 v Leics (Leicester) 1975. BBJPL: 4–22 v Hants (Lydney) 1974. BBBH: 3–32 v Middlesex (Bristol) 1977.

Alastair James HIGNELL (Denstone College and Cambridge) B Cambridge 4/9/1955. RHB, LB. Scored 117* and 78* for England Schools v All India Schools (Birmingham) 1973 and 133 for England Young Cricketers v West Indies Young Cricketers (Arundel) 1974. Debut 1974. Cap 1977. Blue 1975–76–77 (captain). Re-elected University captain for 1978. 1,000 runs (2)—1,140 runs (av 30.81) in 1976 best. Benson & Hedges Gold awards: 1 (for Combined Universities). HS: 149 Cambridge U v Glamorgan (Cambridge) 1977. HSC: 119 v West Indians (Bristol) 1976. HSGC: 85* v Northants (Bristol) 1977. HSJPL: 51 v Northants (Northampton) 1976. HSBH: 51 Combined Universities v Kent (Canterbury) 1977. Blue for rugby 1974–75 (captain) –76–77 (captain). Toured Australia with England Rugby team 1975. 9 caps for England between 1975 and 1976–77.

Martin David PARTRIDGE (Marling School, Stroud) B Birdlip (Glos) 25/10/1954. LHB, RM. Debut 1976. HS: 23 v West Indians (Bristol) 1976. HSJPL: 12 v Leics (Cheltenham) 1976. BBJPL: 5–47 v Kent (Cheltenham) 1977. Studied civil engineering at Bradford University.

Michael John (Mike) PROCTER (Hilton College, Natal) B Durban 15/9/1946. RHB, RF/OB. Vice-captain of South African Schools team to England 1963. Debut for county 1965 in one match v South Africans. Returned home to make debut for Natal in 1965–66 Currie Cup competition. Joined staff in 1968. Cap 1968. *Wisden* 1969. Transferred to Western Province for 1969–70 Currie Cup competition, Rhodesia in 1970–71 and Natal 1976–77. Appointed county captain in 1977. Benefit (£15,500) in 1976. Tests: 7 for South Africa v Australia 1966–67 and 1969–70. Played in 5 matches for Rest of World v England in 1970. 1,000 runs (6)—1,786 runs (av 45.79) in 1971 best. 100 wkts (2)—109 wkts (av 18.04) in 1977 best. Scored 6 centuries in 6 consecutive innings for Rhodesia 1970–71 to equal world record. Scored two centuries in match (114 and 131) for Rhodesia v International Wanderers (Salisbury) 1972–73. Hat-tricks (2): v Essex (Westcliff) 1972—all lbw—and also scored a century in the match, and v Essex (Southend) 1977. Also v Hants (Southampton) in Benson & Hedges Cup, 1977, Had match double of 100 runs and 10 wkts (108 and 13–73) v Worcs (Cheltenham) 1977. Gillette Man of the Match awards: 2. Benson & Hedges Gold awards: 4. HS: 254 Rhodesia v Western Province (Salisbury) 1970–71. HSUK: 167 v Derbyshire (Chesterfield) 1971. HSTC: 48 South Africa v Australia (Cape Town) 1969–70. HSGC: 107 v Sussex (Hove) 1971. HSJPL: 109 v Warwickshire (Cheltenham) 1972. HSBH: 154* v Somerset (Taunton) 1972. BB: 9–71 Rhodesia v Transvaal (Bulawayo) 1972–73. BBUK: 7–35 v Worcs (Cheltenham) 1977. BBTC: 6–73 South Africa v Australia (Port Elizabeth) 1969–70. BBGC: 4–21 v Yorks (Leeds) 1976. BBJPL: 5–8 v Middlesex (Gloucester) 1977. BBBH: 6–13 v Hants (Southampton) 1977.

SADIQ MOHAMMAD B Junagadh (India) 3/5/1945. LHB, LBG. Youngest of family of five cricket-playing brothers which include Hanif and Mushtaq Mohammad. Debut in Pakistan 1959–60 at age of 14 years

GLOUCESTERSHIRE

9 months and has played subsequently for various Karachi sides and Pakistan International Airways. Played for Northants 2nd XI in 1967 and 1968, for Nelson in Lancs League in 1968, and subsequently for Poloc, Glasgow in Scottish Western Union. Played for D. H. Robins' XI v Oxford U 1969 and for Essex v Jamaica XI in 1970. Debut for county 1972. Cap 1973. Played for Tasmania against MCC in 1974–75. Tests: 29 for Pakistan between 1969–70 and 1976–77. Tours: Pakistan to England 1971 and 1974, Australia and New Zealand 1972–73, Australia and West Indies 1976–77. 1,000 runs (4)—1,759 runs (av 47.54) in 1976 best. Scored 1,169 runs (av 41.75) in Australia and New Zealand 1972–73. Scored 4 centuries in 4 consecutive innings in 1976 including two centuries in match (163* and 150) v Derbyshire (Bristol). Gillette Man of Match awards: 1. Benson & Hedges Gold awards: 3. HS: 184* v New Zealanders (Bristol) 1973. HSTC: 166 Pakistan v New Zealand (Wellington) 1972–73. HSGC: 122 v Lancs (Manchester) 1975. HSJPL: 131 v Somerset (Imperial Ground, Bristol) 1975. HSBH: 128 v Minor Counties (Bristol) 1974. BB: 5–29 Pakistan International Airways v Dacca (Dacca) 1964–65 and 5–29 Karachi Blues v Lahore Greens (Karachi) 1970–71. BBUK: 5–37 v Kent (Bristol) 1973. BBGC: 3–19 v Oxfordshire (Bristol) 1975. BBJPL: 3–27 v Hants (Bristol) 1972. BBBH: 3–20 v Minor Counties (Bristol) 1972.

Julian Howard SHACKLETON (Millfield School) B Todmorden (Yorks) 29/1/1952. Son of D. Shackleton, former Hants players. RHB, RM. Debut 1971. HS: 30 v Somerset (Taunton) 1976. HSJPL: 41* v Surrey (Cheltenham) 1977. HSJPL: 18* v Leics (Leicester) 1977. BB: 4–28 v Surrey (Bristol) 1971. BBJPL: 5–20 v Surrey (Cheltenham) 1977. BBBH: 3-26 v Minor Counties (West) (Amersham) 1976.

David Robert SHEPHERD (Barnstaple GS) B Bideford (Devon) 27/12/1940. RHB, RM. Played for Devonshire from 1959 to 1964. Played for Minor Counties v Australians 1964. Debut 1965 scoring 108 in first match v Oxford U. Cap 1969. Joint benefit in 1978 with J. Davey. 1,000 runs (2)—1,079 runs (av 26.97) in 1970 best. Gillette Man of Match awards: 1. Benson & Hedges Gold awards: 1. HS: 153 v Middlesex (Bristol) 1968. HSGC: 72* v Surrey (Bristol) 1973. HSJPL: 81 v Warwickshire (Cheltenham) 1973. HSBH: 81 v Hants (Bristol) 1974. Has played rugby for Bideford.

Andrew Willis STOVOLD (Filton HS) B Bristol 19/3/1953. RHB, WK. Toured West Indies with England Young Cricketers 1972. Played for 2nd XI since 1971. Debut 1973. Cap 1976. Played for Orange Free State in 1974–75 and 1975–76 Currie Cup competition. 1,000 runs (2)— 1,223 runs (av 34.94) in 1977 best. Benson & Hedges Gold awards: 3. HS: 196 v Notts (Nottingham) 1977. HSGC: 35 v Lancs (Manchester) 1975 and 35 v Lancs (Manchester) 1976. HSJPL: 98* v Kent (Cheltenham) 1977. HSBH: 104 v Leics (Leicester) 1977.

Martin Jeffrey VERNON B Middlesex Hospital, St Marylebone 4/7/1951. RHB, RFM. On MCC staff from 1966–72. Debut for Middlesex 1974. Not re-engaged after 1976 season and made debut for Glos for 1977. HS: 27 Middlesex v Sussex (Hove) 1974. HSBH: 15* Middlesex v Minor Counties (South) (Amersham) 1975. BB: 6-58 Middlesex v Somerset (Taunton) 1974. BBJPL: 3–13 Middlesex v Yorks (Leeds) 1974. BBBH: 3–33 Middlesex v Sussex (Hove) 1975.

Syed **ZAHEER ABBAS** B Sialkot (Pakistan) 24/7/1947. RHB, OB. Wears glasses. Debut for Karachi Whites 1965–66, subsequently playing for Pakistan International Airways. *Wisden* 1971. Debut for county 1972. Cap 1975. Tests: 26 for Pakistan between 1969–70 and 1976–77. Played in 5 matches for Rest of the World v Australia 1971–72. Tours: Pakistan to England 1971 and 1974, Australia and New Zealand 1972–73, Australia and West Indies 1976–77, Rest of World to Australia 1971–72. 1,000 runs (6)—2,554 runs (av 75.11) in 1976 best. Scored 1,597 runs (av 84.05) in Pakistan 1973–74—the record aggregate for a Pakistan season. Scored 4 centuries in 4 consecutive innings in 1970–71. Scored two centuries in a match twice in 1976–216* and 156* v Surrey (Oval) and 230* and 104* v Kent (Canterbury) and once in 1977—205* and 108* v Sussex (Cheltenham) to create record of being only player ever to score a double-century and a century in a match on three occasions. Was dismissed, hit the ball twice, for Pakistan International Airways v Karachi Blues (Karachi) 1969–70. Gillette Man of Match awards: 4. HS: 274 Pakistan v England (Birmingham) 1971, sharing in record 2nd wkt partnership for Pakistan first-class cricket 291 with Mushtaq Mohammad. HSC: 230* v Kent (Canterbury) 1977. HSGC: 131* v Leics (Leicester) 1975. HSJPL: 114* v Hants (Bristol) 1976. HSBH: 98 v Surrey (Oval) 1975. BB: 5–15 Dawood Club v Railways (Lahore) 1975–76.

NB J. P. Sullivan who re-appeared in 1977 has not been included as he is unlikely to play again. His career record will be found elsewhere in this Annual.

COUNTY AVERAGES

Schweppes County Championship: Played 20, won 9, drawn 6, lost 5, abandoned 2

All first-class matches: **Played 22, won 9, drawn 7, lost 6, abandoned 2**
BATTING AND FIELDING

Cap		M	I	NO	Runs	HS	Avge	100	50	Ct	St
1975	Zaheer Abbas	20	36	6	1584	205*	52.80	5	9	16	—
1976	A. W. Stovold	22	39	4	1223	196	34.94	1	6	32	6
1977	A. J. Hignell	12	18	2	497	92	31.06	—	4	13	—
1968	M. J. Procter	21	33	2	857	115	27.64	2	3	17	—
1969	D. R. Shepherd	22	32	5	737	142*	27.29	1	4	7	—
1973	Sadiq Mohammad	21	38	1	997	88	26.94	—	6	19	—
—	P. Bainbridge	8	11	0	211	49	19.18	—	—	6	—
—	A. J. Brassington	6	6	3	56	14*	18.66	—	—	12	2
—	J. H. Shackleton	19	23	6	260	41*	15.29	—	—	6	—
—	J. C. Foat	14	23	3	282	44	14.10	—	—	4	—
1976	D. A. Graveney	19	23	3	268	37	13.40	—	—	14	—
—	N. H. Finan	4	2	0	22	18	11.00	—	—	1	—
1977	B. M. Brain	20	25	8	172	35	10.11	—	—	8	—
—	M. D. Partridge	4	5	2	27	17*	9.00	—	—	2	—
1977	J. H. Childs	19	15	8	38	12	5.42	—	—	6	—
—	M. J. Vernon	5	6	0	13	4	2.16	—	—	3	—

Played in two matches: N. H. C. Cooper 7, 19, 25 (1 ct); J. P. Sullivan 5, 21, 0, 0 (2 ct).

Played in one match: A. R. Border 15*; J. Davey 53*, 2*.

81

GLOUCESTERSHIRE
BOWLING

	Type	O	M	R	W	Avge	Best	5 wI	10 wM
M. J. Procter	RF/OB	777.3	226	1967	109	18.04	7–35	9	1
B. M. Brain	RFM	571.1	132	1637	77	21.25	7–51	4	—
D. A. Graveney	SLA	572.5	184	1536	63	24.38	6–70	3	—
J. H. Childs	SLA	468	119	1372	47	29.19	5–41	2	—
J. H. Shackleton	RM	231	54	715	12	59.58	2–19	—	—

Also bowled: J. Davey 17–5–48–0; N. H. Finan 41–9–129–1; J. C. Foat 1–0–6–0; A. J. Hignell 5–0–12–0; M. D. Partridge 20.2–5–58–3; Sadiq Mohammad 84.4–22–288–4; D. R. Shepherd 1–0–8–0; A. W. Stovold 3–0–15–0; J. P. Sullivan 11–2–50–2; M. J. Vernon 54.5–7–217–3; Zaheer Abbas 9–3–23–0.

County Records

First-class cricket

Highest innings totals:	For ......653–6d v Glamorgan (Bristol)	1928
	Agst......774–7d by Australians (Bristol)	1948
Lowest innings totals:	For ......17 v Australians (Cheltenham)	1896
	Agst......12 by Northamptonshire (Gloucester)	1907
Highest individual innings:	For ......318*W.G.Grace v Yorkshire (Cheltenham)	1876
	Agst......296 A. O. Jones for Notts (Nottingham)	1903
Best bowling in an innings:	For ......10–40 G. Dennett v Essex (Bristol)	1906
	Agst......10–66 A. A. Mailey for Aust (Cheltenham)	1921
	and K. Smales for Notts (Stroud)	1956
Best bowling in a match:	For ......17–56 C. W. L. Parker v Essex (Gloucester)	1925
	Agst......15–87 A. J. Conway for Worcestershire (Moreton-in-Marsh)	1914

Most runs in a season: 2860 (av 69.75) W. R. Hammond 1933
runs in a career: 33664 (av 57.05) W.R.Hammond1920–1951
100s in a season: 13 by W. R. Hammond 1938
100s in a career: 113 by W. R. Hammond 1920–1951
wickets in a season: 222 (av 16.80 & 16.37)
T. W. Goddard 1937 & 1947
wickets in a career: 3171 (av 19.43) C. W. L. Parker 1903–1935

RECORD WICKET STANDS

1st	395	D. M. Young & R. B. Nicholls v Oxford U (Oxford)	1962
2nd	256	C. T. M. Pugh & T. W. Graveney v Derbyshire (Chesterfield)	1960
3rd	336	W. R. Hammond & B. H. Lyon v Leicestershire (Leicester)	1933
4th	321	W. R. Hammond & W. L. Neale v Leicestershire (Gloucester)	1937
5th	261	W. G. Grace & W. O. Moberley v Yorkshire (Cheltenham)	1876
6th	320	G. L. Jessop & J. H. Board v Sussex (Hove)	1902
7th	248	W. G. Grace & E. L. Thomas v Sussex (Hove)	1896
8th	239	W. R. Hammond & A. E. Wilson v Lancashire (Bristol)	1938
9th	193	W. G. Grace & S. A. Kitcat v Sussex (Bristol)	1896
10th	131	W. R.Gouldsworthy & J.G. Bessant v Somerset(Bristol)	1923

One-day cricket

Highest innings totals:	Gillette Cup	327–7 v Berkshire (Reading)	1966
	John Player League	255 v Somerset (Imperial Ground, Bristol)	1975
	Benson & Hedges Cup	282 v Hants (Bristol)	1974
Lowest innings totals:	Gillette Cup	86 v Sussex (Hove)	1969
	John Player League	82 v Hants (Lydney)	1974
	Benson & Hedges Cup	62 v Hants (Bristol)	1975
Highest individual innings:	Gillette Cup	131* Zaheer Abbas v Leics (Leicester)	1975
	John Player League	131 Sadiq Mohammad v Somerset (Imperial Ground, Bristol)	1975
	Benson & Hedges Cup	154* M. J. Procter v Somerset (Taunton)	1972
Best bowling figures:	Gillette Cup	5–39 R. D. V. Knight v Surrey (Bristol)	1971
	John Player League	5–8 M. J. Procter v Middlesex (Gloucester)	1977
	Benson & Hedges Cup	6–13 M. J. Procter v Hampshire (Southampton)	1977

HAMPSHIRE

Formation of present club: 1863.
Colours: Blue, gold, and white.
Badge: Tudor rose and crown.
County Champions (2): 1961 and 1973.
Gillette Cup semi-finalists (2): 1966 and 1976.
John Player League Champions: 1975.
Benson & Hedges Cup semi-finalists (2): 1975 and 1977.
Fenner Trophy winners (3): 1975, 1976 and 1977.
Gillette Man of the Match awards: 22.
Benson & Hedges Gold awards: 20.

Secretary: A. K. James, County Cricket
  Ground, Northlands Road, Southampton, SO9 2TY.
Captain: R. M. C. Gilliat.

Nigel Geoffrey COWLEY B Shaftesbury (Dorset) 1/3/1953. RHB, OB. Debut 1974. HS: 109* v Somerset (Taunton) 1977. HSGC: 32 v Middlesex (Lord's) 1977. HSJPL: 29 v Surrey (Southampton) 1977. HSBH: 59 v Glos (Southampton) 1977. BB: 5–94 v Glos (Bristol) 1977. BBJPL: 3–28 v Worcs (Worcester) 1977.

Richard Burtenshaw ELMS (Bexley/Erith Technical HS) B Sutton (Surrey) 5/4/1949. RHB, LFM. Debut for Kent 1970. Not re-engaged after 1976 season and made debut for Hants in 1977. HS: 30 v Essex (Portsmouth) 1977. HSBH: 19 Kent v Sussex (Hove) 1973. BB: 5–38 Kent v Middlesex (Lord's) 1973. BBC: 4–83 v Kent (Canterbury) 1977. BBJPL: 3–27 Kent v Derbyshire (Chesterfield) 1973. BBBH: 3–43 Kent v Sussex (Hove) 1973.

Richard Michael Charles GILLIAT (Charterhouse School and Oxford) B Ware (Herts) 20/5/1944. LHB, LB. Debut for Oxford U 1964. Blue 1964–65–66–67 (capt 1966). Debut for county 1966. Appointed assistant secretary in 1967, county vice-captain in 1969, and captain in 1971. Cap 1969. Benefit in 1978. 1,000 runs (4)—1,386 runs (av 39.60) in 1969 best. Benson & Hedges Gold awards: 1. HS: 223* v Warwickshire (Southampton) 1969. HSGC: 52 v Derbyshire (Southampton) 1976. HSJPL: 89 v Kent (Canterbury) 1976. HSBH: 81 v Glos (Bristol) 1974. Blues for soccer 1964–66 (capt in 1966).

Cuthbert Gordon GREENIDGE B St Peter, Barbados 1/5/1951. RHB, RM. Debut 1970. Cap 1972. Has subsequently played for Barbados. *Wisden* 1976. Tests: 17 for West Indies between 1974–75 and 1976–77. Tours: West Indies to India, Sri Lanka, and Pakistan 1974–75, Australia 1975–76, England 1976. 1,000 runs (7)—1,952 runs (av 55.77) in 1976 best. Scored two centuries in match (134 and 101) West Indies v England (Manchester) 1976. Gillette Man of Match awards: 2. Benson & Hedges Gold awards: 4. HS: 273* D. H. Robins' XI v Pakistanis (Eastbourne) 1974. HSC: 259 v Sussex (Southampton) 1975. HSTC: 134 West Indies v England (Manchester) 1976. HSGC: 177 v Glamorgan (Southampton) 1975—record for all one-day competitions. HSJPL: 102 v Sussex (Hove) 1974 and 102 v Somerset (Weston-super-Mare) 1975. HSBH: 173* v Minor Counties (Amersham) 1973—record for competition—and shared in partnership of 285* for second wicket with D. R. Turner—and the record partnership for all one-day competitions. BB: 5–49 v Surrey (Southampton) 1971.

Trevor Edward JESTY B Gosport 2/6/1948. RHB, RM. Debut 1966. Cap 1971. Played for Border in 1973–74 and Griqualand West in 1974–75 and 1975–76 Currie Cup competitions. 1,000 runs (2)—1,288 runs (av 35.77) in 1976 best. Gillette Man of Match awards: 1. Benson & Hedges Gold awards: 5. Took 3 wkts in 4 balls v Somerset (Portsmouth) 1969. HS: 159* v Somerset (Bournemouth) 1976. HSGC: 69 v Yorks (Bournemouth) 1977. HSJPL: 107 v Surrey (Southampton) 1977. HSBH: 105 v Glamorgan (Swansea) 1977. BB: 7–75 v Worcs (Southampton) 1976. BBGC: 4–32 v Notts (Nottingham) 1972. BBJPL: 6–20 v Glamorgan (Cardiff) 1975. BBBH: 4–28 v Somerset (Taunton) 1974.

Thomas James (Tom) MOTTRAM (Quarry Bank Comprehensive School, Liverpool) B Liverpool 7/9/1945. Tall (6ft 4in). RHB, RM. Played in one John Player League match in 1971. Debut 1972. Plays only in one-day matches. HS: 15* v Notts (Bournemouth) 1973. BB: 6–63 v Warwickshire (Coventry) 1973. BBGC: 3–51 v Lancs (Bournemouth) 1972. BBJPL: 5–21 v Derbyshire (Darley Dale) 1975. BBBH: 3–21 v Glos (Southampton) 1977. Has studied at Edinburgh University and Loughborough College.

Andrew Joseph (Andy) MURTAGH (St Joseph's College, Beulah Hill, London) B Dublin 6/5/1949. RHB, RM. Played for Surrey 2nd XI 1967–68 and for county 2nd XI since 1969. Debut 1973. Played for Eastern Province in 1973–74 Currie Cup competition. HS: 65 v Glos (Bournemouth) 1975.

HSGC: 32 v Derbyshire (Southampton) 1976. HSJPL: 65* v Derbyshire (Bournemouth) 1976. HSBH: 17 v Derbyshire (Southampton) 1976. BBJPL: 5–33 v Yorks (Huddersfield) 1977.

Nicholas Edward Julian POCOCK (Shrewsbury School) B Maracaibo, Venezuela 15/12/1951. RHB, LM. Debut 1976. HS: 68 v Leics (Bournemouth) 1976. HSJPL: 32 v Warwickshire (Basingstoke) 1977.

John Michael RICE (Brockley CGS, London) B Chandler's Ford (Hants) 23/10/1949. RHB, RM. On Surrey staff 1970, but not re-engaged. Debut 1971. Cap 1975. Hat-trick in John Player League v Northants (Southampton) 1975. Gillette Man of the Match awards: 1. Benson & Hedges Gold awards: 1. HS: 96* v Somerset (Weston-super-Mare) 1975. HSGC: 38 v Leics (Leicester) 1976. HSJPL: 54* v Somerset (Street) 1977. HSBH: 43 v Lancs (Southampton) 1977. BB: 7–48 v Worcs (Worcester) 1977. BBGC: 5–35 v Yorks (Bournemouth) 1977. BBJPL: 5–14 v Northants (Southampton) 1975. BBBH: 3–20 v Somerset (Bournemouth) 1975.

Barry Anderson RICHARDS (Durban HS) B Durban 21/7/1945. RHB, OB. Captain of South African Schools team to England 1963. Debut for Natal 1964–65. Appeared for Glos in one match in 1965 v South Africans, but decided not to qualify and returned home. Joined Hants in 1968 and scored 2,395 runs (av 47.90) in first full season, including over 2,000 runs in County Championships. Cap 1968. *Wisden* 1968. Played for South Australia in 1970–71. Benefit in 1977. Tests: 4 for South Africa v Australia 1969–70. Played in 5 matches for Rest of World v England 1970. Scored two centuries in match (130 and 104*) v Northants (Northampton) 1968, and (159 and 108) v Kent (Southampton) 1976. 1,000 runs (9)—2,395 runs (av 47.90) in 1968 best. Has also scored over 1,000 runs in 1969–70, 1971–72, 1972–73, 1973–74 and 1975–76 seasons in South Africa—his aggregate of 1,285 runs (av 80.31) in 1973–74 being a record for a South African. Also scored 1,538 runs (av 109.86) in Australia 1970–71. Gillette Man of Match awards: 3. Benson & Hedges Gold awards: 6. HS: 356 South Australia v Western Australia (Perth) 1970–71 scoring 325* on the first day of match. HSUK: 240 v Warwickshire (Coventry) 1974. HSTC: 140 South Africa v Australia (Durban) 1969–70. HSGC: 129 v Lancs (Bournemouth) 1972 and 129 v Glamorgan (Southampton) 1975. HSJPL: 155* v Yorks (Hull) 1970, record for the competition. HSBH: 129 v Glos (Bristol) 1974. BB: 7–63 v Rest of World (Bournemouth) 1968.

Anderson Montgomery Everton (Andy) ROBERTS B Urlings Village, Antigua 29/1/1951. RHB, RF. Debut for Leeward Islands v Windward Islands 1969–70 and has played subsequently for Combined Islands in Shell Shield competition. Debut 1973. Cap 1974. *Wisden* 1974. Played for New South Wales in 1976–77 Sheffield Shield competition. Tests: 25 for West Indies between 1973–74 and 1976–77. Tours: West Indies to India, Sri Lanka and Pakistan 1974–75, Australia 1975–76, England 1976. Took 119 wkts (av 13.62) in 1974. Took 100th wkt in Test cricket in 1976 in record time of 2 years 144 days. Benson & Hedges Gold awards: 1. HS: 56* West Indians v Middlesex (Lord's) 1976. HSTC: 35 West Indies v Pakistan (Port of Spain) 1976–77. HSC: 39 v Northants (Bournemouth) 1975. HSGC: 14* v Glamorgan (Southampton) 1975. HSJPL: 21* v Surrey (Oval) 1974. HSBH: 29 v Glos (Bristol) 1975. BB: 8–47 v Glamorgan (Cardiff) 1974. BBTC: 7–54 West Indies v Australia (Perth) 1975–76.

BBGC: 3–17 v Glamorgan (Southampton) 1975. BBJPL: 5–13 v Sussex (Hove) 1974. BBBH: 4–12 v Somerset (Bournemouth) 1975.

David John ROCK (Portsmouth GS) B Southsea 20/4/1957. RHB, RM. Debut 1976. HS: 114 v Leics (Leicester) 1977. HSGC: 50 v Middlesex (Lord's) 1977. HSJPL: 68 v Glos (Portsmouth) 1977.

John William SOUTHERN (The William Ellis School, Highgate) B King's Cross, London 2/9/1952. 6ft 3½in tall. RHB. SLA. Debut 1975. HS: 31* v Leics (Leicester) 1977. BB: 6–46 v Glos (Bournemouth) 1975. Obtained BSc degree in Chemistry at Southampton University.

George Robert (Bob) STEPHENSON (Derby School) B Derby 19/11/1942. RHB, WK. Debut for Derbyshire 1967 following injury to R. W. Taylor. Joined Hants by special registration in 1969 following resignation of B. S. V. Timms. Cap 1969. Dismissed 80 batsmen (73 ct 7 st) in 1970. HS: 100* v Somerset (Taunton) 1976. HSGC: 29 v Notts (Nottingham) 1972. HSJPL: 24* v Notts (Nottingham) 1976. HSBH: 29* v Somerset (Taunton) 1974. Soccer for Derby County, Shrewsbury Town, and Rochdale.

Keith STEVENSON (Bemrose GS, Derby) B Derby 6/10/1950. RHB, RM. Debut 1974. HS: 33 v Northants (Chesterfield) 1974. HSGC: 14 v Surrey (Ilkeston) 1976. BB: 7–68 v Warwickshire (Chesterfield) 1977. BBGC: 4–21 v Surrey (Ilkeston) 1976. BBJPL: 3–29 v Surrey (Chesterfield) 1975.

Michael Norman Somerset TAYLOR (Amersham College) B Amersham (Bucks) 12/11/1942. Twin brother of D. J. S. Taylor of Somerset. RHB, RM. Played for Buckinghamshire in 1961–62. Debut for Notts 1964. Cap 1967. Not re-engaged after 1972 season and made debut for Hants in 1973. Cap 1973. Took 99 wkts (av 21.00) in 1968. Hat-trick Notts v Kent (Dover) 1965. Gillette Man of Match awards: 1. Benson & Hedges Gold awards: 1 (for Notts). HS: 105 Notts v Lancs (Nottingham) 1967. HSC: 102 v Essex)Portsmouth) 1977. HSJPL: 58 Notts v Hants (Nottingham) 1972. HSJPL: 44 v Worcs (Worcester) 1973 and 44 v Glos (Bristol) 1976. HSBH: 41 v Minor Counties (South) (Portsmouth) 1974. BB: 7–23 v Notts (Basingstoke) 1977. BBGC: 4–31 Notts v Lancs (Nottingham) 1968. BBJPL: 4–20 Notts v Surrey (Nottingham) 1969. BBBH: 3–15 v Somerset (Taunton) 1974.

Timothy Maurice (Tim) TREMLETT (Richard Taunton College, Southampton) B Wellington (Somerset) 26/7/1956. Son of M. F. Tremlett, former Somerset player. RHB, RM. Debut 1976. HS: 14 v Glamorgan (Cardiff) 1977.

David Roy TURNER B Chippenham (Wilts) 5/2/1949. LHB, RM. Played for Wiltshire in 1965. Debut 1966. Cap 1970. 1,000 runs (5)—1,269 runs (av 36.25) in 1976 best. Gillette Man of Match awards: 1. Benson & Hedges Gold awards: 2. HS: 181* v Surrey (Oval) 1969. HSGC: 86 v Northants (Southampton) 1976. HSJPL: 99* v Glos (Bristol) 1972. HSBH: 123* v Minor Counties (South) (Amersham) 1973.

NB   R. S. Herman who re-appeared in one match in 1977 has not been included as he is unlikely to play again. His career record will be found elsewhere in this Annual.

COUNTY AVERAGES

Schweppes County Championship: **Played 22, won 6, drawn 11, lost 5**
All first-class matches: **Played 22, won 6, drawn 11, lost 5 abandoned 1**
BATTING AND FIELDING

Cap		M	I	NO	Runs	HS	Avge	100	50	Ct	St
1972	C. G. Greenidge	19	32	3	1771	208	(61.06)	6	6	18	—
1968	B. A. Richards	16	25	3	927	115	42.13	2	5	19	—
1971	T. E. Jesty	21	34	3	1230	144	39.67	4	5	12	—
—	N. G. Cowley	18	27	8	687	109*	36.15	1	6	8	—
1969	R. M. C. Gilliat	11	15	4	310	90	28.18	—	1	10	—
1969	G. R. Stephenson	22	23	6	415	76	24.41	—	1	41	3
—	N. E. J. Pocock	7	13	2	265	46*	24.09	—	—	2	—
—	D. J. Rock	11	19	0	454	114	23.89	2	1	5	—
1973	M. N. S. Taylor	21	26	5	467	102	22.23	1	—	11	—
1970	D. R. Turner	18	29	2	567	69	21.00	—	2	5	—
1975	J. M. Rice	21	29	0	566	78	19.51	—	4	19	—
—	A. J. Murtagh	5	7	2	91	41*	18.20	—	—	1	—
—	R. B. Elms	14	14	4	148	30	14.80	—	—	7	—
—	J. W. Southern	22	19	10	94	31*	10.44	—	—	4	—
1974	A. M. E. Roberts	14	13	2	102	19	9.27	—	—	4	—

Played in one match: R. S. Herman 0; T. M. Tremlett 1*, 14 (1 ct).

BOWLING

	Type	O	M	R	W	Avge	Best	5 wI	10 wM
A.M.E. Roberts	RF	349.2	109	793	40	19.82	5–32	2	—
M. N. S. Taylor	RM	394.5	114	1147	42	27.30	7–23	1	—
J. M. Rice	RM	484	139	1224	44	29.40	7–48	2	—
J. W. Southern	SLA	671.1	217	1660	53	31.32	6–81	2	—
R. B. Elms	LFM	287.4	64	926	26	35.61	4–83	—	—
T. E. Jesty	RM	260	72	692	18	38.44	3–62	—	—
N. G. Cowley	OB	400.3	92	1125	29	38.79	5–94	1	—

Also bowled: C. G. Greenidge 1–0–4–0; R. S. Herman 14–1–48–0;
A. J. Murtagh 19–5–66–1; N. E. J. Pocock 6–3–7–0; B. A. Richards
20–3–93–0; D. J. Rock 1–1–0–0; T. M. Tremlett 7–3–13–1; D. R. Turner
2–0–4–0.

County Records

First-class cricket

Highest innings totals:	For .....672–7d v Somerset (Taunton)	1899
	Agst....742 by Surrey (The Oval)	1909
Lowest innings totals:	For .....15 v Warwickshire (Birmingham)	1922
	Agst..23 by Yorkshire (Middlesbrough)	1965
Highest individual innings:	For .....316 R. H. Moore v Warwickshire (Bournemouth)	1937
	Agst..302*P. Holmes for Yorkshire (Portsmouth)	1920
Best bowling in an innings:	For .....9–25 R.M.H.Cottam v Lancs (Manchester)	1965
	Agst..9–21 L.B.Richmond for Notts (Nottingham)	1921
Best bowling in a match:	For .....16–88 J. A. Newman v Somerset (Weston-super-Mare)	1927
	Agst..17–119 W. Mead for Essex (Southampton)	1895

HAMPSHIRE

Most runs in a season: 2854 (av 79.27) C. P. Mead   1928
    runs in a career: 48892 (av 48.84) C. P. Mead   1905–1936
    100s in a season: 12 by C. P. Mead   1928
    100s in a career: 138 by C. P. Mead   1905–1936
    wickets in a season: 190 (av 15.61) A. S. Kennedy   1922
    wickets in a career: 2669 (av 18.22) D. Shackleton 1948–1969

RECORD WICKET STANDS

1st	249	R. E. Marshall & J. R. Gray v Middlesex (Portsmouth)	1960
2nd	321	G. Brown & E. I. M. Barrett v Gloucestershire (Southampton)	1920
3rd	344	C. P. Mead & G. Brown v Yorkshire (Portsmouth)	1927
4th	263	R. E. Marshall & D. A. Livingstone v Middlesex (Lord's)	1970
5th	235	G. Hill & D. F. Walker v Sussex (Portsmouth)	1937
6th	411	R. M. Poore & E. G. Wynyard v Somerset (Taunton)	1899
7th	325	G. Brown & C. H. Abercrombie v Essex (Leyton)	1913
8th	178	C. P. Mead & C. P. Brutton v Worcestershire (Bournemouth)	1925
9th	230	D. A. Livingstone & A. T. Castell v Surrey (Southampton)	1962
10th	192	A. Bowell & W. H. Livsey v Worcestershire (Bournemouth)	1921

NB   A partnership of 334 for the first wicket by B. A. Richards, C. G. Greenidge and D. R. Turner occurred against Kent at Southampton in 1973. Richards retired hurt after 241 runs had been scored and in the absence of any official ruling on the matter, it is a matter of opinion as to whether it should be regarded as the first-wicket record for the county.

One-day cricket

Highest innings totals:	Gillette Cup	371–4 v Glamorgan (Southampton)	1975
	John Player League	288–5 v Somerset (Weston-super-Mare)	1975
	Benson & Hedges Cup	321–1 v Minor Counties (South) (Amersham)	1973
Lowest innings totals:	Gillette Cup	98 v Lancashire (Manchester)	1975
	John Player League	43 v Essex (Basingstoke)	1972
	Benson & Hedges Cup	94 v Glamorgan (Swansea)	1973
Highest individual innings:	Gillette Cup	177 C. G. Greenidge v Glamorgan (Southampton)	1975
	John Player League	155* B. A. Richards v Yorks (Hull)	1970
	Benson & Hedges Cup	173* C. G. Greenidge v Minor Counties (South) (Amersham)	1973
Best bowling figures:	Gillette Cup	7–30 P. J. Sainsbury v Norfolk (Southampton)	1965
	John Player League	6–20 T. E. Jesty v Glamorgan (Cardiff)	1975
	Benson & Hedges Cup	5–24 R. S. Herman v Gloucestershire (Bristol)	1975

KENT

Formation of present club: 1859, reorganised 1870.
Colours: Red and white.
Badge: White horse.
County Champions (5): 1906, 1909, 1910, 1913, and 1970.
Joint Champions: 1977.
Gillette Cup winners (2): 1967 and 1974.
Gillette Cup finalists: 1971.
John Player League Champions (3): 1972, 1973 and 1976.
Benson & Hedges Cup winners (2): 1973 and 1976.
Benson & Hedges Cup finalists: 1977.
Fenner Trophy winners (2): 1971 and 1973.
Gillette Man of the Match awards: 21.
Benson & Hedges Gold awards: 22.

Secretary: M. D. Fenner, St Lawrence Ground, Canterbury, CT1 3NZ.
Captain: Asif Iqbal.

ASIF IQBAL RAZVI (Osmania University, Hyderabad, India) B Hyderabad 6/6/1943. Nephew of Ghulam Ahmed, former Indian off-break bowler and Test cricketer. RHB, RM. Debut 1959–60 for Hyderabad in Ranji Trophy. Migrated to Pakistan in 1961 and has since appeared for various Karachi teams and Pakistan International Airways. Captained Pakistan under-25 v England under-25 in 1966–67. Debut for county and cap 1968. *Wisden* 1967. Appointed county captain in 1977. Tests: 45 for Pakistan between 1964–65 and 1976–77. Tours: Pakistan to Australia and New Zealand 1964–65, 1972–73 (vice-captain), England 1967, 1971 (vice-captain) and 1974 (vice-captain) Australia and West Indies 1976–77, Pakistan Eaglets to England 1963, Pakistan 'A' to Ceylon 1964, Pakistan International Airways to East Africa 1964. 1,000 runs (6)—1,379 runs (av 39.40) in 1970 best. Scored 1,029 runs (av 41.16) in Australia and New Zealand 1972–73. Scored 146 v England (Oval) 1967 sharing in 9th wkt partnership of 190 with Intikhab Alam after Pakistan were 65–8—record 9th wkt stand in Test cricket. Gillette Man of Match awards: 2. Benson & Hedges Gold awards: 3. HS: 196 National Bank v Pakistan International Airways (Lahore) 1976–77. HSTC: 175 Pakistan v New Zealand (Dunedin) 1972–73. HSUK: 159 v Northants (Northampton) 1969. HSGC: 89 v Lancs (Lord's) 1971. HSJPL: 106 v Glos (Maidstone) 1976. HSBH: 75 v Middlesex (Canterbury) 1973. BB: 6–45 Pakistan Eaglets v Cambridge U (Cambridge) 1963. BBTC: 5–48 Pakistan v New Zealand (Wellington) 1964–65. BBC: 4–11 v Lancs (Canterbury) 1968. BBJPL: 3–3 v Northants (Tring) 1977. BBBH: 4–43 v Worcs (Lord's) 1973.

Grahame Selvey CLINTON (Chislehurst and Sidcup GS) B Sidcup 5/5/1953. LHB, RM. Toured West Indies v England Young Cricketers 1972. Debut 1974. Benson & Hedges Gold awards: 1. HS: 88 v Leics (Leicester) 1977. HSJPL: 21 v Leics (Maidstone) 1976. HSBH: 66 v Surrey (Canterbury) 1976.

KENT

Christopher Stuart COWDREY (Tonbridge School) B Farnborough (Kent) 20/10/1957. Eldest son of M. C. Cowdrey. RHB, RM. Played for 2nd XI at age of 15. Captain of England Young Cricketers team to West Indies 1976. Played in one John Player League match in 1976. Debut 1977. Benson & Hedges Gold awards: 1. HS: 101* v Glamorgan (Swansea) 1977. HSJPL: 19 v Notts (Canterbury) 1977. HSBH: 114 v Sussex (Canterbury) 1977.

Graham Roy DILLEY B Dartford 18/5/1959. 6ft 3ins tall. LHB, RM. Debut 1977. One match v Cambridge U (Canterbury). HS: 16 v Cambridge U (Canterbury) 1977.

Paul Rupert DOWNTON (Sevenoaks School) B Farnborough (Kent) 4/4/1957. Son of G. Downton, former Kent player. RHB, WK. Played for 2nd XI at age of 16. Vice-captain of England Young Cricketers team to West Indies 1976, Debut 1977. Tour: Pakistan and New Zealand 1977–78. HS: 31* v Surrey (Maidstone) 1977. Is studying law at Exeter University.

Alan George Ernest EALHAM B Ashford (Kent) 30/8/1944. RHB, OB. Debut 1966. Cap 1970. 1,000 runs (3)—1,363 runs (av 34.94) in 1971 best. Held 5 catches in innings v Glos (Folkestone) 1966, all in outfield off D. L. Underwood. Benson & Hedges Gold awards: 2. HS: 134* v Notts (Nottingham) 1976. HSGC: 46 v Leics (Canterbury) 1974. HSJPL: 83 v Leics (Leicester) 1977. HSBH: 94* v Sussex (Canterbury) 1977.

Richard William HILLS B Borough Green (Kent) 8/1/1951. RHB, RM. Debut 1973. Cap 1977. HS: 45 v Hants (Canterbury) 1975. HSJPL: 25 v Northants (Tring) 1977. HSBH: 34 v Surrey (Canterbury) 1977. BB: 5–44 v Notts (Canterbury) 1977. BBJPL: 4–29 v Sussex (Maidstone) 1977. BBBH: 5–28 v Combined Universities (Oxford) 1976.

James Alan HOWGEGO B Folkestone 3/8/1948. RHB, LB. Debut 1977. One match v Cambridge U (Canterbury). HS: 52 v Cambridge U (Canterbury) 1977.

Kevin Bertram Sidney JARVIS (Springhead School, Northfleet) B Dartford 23/4/1953. 6ft 3in tall. RHB, RFM. Debut 1975. Cap 1977. Benson & Hedges Gold awards: 1. HS: 12* v Cambridge U (Canterbury) 1977. BB: 7–58 v Northants (Northampton) 1977. BBGC: 3–53 v Sussex (Canterbury) 1976. BBJPL: 4–27 v Surrey (Maidstone) 1977. BBBH: 4–34 v Worcs (Lord's) 1976.

Graham William JOHNSON (Shooters Hill GS) B Beckenham 8/11/1946. RHB, OB. Debut 1965. Cap 1970. Appointed county vice-captain in 1977. 1,000 runs (3)—1,438 runs (av 31.26) in 1973 and 1,438 runs (av 35.95) in 1975 best. Gillette Man of Match awards: 1. Benson & Hedges Gold awards: 3. HS: 168 v Surrey (Oval) 1976. HSGC: 120* v Bucks (Canterbury) 1974. HSJPL: 89 v Sussex (Hove) 1976. HSBH: 85* v Minor Counties (South) (Canterbury) 1975. BB: 6–35 (12–151 match) v Surrey (Blackheath) 1970. BBJPL: 5–26 v Surrey (Oval) 1974. Studied at London School of Economics.

Nicholas John KEMP (Tonbridge School) B Bromley 16/12/1956. RHB, RM. Played for 2nd XI since 1974. Toured West Indies with England Young Cricketers 1976. Debut 1977. Played in two matches v Australians and Cambridge U and also in one John Player League match.

Alan Philip Eric KNOTT B Belvedere 9/4/1946. RHB, WK. Can bowl OB. Debut 1964. Cap 1965. Elected Best Young Cricketer of the Year in 1965 by Cricket Writers Club. *Wisden* 1969. Played for Tasmania 1969–70 whilst coaching there. Benefit (£27,037) in 1976. Tests: 89 between 1967 and 1977. Played in 5 matches against Rest of World in 1970. Tours: Pakistan 1966–67, West Indies, 1967–68 and 1973–74, Ceylon and Pakistan 1968–69, Australia and New Zealand 1970–71, 1974–75, India, Sri Lanka and Pakistan 1972–73, India, Sri Lanka and Australia 1976–77. 1,000 runs (2)—1,209 runs (av 41.68) in 1971 best. Scored two centuries in match (127* and 118*) v Surrey (Maidstone) 1972. Gillette Man of Match awards: 2. Benson & Hedges Gold awards: 1. HS: 156 MCC v South Zone (Bangalore) 1972–73. HSUK: 144 v Sussex (Canterbury) 1976. HSTC: 135 v Australia (Nottingham) 1977. HSGC: 46 v Notts (Nottingham) 1975. HSJPL: 60 v Hants (Canterbury) 1969. HSBH: 65 v Combined Universities (Oxford) 1976. Dismissed 84 batsmen (74 ct 10 st) in 1965. 81 batsmen (73 ct 8 st) in 1966, and 98 batsmen (90 ct 8 st) in 1967. Dismissed 7 batsmen (7 ct) on debut in Test cricket v Pakistan (Nottingham) 1967. Holds record for most dismissals in Test cricket.

Brian William LUCKHURST B Sittingbourne 5/2/1939. RHB, SLA. Joined staff 1954. Debut 1958. Cap 1963. *Wisden* 1970. Benefit (£18,231) in 1973. Retired after 1976 season and became 2nd XI captain. May re-appear in 1978. Tests: 21 between 1970–71 and 1974–75. Played in 5 matches against Rest of the World 1970. Tours: Australia and New Zealand 1970–71, 1974–75. 1,000 runs (14)—1,914 runs (av 47.85) in 1969 best. Scored 1,061 runs (av 46.13) in all limited-over cricket in 1974—the first batsman to do so. Scored two centuries in match (113 and 100*) v Rest of World (Canterbury) 1968. Gillette Man of Match awards: 4. Benson & Hedges Gold awards: 2. HS: 215 v Derbyshire (Derby) 1973. HSTC: 131 v Australia (Perth) 1970–71. HSGC: 129 v Durham (Canterbury) 1974. HSJPL: 142 v Somerset (Weston-super-Mare) 1970. HSBH: 111 v Leics (Canterbury) 1974. BB: 4–32 v Somerset (Gravesend) 1962. BBGC: 3–22 v Hants (Portsmouth) 1965.

David NICHOLLS (Gravesend GS) B East Dereham (Norfolk) 8/12/1943. LHB, reserve WK, LB. Debut 1960. Cap 1969. Scored 1,000 runs (av 32.25) in 1971. HS: 211 v Derbyshire (Folkestone) 1963. HSGC: 43 v Warwickshire (Canterbury) 1971. HSJPL: 64 v Glos (Gillingham) 1971. HSBH: 51 v Essex (Chelmsford) 1972.

Charles James Castell ROWE (King's School, Canterbury) B Hong Kong 27/11/1951. RHB, OB. Debut 1974. Cap 1977. HS: 103 v Sussex (Tunbridge Wells) 1977. HSGC: 11 v Sussex (Canterbury) 1976. HSJPL: 78* v Notts (Canterbury) 1977. HSBH: 40 v Combined Universities (Canterbury) 1977. BB: 6–46 v Derbyshire (Dover) 1976. BBJPL: 5–32 v Worcs (Worcester) 1976.

John Neil SHEPHERD (Alleyn's School, Barbados) B St Andrew, Barbados 9/11/1943. RHB, RM. Debut 1964–65 in one match for Barbados v Cavaliers and has played subsequently for Barbados in Shell Shield competition. Debut for county 1966. Cap 1967. Played for Rhodesia in 1975–76 Currie Cup competition. Tests: 5 for West Indies in 1969 and 1970–71. Tour: West Indies to England 1969. Scored 1,157 runs (av 29.66) and took 96 wkts (av 18.72) in 1968. Gillette Man of the Match awards: 1. Benson & Hedges Gold awards: 1. HS: 170 v Northants (Folkestone) 1968. HSTC: 32 West Indies v England (Lord's) 1969. HSGC: 101 v Middlesex (Canterbury) 1977. HSJPL: 65 v Surrey (Oval) 1971. HSBH: 96 v Middlesex (Lord's) 1975. BB: 8–40 West Indians v Glos (Bristol) 1969. BBTC: 5–104 West Indies v England (Manchester) 1969. BBC: 8–83 v Lancs (Tunbridge Wells) 1977. BBGC: 4–23 v Essex (Leyton) 1972. BBJPL: 4–18 v Hants (Portsmouth) 1972. BBBH: 3–21 v Essex (Canterbury) 1973 and 3-12 v Middlesex (Lord's) 1975.

Christopher James (Chris) TAVARE (Sevenoaks School and Oxford) B Orpington 27/10/1954. RHB, RM. Scored 124* for English Schools v All-India Schools (Birmingham) 1973. Debut 1974. Blue 1975–76–77. Scored 1,229 runs (av 40.96) in 1976. Benson & Hedges Gold awards: 2 (for Combined Universities). HS: 124* v Notts (Canterbury) 1977. HSJPL: 60 v Glos (Cheltenham) 1977. HSBH: 89 Combined Universities v Surrey (Oval) 1976.

Derek Leslie UNDERWOOD (Beckenham and Penge GS) B Bromley 8/6/1945. RHB, LM. Debut 1963, taking 100 wkts and being the youngest player ever to do so in debut season. Cap 1964 (second youngest Kent player to have received this award). Elected Best Young Cricketer of the Year in 1966 by the Cricket Writers' Club. Wisden 1968. Benefit (£24,114) in 1975. Took 1,000th wkt in first-class cricket in New Zealand 1970–71 at age of 25 years 264 days—only W. Rhodes (in 1902) and G. A. Lohmann (in 1890) have achieved the feat at a younger age. Took 200th wkt in Test cricket against Australia in 1977. Tests: 74 between 1966 and 1977. Played in 3 matches against Rest of World in 1970. Tours: Pakistan 1966–67, Ceylon and Pakistan 1968–69, Australia and New Zealand 1970–71, 1974–75, India, Sri Lanka and Pakistan 1972–73, West Indies 1973–74, India, Sri Lanka and Australia 1976–77. 100 wkts (7)—157 wkts (av 13.80) in 1966 best. Hat-trick v Sussex (Hove) 1977. HS: 80 v Lancs (Manchester) 1969. HSTC: 45* v Australia (Leeds) 1968. HSGC: 28 v Sussex (Tunbridge Wells) 1963. HSJPL: 22 v Worcs (Dudley) 1969. HSBH: 17 v Essex (Canterbury) 1973. BB: 9-28 v Sussex (Hastings) 1964 and 9-37 v Essex (Westcliff) 1966. BBTC: 8–51 v Pakistan (Lord's) 1974. BBGC: 4–57 v Leics (Canterbury) 1974. BBJPL: 5–19 v Glos (Maidstone) 1972. BBBH: 5–35 v Surrey (Oval) 1976.

Robert Andrew (Bob) WOOLMER (Skinners' School, Tunbridge Wells) B Kanpur (India) 14/5/1948. RHB, RM. Debut 1968. Cap 1970. Wisden 1975. Played for Natal between 1973–74 and 1975–76 in Currie Cup competition. Tests: 15 between 1975 and 1977. Tour: India, Sri Lanka and Australia 1976–77. 1,000 runs (3)—1,749 runs (av 47.27) in 1976 best. Hat-trick for MCC v Australians (Lord's) 1975. Gillette Man of Match awards: 2. Benson & Hedges Gold awards: 2. HS: 149 England v Australia (Oval) 1975. HSC: 143 v Notts (Nottingham) 1976. HSGC: 78 v Notts (Nottingham) 1975. HSJPL: 64 v Lancs (Manchester) 1976. HSBH: 64 v Glos (Lord's) 1977. BB: 7–47 v Sussex (Canterbury) 1969. BBGC: 4–37 v Leics (Leicester) 1971. BBJPL: 5–26 v Somerset (Canterbury) 1973. BBBH: 4–14 v Sussex (Tunbridge Wells) 1972.

NB The following players whose particulars appeared in the 1977 Annual have been omitted: J. N. Graham (retired), B. D. Julien (not re-engaged) and A. O. C. Verrinder (not re-engaged). The career records of all these players appear elsewhere in this Annual.

COUNTY AVERAGES

Schweppes County Championship: Played 21, won 9, drawn 10, lost 2, abandoned 1

All first-class matches: Played 23, won 9, drawn 12, lost 2, abandoned 1

BATTING AND FIELDING

Cap		M	I	NO	Runs	HS	Avge	100	50	Ct	St
1965	A. P. E. Knott	11	13	2	516	109	46.90	1	3	35	3
1970	R. A. Woolmer	15	22	3	844	122	44.42	4	3	8	—
1970	A. E. G. Ealham	22	33	5	1116	99	39.85	—	10	16	—
1968	Asif Iqbal	22	33	2	1224	116	39.48	1	7	14	—
—	G. S. Clinton	18	28	1	828	88	30.66	—	7	6	—
—	C. J. Tavare	12	22	4	529	124*	29.38	1	2	12	—
—	C. S. Cowdrey	14	19	4	386	101*	25.73	1	1	8	—
1972	B. D. Julien	16	21	3	451	55*	25.05	—	2	4	—
1969	D. Nicholls	7	8	2	142	48	23.66	—	—	17	1
1977	R. W. Hills	17	14	3	247	43	22.45	—	—	3	—
—	P. R. Downton	7	7	3	87	31*	21.75	—	—	18	4
1967	J. N. Shepherd	20	25	4	446	77	21.23	—	2	18	—
1977	C. J. C. Rowe	20	29	3	540	103	20.76	1	2	3	—
1970	G. W. Johnson	11	18	1	229	58*	13.47	—	1	11	—
1977	K. B. S. Jarvis	21	14	11	20	12*	6.66	—	—	5	—
—	N. J. Kemp	2	3	0	16	14	5.33	—	—	1	—
1964	D. L. Underwood	12	13	4	25	8	2.77	—	—	4	—

Played in two matches: J. N. Graham 10 (2 ct).

Played in one match: G. R. Dilley 16, 15; J. A. Howgego 52, 39; A. O. C. Verrinder 23, 1* (1 ct).

BOWLING

	Type	O	M	R	W	Avge	Best	5 wI	10 wM
R. A. Woolmer	RM	118.1	45	258	18	14.33	3-7	—	—
D. L. Underwood	LM	267.1	103	534	33	16.18	7-43	2	—
R. W. Hills	RM	215.3	60	566	33	17.15	5-44	1	—
J. N. Shepherd	RM	738.4	216	1734	87	19.93	8-83	6	—
K. B. S. Jarvis	RFM	440.4	107	1304	55	23.70	7-58	3	—
B. D. Julien	LM	421.4	119	1076	27	39.08	4-42	—	—
C. J. C. Rowe	OB	192.5	49	545	15	36.33	5-85	1	—
G. W. Johnson	OB	148	42	441	12	36.75	5-77	1	—

Also bowled: Asif Iqbal 72–22–192–4; C. S. Cowdrey 10–0–54–1; G. R. Dilley 6–0–23–0; J. N. Graham 46–13–83–2; N. J. Kemp 19–7–48–0; A. O. C. Verrinder 8–0–39–0.

County Records

First-class cricket

Highest innings totals:	For ....803–4d v Essex (Brentwood)	1934
	Agst....676 by Australians (Canterbury)	1921
Lowest innings totals:	For ....18 v Sussex (Gravesend)	1867
	Agst....16 by Warwickshire (Tonbridge)	1913
Highest individual innings:	For ....332 W. H. Ashdown v Essex (Brentwood)	1934
	Agst....344 W. G. Grace for MCC (Canterbury)	1876

KENT

Best bowling in an innings:	For ....10–30 C. Blythe v Northamptonshire (Northampton)	1907
	Agst....10–48 C.H.G.Bland for Sussex (Tonbridge)	1899
Best bowling in a match:	For ....17–48 C. Blythe v Northamptonshire (Northampton)	1907
	Agst....17–106 T. W. Goddard for Gloucestershire (Bristol)	1939
Most runs in a season:	2894 (av 59.06) F. E. Woolley	1928
runs in a career:	48483 (av 42.05) F. E. Woolley	1906–1938
100s in a season:	10 by F. E. Woolley	1928 & 1934
100s in a career:	112 by F. E. Woolley	1906–1938
wickets in a season:	262 (av 14.74) A. P. Freeman	1933
wickets in a career:	3359 (av 14.45) A. P. Freeman	1914–1936

RECORD WICKET STANDS

1st	283	A. E. Fagg & P. R. Sunnucks v Essex (Colchester)	1938
2nd	352	W. H. Ashdown & F. E. Woolley v Essex (Brentwood)	1934
3rd	321	A. Hearne & J. R. Mason v Nottinghamshire (Nottingham)	1899
4th	297	H. T. W. Hardinge & A. P. F. Chapman v Hampshire (Southampton)	1926
5th	277	F. E. Woolley & L. E. G. Ames v New Zealanders (Canterbury)	1931
6th	284	A.P.F.Chapman & G.B.Legge v Lancashire (Maidstone)	1927
7th	248	A. P. Day & E. Humphreys v Somerset (Taunton)	1908
8th	157	A. L. Hilder & C. Wright v Essex (Gravesend)	1924
9th	161	B. R. Edrich & F. Ridgway v Sussex (Tunbridge Wells)	1949
10th	235	F.E.Woolley & A.Fielder v Worcestershire (Stourbridge)	1909

One-day cricket

Highest innings totals:	Gillette Cup	297–3 v Worcestershire (Canterbury)	1970
	John Player League	278–5 v Gloucestershire (Maidstone)	1976
	Benson & Hedges Cup	280–3 v Surrey (Oval)	1976
Lowest innings totals:	Gillette Cup	110 v Gloucestershire (Bristol)	1968
	John Player League	84 v Gloucestershire (Folkestone)	1969
	Benson & Hedges Cup	118 v Essex (Chelmsford)	1975
Highest individual innings:	Gillette Cup	129 B. W. Luckhurst v Durham (Canterbury)	1974
	John Player League	142 B. W. Luckhurst v Somerset (Weston-super-Mare)	1970
	Benson & Hedges Cup	114 C. S. Cowdrey v Sussex (Canterbury)	1977
Best bowling figures:	Gillette Cup	7–15 A. L. Dixon v Surrey (Oval)	1967
	John Player League	5–7 J. N. Graham v Northants (Tring)	1975
	Benson & Hedges Cup	5–21 B. D. Julien v Surrey (Oval)	1973

94

LANCASHIRE

Formation of present club: 1864.
Colours: Red, green, and blue.
Badge: Red Rose.
County Champions (8): 1881, 1897, 1904, 1926,
1927, 1928, 1930 and 1934.
Joint Champions (5): 1875, 1879, 1882, 1889, and
1950.
Gillette Cup Winners (4): 1970, 1971, 1972 and 1975.
Gillette Cup Finalists (2): 1974 and 1976.
John Player League Champions (2): 1969 and 1970.
Benson & Hedges Cup semi-finalists (2): 1973 and 1974.
Gillette Man of the Match awards: 32.
Benson & Hedges Gold awards: 17.

Secretary: c/o Old Trafford, Manchester, M16 0PX.
Captain: F. C. Hayes.

John ABRAHAMS (Heywood GS) B Cape Town, South Africa 21/7/
1952. LHB, OB. Son of Cecil J. Abrahams, former professional for
Milnrow and Radcliffe in Central Lancashire League. Has lived in this
country since 1962. Debut 1973. HS: 101* v Yorks (Manchester) 1977.
HSGC: 46 v Northants (Lord's) 1976. HSJPL: 58 v Worcs (Worcester)
1976. HSBH: 22 v Hants (Southampton) 1977.

Robert (Bob) ARROWSMITH B Denton (Lancs) 21/5/1952. RHB, SLA.
Played in one John Player League match in 1975. Debut 1976. HS: 30* v
Australians (Manchester) 1977. BB: 6–29 v Oxford U (Oxford) 1977.

Colin Everton Hunte CROFT (Central High School, Georgetown) B
Lancaster Village, Demarara, British Guiana 15/3/1953. 6ft 4ins tall.
RHB, RFM. Debut for Guyana in 1971–72 Shell Shield competition.
Played for Warwickshire 2nd XI in 1972. Debut for county 1977. Tests:
5 for West Indies in 1976–77, taking 33 wkts against Pakistan to equal
West Indies record for any series. HS: 46* v Worcs (Worcester) 1977.
HSJPL: 10* v Surrey (Oval) 1977. BB: 8–29 West Indies v Pakistan
(Port of Spain) 1976–77. BBUK: 7–54 v Notts (Nottingham) 1977.

Frank Charles HAYES (De La Salle College, Salford) B Preston
6/12/1946. RHB, RM. Debut 1970 scoring 94 and 99 in first two matches
after scoring 203* for 2nd XI v Warwickshire 2nd XI (Birmingham).
Cap 1972. Appointed county captain for 1978. Tests: 9 between 1973 and
1976. Tour: West Indies 1973–74. 1,000 runs (4)—1,311 runs (av 35.43)
in 1974 best. Scored 34 in one over (6 4 6 6 6 6) off M. A. Nash v Glamorgan (Swansea) 1977. Gillette Man of Match awards: 1. Benson & Hedges
Gold awards: 2. HS: 187 v Indians (Manchester) 1974. HSTC: 106* v
West Indies (Oval) 1973 in second innings on Test debut. HSGC: 93
v Warwickshire (Birmingham) 1976. HSJPL: 68 v Middlesex (Lord's)
1974. HSBH: 102 v Minor Counties (North) (Manchester) 1973. Amateur
soccer player. Studied at Sheffield University.

LANCASHIRE

William (Willie) HOGG (Ulverston Comprehensive School) B Ulverston 12/7/1955. RHB, RFM. Debut 1976 after playing as professional for Preston in Northern League. HS: 17 v Middlesex (Blackpool) 1977. BB: 3–48 v Notts (Liverpool) 1977. BBJPL: 3–41 v Glos (Bristol) 1977.

David Paul HUGHES (Newton-le-Willows GS) B Newton-le-Willows (Lancs) 13/5/1947. RHB, SLA. Debut 1967. Cap 1970. Played for Tasmania in 1975–76 and 1976–77 whilst coaching there. Gillette Man of Match awards: 1. HS: 101 v Cambridge U (Cambridge) 1975. HSGC: 42* v Middlesex (Lord's) 1974. HSJPL: 84 v Essex (Leyton) 1973. HSBH: 39* v Somerset (Bath) 1977. BB: 7–24 v Oxford U (Oxford) 1970. BBGC: 4–61 v Somerset (Manchester) 1972. BBJPL: 6–29 v Somerset (Manchester) 1977.

Andrew KENNEDY (Nelson GS) B Blackburn 4/11/1949. LHB, RM. Debut 1970. Cap 1975. Elected Best Young Cricketer of the Year in 1975 by the Cricket Writers' Club. Scored 1,022 runs (av 42.58) in 1975. HS: 176* v Leics (Leicester) 1976. HSGC: 51 v Middlesex (Lord's) 1975. HSJPL: 87* v Notts (Nottingham) 1974. HSBH: 31 v Leics (Leicester) 1975.

Peter Granville LEE B Arthingworth (Northants) 27/8/1945. RHB, RFM. Debut for Northants 1967. Joined Lancs in 1972. Cap 1972. *Wisden* 1975. 100 wkts (2)—112 wkts (av 18.45) in 1975 best. HS: 26 Northants v Glos (Northampton) 1969. HSGC: 10* v Middlesex (Lord's) 1974. HSJPL: 27* Northants v Derbyshire (Chesterfield) 1971. BB: 8–53 v Sussex (Hove) 1973. BBGC: 4–7 v Cornwall (Truro) 1977. BBJPL: 4–17 v Derbyshire (Chesterfield) 1972. BBBH: 4–32 v Worcs (Manchester) 1973.

Clive Hubert LLOYD (Chatham HS, Georgetown) B Georgetown, British Guiana 31/8/1944. Cousin of L. R. Gibbs. LHB, RM. Wears glasses. Debut 1963–64 for Guyana (then British Guiana). Played for Haslingden in Lancashire League in 1967 and also for Rest of World XI in 1967 and 1968. Debut for county v Australians 1968. Cap 1969. *Wisden* 1970. Appointed county vice-captain in 1973. Testimonial in 1977. Tests: 63 for West Indies between 1966–67 and 1976–77, captaining West Indies in 28 Tests. Played in 5 matches for Rest of World 1970 and 2 in 1971–72. Scored 118 on debut v England (Port of Spain) 1967–68, 129 on debut v Australia (Brisbane) 1968–69, and 82 and 78* on debut v India (Bombay) 1966–67. Tours: West Indies to India and Ceylon 1966–67, Australia and New Zealand 1968–69, England 1969, 1973 and 1976 (captain). Rest of World to Australia 1971–72 (returning early owing to back injury), India, Sri Lanka, and Pakistan 1974–75 (captain), Australia 1975–76 (captain). 1,000 runs (7)—1,603 runs (av 47.14) in 1970 best. Also scored 1,000 runs in Australia and New Zealand 1968–69 and in India, Sri Lanka and Pakistan 1974–75. Scored 201* in 120 minutes for West Indians v Glamorgan (Swansea) 1976 to equal record for fastest double century in first class cricket. Gillette Man of Match awards: 6. HS: 242* West Indies v India (Bombay) 1974–75. HSUK: 217* v Warwickshire (Manchester) 1971. HSGC: 126 v Warwickshire (Lord's) 1972. HSJPL: 134* v Somerset (Manchester) 1970. HSBH: 73 v Notts (Manchester) 1974 BB: 4–48 v Leics (Manchester) 1970. BBGC: 3–39 v Somerset (Taunton) 1970. BBJPL: 4–33 v Middlesex (Lord's) 1971. BBBH: 3–23 v Derbyshire (Manchester) 1974.

David LLOYD (Accrington Secondary TS) B Accrington 18/3/1947. LHB, SLA. Debut 1965. Cap 1968. County captain from 1973 to 1977. Benefit in 1978. Tests: 9 in 1974 and 1974–75. Tour: Australia and New Zealand 1974–75. 1,000 runs (7)—1,510 runs (av 47.18) in 1972 best. Gillette Man of Match awards: 2. HS: 214* England v India (Birmingham) 1974. HSC: 195 v Glos (Manchester) 1973. HSGC: 94 v Somerset (Taunton) 1971. HSJPL: 103* v Northants (Bedford) 1974. HSBH: 113 v Minor Counties (North) (Manchester) 1973. BB: 7–38 v Glos (Lydney) 1966.

John LYON (St Helen's Central County Secondary School) B St Helens 17/5/1951. RHB, WK. Played for 2nd XI since 1971. Debut 1973. Cap 1975. HS: 60 v Somerset (Weston-super-Mare) 1976. HSJPL: 31 v Glos (Gloucester) 1975.

Harry PILLING (Ashton TS) B Ashton-under-Lyne (Lancs) 23/2/1943. 5ft 3in tall. RHB, OB. Debut 1962. Cap 1965. Testimonial (£9,500) 1974. 1,000 runs (8)—1,606 runs (av 36.50) in 1967 best. Scored two centuries in match (119* and 104*) v Warwickshire (Manchester) 1970. Gillette Man of Match awards: 3. Benson & Hedges Gold awards: 3. HS: 149* v Glamorgan (Liverpool) 1976. HSGC: 90 v Middlesex (Lord's) 1973. HSJPL: 85 v Sussex (Hove) 1970. HSBH: 109* v Glamorgan (Manchester) 1973.

Robert Malcolm (Bob) RATCLIFFE B Accrington 29/11/1951. RHB, RM. Joined staff 1971. Debut 1972. Cap 1976. Gillette Man of Match awards: 1. HS: 47* v Derbyshire (Manchester) 1975. HSGC: 17 v Cornwall (Truro) 1977. HSJPL: 28 v Essex (Manchester) 1976. HSBH: 14 v Derbyshire (Southport) 1976. BB: 7–67 v Somerset (Weston-super-Mare) 1976. BBGC: 4–25 v Hants (Manchester) 1975. BBJPL: 4–25 v Sussex (Blackpool) 1976. BBBH: 3–33 v Warwickshire (Birmingham) 1976.

Bernard Wilfrid REIDY (St Mary's College, Blackburn) B Bramley Meade, Whalley (Lancs) 18/9/1953. LHB, SLA. Toured West Indies with England Young Cricketers 1972. Played for 2nd XI since 1971. Debut 1973. HS: 80 v Cambridge U (Cambridge) 1975. HSGC: 18 v Glos (Manchester) 1975. HSJPL: 58* v Somerset (Manchester) 1975.

Christopher John SCOTT (Ellesmere Port HS) B Swinton, Manchester 16/9/1959. LHB, WK. Played for 2nd XI since 1975. Debut 1977 aged 17 years 8 months. HS: 10 v Oxford U (Oxford) 1977.

Jack SIMMONS (Accrington Secondar TS and Blackburn TS) B Clayton-le-Moors (Lancs) 28/3/1941. RHB, OB. Debut for 2nd XI 1959. Played for Blackpool in Northern League as professional. Debut 1968. Cap 1971. Played for Tasmania from 1972–73 to 1977–78 whilst coaching there. Hat-trick v Notts (Liverpool) 1977. Benson & Hedges Gold awards: 1. HS: 112 v Sussex (Hove) 1970. HSGC: 37* v Cornwall (Truro) 1977. HSJPL: 47* v Warwickshire (Birmingham) 1977. HSBH: 31 v Derbyshire (Manchester) 1974. BB: 7–64 v Hants (Southport) 1973. BBGC: 5–49 v Worcs (Worcester) 1974. BBJPL: 5–28 v Northants (Peterborough) 1972. BBBH: 4–31 v Yorks (Manchester) 1975. Has played soccer in Lancs Combination.

LANCASHIRE

Geoffrey Edward **TRIM** B Openshaw Manchester 6/4/1956. RHB, LB. Joined staff 1974. Played in last John Player League match of 1975 season. Debut 1976 (two matches). Did not play in 1977. HS: 15 v Notts (Nottingham) 1976.

Barry **WOOD** B Ossett (Yorks) 26/12/1942. RHB, RM. Brother of R. Wood who played occasionally for Yorkshire some years ago. Debut for Yorks 1964. Joined Lancs by special registration, making debut for county in 1966. Cap 1968. Played for Eastern Province in Currie Cup in 1971–72 and 1973–74. Tests: 11 between 1972 and 1976. Tours: India, Pakistan, and Sri Lanka 1972–73, New Zealand 1974–75 (flown out as reinforcement). Scored centuries in both 'Roses' matches in 1970 against his native county. 1,000 runs (6)—1,492 runs (av 38.25) in 1971 best. Gillette Man of Match awards: 6. Benson & Hedges Gold awards: 8. HS: 198 v Glamorgan (Liverpool) 1976. HSTC: 90 v Australia (Oval) 1972. HSGC: 105 v Warwickshire (Birmingham) 1976. HSJPL: 90* v Notts (Manchester) 1977. HSBH: 79 v Minor Counties (North) (Longton) 1975. BB: 7–52 v Middlesex (Manchester) 1968. BBGC: 4–17 v Hants (Manchester) 1975. BBJPL: 5–19 v Kent (Manchester) 1971. BBBH: 5–12 v Derbyshire (Southport) 1976.

NB The following players whose particulars appeared in the 1977 Annual have been omitted: F. M. Engineer, A. J. Good (left staff) and P. Lever (left staff).

COUNTY AVERAGES

Schweppes County Championship: Played 21, won 2, drawn 15, lost 4, abandoned 1
All first-class matches: Played 23, won 3, drawn 15, lost 5, abandoned 1

BATTING AND FIELDING

Cap		M	I	NO	Runs	HS	Avge	100	50	Ct	St
1969	C. H. Lloyd	5	3	1	164	95	82.00	—	1	—	—
1968	B. Wood	23	34	6	1439	155*	51.39	3	7	21	—
1972	F. C. Hayes	20	26	3	1152	157*	50.08	3	4	7	—
1968	D. Lloyd	22	32	5	996	119*	36.88	1	6	29	—
—	J. Abrahams	22	28	5	652	101*	28.34	1	3	10	—
1965	H. Pilling	23	34	5	784	105*	27.03	1	3	7	—
—	B. W. Reidy	9	12	3	240	78	26.66	—	1	1	—
1971	J. Simmons	22	24	6	377	64*	20.94	—	1	17	—
1970	D. P. Hughes	9	11	3	166	39*	20.75	—	—	7	—
1975	A. Kennedy	7	9	0	166	37	18.44	—	—	7	—
—	C. E. H. Croft	19	16	4	200	46*	16.66	—	—	2	—
1975	J. Lyon	20	19	2	172	34	10.11	—	—	33	4
1972	P. G. Lee	23	18	6	100	25	8.33	—	—	5	—
—	R. Arrowsmith	17	15	3	81	30*	6.75	—	—	5	—
—	W. Hogg	6	4	1	19	17	6.33	—	—	2	—
—	C. J. Scott	3	3	0	16	10	5.33	—	—	3	2
1976	R. M. Ratcliffe	3	1	0	0	0	0.00	—	—	—	—

BOWLING

	Type	O	M	R	W	Avge	Best	5 wI	10 wM
B. Wood	RM	120.3	40	306	15	20.40	6–19	1	—
J. Simmons	OB	592.2	199	1313	61	21.52	6–74	3	—
D. P. Hughes	SLA	154	40	401	18	22.27	4–9	—	—
P. G. Lee	RFM	580.5	120	1673	71	23.56	7–24	3	3
R. Arrowsmith	SLA	480.2	170	1192	44	27.09	6–29	2	—
C. E. H. Croft	RFM	476	120	1335	47	28.40	7–54	1	—
W. Hogg	RFM	93.2	20	303	7	43.28	3–48	—	—

Also bowled: D. Lloyd 21–7–57–1; R. M. Ratcliffe 5–2–9–0.

County Records

First-class cricket

Highest innings totals:	For —801 v Somerset (Taunton)	1895
	Agst—634 v Surrey (The Oval)	1898
Lowest innings totals:	For —25 v Derbyshire (Manchester)	1871
	Agst—22 by Glamorgan (Liverpool)	1924
Highest individual innings:	For —424 A. C. MacLaren v Somerset (Taunton)	1895
	Agst—315* T. Hayward for Surrey (The Oval)	1898
Best bowling in an innings:	For —10–55 J. Briggs v Worcestershire (Manchester)	1900
	Agst—10–40 G. O. Allen for Middlesex (Lord's)	1929
Best bowling in a match:	For —17–91 H. Dean v Yorkshire (Liverpool)	1913
	Agst—16–65 G. Giffen for Australians (Manchester)	1886
Most runs in a season:	2633 (av 56.02) J. T. Tyldesley	1901
runs in a career:	34222 (av 45.02) E. Tyldesley	1909–1936
100s in a season:	11 by C. Hallows	1928
100s in a career:	90 by E. Tyldesley	1909–1936
wickets in a season:	198 (av 18.55) E. A. McDonald	1925
wickets in a career:	1816 (av 15.12) J. B. Statham	1950–1968

RECORD WICKET STANDS

1st	368	A. C. MacLaren & R. H. Spooner v Gloucestershire (Liverpool)	1903
2nd	371	F. Watson & E. Tyldesley v Surrey (Manchester)	1928
3rd	306	E. Paynter & N. Oldfield v Hampshire (Southampton)	1938
4th	324	A. C. MacLaren & J. T. Tyldesley v Nottinghamshire (Nottingham)	1904
5th	249	B. Wood & A. Kennedy v Warwickshire (Birmingham)	1975
6th	278	J. Iddon & H. R. W. Butterworth v Sussex (Manchester)	1932
7th	245	A. H. Hornby & J. Sharp v Leicestershire (Manchester)	1912
8th	150	A. Ward & C. R. Hartley v Leicestershire (Leicester)	1900
9th	142	L. O. S. Poidevin & A. Kermode v Sussex (Eastbourne)	1907
10th	173	J. Briggs & R. Pilling v Surrey (Liverpool)	1885

One-day cricket

Highest innings totals:	Gillette Cup	304–9 v Leicestershire (Manchester)	1963
	John Player League	255–5 v Somerset (Manchester)	1970
	Benson & Hedges Cup	275–5 v Minor Counties (North) (Manchester)	1973
Lowest innings totals:	Gillette Cup	59 v Worcestershire (Worcester)	1963
	John Player League	76 v Somerset (Manchester)	1972
	Benson & Hedges Cup	82 v Yorks (Bradford)	1972
Highest individual innings:	Gillette Cup	126 C. H. Lloyd v Warwicks (Lord's)	1972
	John Player League	134* C. H. Lloyd v Somerset (Manchester)	1970
	Benson & Hedges Cup	113 D. Lloyd v Minor Counties (North) (Manchester)	1973
Best bowling figures:	Gillette Cup	5–28 J. B. Statham v Leics (Manchester)	1963
	John Player League	6–29 D. P. Hughes v Somerset (Manchester)	1977
	Benson & Hedges Cup	5–12 B. Wood v Derbyshire (Southport)	1976

LEICESTERSHIRE

Formation of present club: 1879.
Colours: Scarlet and dark green.
Badge: Running fox (gold) on green background.
County Champions: 1975.
Gillette Cup semi-finalists: 1977.
John Player League Champions (2): 1974 and 1977.
Benson & Hedges Cup Winners (2): 1972 and 1975.
Benson & Hedges Cup finalists: 1974.
Gillette Man of the Match awards: 11.
Benson & Hedges Gold awards: 25.

Secretary: F. M. Turner, County Ground, Grace Road, Leicester, LE2 8AD.
Captain: R. Illingworth CBE.

John Christopher (Chris) BALDERSTONE B Huddersfield 16/11/1940. RHB, SLA. Played for Yorks from 1961 to 1970. Specially registered and made debut for Leics in 1971. Cap 1973. Tests: 2 in 1976. 1,000 runs (4)— 1,409 runs (av 33.54) in 1976 best. Hat-trick v Sussex (Eastbourne) 1976. Gillette Man of Match awards: 1. Benson & Hedges Gold awards: 5.

HS: 178* v Notts (Nottingham) 1977. HSTC: 35 v West Indies (Leeds) 1976. HSGC: 119* v Somerset (Taunton) 1973. HSJPL: 96 v Northants (Leicester) 1976. HSBH: 101* v Hants (Leicester) 1975. BB: 6–84 v Derbyshire (Leicester) 1971. BBGC: 4–33 v Herts (Leicester) 1977. BBJPL: 3–29 v Worcs (Leicester) 1971. Soccer for Huddersfield Town, Carlisle United and Doncaster Rovers.

Jack BIRKENSHAW (Rothwell GS) B Rothwell (Yorks) 13/11/1940. LHB, OB. Played for Yorks 1958 to 1960. Specially registered and made debut for Leics in 1961. Cap 1965. Benefit (£13,100) in 1974. Scored 951 runs (av 30.67) in 1969. Tests: 5 in 1972–73 and 1973–74. Tours: India Pakistan and Sri Lanka 1972-73, West Indies 1973-74. 100 wkts (2)— 111 wkts (av 21.41) in 1967 best. Hat-tricks (2) v Worcs (Worcester) 1967 and v Cambridge U (Cambridge) 1968. Shared in 7th wkt partnership record for county, 206 with B. Dudleston v Kent (Canterbury) 1969. HS: 131 v Surrey (Guildford) 1969. HSTC: 64 v India (Kanpur) 1972–73. HSGC: 101* v Hants (Leicester) 1976. HSJPL: 61 v Hants (Leicester) 1970. HSBH: 35* v Worcs (Worcester) 1972. BB: 8–94 v Somerset (Taunton) 1972. BBGC: 3–19 v Somerset (Leicester) 1968. BBJPL: 5–20 v Essex (Leicester) 1975.

Peter BOOTH (Whitcliffe Mount GS, Cleckheaton) B Shipley (Yorks) 2/11/1952. RHB, RFM. Played for MCC Schools at Lord's 1970 and 1971. Toured West Indies with England Youth Team 1972. Debut 1972. Cap 1976. HS: 58* v Lancs (Leicester) 1976. HSGC: 40* v Glamorgan (Swansea) 1977. HSJPL: 22* v Derbyshire (Leicester) 1976. BB: 4–18 v Oxford U (Oxford) 1972. BBGC: 5–33 v Northants (Northampton) 1977. BBJPL: 4–20 v Warwickshire (Leicester) 1977. BBBH: 3–27 v Hants (Leicester) 1975. Trained as a teacher at Loughborough College.

Nigel Edwin BRIERS (Lutterworth GS) B Leicester 15/1/1955. RHB, Cousin of N. Briers who played once for county in 1967. Debut 1971 at age of 16 years 104 days. Youngest player ever to appear for county. HS: 87 v Notts (Nottingham) 1976. HSJPL: 45 v Glos (Leicester) 1975.

Patrick Bernard (Paddy) CLIFT (St George's College, Salisbury) B Salisbury, Rhodesia 14/7/1953. RHB, RM. Debut for Rhodesia 1971–72. Debut for county 1975. Cap 1976. Hat-trick v Yorks (Leicester) 1976. HS: 75* Rhodesia v Eastern Province (Bulawayo) 1972–73. HSUK: 64 v Somerset (Leicester) 1977. HSGC: 23* v Herts (Leicester) 1977. HSJPL: 49* v Sussex (Eastbourne) 1976. HSBH: 58 v Worcs (Worcester) 1976. BB: 8–17 v MCC (Lord's) 1976. BBJPL: 4–20 v Hants (Leicester) 1976.

Graham Frederick CROSS B Leicester 15/11/1943. RHB, RM. Debut 1961. Re-appeared in 1975 after not having played since 1971. Played in one Benson & Hedges match in 1977. Has played soccer for Leicester City and Brighton and Hove Albion and made 11 appearances for England in under-23 international matches in 1962–63, 1963–64 and 1965–66 seasons. HS: 78 v Hants (Portsmouth) 1964. HSGC: 53* v Surrey (Leicester) 1966. HSJPL: 57* v Derbyshire (Leicester) 1971. HSBH: 27 v Worcs (Leicester) 1976. BB: 4–28 v Lancs (Manchester) 1970. BBGC:3–36 v Surrey (Leicester) 1966. BBJPL: 4–11 v Warwickshire (Birmingham) 1976. BBBH: 3–20 v Minor Counties (West) (Leicester) 1976.

LEICESTERSHIRE

Brian Fettes DAVISON (Gifford Technical HS, Rhodesia) B Bulawayo, Rhodesia 21/12/1946. RHB, RM. Debut for Rhodesia 1967–68 in Currie Cup competition. Debut for county 1970 after having played for International Cavaliers. Cap 1971. 1,000 runs (7)—1,818 runs (av 56.81) in 1976 best. Gillette Man of Match awards: 1. Benson & Hedges Gold awards: 5. HS: 189 v Australians (Leicester) 1975. HSGC: 99 v Essex (Southend) 1977. HSJPL: 85* v Glamorgan (Cardiff) 1974. HSBH: 158* v Warwickshire (Coventry) 1972. BB: 5–52 Rhodesia v Griqualand West (Bulawayo) 1967–68. BBUK: 4–99 v Northants (Leicester) 1970. BBJPL: 4–29 v Glamorgan (Neath) 1971. Has played hockey for Rhodesia.

Barry DUDLESTON (Stockport School) B Bebington (Cheshire) 16/7/1945. RHB, SLA. Debut 1966. Cap 1969. Played for Rhodesia in 1976–77 and 1977–78 Currie Cup competitions. 1,000 runs (7)—1,374 runs (av 31.22) in 1970 best. Gillette Man of Match awards: 1. Benson & Hedges Gold awards: 3. Shared in 7th wkt partnership record for county 206 with J. Birkenshaw v Kent (Canterbury) 1969. HS: 172 v Glamorgan (Leicester) 1975. HSGC: 118 v Staffs (Longton) 1975. HSJPL: 152 v Lancs (Manchester) 1975. HSBH: 90 v Warwickshire (Leicester) 1973. BB: 4–6 v Surrey (Leicester) 1972.

David Ivon GOWER (King's School, Canterbury) B Tunbridge Wells 1/4/1957. LHB, OB. Toured South Africa with English Schools XI 1974–75 and West Indies with England Young Cricketers 1976. Debut 1976. Cap 1977. Gillette Man of Match awards: 1. HS: 144* v Hants (Leicester) 1977. HSGC: 117* v Herts (Leicester) 1977. HSJPL: 135* v Warwickshire (Leicester) 1977. HSBH: 48 v Lancs (Liverpool) 1977. BB: 3–47 v Essex (Leicester) 1977.

Kenneth (Ken) HIGGS B Sandyford (Staffordshire) 14/1/1937. LHB RFM. Played for Staffordshire 1957. Debut for Lancs 1958. Cap 1959. Wisden 1967. Benefit (£8,390) in 1968. Retired after 1969 season. Re-appeared for Leics in 1972. Cap 1972. Appointed county vice-captain in 1973. Tests: 15 between 1965 and 1968. Shared in 10th wkt partnership of 128 with J. A. Snow v WI (Oval) 1966—2 runs short of then record 10th wkt partnership in Test cricket. Also shared in 10th wkt partnership record for county, 228 with R. Illingworth v Northants (Leicester) 1977. Tours: Australia and New Zealand 1965–66, West Indies 1967–68. 100 wkts (5)—132 wkts (av 19.42) in 1960 best. Hat-tricks (3): Lancs v Essex (Blackpool) 1960, Lancs v Yorks (Leeds) 1968 and v Hants (Leicester) 1974. Hat-trick also in Benson & Hedges Cup Final v Surrey (Lord's) 1974. Benson & Hedges Gold awards: 1. HS: 98 v Northants (Leicester) 1977. HSTC: 63 England v West Indies (Oval) 1966. HSGC: 25 Lancs v Somerset (Taunton) 1966, HSJPL: 17* v Notts (Nottingham) 1975. BB: 7–19 Lancs v Leics (Manchester) 1965. BBTC: 6–91 v West Indies (Lord's) 1966. BBC: 6–62 v Somerset (Leicester) 1975. BBGC: 6–20 v Staffs (Longton) 1975. BBJPL: 6–17 v Glamorgan (Leicester) 1973. BBBH: 4–10 v Surrey (Lord's) 1974. Soccer for Port Vale.

Raymond (Ray) ILLINGWORTH B Pudsey 8/6/1932. RHB, OB. Debut for Yorks 1951. Cap 1955. Wisden 1959. Benefit (£6,604) in 1965. Left Yorks after 1968 season and joined Leics by special registration in 1969 being appointed county captain. Cap 1969. Awarded CBE in 1973 New Years Honours list. Benefit in 1977. Tests: 61 between 1958 and 1973 captaining England in 31 Test matches between 1969 and 1973. Played in 5 matches as captain against Rest of World in 1970. Tours: West Indies 1959–60, Australia and New Zealand 1962–63, 1970–71 (captain). 1,000 runs (8)—1,726 runs (av 46.64) in 1959 best. Shared in 10th wkt partnership record for county, 228 with K. Higgs v Northants (Leicester) 1977. 100 wkts (10)—131 wkts (av 14.36) in 1968 best. Hat-trick v Surrey (Oval) 1975. Doubles (6): 1957, 1959–62 and 1964. Had match double of 100 runs and 10 wkts Yorks v Kent (Dover) 1964 (135 and 14–101). Gillette Man of Match awards: 1 (for Yorks). Benson & Hedges Gold awards: 3. HS: 162 Yorks v Indians (Sheffield) 1959. HSTC: 113 v West Indies (Lord's) 1969. HSC: 153* v Essex (Leicester) 1965. HSGC: 59 v Notts (Leicester) 1970. HSJPL: 79 v Yorks (Leicester) 1970. HSBH: 43* v Worcs (Worcester) 1975. BB: 9–42 Yorks v Worcs (Worcester) 1967. BBTC: 6–29 v India (Lord's) 1967. BBC: 8–38 v Glamorgan (Swansea) 1976. BBGC: 5–29 Yorks v Surrey (Lord's) 1965. BBJPL: 5–31 v Yorks (Bradford) 1977. BBBH: 5-20 v Somerset (Leicester) 1974.

Norman Michael McVICKER (Stand GS, Whitefield, Manchester) B Radcliffe (Lancs) 4/11/1940. RHB, RFM. Played for Lincolnshire from 1963 to 1968, and was captain in 1967–68. Debut for Minor Counties v South Africans (Jesmond) 1965. Debut for Warwickshire 1969. Cap 1971. Debut for Leics 1974. Cap 1974. Left staff after 1976 season, but re-appeared in 7 one-day matches in 1977. Hat-trick Warwickshire v Lincs (Birmingham) 1971 in Gillette Cup competition. Gillette Man of Match awards: 2 (for Warwickshire). Benson & Hedges Gold awards: 1. HS: 83* v Kent (Tunbridge Wells) 1975. HSGC: 42 Warwickshire v Glamorgan (Birmingham) 1972. HSJPL: 45 Warwickshire v Notts (Birmingham) 1971. HSBH: 23 Warwickshire v Leics (Leicester) 1972. BB: 7–29 Warwickshire v Northants (Birmingham) 1969. BBC: 6–19 v Middlesex (Lord's) 1969. BBGC: 5–26 Warwickshire v Lincs (Birmingham) 1971. BBJPL: 5–19 v Glos (Leicester) 1975. BBBH: 5–32 Warwickshire v Oxford U (Oxford) 1973.

Martin SCHEPENS (Rawlins School, Quorn) B Barrow-upon-Soar (Leics) 12/8/1955. RHB, LB. Played for 2nd XI since 1971. Debut 1973 aged 17 years 8 months. HS: 39 v Middlesex (Lord's) 1976.

Kenneth (Ken) SHUTTLEWORTH B St Helens 13/11/1944. RHB, RFM. Debut for Lancs 1964. Cap 1968. Joint testimonial (£12,500) with J. Sullivan in 1975. Did not play in 1976. Not re-engaged at end of season and made debut for county in 1977. Cap 1977. Tests: 5 in 1970–71 and 1971. Played in one match v Rest of World 1970. Tour: Australia and New Zealand 1970–71. Hat-trick v Surrey (Oval) 1977. HS: 71 Lancs v Glos (Cheltenham) 1967. HSTC: 21 v Pakistan (Birmingham) 1971. HSC: 30* v Somerset (Leicester) 1977. HSGC: 23 Lancs v Somerset (Manchester) 1967. HSJPL: 19* Lancs v Notts (Manchester) 1969. HSBH: 12* Lancs v Derbyshire (Manchester) 1974. BB: 7–41 Lancs v Essex (Leyton) 1968. BBTC: 5–47 v Australia (Brisbane) 1970–71. BBC: 6–17 v Essex (Leicester) 1977. BBGC: 4–26 Lancs v Essex (Chelmsford) 1971. BBJPL: 5–13 Lancs v Notts (Nottingham) 1972. BBBH: 3–15 Lancs v Notts (Manchester) 1972.

John Frederick STEELE B Stafford 23/7/1946. Younger brother of D. S. Steele of Northants. RHB, SLA. Debut 1970. Was 12th man for England v

Rest of World (Lord's) a month after making debut. Cap 1971. Played for Natal in 1973–74 Currie Cup competition. 1,000 runs (4)—1,347 runs (av 31.32) in 1972 best. Gillette Man of Match awards: 2. Benson & Hedges Gold awards: 4. HS: 195 v Derbyshire (Leicester) 1971. HSGC: 108* v Staffs (Longton) 1975. HSJPL: 92 v Essex (Leicester) 1973. HSBH: 91 v Somerset (Leicester) 1974. BB: 7–29 Natal B v Griqualand West (Umzinto) 1973–74. BBUK: 6–33 v Northants (Northampton) 1975. BBGC: 5–19 v Essex (Southend) 1977. BBJPL: 4–27 v Derbyshire (Burton-on-Trent) 1973. BBBH: 3–17 v Cambridge U (Leicester) 1972.

Leslie Brian **TAYLOR** (Heathfield HS, Earl Shilton) B Earl Shilton (Leics) 25/10/1953. 6ft 3½ins tall. RHB, RM. Debut 1977. Played in two matches and four John Player League matches. BBJPL: 3–32 v Northants (Luton) 1977.

Jeffrey Graham (Jeff) **TOLCHARD** (Malvern College) B Torquay 17/3/1944. Brother of R. W. Tolchard. RHB, RM. Occasional WK. Good cover point. Played for Devon in 1963 and from 1966 to 1969. Debut 1970. HS: 78 v Derbyshire (Burton-on-Trent) 1977. HSGC: 18 v Kent (Canterbury) 1974. HSJPL: 46* v Surrey (Leicester) 1975. HSBH: 28 v Oxford U (Oxford) 1973. Studied at Loughborough College. Has played soccer for Torquay United and Exeter City.

Roger William **TOLCHARD** (Malvern College) B Torquay 15/6/1946. RHB, WK. Played for Devon in 1963 and 1964. Also played for Hants 2nd XI and Public Schools v Combined Services (Lord's) in 1964. Debut 1965. Cap 1966. Appointed vice-captain in 1970. Relinquished appointment in 1973. Tests: 4 in 1976–77. Tours: India, Pakistan, and Sri Lanka 1972–73, India, Sri Lanka and Australia 1976–77. Scored 998 runs (av 30.24) in 1970. Benson & Hedges Gold awards: 3. HS: 126* v Cambridge U (Cambridge) 1970. HSGC: 86* v Glos (Leicester) 1975. HSJPL: 103 v Middlesex (Lord's) 1972 and was dismissed obstructing the field. HSBH: 92* v Worcs (Worcester) 1976. Has had soccer trial for Leicester City.

Alan **WARD** B Dronfield (Derbyshire) 10/8/1947. RHB, RF. Debut for Derbyshire 1966. Cap 1969. Elected Best Young Cricketer of the Year in 1969 by the Cricket Writers Club. Played for Border in 1971–72 Currie Cup competition. Was sent off the field for refusing to bowl against Yorks at Chesterfield in June 1973. Left staff afterwards, but rejoined in 1974. Not re-engaged after 1976 season and made debut for Leics in 1977. Cap 1977. Tests: 5 between 1969 and 1976. Also played in 1 match v Rest of World in 1970. Tour: Australia 1970–71 returning home early owing to injury. Took 4 wickets in 4 balls in John Player League match, Derbyshire v Sussex (Derby) 1970. Benson & Hedges Gold awards: 1. HS: 44 Derbyshire v Notts (Ilkeston) 1969. HSTC: 21 v New Zealand (Oval) 1969. HSC: 19 v Surrey (Oval) 1977. HSGC: 17 Derbyshire v Yorks (Lord's) 1969. HSJPL: 21* Derbyshire v Somerset (Buxton) 1969. BB: 7–42 Derbyshire v Glamorgan (Burton-on-Trent) 1974. BBTC: 4–61 v New Zealand (Nottingham) 1969. BBC: 4–37 v Notts (Leicester) 1977. BBGC: 3–31 Derbyshire v Yorks (Lord's) 1969. BBJPL: 6–24 Derbyshire v Essex (Ilkeston) 1976. BBBH: 4–14 Derbyshire v Lancs (Manchester) 1974.

COUNTY AVERAGES

Schweppes County Championship: Played 22, won 6, drawn 12, lost 4
All first-class matches: Played 25, won 6, drawn 15, lost 4

BATTING AND FIELDING

Cap		M	I	NO	Runs	HS	Avge	100	50	Ct	St
1973	J. C. Balderstone	25	38	8	1297	178*	43.23	2	8	17	—
1971	B. F. Davison	24	32	4	1075	141	38.39	2	7	21	—
1972	K. Higgs	23	16	11	186	98	37.20	—	1	19	—
1966	R. W. Tolchard	17	22	6	524	76	32.75	—	4	20	4
—	N. E. Briers	6	11	1	307	62	30.70	—	2	4	—
1971	J. F. Steele	24	39	7	961	124	30.03	1	4	15	—
—	J. G. Tolchard	7	10	2	229	78	28.62	—	3	7	—
1969	B. Dudleston	11	15	4	306	93	27.81	—	2	15	5
1965	J. Birkenshaw	25	27	6	550	76	26.19	—	2	25	—
1969	R. Illingworth	25	24	3	506	119*	24.09	1	1	11	—
1977	D. I. Gower	24	33	2	720	144*	23.22	1	3	8	—
1976	P. B. Clift	15	17	2	243	64	16.20	—	1	5	—
1977	K. Shuttleworth	13	15	4	154	30*	14.00	—	—	10	—
—	M. Schepens	3	4	1	40	23*	13.33	—	—	—	—
1976	P. Booth	11	6	0	65	32	10.83	—	—	7	—
1977	A. Ward	20	15	4	81	19	7.36	—	—	6	—

Played in two matches: L. B. Taylor 1, 1*.*

BOWLING

	Type	O	M	R	W	Avge	Best	5 wI	10 wM
P. Booth	RFM	179	37	494	25	19.76	4–39	—	—
K. Shuttleworth	RFM	293.4	57	825	40	20.62	6–17	3	—
R. Illingworth	OB	388.4	143	777	37	21.00	5–32	1	—
P. B. Clift	RM	379.5	100	949	44	21.56	5–19	4	—
J. C. Balderstone	SLA	373.3	112	933	38	24.55	4–33	—	—
J. Birkenshaw	OB	641.1	188	1516	59	25.69	6–74	1	—
K. Higgs	RFM	449.1	119	1001	38	26.34	5–45	2	—
A. Ward	RF	316.5	62	956	33	28.96	4–37	—	—
J. F. Steele	SLA	195	67	446	12	37.16	3–19	—	—

Also bowled: B. F. Davison 10–1–42–1; D. I. Gower 14–2–59–3; L. B. Taylor 61–18–140–3; R. W. Tolchard 2–0–6–0.

County Records

First-class cricket

Highest innings totals:	For ......701–4d v Worcestershire (Worcester)	1906
	Agst......739–7d by Nottinghamshire (Notingham)	1903
Lowest innings totals:	For ......25 v Kent (Leicester)	1912
	Agst......24 by Glamorgan (Leicester)	1971
Highest individual innings:	For ......252* S. Coe v Northants (Leicester)	1914
	Agst......341 G. H. Hirst for Yorkshire (Leicester)	1905
Best bowling in an innings:	For ......10–18 G. Geary v Glamorgan (Pontypridd)	1929
	Agst......10–32 H. Pickett for Essex (Leyton)	1895
Best bowling in a match:	For ......16–96 G, Geary v Glamorgan (Pontypridd)	1929
	Agst......16–102 C. Blythe for Kent (Leicester)	1909

LEICESTERSHIRE

Most runs in a season: 2446 (av 52.04) L. G. Berry   1937
    runs in a career: 30143 (av 30.32) L. G. Berry 1924–1951
    100s in a season: 7 by L. G. Berry and
                            W. Watson 1937 and 1959
    100s in a career: 45 by L. G. Berry   1924–1951
    wickets in a season: 170 (av 18.96) J. E. Walsh   1948
    wickets in a career: 2130 (av 23.19) W. E. Astill 1906–1939

RECORD WICKET STANDS

1st	380	C. J. B. Wood & H. Whitehead v Worcestershire (Worcester)	1906
2nd	287	W. Watson & A. Wharton v Lancashire (Leicester)	1961
3rd	316*	W. Watson & A. Wharton v Somerset (Taunton)	1961
4th	270	C. S. Dempster & G. S. Watson v Yorkshire (Hull)	1937
5th	226*	R. MacDonald & F. Geeson v Derbyshire (Glossop)	1901
6th	262	A. T. Sharpe & G. H. S. Fowke v Derbyshire (Chesterfield)	1911
7th	206	B. Dudleston & J. Birkenshaw v Kent (Canterbury)	1969
8th	164	M. R. Hallam & C. T. Spencer v Essex (Leicester)	1964
9th	160	W. W. Odell & R. T. Crawford v Worcestershire (Leicester)	1902
10th	228	R. Illingworth & K. Higgs v Northamptonshire (Leicester)	1977

One-day cricket

Highest innings totals:	Gillette Cup	313–5 v Hertfordshire (Leicester)	1977
	John Player League	262–6 v Somerset (Frome)	1970
	Benson & Hedges Cup	327–4 v Warwickshire (Coventry)	1972
Lowest innings totals:	Gillette Cup	56 v Northamptonshire (Leicester)	1964
	John Player League	36 v Sussex (Leicester)	1973
	Benson & Hedges Cup	82 v Hampshire (Leicester)	1973
Highest individual innings:	Gillette Cup	119* J. C. Balderstone v Somerset (Taunton)	1973
	John Player League	152 B. Dudleston v Lancs (Manchester)	1975
	Benson & Hedges Cup	158* B. F. Davison v Warwicks (Coventry)	1972
Best bowling figures:	Gillette Cup	6–20 K. Higgs v Staffs (Longton)	1975
	John Player League	6–17 K. Higgs v Glamorgan (Leicester)	1973
	Benson & Hedges Cup	5–20 R. Illingworth v Somerset (Leicester)	1974

MIDDLESEX

Formation of present club: 1863.
Colours: Blue.
Badge: Three seaxes.
County Champions (6): 1878, 1903, 1920, 1921, 1947 and 1976.
Joint Champions (2): 1949 and 1977.
Gillette Cup Winners: 1977.
Gillette Cup finalists: 1975.
Best position in John Player League: 3rd in 1977.
Benson & Hedges Cup finalists: 1975.
Gillette Man of the Match awards: 21.
Benson & Hedges Gold awards: 11.

Secretary: A. W. Flower, Lord's Cricket Ground, St John's Wood Road, London NW8 8QN.
Captain: J. M. Brearley, OBE.

Graham Derek BARLOW (Ealing GS) B Folkestone 26/3/1950. LHB, RM. Played in MCC Schools matches at Lord's 1968. Debut 1969. Cap 1976. Tests: 3 in 1976–77 and 1977. Tour: India, Sir Lanka and Australia 1976–77. Scored 1,478 runs (av 49.26) in 1976. Gillette Man of Match awards: 1. Benson & Hedges Gold awards: 1. HS: 160* v Derbyshire (Lord's) 1976. HSTC: 7* v India (Calcutta) 1976–77. HSGC: 76* v Warwickshire (Birmingham) 1975. HSJPL: 104 v Somerset (Bath) 1976. HSBH: 129 v Northants (Northampton) 1977. Studied at Loughborough College for whom he played rugby.

John Michael (Mike) BREARLEY (City of London School and Cambridge) B Harrow 28/4/1942. RHB. Occasional WK. Debut 1961 scoring 1,222 runs (av 35.94) in first season. Blue 1961–64. Cap 1964. Elected Best Young Cricketer of the Year in 1964 by the Cricket Writers' Club. Did not play in 1966 or 1967, but reappeared in latter half of each season between 1968 and 1970. Appointed county captain in 1971. Wisden 1976. Benefit in 1978. Tests: 13 between 1976 and 1977. Tours: South Africa 1964–65, Pakistan 1966–67 (captain), India, Sri Lanka and Australia (vice-captain) 1976–77, Pakistan and New Zealand 1977–78 (captain). 1,000 runs (8)—2,178 runs (av 44.44) in 1964 best. Holds record for most runs scored for Cambridge University (4,310 runs, av 38.48). Gillette Man of Match awards: 2. Benson & Hedges Gold awards: 1 HS: 312* MCC under-25 v North Zone (Peshawar) 1966–67. HSUK: 173* v Glamorgan (Cardiff) 1974. HSTC: 91 v India (Bombay) 1976–77 HSGC: 124* v Bucks (Lord's) 1975. HSJPL: 75* v Glamorgan (Lord's) 1974. HSBH: 88 v Notts (Newark) 1976. Awarded OBE in 1978 New Year honours list.

Roland Orlando BUTCHER B East Point, St Philip, Barbados 14/10/1953. RHB, RM. Debut 1974. Played for Barbados in 1974–75 Shell Sheild competition. HS: 74 v Worcs (Worcester) 1976. HSJPL: 33 v Northants (Lord's) 1974.

107

MIDDLESEX

Wayne Wendell **DANIEL** B St Philip, Barbados 16/1/1956. RHB, RF. Toured England with West Indies Schoolboys team 1974. Played for 2nd XI in 1975. Debut for Barbados 1975–76. Debut for county and cap 1977. Tests: 5 for West Indies in 1975–76 and 1976. Tour: West Indies to England 1976. Gillette Man of Match awards: 1. HS: 30 West Indians v Sussex (Hove) 1976. HSC: 28 v Sussex (Lord's) 1977. HSTC: 11 West Indies v India (Kingston) 1975–76. BB: 6–21 West Indians v Yorks (Sheffield) 1976. BBC: 6–33 v Sussex (Lord's) 1977. BBTC: 4–53 West Indies v England (Nottingham) 1976. BBGC: 4–24 v Somerset (Lord's) 1977. BBJPL: 3–30 v Leics (Lord's) 1977.

Phillippe Henri (Phil) **EDMONDS** (Gilbert Rennie HS, Lusaka Skinner's School, Tunbridge Wells, Cranbrook School and Cambridge) B Lusaka, Northern Rhodesia (now Zambia) 8/3/1951. RHB, SLA. Debut for Cambridge U and county 1971. Blue 1971–73 (capt in 1973). Cap 1974. Elected Best Young Cricketer of the Year in 1974 by the Cricket Writers' Club. Played for Eastern Province in 1975–76 Currie Cup competition. Tests: 2 in 1975. Tour: Pakistan and New Zealand 1977–78. HS: 103* T. N. Pearce's XI v West Indians (Scarborough) 1976. HSC: 93 v Northants (Lord's) 1976. HSTC: 13* v Australia (Leeds) 1975. HSGC: 35 v Kent (Canterbury) 1977. HSJPL: 43 v Leics (Lord's) 1977. HSBH: 44* v Notts (Newark) 1976. BB: 8–132 (14–150 match) v Glos (Lord's) 1977. BBTC: 5–28 v Australia (Leeds) 1975. BBGC: 3–47 v Bucks (Lord's) 1975. BBJPL: 3–19 v Leics (Lord's) 1973. BBBH: 4–11 v Kent (Lord's) 1975. Has also played rugby for University and narrowly missed obtaining Blue.

John Ernest **EMBUREY** B Peckham 20/8/1952. RHB, OB. Played for Surrey Young Cricketers 1969–70. Joined county staff 1972. Debut 1973. Cap 1977. HS: 48 v Warwickshire (Lord's) 1977. HSJPL: 29* v Essex (Southend) 1977. BB: 7–36 v Cambridge U (Cambridge) 1977. BBJPL: 4–43 v Worcs (Worcester) 1976.

Norman George (Smokey) **FEATHERSTONE** (King Edward VII High School, Johannesburg) B Que Que, Rhodesia 20/8/1949. RHB, OB. Member of South African Schools Team to England 1967. Debut for Transvaal B 1967–68 in Currie Cup competition. Debut for county 1968. Cap 1971. Asked to be released from contract after 1972 season, but subsequently changed his decision. 1,000 runs (2)—1,156 runs (av 35.03) in 1975 best. Scored two centuries in match (127* and 100*) v Kent (Canterbury) 1975. Gillette Man of Match awards: 1. Benson & Hedges Gold awards: 1. HS: 147 v Yorks (Scarborough) 1975. HSGC: 72* v Worcs (Worcester) 1975. HSJPL: 82* v Notts (Lord's) 1976. HSBH: 56* v Sussex (Hove) 1975 and 56 v Kent (Lord's) 1975. BB: 5–58 v Surrey (Oval) 1976. BBGC: 3–17 v Glamorgan (Lord's) 1977. BBJPL: 4–33 v Derbyshire (Derby) 1971. BBBH: 4–35 v Minor Counties (East) (Lord's) 1976.

Michael William (Mike) **GATTING** (John Kelly Boys HS, Cricklewood) B Kingsbury (Middlesex) 6/6/1957. RHB, RM. Represented England Young Cricketers 1974. Debut 1975. Toured West Indies with England Young Cricketers 1976. Cap 1977. Tour: Pakistan and New Zealand 1977–78. Scored 1,095 runs (av 33.18) in 1977. HS: 94 v Sussex (Lord's) 1976. HSGC: 62 v Kent (Canterbury) 1977. HSJPL: 85 v Notts (Lord's) 1976. HSBH: 31 v Essex (Chelmsford) 1976. BB: 3–15 v Sussex (Lord's) 1976. BBJPL: 3–22 v Kent (Lord's) 1976. BBBH: 3–35 v Minor Counties (East) (Lord's) 1976.

Ian James GOULD B Slough (Bucks) 19/8/1957. LHB, WK. Joined staff 1972. Debut 1975. Toured West Indies with England Young Cricketers 1976. Cap 1977. HS: 47* v Glos (Gloucester) 1976. HSGC: 12 v Warwickshire (Lord's) 1977. HSJPL: 36* v Yorks (Lord's) 1975.

Allan Arthur JONES (St John's College, Horsham) B Horley (Surrey) 9/12/1947. RHB, RFM. Tall (6ft 4in). Debut for Sussex 1966. Cap 1972. Played for Northern Transvaal in 1972–73 Currie Cup competition and for Orange Free State in 1976–77. Left Somerset after 1975 season and made debut for Middlesex in 1976. Cap 1976. Took 3 wkts in 4 balls Somerset v Notts (Nottingham) 1972. Hat-trick in Benson & Hedges Cup v Essex (Lord's) 1977. Benson & Hedges Gold awards: 3 (1 for Somerset). HS: 27 Somerset v Northants (Taunton) 1975. HSC: 22 v Oxford U (Oxford) 1976. HSJPL: 18* Somerset b Sussex (Hove) 1973. HSBH: 13 Somerset v Glos (Bristol) 1973. BB: 9–51 Somerset v Sussex (Hove) 1972. BBC: 6–120 v Essex (Chelmsford) 1976. BBGC: 5–23 v Kent (Canterbury) 1977. BJPL: 6–34 Somerset v Essex (Westcliff) 1971. BBBH: 5–16 v Minor Counties (East) (Lakenham) 1977.

Roger Peter MOULDING (Haberdashers' Aske's School, Elstree) B Enfield 3/1/1958. RHB, LB. Debut 1977. One match v Cambridge U (Cambridge). HS: 26* v Cambridge U (Cambridge) 1977. Entered Oxford University in 1977.

Ashok Sitaram PATEL (Willesden Lane GS) B Nairobi, Kenya 23/9/1956. LHB, SLA. Toured West Indies with England Young Cricketers 1976. Played in two John Player League matches in 1977, but has yet to appear in first-class cricket. HSJPL: 27* v Northants (Lord's) 1977. BBJPL: 3–26 v Northants (Lord's) 1977. Is studying at Durham University.

Clive Thornton RADLEY (King Edward VI GS, Norwich) B Hertford 13/5/1944. RHB, LB. Debut 1974. Cap 1967. Benefit in 1977. 1,000 runs (11)—1,414 runs (av 38.21) in 1969 and 1,413 runs (av 41.55) in 1972 best. Shared in 6th wkt partnership record for county, 227 with F. J. Titmus v South Africans (Lord's) 1965. Gillette Man of March awards: 2. Benson & Hedges Gold awards: 2. HS: 171 v Cambridge U (Cambridge) 1976. HSGC: 105* v Worcs (Worcester) 1975. HSJPL: 133* v Glamorgan (Lord's) 1969. HSBH: 121* v Minor Counties (East) (Lord's) 1976.

Michael Walter William (Mike) SELVEY (Battersea GS and Manchester and Cambridge Universities) B Chiswick 25/4/1948. RHB, RFM. Debut for Surrey 1968. Debut for Cambridge U and Blue 1971. Debut for Middlesex 1972. Cup 1973. Played for Orange Free State in 1973–74 Currie Cup competition. Tests: 3 in 1976 and 1976–77. Tour: India, Sri Lanka and Australia 1976–77. Benson & Hedges Gold awards: 1. HS: 42 Cambridge U v Pakistanis (Cambridge) 1971. HSC: 37* v Worcs (Worcester) 1974. HSJPL: 38 v Essex (Southend) 1977. HSBH: 27* v Surrey (Lord's) 1973. BB: 7–20 v Glos (Gloucester) 1976. BBTC: 4–41 v West Indies (Manchester) 1976. BBGC: 3–32 v Somerset (Lord's) 1977. BBJPL: 5–18 v Glamorgan (Cardiff) 1975. BBBH: 5–39 v Glos (Lord's) 1972. Played soccer for University.

109

MIDDLESEX

Wilfred Norris SLACK B Troumaca, St. Vincent 12/12/1954. LHB,
RM. Played for Buckinghamshire in 1976. Debut 1977. HS: 30 v Sussex
(Hove) 1977.

Michael John (Mike) SMITH (Enfield GS) B Enfield 4/1/1942. RHB,
SLA. Debut 1959. Cap 1967. Benefit (£20,000) in 1976. 1,000 runs (10)—
1,705 runs (av 39.65) in 1970 best. Gillette Man of Match awards: 2.
Benson & Hedges Gold awards: 1. HS: 181 v Lancs (Manchester) 1967.
HSGC: 123 v Hants (Lord's) 1977. HSJPL: 101 v Lancs (Lord's) 1971.
HSBH: 105 v Minor Counties (East) (Lord's) 1976. BB: 4—13 v Glos
(Lord's) 1961.

Keith Patrick TOMLINS (St. Benedict's School, Ealing) B Kingston-
upon-Thames 23/10/1957. RHB, RM. Debut 1977 (two matches). Is
studying at Durham University.

NB The following players whose particulars appeared in the 1977
Annual have been omitted: N. P. D. Ross (left staff) and C. J. Whiteside.
The career record of Ross will be found elsewhere in this Annual. In
addition T. M. Lamb has joined Northamptonshire and his particulars
will be found under that county.

COUNTY AVERAGES

Schweppes County Championship: Played 22, won 9, drawn 8, lost 5
All first-class matches: Played 26, won 10, drawn 11, lost 5

BATTING AND FIELDING

Cap		M	I	NO	Runs	HS	Avge	100	50	Ct	St
1964	J. M. Brearley	14	20	4	953	152	59.56	3	4	8	—
1967	C. T. Radley	26	40	5	1309	85	37.40	—	9	29	—
1977	M. W. Gatting	26	40	7	1095	82	33.18	—	11	24	—
1967	M. J. Smith	25	42	2	1278	141	31.95	3	6	13	—
1971	N. G. Featherstone	26	36	2	775	115	22.79	1	5	12	—
1976	G. D. Barlow	21	30	4	577	80	22.19	—	3	16	—
—	R. O. Butcher	8	15	0	298	42	19.86	—	—	6	—
—	N. P. D. Ross	10	13	1	238	53	19.83	—	2	7	—
1974	P. H. Edmonds	25	36	7	518	49	17.86	—	30	—	—
1977	J. E. Emburey	18	23	8	228	48	15.20	—	22	—	—
1977	I. J. Gould	21	30	5	330	41	13.20	—	42	8	—
—	W. N. Slack	3	5	0	65	30	13.00	—	—	—	—
1973	M. W. W. Selvey	24	26	8	215	41*	11.94	—	10	—	—
1977	W. W. Daniel	23	19	9	106	28	10.60	—	4	—	—
—	T. M. Lamb	4	4	1	19	8	6.33	—	1	—	—
1976	A. A. Jones	8	4	1	17	14	5.66	—	1	—	—
—	K. P. Tomlins	3	3	0	1	1	0.33	—	1	—	—

Played in one match: R. P. Moulding 26*.

BOWLING

	Type	O	M	R	W	Avge	Best	5 wI	10 wM
W. W. Daniel	RF	516.1	142	1233	75	16.44	6–33	6	2
A. A. Jones	RFM	109.4	25	309	18	17.16	4–27	—	—
J. E. Emburey	OB	686.1	205	1488	81	18.37	7–36	9	3
M. W. W. Selvey	RFM	629.1	158	1540	78	19.74	5–19	3	—
P. H. Edmonds	SLA	868.3	289	1843	80	23.03	8–132	3	1
M. W. Gatting	RM	148.2	36	426	14	30.42	2–1	—	—
N. G. Featherstone	OB	275.4	62	801	26	30.80	5–65	1	—

Also bowled: T. M. Lamb 62–15–151–3; N. P. D. Ross 7–1–13–0;
M. J. Smith 2–0–2–0.

County Records

Highest innings totals:	For	642–3d v Hampshire (Southampton)	1923
	Agst	665 by West Indians (Lord's)	1939
Lowest innings totals:	For	20 v MCC (Lord's)	1864
	Agst	31 by Gloucestershire (Bristol)	1924
Highest individual innings:	For	331* J. D. Robertson v Worcs (Worcester)	1949
	Agst	316* J. B. Hobbs for Surrey (Lord's)	1926
Best bowling in an innings:	For	10–40 G. O. Allen v Lancs (Lord's)	1929
	Agst	9–38 R. C. Robertson-Glasgow for Somerset (Lord's)	1924
Best bowling in a match:	For	16–114 { G. Burton v Yorks (Sheffield)	1888
		{ J. T. Hearne v Lancs (Manchester)	1898
	Agst	16–109 C. W. L. Parker for Glos (Cheltenham)	1930
Most runs in a season:		2650 (av 85.48) W. J. Edrich	1947
runs in a career:		40302 (av 49.81) E. H. Hendren	1907–1937
100s in a season:		13 by D. C. S. Compton	1947
100s in a career:		119 by E. H. Hendren	1907–1937
wickets in a season:		158 (av 14.63) F. J. Titmus	1955
wickets in a career:		2343 (av 21.18) F. J. Titmus	1949–1976

RECORD WICKET STANDS

1st	310	W. E. Russell & M. J. Harris v Pakistanis (Lord's)	1967
2nd	380	F. A. Tarrant & J. W. Hearne v Lancashire (Lord's)	1914
3rd	424*	W. J. Edrich & D. C. S. Compton v Somerset (Lord's)	1948
4th	325	J. W. Hearne & E. H. Hendren v Hampshire (Lord's)	1919
5th	338	R. S. Lucas & T. C. O'Brien v Sussex (Hove)	1895
6th	227	C. T. Radley & F. J. Titmus v South Africans (Lord's)	1965
7th	271*	E. H. Hendren & F. T. Mann v Nottinghamshire (Nottingham)	1925
8th	182*	M. H. C. Doll & H. R. Murrell v Nottinghamshire (Lord's)	1913
9th	160*	E. H. Hendren & T. J. Durston v Essex (Leyton)	1927
10th	230	R. W. Nicholls & W. Roche v Kent (Lord's)	1899

One-day cricket

Highest innings totals:	Gillette Cup	280–8 v Sussex (Lord's)	1965
	John Player League	256–9 v Worcestershire (Worcester)	1976
	Benson & Hedges Cup	303–7 v Northants (Northampton)	1977
Lowest innings totals:	Gillette Cup	41 v Essex (Westcliff)	1972
	John Player League	23 v Yorkshire (Leeds)	1974
	Benson & Hedges Cup	97 v Northamptonshire (Lord's)	1976
Highest individual innings:	Gillette Cup	124* J. M. Brearley v Buckinghamshire (Lord's)	1975
	John Player League	133* C. T. Radley v Glamorgan (Lord's)	1969
	Benson & Hedges Cup	129 G. D. Barlow v Northants (Northampton)	1977
Best bowling figures:	Gillette Cup	6–28 K. V. Jones v Lancashire (Lord's)	1974
	John Player League	6–6 R. W. Hooker v Surrey (Lord's)	1969
	Benson & Hedges Cup	5–16 A. A. Jones v Minor Counties (East) (Lakenham)	1977

NORTHAMPTONSHIRE

Formation of present club: 1820, reorganised 1878.
Colours: Maroon.
Badge: Tudor Rose.
County Championship runners-up (4):
    1912, 1957, 1965 and 1976.
Gillette Cup winners: 1976.
Best final position in John Player League: 4th in 1974.
Benson & Hedges Cup semi-finalists: 1977.
Gillette Man of the Match awards: 13.
Benson & Hedges Gold awards: 8.

Secretary: K. C. Turner, County Ground, Wantage Rd, Northampton, NN1 4TJ.
Captain: P. J. Watts.

Geoffrey (Geoff) COOK (Middlesbrough HS) B Middlesbrough 9/10/1951. RHB, SLA. Debut 1971. Cap 1975. Gillette Man of Match awards: 1. 1,000 runs (3)—1,201 runs (av 33.36) in 1977 best. HS: 126 v Leics (Leicester) 1977. HSGC: 95 v Leics (Northampton) 1977. HSJPL: 85 v Leics (Leicester) 1976. HSBH: 54 v Cambridge U (Cambridge) 1972.

Vincent Anthony FLYNN (Aylesbury GS) B Aylesbury (Bucks) 3/10/1955. RHB, WK. Debut 1976. One match v Oxford U (Oxford). Did not play in 1977. Studied at Leeds University.

112

Brian James (Jim) GRIFFITHS B Wellingborough 13/6/1949. RHB, RM. Debut 1974. HS: 6 v Somerset (Taunton) 1974. BB: 5–69 v Worcs (Worcester) 1977. BBJPL: 4–22 v Somerset (Weston-super-Mare) 1977. BBBH: 4–36 v Warwickshire (Northampton) 1977.

Alan HODGSON (Annfield Plain GTS) B Moorside Consett, County Durham 27/10/1951. Tall (6ft 4½in.) LHB, RFM. Joined staff 1969. Debut 1970. Cap 1976. Hat-trick in John Player League v Somerset (Northampton) 1976. HS: 41 v New Zealanders (Northampton) 1973 and 41* v Glos (Northampton) 1976. HSGC: 20 v Kent (Canterbury) 1971. HSJPL: 26 v Middlesex (Lord's) 1973. HSBH: 17 v Worcs (Northampton) 1975. BB: 5–30 v Oxford U (Oxford) 1976. BBGC: 4–32 v Leics (Northampton) 1977. BBJPL: 7–39 v Somerset (Northampton) 1977. BBBH: 3–58 v Kent (Northampton) 1977.

Alan Joseph LAMB (Wynberg Boys' High School) B Langebaanweg, Cape Province, South Africa 20/6/1954. RHB. Debut for Western Province in Currie Cup 1972–73. Has joined Northants for 1978 on two-year contract. HS: 109 Western Province v Rhodesia (Bulawayo) 1976–77.

Hon. Timothy Michael LAMB (Shrewsbury School and Oxford) B Hartford (Cheshire) 24/3/1953. Younger son of Lord Rochester. RHB, RM. Debut for Oxford U 1973. Blue 1973-74. Debut for Middlesex 1974. Has joined Northants for 1978. HS: 77 Middlesex v Notts (Lord's) 1976. HSGC: 11* Middlesex v Lancs (Lord's) 1975. HSJPL: 27 Middlesex v Hants (Basingstoke) 1976. BB: 6–49 Middlesex v Surrey (Lord's) 1975. BBJPL: 3–24 Middlesex v Essex (Chelmsford) 1975. BBBH: 5–44 Middlesex v Yorks (Lord's) 1975.

Wayne LARKINS B Roxton (Beds) 22/11/1953. RHB, RM. Joined staff 1969. Debut 1972. Cap 1976. Benson & Hedges Gold awards: 1. HS: 167 v Warwickshire (Birmingham) 1976. HSGC: 22 v Leics (Northampton) 1977. HSJPL: 74* v Lancs (Manchester) 1977. HSBH: 73* v Essex (Chelmsford) 1977. BB: 3–34 v Somerset (Northampton) 1976. BBJPL: 4–38 v Kent (Tring) 1977. BBBH: 3–13 v Essex (Chelmsford) 1977.

Ian Michael RICHARDS (Grangefield GS and Stockton VIth Form College) B Stockton-on-Tees 9/12/1957. LHB, RM. Debut 1976. Played in three John Player League matches only in 1977. HS: 50 vNotts)Z orth- ampton) 1976. HSJPL: 10 v Surrey (Guildford) 1977.

SARFRAZ NAWAZ (Government College, Lahore) B Lahore, Pakistan 1/12/1948. RHB, RFM. Debut 1967–68 for West Pakistan Govenor's l'XI v Punjab University at Lahore and subsequently played for various Lahore sides. Debut for county 1969. Not re-engaged after 1971 season, but rejoined staff in 1974. Cap 1975. Tests: 22 for Pakistan between 1968–69 and 1976–77. Tours: Pakistan to England 1971 and 1974, Australia and New Zealand 1972–73, Australia and West Indies 1976–77. Took 101 wkts (av 20.30) in 1975. Gillette Man of Match awards:1. Benson & Hedges Gold awards: 1. HS: 86 v Essex (Chelmsford) 1975. HSTC: 53 Pakistan v England (Leeds) 1974. HSGC: 22 v Cambs (March) 1975. HSJPL: 43* v Lancs (Manchester) 1975. HSBH: 50 v Kent (Northampton) 1977. BB: 8–27 Pakistanis v Notts (Nottingham) 1974. BBC: 7–37 v Somerset (Weston-super-Mare) 1977. BBTC: 6–89 Pakistan v West Indies (Lahore)

1974–75. BBGC: 4–17 v Herts (Northampton) 1976. BBJPL: 5–15 v
Yorks (Northampton) 1975. BBBH: 3–11 v Minor Counties (East)
(Horton) 1977.

George SHARP B West Hartlepool 12/3/1950. RHB, WK. Can also
bowl LM. Debut 1968. Cap 1973. HS: 85 v Warwickshire (Birmingham)
1976. HSGC: 35* v Durham (Northampton) 1977. HSJPL: 47 v Sussex
(Hove) 1974. HSBH: 36 v Warwickshire (Coventry) 1973.

David Stanley STEELE B Stoke-on-Trent 29/9/1941. Cousin of B. S.
Crump, former Northants player, and brother of J. F. Steele of Leics.
Wears glasses. RHB, SLA. Played for Staffordshire from 1958 to 1962.
Tests: 8 in 1975 and 1976. Debut for Northants 1963. Cap 1965. Benefit
(£25,500) in 1975. *Wisden* 1975. 1,000 runs (8)—1,756 runs (av 48.77) in
1975 best. Gillette Man of Match awards: 1. HS: 140* v Worcs (Wor-
cester) 1971. HSTC: 106 v West Indies (Nottingham) 1976. HSGC: 109 v
Cambs (March) 1975. HSJPL: 76 v Sussex (Hove) 1974. HSBH: 69 v
Warwickshire (Northampton) 1974. BB: 8–29 v Lancs (Northampton)
1966.

Patrick James (Jim) WATTS (Stratton School, Biggleswade) B
Henlow (Beds) 16/6/1940. Brother of P. D. Watts who also played for
county. LHB, RM. Debut 1959, scoring 1,118 runs (av 28.66) in his first
season. Cap 1962. Left staff after 1966 season, but rejoined staff in 1970.
County captain from 1971 to 1974. Benefit (£6,351) in 1974. Left staff
after 1974 season to train as a teacher. Played occasionally in 1975, but
did not appear in 1976 and 1977. Re-appointed county captain for 1978.
1,000 runs (7)—1,798 runs (av 43.85) in 1962 best. Benson & Hedges Gold
awards: 1. HS: 145 v Hants (Bournemouth) 1962. HSGC: 40 v Glamorgan
(Northampton) 1972. HSJPL: 83 v Lancs (Bedford) 1971. HSBH: 40 v
Middlesex (Lord's) 1974. BB: 6–18 v Somerset (Taunton) 1965. BBGC:
4–58 v Warwickshire (Northampton) 1964. BBJPL: 5–24 v Notts
(Peterborough) 1971. BBBH: 4–11 v Middlesex (Lord's) 1974.

Peter WILLEY B Sedgefield (County Durham) 6/12/1949. RHB, OB.
Debut 1966 aged 16 years 5 months scoring 78 in second innings of first
match v Cambridge U (Cambridge). Cap 1971. Tests: 2 in 1976. Scored
1,115 runs (av 41.29) in 1976. Shared in 4th wkt partnership record for
county, 370 with R. T. Virgin v Somerset (Northampton) 1976. Gillette
Man of Match awards: 2. HS: 227 v Somerset (Northampton) 1976.
HSTC: 45 v West Indies (Leeds) 1976. HSGC: 65 v Lancs (Lord's) 1976.
HSJPL: 107 v Warwickshire (Birmingham) 1975 and 107 v Hants (Tring)
1976. HSBH: 58 v Warwickshire (Northampton) 1974. BB: 7–37 v
Oxford U (Oxford) 1975. BBGC: 3–37 v Cambs (March) 1975. BBJPL:
4–59 v Kent (Northampton) 1971. BBBH: 3–12 v Minor Counties (East)
(Horton) 1977.

Richard Grenville WILLIAMS (Ellesmere Port GS) B Bangor (Caernarvonshire) 10/8/1957. RHB, OB. Debut for 2nd XI in 1972, aged
14 years 11 months. Debut 1974, aged 16 years 10 months. Toured West
Indies with England Young Cricketers 1976. HS: 64 v Oxford U (Oxford)
1974. HSGC: 51 v Durham (Northampton) 1977. HSJPL: 65* v Glamorgan (Cardiff) 1976. HSBH: 10* v Minor Counties (East) (Longton) 1976.

Thomas James (Jim) YARDLEY (King Charles I GS, Kidderminster) B Chaddesley Corbett (Worcs) 27/10/1946. LHB, RM. Occasional WK. Debut for Worcs 1967. Cap 1972. Not re-engaged after 1975 season and made debut for Northants in 1976. Scored 1,066 runs (av 30.45) in 1971. HS: 135 Worcs v Notts (Worcester) 1973. HSC: 74 v Essex (Westcliff) 1976. HSGC: 52 Worcs v Warwickshire (Birmingham) 1972 and 52* Worcs v Warwickshire (Birmingham) 1973. HSJPL: 66* v Middlesex (Lord's) 1977. HSBH: 75* Worcs v Warwickshire (Worcester) 1972.

NB The following players whose particulars appeared in the 1977 Annual have been omitted. B. S. Bedi (not re-engaged), J. C. J. Dye (not re-engaged), Mushtaq Mohammad (not re-engaged) and R. T. Virgin (not re-engaged).

The career records of all these players will be found elsewhere in this Annual.

COUNTY AVERAGES

Schweppes County Championship: Played 20, won 6, drawn 8, lost 6, abandoned 2

All first-class matches: Played 21, won 6, drawn 9, lost 6, abandoned 2

BATTING AND FIELDING

Cap		M	I	NO	Runs	HS	Avge	100	50	Ct	St
1967	Mushtaq Mohammad	21	37	5	1469	147	45.90	5	7	9	—
1975	G. Cook	21	37	1	1201	126	33.36	2	5	30	—
1965	D. S. Steele	19	33	4	938	117*	32.34	2	3	21	—
1974	R. T. Virgin	21	37	2	992	107	28.34	3	3	12	—
1976	W. Larkins	21	34	2	793	110	24.78	2	—	11	—
1973	G. Sharp	21	31	9	474	53*	21.54	—	1	37	10
1975	Sarfraz Nawaz	18	28	5	450	61	19.56	—	1	14	—
1971	P. Willey	19	33	1	571	73	17.84	—	1	6	—
—	R. G. Williams	7	13	2	135	43	12.27	—	—	2	—
1972	B. S. Bedi	19	22	7	172	38	11.46	—	—	5	—
—	T. J. Yardley	7	11	1	112	37	11.20	—	—	2	—
1976	A. Hodgson	18	24	4	199	40	9.95	—	—	5	—
1972	J. C. J. Dye	9	9	4	49	29	9.80	—	—	1	—
—	B. J. Griffiths	10	11	6	3	2*	0.60	—	—	2	—

BOWLING

	Type	O	M	R	W	Avge	Best	5 wI	10 wM
Sarfraz Nawaz	RFM	486.4	130	1246	73	17.06	7-37	4	—
B. S. Bedi	SLA	667.1	195	1554	68	22.85	6-83	4	1
J. C. J. Dye	LFM	195	45	581	24	24.20	4-55	—	—
P. Willey	OB	518	141	1216	45	27.02	5-14	2	—
A. Hodgson	RFM	321.4	75	965	35	27.57	4-15	—	—
B. J. Griffiths	RM	169	44	488	17	28.70	5-69	1	—
Mushtaq Mohammad	LBG	286.4	71	870	27	32.22	6-63	1	—

Also bowled: G. Cook 2-0-2-0; W. Larkins 40-10-135-1; D. S. Steele 29.3-11-68-1; R. T. Virgin 1.4-1-7-0; R. G. Williams 10-3-49-0.

NORTHAMPTONSHIRE

County Records

First-class cricket

Highest innings totals:	For ......557–6d v Sussex (Hove)	1914
	Agst .....670–9d by Sussex (Hove)	1921
Lowest innings totals:	For ......12 v Gloucestershire (Gloucester)	1907
	Agst .....43 by Leicestershire (Peterborough)	1968
Highest individual innings:	For ......300 R. Subba Row v Surrey (The Oval)	1958
	Agst .....333 K. S. Duleepsinhji for Sussex (Hove)	1930
Best bowling in an innings:	For ......10–127 V. W. C. Jupp v Kent (Tunbridge Wells)	1932
	Agst .....10–30 C. Blythe for Kent (Northampton)	1907
Best bowling in a match:	For ......15–31 G. E. Tribe v Yorkshire (Northampton)	1958
	Agst .....17–48 C. Blythe for Kent (Northampton)	1907
Most runs in a season:	2198 (av 51.11) D. Brookes	1952
runs in a career:	28980 (av 36.13) D. Brookes	1934–1959
100s in a season:	8 by R. Haywood	1921
100s in a career:	67 by D. Brookes	1934–1959
wickets in a season:	175 (av 18.70) G. E. Tribe	1955
wickets in a career:	1097 (av 21.31) E. W. Clark	1922–1947

RECORD WICKET STANDS

1st	361	N. Oldfield & V. Broderick v Scotland (Peterborough)	1953
2nd	299*	T. L. Livingston & D. Barrick v Sussex (Northampton)†	1953
3rd	320	T. L. Livingston & F. Jakeman v South Africans (Northampton)	1951
4th	370	R. T. Virgin & P. Willey v Somerset (Northampton)	1976
5th	347	D. Brookes & D. Barrick v Essex (Northampton)	1952
6th	376	R. Subba Row & A. Lightfoot v Surrey (The Oval)	1958
7th	229	W. W. Timms & F. A. Walden v Warwickshire (Northampton)	1926
8th	155	F. R. Brown & A. E. Nutter v Glamorgan (Northampton)	1952
9th	156	R. Subba Row & S. Starkie v Lancashire (Northampton)	1955
10th	148	R. Bellamy & V. Murdin v Glamorgan (Northampton)	1925

†307 runs in all were added for this wicket, N. Oldfield retiring hurt after 8 runs had been scored.

One-day cricket

Highest innings totals:	Gillette Cup	275–5 v Nottinghamshire (Nottingham)	1976
	John Player League	239–3 v Kent (Dover)	1970
	Benson & Hedges Cup	249–3 v Warwickshire (Northampton)	1974
Lowest innings totals:	Gillette Cup	62 v Leics (Leicester)	1974
	John Player League	41 v Middlesex (Northampton)	1972
	Benson & Hedges Cup	113 v Worcs (Northampton)	1974
Highest individual innings:	Gillette Cup	109 D. S. Steele v Cambs (March)	1975
	John Player League	115* H. M. Ackerman v Kent (Dover)	1970

	Benson & Hedges Cup	131 Mushtaq Mohammad v Minor Counties (East) (Longton)	1976
Best bowling figures:	Gillette Cup	5–24 J. D. F. Larter v Leicestershire (Leicester)	1964
	John Player League	7–39 A. Hodgson v Somerset (Northampton)	1976
	Benson & Hedges Cup	5–30 J. C. J. Dye v Worcestershire (Northampton)	1975

NOTTINGHAMSHIRE

Formation of present club: 1841, reorganized 1866.
Colours: Green and gold.
Badge: County Badge of Nottinghamshire.
County Champions (6): 1883, 1884, 1885, 1886, 1907 and 1929.
Joint champions (6): 1873, 1875, 1879, 1880, 1882, and 1889.
Gillette Cup semi-finalists: 1969.
Best final position in John Player League: 5th in 1975.
Benson & Hedges Cup quarter-finalists (2): 1973 and 1976.
Gillette Man of the Match awards: 10.
Benson & Hedges Gold awards: 13.

Chief Executive: P. G. Carling, County Cricket Ground, Trent Bridge, Nottingham, NG2 6AG.
 Ground, Trent Bridge, Nottingham, NG2 6AG.
Captain: C. E. B. Rice.

Mark Edward ALLBROOK (Tonbridge School and Cambridge) B Frimley (Surrey) 15/11/1954. RHB, OB. Played for Kent 2nd XI 1974–75. Debut for Cambridge U 1975. Blue 1975–76–77. Debut for county 1976. Played only for University in 1977. HS: 39 Cambridge U v Yorks (Cambridge) 1976. HSC: 13 v Yorks (Bradford) 1976. BB: 4–26 Cambridge U v Oxford U (Lord's) 1977. BBC: 4–106 v Northants (Northampton) 1976.

John Dennis BIRCH B Nottingham 18/6/1955. RHB, RM. Debut 1973. HS: 86 v Glamorgan (Worksop) 1977. HSGC: 10 v Hants (Southampton) 1977. HSJPL: 31 v Sussex (Nottingham) 1977. HSBH: 16 v Kent (Nottingham) 1977. BB: 6–64 v Hants (Bournemouth) 1975. BBJPL: 3–29 v Glamorgan (Swansea) 1976.

Kevin COOPER B Hucknall (Notts) 27/12/1957. LHB, RFM. Debut 1976. HS: 18 v Surrey (Nottingham) 1977. BB: 5–24 v Yorks (Worksop) 1976. BBJPL: 4–25 v Hants (Nottingham) 1976.

David Edward COOTE (Magnus GS, Newark) B Winkburn (Notts) 8/4/1955. LHB. Debut 1977. Played in one match and also one John Player League match. HS: 20 v Yorks (Nottingham) 1977. HSJPL: 13 v Glos (Nottingham) 1977.

117

Roy Evatt **DEXTER** (Nottingham High School) B Nottingham 13/4/1955. RHB. Debut 1975. HS: 48 v Derbyshire (Ilkeston) 1977.

Dilip Rasiklal **DOSHI** (J. J. Ajmera HS and Calcutta University) B Rajkot, India 22/12/1947. LHB, SLA. Debut 1968–69 for Vasir Sultan Colts XI v State Bank of India in Moin-ud-Dowlah Tournament at Hyderabad. Subsequently appeared for Bengal in Ranji Trophy and East Zone in the Duleep Trophy. Played for Sussex 2nd XI in 1972 and Lancs and Notts 2nd XIs in 1973. Also played for Meltham in Huddersfield League in 1973. Debut for county 1973 in two matches v West Indians and Cambridge U. Not re-engaged after 1974 season. Played as professional for Hertfordshire in 1976. Rejoined staff in 1977. Cap 1977. Gillette Man of Match awards: 1 (for Herts). HS: 31* Bengal v Assam (Gauhati) 1972–73. HSUK: 18 v Northants (Nottingham) and 18 v Leics (Nottingham) 1977. HSBH: 10* v Sussex (Hove) 1977. BB: 7–29 Bengal v Assam (Nowgong) 1970–71. BBUK: 6–97 v Somerset (Bath) 1977. BBGC: 4–23 Herts v Essex (Hitchin) 1976.

Bruce Nicholas **FRENCH** (The Meden Comprehensive School, Warsop) B Warsop (Notts) 13/8/1959. RHB, WK. Debut 1976 aged 16 years 10 months. HS: 24 v Oxford U (Oxford) 1977.

Peter John **HACKER** B Lenton Abbey, Nottingham 16/7/1952. RHB, LFM. Debut 1974. HS: 35 v Kent (Canterbury) 1977. BB: 3–27 v Oxford U (Oxford) 1977.

William Henry (Dusty) **HARE** (Magnus GS, Newark) B Newark 29/11/1952. RHB. Debut 1971. Left staff after 1974 season. Re-appeared in one match in 1977. HS: 36 v Warwickshire (Coventry) 1974. HSJPL: 24 v Glos (Nottingham) 1975. Plays rugby (full-back) for Newark and East Midlands and appeared for England v Wales 1973–74.

Michael John (Mike, Pasty) **HARRIS** B St Just-in-Roseland (Cornwall) 25/5/1944. RHB, WK. Can bowl LBG. Debut for Middlesex 1964. Cap 1967. Left staff after 1968 season and joined Notts by special registration in 1969. Cap 1970. Played for Eastern Province in 1971–72 Currie Cup competition. Played for Wellington in New Zealand Shell Shield competition in 1975–76. Benefit in 1977. 1,000 runs (9)—2,238 runs (av 50.86) in 1971 best. Scored 9 centuries in 1971 to equal county record. Scored two centuries in match twice in 1971, 118 and 123 v Leics (Leicester) and 107 and 131* v Essex (Chelmsford). Shared in 1st wkt partnership record for Middlesex, 312 with W. E. Russell v Pakistanis (Lord's) 1967. Benson & Hedges Gold awards: 2. HS: 201* v Glamorgan (Nottingham) 1973. HSGC: 101 v Somerset (Nottingham) 1970. HSJPL: 104* v Hants (Nottingham) 1970. HSBH: 101 v Yorks (Hull) 1973. BB: 4–16 v Warwickshire (Nottingham) 1969.

Basharat **HASSAN** (City HS, Nairobi) B Nairobi (Kenya) 24/3/1944. RHB, RM, occasional WK. Debut for East Africa Invitation XI v MCC 1963–64. Played for Coast Invitation XI v Pakistan International Airways 1964. Also played for Kenya against these and other touring sides. Debut for county 1966. Cap 1970. Benefit in 1978. 1,000 runs (5)—1,395 runs (av 32.44) in 1970 best. Scored century with aid of a runner v Kent (Canterbury) 1977—a rare achievement in first-class cricket. HS: 182* v

Glos (Nottingham) 1977. HSGC: 79 v Hants (Southampton) 1977. HSJPL: 111 v Surrey (Oval) 1977. HSBH: 98* v Minor Counties (North) (Nottingham) 1973. BB: 3–33 v Lancs (Manchester) 1976. BBGC: 3–20 v Durham (Chester-le-Street) 1967.

Nirmal NANAN B Preysal Village, Couva, Trinidad 19/8/1951. RHB, LBG. Toured England with West Indian schoolboy team 1970. Debut 1969–70 for South Trinidad v North Trinidad (Pointe-a-Pierre). Debut for county 1971. HS: 72 v Oxford U (Oxford) 1971. HSGC: 16 v Hants (Southampton) 1977. HSJPL: 58 v Somerset (Torquay) 1972. BB: 3–12 v Oxford U (Oxford) 1971.

Derek William RANDALL B Retford 24/2/1951. RHB, RM. Played in one John Player League match in 1971. Debut 1972. Cap 1973. Tests: 10 in 1976–77 and 1977. Tours: India, Sri Lanka and Australia 1976–77, Pakistan and New Zealand 1977–78. 1,000 runs (3)—1,546 runs (av 42.94) in 1976 best. Benson & Hedges Gold awards: 2. HS: 204* v Somerset (Nottingham) 1976. HSTC: 174 v Australia (Melbourne) 1976–77. HSGC: 73 v Northants (Nottingham) 1976. HSJPL: 107* v Middlesex (Lord's) 1976. HSBH: 60* v Minor Counties (East) (Nottingham) 1976.

Clive Edward Butler RICE (St John's College, Johannesburg) B Johannesburg 23/7/1949. RHB, RFM. Debut for Transvaal 1969–70. Professional for Ramsbottom in Lancashire League in 1973. Played for D. H. Robins' XI v West Indians 1973 and Pakistanis 1974. Debut for county and cap 1975. Appointed county captain for 1978. 1,000 runs (3)—1,438 runs (av 42.29) in 1976 best. Benson & Hedges Gold awards: 2. HS: 246 v Sussex (Hove) 1976. HSGC: 46 v Kent (Nottingham) 1975. Scored 157 for Transvaal v Orange Free State (Bloemfontein) 1975–76 in South African Gillette Cup competition. HSJPL: 116 v Lancs (Manchester) 1977. HSBH: 94 v Middlesex (Newark) 1976. BB: 7-62 Transvaal v Western Province (Johannesburg) 1975-76. BBUK: 6–16 v Worcs (Worcester) 1977. BBGC: 3–29 v Sussex (Nottingham) 1975. BBJPL: 4–23 v Glamorgan (Nottingham) 1975. BBBH: 4–9 v Combined Universities (Nottingham) 1977.

Michael John (Mike) SMEDLEY (Woodhouse GS, Sheffield) B Maltby (Yorks) 28/10/1941. RHB, OB. Played for Yorkshire 2nd XI 1960 to 1962. Debut 1964. Cap 1966. Appointed county vice-captain in 1973 and county captain from 1975 to 1977. Benefit (£8,500) in 1975. 1,000 runs in season (9)—1,718 runs (av 38.17) in 1971 best. Scored two centuries in match (119 and 109) v Lancs (Manchester) 1971. Shared in 7th wkt partnership record for county, 204 with R. A. White v Surrey (Oval) 1976. Gillette Man of Match awards: 1. Benson & Hedges Gold awards: 1. HS: 149 v Glamorgan (Cardiff) 1970. HSGC: 75 v Glos (Nottingham) 1968. HSJPL: 69 v Kent (Dover) 1975. HSBH: 66 v Minor Counties (Nottingham) 1973.

Barry STEAD B Leeds 21/6/1939. LHB, LFM. Debut for Yorks 1959, taking 7–76 v Indians (Bradford) in his first match. Played for Combined Services in 1960 and 1961. Debut for Notts 1962. Cap 1969. Played for Northern Transvaal in 1975–76 Currie Cup competition. Benefit (£7,500) in 1976. Played only in two Benson & Hedges Cup matches and one Gillette Cup match in 1977. Took 98 wkts (av 20.38) in 1972. Hat-trick v Somerset (Nottingham) 1972. Benson & Hedges Gold awards: 1. HS: 58 v Glos (Bristol) 1972. HSGC: 24 v Worcs (Worcester) 1974. HSJPL: 33 v Worcs (Nottingham) 1974. HSBH: 35* v Middlesex (Newark) 1976. BB: 8–44 v Somerset (Nottingham) 1972. BBGC: 5–44 v Worcs (Worcester) 1974. BBJPL: 5–26 v Essex (Nottingham) 1975. BBBH: 5–26 v Minor Counties (Newark) 1975.

William (Bill) TAYLOR B Manchester 24/1/1947. RHB, RFM. Played for Lancs 2nd XI 1964–65. Professional for Leek in North Staffs and South Cheshire League 1967–70. Debut 1971. Cap 1975. Gillette Man of Match awards: 1. Benson & Hedges Gold awards: 2. HS: 26* v Leics (Nottingham) 1972. HSGC: 63 v Sussex (Nottingham) 1975. HSJPL: 15 v Glamorgan (Nottingham) 1977. HSBH: 17* v Derbyshire (Chesterfield) 1973. BB: 6–42 v Warwickshire (Nottingham) 1972. BBJPL: 4–11 v Sussex (Nottingham) 1972. BBBH: 5–37 v Surrey (Oval) 1977.

Paul Adrian TODD B Morton (Notts) 12/3/1953. RHB, RM. Debut 1972. Cap 1977. Scored 1,008 runs (av 27.24) in 1976. HS: 178 v Glos (Nottingham) 1975. HSGC: 41 v Middlesex (Lord's) 1973. HSJPL: 58 v Glamorgan (Nottingham) 1973. HSBH: 45 v Essex (Ilford) 1976.

Howard Trevor TUNNICLIFFE (Malvern College) B Derby 4/3/1950 RHB, RM. Debut 1973. Is training as a teacher and is only available for one-day matches in first half of season. HS: 87 v Derbyshire (Nottingham) 1974. HSGC: 27 v Warwickshire (Birmingham) 1974. HSJPL: 36* v Derbyshire (Ilkeston) 1975. HSBH: 32 v Kent (Canterbury) 1976. BB: 3–48 v Leics (Nottingham) 1975. BBJPL: 3–17 v Sussex (Nottingham) 1975.

William Kenneth (Ken) WATSON (Dale College, Kingwilliamstown) B Port Elizabeth 21/5/1955. RHB, RFM. Debut for Border 1974–75. Played for Northern Transvaal 1975–76 and for Eastern Province in 1976–77. Debut for county 1976. Played only in John Player League matches in 1977. HS: 18 Eastern Province v Transvaal (Johannesburg) 1976–77. HSUK: 10* v West Indians (Nottingham) 1976. BB: 5–54 Northern Transvaal v Orange Free State (Bloemfontein) 1975–76. BBUK: 4–23 v West Indians (Nottingham) 1976. BBJPL: 3–20 v Hants (Bournemouth) 1977.

Robert Arthur (Bob) WHITE (Chiswick GS) B Fulham 6/10/1936. LHB, OB. Debut for Middlesex 1958. Cap 1963. Debut for Notts after special registration in 1966 and developed into useful off-break bowler. Cap 1966. Benefit (£11,000) in 1974. Scored 1,355 runs (av 33.87) in 1963. HS: 116* v Surrey (Oval) 1967, sharing in 7th wkt partnership record for county, 204 with M. J. Smedley. HSGC: 39 v Worcs (Worcester) 1966. HSJPL: 86* v Surrey (Guildford) 1973. HSBH: 52* v Worcs (Worcester) 1973. BB: 7–41 v Derbyshire (Ilkeston) 1971. BBGC: 3–43 v Worcs (Worcester) 1968. BBJPL: 4–15 v Somerset (Bath) 1975. BBBH: 3–27 v Northants (Northampton) 1976.

NB The following players whose particulars appeared in the 1977 Annual have been omitted: P. D. Johnson (left staff) and P. A. Wilkinson (left staff).

The career records of both these players will be found elsewhere in this Annual.

COUNTY AVERAGES

Schweppes County Championship: Played 22, won 1, drawn 10, lost 11
All first-class matches: Played 25, Won 2, drawn 11, lost 12

BATTING AND FIELDING

Cap		M	I	NO	Runs	HS	Avge	100	50	Ct	St
1975	C. E. B. Rice	25	42	5	1300	114	35.13	1	9	19	—
1966	M. J. Smedley	23	38	8	942	130*	31.40	1	4	9	—
1970	S. B. Hassan	23	42	4	1141	182*	30.02	2	2	14	—
1975	P. D. Johnson	18	32	4	719	106*	25.67	1	4	3	—
1977	P. A. Todd	17	30	1	743	86	25.62	—	6	19	—
1966	R. A. White	25	34	5	642	90	22.13	—	2	6	—
—	R. E. Dexter	3	5	0	102	48	20.40	—	—	1	—
—	J. D. Birch	16	27	2	484	86	19.36	—	3	10	—
—	H. T. Tunnicliffe	4	8	1	133	64*	19.00	—	1	1	—
1973	D. W. Randall	13	23	1	401	63	18.22	—	2	7	—
—	P. J. Hacker	15	21	8	220	35	16.92	—	—	5	—
1974	P. A. Wilkinson	14	19	4	216	40*	14.40	—	4	—	—
1970	M. J. Harris	14	22	4	250	37	13.88	—	—	15	3
—	B. N. French	20	28	11	146	24	8.58	—	—	25	5
1975	W. Taylor	9	13	2	79	23	7.18	—	—	—	—
—	K. Cooper	8	9	1	48	18	6.00	—	—	1	—
1977	D. R. Doshi	25	29	3	150	18	5.76	—	—	5	—

Played in one match: D. E. Coote 20; W. H. Hare 13, 2; N. Nanan 55, 54 (1 ct)

BOWLING

	Type	O	M	R	W	Avge	Best	5 wI	10 wM
C. E. B. Rice	RFM	395.1	98	1113	50	22.26	6–16	3	—
P. A. Wilkinson	RM	351	100	877	30	29.23	6–81	1	—
D. R. Doshi	SLA	950.5	288	2442	82	29.78	6–97	2	—
R. A. White	OB	660.4	179	1721	55	31.29	6–49	3	—
J. D. Birch	RM	115.5	17	410	13	31.53	3–42	—	—
K. Cooper	RFM	143	38	399	10	39.90	4–75	—	—
W. Taylor	RFM	106	22	331	8	41.37	3–43	—	—
P. J. Hacker	LFM	262.3	54	846	20	42.30	3–27	—	—

Also bowled: P. D. Johnson 0.1–0–0–0; D. W. Randall 1–0–1–0; M. J. Smedley 1–1–0–0; H. T. Tunnicliffe 17–3–79–0

County Records

First-class records

Highest innings totals:	For .....739–7d v Leicestershire (Nottingham)	1903
	Agst.....706–4d by Surrey (Nottingham)	1947
Lowest innings totals:	For .....13 v Yorkshire (Nottingham)	1901
	Agst.....16 by Derbyshire (Nottingham) and Surrey (The Oval)	1879 & 1880

NOTTINGHAMSHIRE

Highest individual innings:	For .....312* W.W. Keeton v Middlesex (The Oval)	1939
	Agst.....345 C.G.Macartney for Australians (Nottm)	1921
Best bowling in an innings:	For ....10–66 K. Smales v Gloucestershire (Stroud)	1956
	Agst....10–10 H. Verity for Yorkshire (Leeds)	1932
Best bowling in a match:	For ....17–89 F.C.L. Matthews v Northants (Nottm)	1923
	Agst....17–89 W. G. Grace for Glos (Cheltenham)	1877
Most runs in a season:	2620 (av 53.46) W. W. Whysall	1929
runs in a career:	31327 (av 36.71) G. Gunn	1902–1928
100s in a season:	9 by W. W. Whysall	1928
	and M. J. Harris	1971
100s in a career:	62 by J. Hardstaff	1930–1955
wickets in a season:	181 (av 14.96) B. Dooland	1954
wickets in a career:	1653 (av 20.40) T. Wass	1896–1914

RECORD WICKET STANDS

1st	391	A. O. Jones & A. Shrewsbury v Gloucestershire (Bristol)	1899
2nd	398	W. Gunn & A. Shrewsbury v Sussex (Nottingham)	1890
3rd	369	J. Gunn & W. Gunn v Leicestershire (Nottingham)	1903
4th	361	A. O. Jones & J. Gunn v Essex (Leyton)	1905
5th	266	A. Shrewsbury & W. Gunn v Sussex (Hove)	1884
6th	303*	H. Winrow & P. F. Harvey v Derbyshire (Nottingham)	1947
7th	204	M. J. Smedley & R A. White v Surrey (Oval)	1967
8th	220	G. F. H. Heane & R. Winrow v Somerset (Nottingham)	1933
9th	167	W. McIntyre & G. Wootton v Kent (Nottingham)	1869
10th	152	E. Alletson & W. Riley v Sussex (Hove)	1911

One-day cricket

Highest innings totals:	Gillette Cup	271 v Gloucestershire (Nottingham)	1968
	John Player League	260–5 v Warwickshire (Birmingham)	1976
	Benson & Hedges Cup	245–7 v Essex (Ilford)	1976
Lowest innings totals:	Gillette Cup	123 v Yorkshire (Scarborough)	1969
	John Player League	66 v Yorks (Bradford)	1969
	Benson & Hedges Cup	94 v Lancashire (Nottingham)	1975
Highest individual innings:	Gillette Cup	107 M. Hill v Somerset (Taunton)	1964
	John Player League	116* G. St. A. Sobers v Worcestershire (Newark)	1971
		116 C. E. B. Rice v Lancs (Manchester)	1977
	Benson & Hedges Cup	101 M. J. Harris v Yorks (Hull)	1973
Best bowling figures:	Gillette Cup	5–44 B. Stead v Worcestershire (Worcester)	1974
	John Player League	5–23 C. Forbes v Glos (Bristol)	1969
	Benson & Hedges Cup	5–26 B. Stead v Minor Counties (North) (Newark)	1975

SOMERSET

Formation of present club: 1875, reorganised 1885.
Colours: Black, white and maroon.
Badge: Wessex Wyvern.
Best final position in Championship: Third (4): 1892, 1958, 1963, and 1966.
Gillette Cup finalists: 1967.
John Player League runners-up (2): 1974 and 1976.
Benson & Hedges Cup semi-finalists: 1974.
Gillette Man of the Match awards: 18.
Benson & Hedges Gold awards: 13.
Secretary: R. Stevens, County Cricket Ground, St James's Street, Taunton, TA1 1JT.
Captain: B. C. Rose.

Ian Terrence BOTHAM B Heswall (Cheshire) 24/11/1955. RHB, RM. Played for 2nd XI in 1971. On MCC staff 1972–73. Played for county in last two John Player League matches of 1973. Debut 1974. Cap 1976. Elected Best Young Cricketer of the Year in 1977 by the Cricket Writers' Club. Tests: 2 in 1977. Tour: Pakistan and New Zealand 1977–78. Scored 1,022 runs (av 34.06) in 1976. Gillette Man of Match awards: 1. Benson & Hedges Gold awards: 1. HS: 167* v Notts (Nottingham) 1976. HSTC: 25 v Australia (Nottingham) 1977. HSGC: 91* v Northumberland 1977. HSJPL: 69 v Hants (Street) 1977. HSBH: 45* v Hants (Taunton) 1974, BB: 6–16 v Hants (Bournemouth) 1976. BBTC: 5–21 v Australia (Leeds) 1977. BBJPL: 4–41 v Middlesex (Bath) 1976. BBBH: 3–56 v Hants (Southampton) 1975. Plays soccer in Somerset Senior League.

Dennis BREAKWELL (Ounsdale Comprehensive School, Wombourne, Wolverhampton) B Brierley Hill (Staffs) 2/7/1948. LHB, SLA. Debut for Northants 1969 after being on staff for some years. Left county after 1972 season and joined Somerset by special registration in 1973. Cap 1976. HS: 97 Northants v Derbyshire (Chesterfield) 1970. HSC: 67 v Sussex (Hove) 1974. HSGC: 19* v Essex (Westcliff) 1974. HSJPL: 44* v Notts (Nottingham) 1976. HSBH: 28* v Minor Counties (West) (Chippenham) 1976. BB: 8–39 Northants v Kent (Dover) 1970. BBC: 6–78 v Warwickshire (Taunton) 1976. BBJPL: 4–10 Northants v Derbyshire (Northampton) 1970.

Graham Iefvion BURGESS (Millfield School) B Glastonbury 5/5/1943. RHB, RM. Debut 1966. Cap 1968. Testimonial in 1977. Gillette Man of Match awards: 2. HS: 129 v Glos (Taunton) 1973. HSGC: 73 v Leics (Taunton) 1967. HSJPL: 66* v Glos (Bristol) 1971. HSBH: 58 v Hants (Yeovil) 1972. BB: 7–43 (13–75 match) v Oxford U (Oxford) 1975. BBGC: 3–54 v Essex (Westcliff) 1974. BBJPL: 6–25 v Glamorgan (Glastonbury) 1972. BBBH: 4–12 v Glamorgan (Pontypridd) 1972. Plays soccer.

Robert John (Bob) CLAPP B Weston-super-Mare 12/12/1948. RHB, RM. Debut 1972. Is a schoolteacher and plays only occasionally. Played in one Championship match in 1977. Took 51 wkts (av 15.90) in one-day matches in 1974 and is the only bowler to take 50 wkts in these matches in one season. HS: 32 v Lancs (Manchester) 1975. BB: 3–15 v Northants (Northampton) 1975. BBJPL: 5–38 v Worcs (Worcester) 1974. BBBH: 4–32 v Glos (Taunton) 1974.

Peter William (Pete) DENNING (Millfield School) B Chewton Mendip (Somerset) 16/12/1949. LHB. OB. Debut 1969. Cap 1973. 1,000 runs (3) —1,199 runs (av 32.40) in 1975 best. Scored two centuries in match (122 and 107) v Glos (Taunton) 1977. Gillette Man of Match awards: 2. Benson & Hedges Gold awards: 1. HS: 122 v Glos (Taunton) 1977. HSGC: 112 v Surrey (Taunton) 1974. HSJPL: 100 v Northants (Brackley) 1974. HSBH: 87 v Glos (Taunton) 1974. Trained as a teacher at St Luke's College, Exeter.

Colin Herbert DREDGE B Frome 4/8/1954. LHB, RM. 6ft 5in. tall. Debut 1976. HS: 56* v Yorks (Harrogate) 1977. HSJPL: 13* v Lancs (Weston-super-Mare) 1976. BB: 4–42 v Worcs (Worcester) 1977. Played soccer for Bristol City Reserves.

Trevor GARD (Huish Episcopi School, Langport) B West Lambrook, near South Petherton (Somerset) 2/6/1957. RHB, WK. Played for 2nd XI since 1972. Debut 1976. Played in two Championship matches only in 1977. HS: 7 v West Indians (Taunton) 1976.

Joel GARNER B Barbados 16/12/1952. RHB, RFM. 6ft 8ins tall. Debut for Barbados in Shell Shield competition 1975–76. Debut for county 1977 in mid-week matches whilst playing as a professional for Littleborough in Central Lancashire League. Tests: 5 for West Indies in 1976–77. HS: 44* Barbados v Guyana (Bridgetown) 1976–77. HSTC: 43 West Indies v Pakistan (Bridgetown) 1976–77. HSUK: 37 v Surrey (Weston-super-Mare) 1977. BB: 8–31 v Glamorgan (Cardiff) 1977. BBTC: 4–48 West Indies v Pakistan (Georgetown) 1977. BBGC: 5–30 v Derbyshire (Ilkeston) 1977.

David Roberts GURR (Aylesbury GS and Oxford) B Whitchurch (Bucks) 27/3/1956. RHB, RFM. 6ft 3½in tall. Played for Middlesex 2nd XI in 1974. Debut for both Oxford U and county in 1976. Blue 1976–77. HS: 46* Oxford U v Cambridge U (Lord's) 1977. HSC: 21 v Glos (Bristol) 1976. HSBH: 29*. Combined Universities v Sussex (Oxford) 1977. BB: 6–82 Oxford U v Warwickshire (Birmingham) 1976. BBC: 5–30 v Lancs (Weston-super-Mare) 1976. BBBH: 3–42 Combined Universities v Kent (Oxford) 1976.

Keith Francis JENNINGS B Wellington 5/10/1953. RHB, RM. Formerly on MCC staff. Debut 1975. HS: 49 v West Indians (Taunton) 1976. HSJPL: 51* v Notts (Nottingham) 1976. BB: 3–23 v Glamorgan (Cardiff) 1977. BBJPL: 4–33 v Hants (Portsmouth) 1976. BBBH: 3–28 v Hants (Bournemouth) 1977.

Mervyn John KITCHEN B Nailsea (Somerset) 1/8/1940. LHB, RM. Joined staff 1957. Debut 1960. Cap 1966. Testimonial (£6,000) in 1973.

Left staff after 1974 season, but rejoined county in 1976. 1,000 runs (7)—1,730 runs (av 36.04) in 1968 best. Gillette Man of Match awards: 2. Benson & Hedges Gold awards: 1. HS: 189 v Pakistanis (Taunton) 1967. HSGC: 116 v Lancs (Manchester) 1972. HSJPL: 82 v Glamorgan (Yeovil) 1977. HSBH: 70 v Minor Counties (West) (Chippenham) 1976.

Victor James (Vic) MARKS (Blundell's School and Oxford) B Middle Chinnock (Somerset) 25/6/1955. RHB, OB. Debut for both Oxford U and county 1975. Blue 1975–76 (captain in last two seasons). Scored 215 for Oxford U v Army (Aldershot) in non-first-class match. HS: 105 Oxford U v Worcs (Oxford) 1976. HSC: 98 v Essex (Leyton) 1976. HSJPL: 32* v Hants (Weston-super-Mare) 1976. HSBH: 47* Combined Universities v Yorks (Barnsley) 1976. BB: 5–50 v Surrey (Weston-super-Mare) 1977. Half-blue for Rugby Fives 1975–76.

Hallam Reynold MOSELEY B Christchurch, Barbados 28/5/1948. RHB, RFM. Toured England with Barbados team in 1969 and made debut v Notts (Nottingham). Has played for Barbados in Shell Shield since 1969–70. Joined county in 1970 and made debut in 1971. Cap 1972. HS: 67 v Lancs (Taunton) 1972. HSGC: 15 v Lancs (Manchester) 1972. HSJPL: 24 v Notts (Torquay) 1972 and 24 v Hants (Weston-super-Mare) 1975. HSBH: 33 v Hants (Bournemouth) 1973. BB: 6–34 v Derbyshire (Bath) 1975. BBGC: 4–31 v Surrey (Taunton) 1974. BBJPL: 5–30 v Middlesex (Lord's) 1973. BBBH: 3–17 v Leics (Taunton) 1977.

Martin OLIVE (Millfield School) B Watford (Herts) 18/4/1958. RHB, RM. Played for 2nd XI since 1974. Debut 1977. HS: 15 v Leics (Leicester) 1977.

Isaac Vivian Alexander (Viv) RICHARDS (Antigua Grammar School) B St John's, Antigua 7/3/1952. RHB, OB. Debut 1971–72 for Leeward Islands v Windward Islands and subsequently played for Combined Islands in Shell Shield tournament. Debut for county and cap 1974. *Wisden* 1976. Played for Queensland in 1976–77 Sheffield Shield competition. Tests: 26 for West Indies between 1974–75 and 1976–77. Tours: West Indies to India, Sri Lanka and Pakistan 1974–75, Australia 1975–76, England 1976. 1,000 runs (4)—2,161 runs (av 65.48) in 1977 best. Also scored 1,267 runs (av 60.33) on 1974–75 tour and 1,107 runs (av 58.26) on 1975–76 tour. Scored 1,710 in 11 Test matches in 1976 including 829 runs in 4 Tests against England - record aggregate for a year and fourth highest aggregate for a Test series. Shared in 4th wkt partnership record for county, 251 with P. M. Roebuck v Surrey (Weston-super-Mare) 1977. Benson & Hedges Gold awards: 2. HS: 291 West Indies v England (Oval) 1976. HSC: 241* v Glos (Bristol) 1977. HSGC: 49 v Derbyshire (Taunton) 1975. HSJPL: 126* v Glos (Bristol, Imperial Ground) 1975. HSBH: 81* v Glamorgan (Swansea) 1974. BB: 3–15 v Surrey (Weston-super-Mare) 1977.

Peter James ROBINSON B Worcester 9/2/1943. Nephew of R. O. Jenkins, former Worcestershire player. LHB, SLA. Debut for Worcs 1963. Left county after 1964 season and made debut for Somerset in 1965. Cap

1966. Testimonial in 1974. Is now groundsman at county ground and re-appeared in one championship match in 1977. Scored 1,158 runs (av 26.93) in 1970. HS: 140 v Northants (Northampton) 1970. HSGC: 67 v Leics (Taunton) 1973. HSJPL: 71* v Warwickshire (Birmingham) 1973. HSBH: 15 v Minor Counties (South) (Taunton) 1973. BB: 7–10 v Notts (Nottingham) 1966. BBBH: 3–17 v Minor Counties (South) (Plymouth) 1972. Played soccer for Worcester City.

Peter Michael ROEBUCK (Millfield School and Cambridge) B Oxford 6/3/1956. RHB, LB. Played for 2nd XI in 1969 at age of 13. Debut 1974. Blue 1975–76–77. Shared in 4th wkt partnership record for county, 251 with I. V. A. Richards v Surrey (Weston-super-Mare) 1977. HS: 158 Cambridge U v Oxford U (Lord's) 1975. HSC: 112 v Surrey (Weston-super-Mare) 1977. HSGC: 16 v Warwickshire (Birmingham) 1976. HSJPL: 29* v Hants (Street) 1977. HSBH: 48 Combined Universities v Kent (Oxford) 1976. BB: 6–50 Cambridge U v Kent (Canterbury) 1977.

Brian Charles ROSE (Weston-super-Mare GS) B Dartford (Kent) 4/6/1950. LHB, LM. Played for English Schools CA at Lord's 1968. Debut 1969. Cap 1975. Appointed county captain for 1978. Tour: Pakistan and New Zealand 1977–78. 1,000 runs (3)—1,624 runs (av 46.40) in 1976 best. Gillette Man of Match awards: 1. HS: 205 v Northants (Weston-super-Mare) 1977. HSGC: 128 v Derbyshire (Ilkeston) 1977. HSJPL: 80 v Derbyshire (Heanor) 1976. HSBH: 68 v Glos (Street) 1975. BB: 3–9 v Glos (Taunton) 1975. BBJPL: 3–25 v Lancs (Manchester) 1975. Trained as a teacher at Borough Road College, Isleworth.

Philip Anthony SLOCOMBE (Weston-super-Mare GS and Millfield School) B Weston-super-Mare 6/9/1954. RHB, RM. Played for 2nd XI in 1969 at age of 14. Joined staff 1974. Debut 1975 scoring 1,125 runs (av 35.15) in debut season. HS: 132 v Notts (Taunton) 1975. HSGC: 42 v Surrey (Oval) 1975. HSJPL: 39 v Glamorgan (Yeovil) 1977. HSBH: 11 v Minor Counties (West) (Chippenham) 1976. Plays soccer for Weston-super-Mare in Western League.

Derek John Somerset TAYLOR (Amersham College) B Amersham (Bucks) 12/11/1942. Twin brother of M. N. S. Taylor of Hants. RHB, WK. Debut for Surrey 1966. Cap 1969. Left staff after 1969 season and made debut for Somerset in 1970. Cap 1971. Benefit in 1978. Played for Griqualand West in Currie Cup competition 1970–71 and 1971–72. Scored 1,121 runs (av 28.02) in 1974. HS: 179 v Glamorgan (Swansea) 1974. HSGC: 49 v Kent (Canterbury) 1974. HSJPL: 93 v Surrey (Guildford) 1975. HSBH: 83* v Glos (Street) 1975. Has played soccer for Corinthian Casuals.

NB The following player whose particulars appeared in the 1977 Annual has been omitted: D. B. Close (retired). His career record will be found elsewhere in this Annual.

COUNTY AVERAGES

Schweppes County Championship: Played 21, won 6, drawn 11, lost 4, abandoned 1

All first-class matches: Played 22, won 7, drawn 11, lost 4, abandoned 1

BATTING AND FIELDING

Cap		M	I	NO	Runs	HS	Avge	100	50	Ct	St
1974	I. V. A. Richards	20	35	2	2161	241*	65.48	7	9	16	—
1973	P. W. Denning	17	29	3	1032	122	39.69	3	4	8	—
1975	B. C. Rose	19	33	2	1119	205	36.09	3	3	6	—
—	D. R. Gurr	6	5	4	35	16*	35.00	—	—	4	—
—	V. J. Marks	9	13	2	347	69	31.54	—	3	1	—
1966	M. J. Kitchen	20	33	1	1005	143*	31.40	3	2	16	—
1976	I. T. Botham	13	22	1	650	114	30.95	1	4	9	—
—	P. A. Slocombe	12	19	3	437	55*	27.31	—	2	4	—
—	P. M. Roebuck	6	8	2	159	112	26.50	1	—	2	—
1971	D. J. S. Taylor	20	28	9	496	84*	26.10	—	2	51	5
1971	D. B. Close	16	25	2	438	87	19.04	—	2	19	—
—	J. Garner	5	6	1	91	37	18.20	—	—	4	—
1976	D. Breakwell	17	26	5	368	51	17.52	—	1	4	—
—	C. H. Dredge	20	26	7	287	56*	15.10	—	1	11	—
1972	H. R. Moseley	14	13	10	45	10*	15.00	—	—	3	—
1968	G. I. Burgess	13	15	2	163	32	12.53	—	—	7	—
—	M. Olive	3	5	1	24	15	6.00	—	—	4	—
—	K. F. Jennings	8	12	2	42	14	4.20	—	—	8	—

Played in two matches: T. Gard 3, 0 (2 ct).

Played in one match: P. J. Robinson 0* (1 ct); R. J. Clapp did not bat.

BOWLING

	Type	O	M	R	W	Avge	Best	5 wI	10 wM
J. Garner	RFM	215.1	60	539	27	19.96	8-31	1	—
I. T. Botham	RM	535.5	118	1648	70	23.54	6-50	4	1
H. R. Moseley	RFM	451.2	107	1089	42	25.92	4-50	—	—
G. I. Burgess	RM	367.1	101	1043	38	27.44	5-25	1	—
D. R. Gurr	RFM	143.1	22	494	17	29.05	5-60	1	—
D. Breakwell	SLA	355	110	890	29	30.68	4-44	—	—
I. V. A. Richards	OB	89.5	24	248	7	35.42	3-15	—	—
P. M. Roebuck	OB	92.5	26	261	7	37.28	2-65	—	—
C. H. Dredge	RM	464	98	1396	37	37.72	4-42	—	—
V. J. Marks	OB	263.1	80	729	19	38.36	5-50	1	—
K. F. Jennings	RM	139.3	41	386	8	48.25	3-23	—	—

Also bowled: R. J. Clapp 19.1–8–37–4; D. B. Close 0.2–0–8–0; P. J. Robinson 13–3–32–3; B. C. Rose 10–1–52–0; P. A. Slocombe 3–1–14–0.

County Records

First-class cricket

Highest innings totals:	For .....675–9d v Hampshire (Bath)	1924
	Agst.....811 by Surrey (The Oval)	1899
Lowest innings totals:	For .....25 v Gloucestershire (Bristol)	1947
	Agst.....22 by Gloucestershire (Bristol)	1920
Highest individual innings:	For .....310 H. Gimblett v Sussex (Eastbourne)	1948
	Agst.....424 A. C. MacLaren for Lancs (Taunton)	1895

SOMERSET

Best bowling in an innings:	For ....10–49 E. J. Tyler v Surrey (Taunton)	1895
	Agst.....10–35 A. Drake for Yorkshire (Weston-super-Mare)	1914
Best bowling in a match:	For ....16–83 J. C. White v Worcestershire (Bath)	1919
	Agst....17–137 W. Brearley for Lancashire (Manchester)	1905
Most runs in a season:	2761 (av 56.82) W. E. Alley	1961
runs in a career:	21108 (av 37.09) H. Gimblett	1935–1954
100s in a season:	10 by W. E. Alley	1961
100s in a career:	49 by H. Gimblett	1935–1954
wickets in a season:	169 (av 19.24) A. W. Wellard	1938
wickets in a career:	2153 (av 18.10) J. C. White	1909–1937

RECORD WICKET STANDS

1st	346	H. T. Hewett & L. C. H. Palairet v Yorkshire (Taunton)	1892
2nd	286	J. C. W. MacBryan & M. D. Lyon v Derbyshire (Buxton)	1924
3rd	300	G. Atkinson & P. B. Wight v Glamorgan (Bath)	1960
4th	251	I. V. A. Richards & P. M. Roebuck v Surrey (Weston-super-Mare)	1977
5th	235	J. C. White & C. C. C. Case v Gloucestershire (Taunton)	1927
6th	265	W. E. Alley & K. E. Palmer v Northamptonshire (Northampton)	1961
7th	240	S. M. J. Woods & V. T. Hill v Kent (Taunton)	1898
8th	143*	E. F. Longrigg & C. J. P. Barnwell v Gloucestershire (Bristol)	1938
9th	183	C. Greetham & H. W. Stephenson v Leicestershire (Weston-super-Mare)	1963
10th	143	J. J. Bridges & H. Gibbs v Surrey (Weston-super-Mare)	1919

One-day cricket

Highest innings totals:	Gillette Cup	257–5 v Surrey (Taunton)	1974
	John Player League	270–4 v Gloucestershire (Bristol, Imperial)	1975
	Benson & Hedges Cup	265–8 v Gloucestershire (Taunton)	1974
Lowest innings	Gillette Cup	59 v Middlesex (Lord's)	1977
	John Player League	58 v Essex (Chelmsford)	1977
	Benson & Hedges Cup	105 v Hampshire (Bournemouth)	1975
Highest indi-	Gillette Cup	128 B. C. Rose v Derbyshire (Ilkeston)	1977
	John Player League	131 D. B. Close v Yorkshire (Bath)	1974
	Benson & Hedges Cup	95 R. C. Cooper v Minor Counties (Plymouth)	1972
Best bowling figures:	Gillette Cup	5–18 R. Palmer v Lancashire (Taunton)	1966
	John Player League	6–25 G. I. Burgess v Glamorgan (Glastonbury)	1972
	Benson & Hedges Cup	4–12 G. I. Burgess v Glamorgan (Pontypridd)	1972

SURREY

Formation of present club: 1845.
Colours: Chocolate.
Badge: Prince of Wales' Feathers
County Champions (17): 1887, 1888, 1890, 1891, 1892, 1894, 1895, 1899, 1914, 1952, 1953, 1954, 1955, 1956, 1957, 1958, and 1971.
Joint Champions (2): 1889 and 1950.
Gillette Cup finalists: 1965.
Best final position in John Player League: 5th in 1969
Benson & Hedges Cup winners: 1974.
Gillette Man of the Match awards: 13.
Benson & Hedges Gold awards: 18.
Secretary: I. F. B. Scott-Browne, Kennington Oval, London, SE11, 5SS.
Captain: R. D. V. Knight.

Raymond Paul (Ray) BAKER (Wallington HS) B Carshalton (Surrey) 9/4/1954. RHB, RM. Played for 2nd XI since 1971. Debut 1973. HS: 77* v Glos (Cheltenham) 1977. HSGC: 25* v Lancs (Manchester) 1977. HSJPL: 48* v Middlesex (Oval) 1977. BB: 6–29 v Essex (Ilford) 1974. BBJPL: 4–39 v Somerset (Byfleet) 1977.

Alan Raymond BUTCHER (Heath Clark GS, Croydon) B Croydon 7/1/1954. LHB, LM. Played in two John Player League matches in 1971. Debut 1972. Cap 1975. Scored 977 runs (av 25.71) in 1976. Benson & Hedges Gold awards: 3. HS: 112 v Glamorgan (Cardiff) 1977. HSGC: 51 v Derbyshire (Ilkeston) 1976. HSJPL: 103* v Derbyshire (Oval) 1976. HSBH: 61 v Kent (Canterbury) 1976. BB: 6–48 v Hants (Guildford) 1972. BBJPL: 5–19 v Glos (Bristol) 1975. BBBH: 3–11 v Lancs (Manchester) 1974.

John Hugh EDRICH B Blofield (Norfolk) 21/6/1937. LHB, RM. Cousin of W. J. Edrich. Played for Norfolk in 1954 and Surrey 2nd XI in 1955. Debut 1956 for Combined Services. Debut for Surrey 1958. Cap 1959. *Wisden* 1965. Benefit (£10,551) in 1968. Appointed county captain in 1973. Testimonial (£20,000) in 1975. Awarded MBE in 1977 Birthday Honours list. Tests: 77 between 1963 and 1976. Scored century (120) on debut v Australia at Lord's 1964. Tours: India 1963–64, Australia and New Zealand 1965–66, 1970–71 and 1974–75 (vice-captain), West Indies 1967–68, Ceylon and Pakistan 1968–69. 1,000 runs (19)—2,482 runs (av 51.70) in 1962 best. Also scored 1,060 runs (av 44.16) on 1965–66 tour and 1,136 runs (av 56.80) in 1970–71. Scored 1,799 runs (av 52.91) in 1959 in first full season, despite absence through injury for a few matches. Scored two centuries in match v Notts (Nottingham) 1959 (171 and 124) v Worcs (Worcester) 1970 (143 and 113*), v Warwickshire (Oval) 1971 (111 and 124) and v Kent (Oval) 1977 (140 and 115). Scored 1,311 runs in 9 consecutive innings all over 50 including three consecutive centuries in 1965. Completed 30,000 runs in 1971 and scored 100th century in 1977. Gillette

Man of Match awards: 2. Benson & Hedges Gold awards: 7. HS: 310*
England v New Zealand (Leeds) 1965 sharing in 2nd wkt partnership of
369 with K. F. Barrington. HSC: 226* v Middlesex (Oval) 1967. HSGC:
96 v Glos (Oval) 1964. HSJPL: 108* v Derbyshire (Derby) 1972. HSBH:
83* v Sussex (Oval) 1973.

Thomas Michael Geoffrey (Tom) HANSELL (Millfield School) B Sutton
Coldfield (Warwickshire) 24/8/1954. LHB, SLA. Joined staff 1974.
Debut 1975. HS: 54 v Notts (Oval) 1976. HSJPL: 26 v Northants (Guild-
ford) 1977.

Geoffrey Philip (Geoff) HOWARTH (Auckland GS) B Auckland
29/3/1951. Younger brother of H. J. Howarth, New Zealand Test cricketer.
RHB, OB. Debut for New Zealand under-23 XI v Auckland (Auckland)
1968–69. Joined Surrey staff 1969. Debut 1971. Cap 1974. Tests: 8 between
1974–75 and 1976–77. Tour: New Zealand to Pakistan and India 1976–77.
Scored 1,554 runs (av 37.90) in 1976. Benson & Hedges Gold awards: 1.
HS: 159 v Kent (Maidstone) 1973. HSTC: 59 New Zealand v Australia
(Auckland) 1976–77. HSGC: 34 v Lancs (Manchester) 1977. HSJPL: 122
v Glos (Oval) 1976. HSBH: 80 v Yorks (Oval) 1974. BB: 5–32 Auckland
v Central Districts (Auckland) 1973–74. BBUK: 3–20 v Northants (North-
hampton) 1976.

INTIKHAB ALAM B Hoshiarpur, India 28/12/1941. RHB, LBG.
Debut for Karachi 1957–58 aged 16 years 9 months and has played
continuously for various Karachi sides and Pakistan International
Airways since. Professional for West of Scotland Club in Scottish Western
Union for some seasons. Debut for county and cap 1969. Benefit in 1978.
Tests: 47 for Pakistan between 1959–60 and 1976–77, captaining country
in 17 Tests. Played in 5 matches for Rest of World in 1970 and 5 in 1971–
72. Took wkt of C. C. McDonald with first ball he bowled in Test cricket.
Tours: Pakistan to India 1960–61, England 1962, 1967, 1971 and 1974
(captain on last two tours), Ceylon 1964, Australia and New Zealand
1964–65, 1972–73 (captain), Australia and West Indies 1976–77, Pakistan
Eaglets to England 1963, Pakistan International Airways to East Africa
1964, Rest of World to Australia 1971–72 (vice captain). Took 104 wkts
(av 28,36) in 1971. Hat-trick v Yorks (Oval) 1972. HS: 182 Karachi
Blues v Pakistan International Airways B (Karachi) 1970–71. HSUK:
139 v Glos (Oval) 1973. HSTC: 138 Pakistan v England (Hyderabad)
1972–73. HSGC: 50 v Somerset (Oval) 1975. HSJPL: 62 v Northants
(Tolworth) 1973. HSBH: 32 v Middlesex (Lord's) 1973. BB: 8–54 Pakistanis v Tasmania (Hobart) 1972–73. BBUK: 8–61 Pakistanis v Minor
Counties (Swindon) 1967. BBTC: 7–52 Pakistan v New Zealand (Dunedin) 1972–73. BBC: 8–74 v Middlesex (Oval) 1970. BBJPL: 6–25 v
Derbyshire (Oval) 1974. BBBH: 3–42 v Essex (Chelmsford) 1973.

Robin David JACKMAN (St Edmund's School, Canterbury) B Simla
(India) 13/8/1945. RHB, RFM. Debut 1964. Cap 1970. Played for Western
Province in 1971–72 and Rhodesia from 1972–73 to 1976–77 in Currie Cup
competition. Hat-tricks (3): v Kent (Canterbury) 1971, Western Province
v Natal (Pietermaritzburg) 1971–72 and v Yorks (Leeds) 1973. Gillette
Man of Match awards: 1. HS: 92* v Kent (Oval) 1974. HSGC: 18* v

Glamorgan (Cardiff) 1977. HSJPL: 43 v Kent (Maidstone) 1977. HSBH: 36 v Leics (Lord's) 1974. BB: 8–40 Rhodesia v Natal (Durban) 1972–73. BBUK: 8–79 v Hants (Oval) 1976. BBGC: 7–33 v Yorks (Harrogate) 1970. BBJPL: 6–34 v Derbyshire (Derby) 1973. BBBH: 4–31 v Kent (Canterbury) 1974.

Roger David Verdon KNIGHT (Dulwich College and Cambridge) B Streatham 6/9/1946. LHB, RM. Debut for Cambridge U 1967. Blues 1967–70. Debut for Surrey 1968. Debut for Glos by special registration 1971. Cap 1971. Left county after 1975 season and made debut for Sussex in 1976. Cap 1976. 1,000 runs (7)—1,350 runs (av 38.57) in 1974 best. Gillette Man of Match awards: 3 (for Glos). Benson & Hedges Gold awards: 3 (2 for Glos). HS: 165* v Middlesex (Hove) 1976. HSGC: 75 Glos v Glamorgan (Cardiff) 1973. HSJPL: 127 v Hants (Hove) 1976. HSBH: 117 v Surrey (Oval) 1977. BB: 6–44 Glos v Northants (Northampton) 1974. BBC: 4–46 v Worcs (Hove) 1977. BBGC: 5–39 Glos v Surrey (Bristol) 1971. BBJPL: 5–42 v Notts (Nottingham) 1977. BBBH: 3–19 v Surrey (Oval) 1977.

Monte Alan LYNCH (Ryden's School, Walton-on-Thames) B Georgetown, British Guiana 21/5/1958. RHB, RM/OB. Debut 1977. HS: 44 v Somerset (Weston-super-Mare) 1977. HSJPL: 11* v Lancs (Oval) 1977.

Andrew NEEDHAM (Paisley GS and Watford GS) B Calow (Derbyshire) 23/3/1957. RHB, OB. Debut 1977. HS: 15* v Somerset (Weston-super-Mare) 1977. BB: 3–25 v Oxford U (Oxford) 1977.

Ian Roger PAYNE (Emanuel School) B Lambeth Hospital, Kennington 9/5/1958. RHB, RM. Debut 1977. HS: 29 v Kent (Oval) 1977. HSJPL: 20 v Kent (Maidstone) 1977. BBJPL: 4–31 v Northants (Guildford) 1977.

Patrick Ian (Pat) POCOCK (Wimbledon Technical School) B Bangor (Caernarvonshire) 24/9/1946. RHB, OB. Debut 1964. Benefit in 1977. Played for Northern Transvaal in 1971–72 Currie Cup competition. Tests: 17 between 1967–68 and 1976. Tours: Pakistan 1966–67, West Indies 1967–68 and 1973–74, Ceylon and Pakistan 1968–69, India, Pakistan, and Sri Lanka 1972–73. Took 112 wkts (av 18.22) in 1967. Took 4 wkts in 4 balls, 5 in 6, 6 in 9, and 7 in 11 (the last two being first-class records) v Sussex (Eastbourne) 1972. Hat-tricks (2): as above and v Worcs (Guildford) 1971. Benson & Hedges Gold awards: 2. HS: 75* v Notts (Oval) 1968. HSTC: 33 v Pakistan (Hyderabad) 1972–73. HSGC: 11* v Somerset (Taunton) 1974. HSJPL: 22 v Notts (Nottingham) 1971. HSBH: 19 v Middlesex (Oval) 1972. BB: 7–57 v Essex (Romford) 1968. BBTC: 6–79 v Australia (Manchester) 1968. BBGC: 3–34 v Somerset (Oval) 1975. BBJPL: 4–27 v Essex (Chelmsford) 1974. BBBH: 4–20 v Combined Universities (Cambridge) 1977.

Clifton James (Jack) RICHARDS (Humphrey Davy GS, Penzance) B Penzance 10/8/1958. RHB, WK. Debut 1976. HS: 33* v Sussex (Oval) 1977. HSJPL: 18* v Glos (Cheltenham) 1977.

SURREY

Graham Richard James ROOPE (Bradfield College) B Fareham (Hants) 12/7/1946. RHB, RM. Played for Public Schools XI v Comb. Services (Lord's) 1963 and 1964. Played for Berkshire 1963 scoring century against Wiltshire. Joined county staff and debut 1964. Cap 1969. Played for Griqualand West in 1973–74 Currie Cup competition. Tests: 11 between 1972–73 and 1977. Tours: India, Pakistan and Sri Lanka 1972–73, Pakistan and New Zealand 1977–78. 1,000 runs (8)—1,641 runs (av 44.35) in 1971 best. Scored two centuries in match (109 and 103*) v Leics (Leicester) 1971. Held 59 catches in 1971. Benson & Hedges Gold awards: 3. HS: 171 v Yorks (Oval) 1971. HSTC: 77 v Australia (Oval) 1975. HSGC: 66 v Somerset (Oval) 1975. HSJPL: 120* v Worcs (Byfleet) 1973. HSBH: 115* v Essex (Chelmsford) 1973. BB: 5–14 v West Indians (Oval) 1969. BBGC: 5–23 v Derbyshire (Oval) 1967. BBJPL: 4–31 v Glamorgan (Oval) 1974. BBBH: 3–45 v Somerset (Oval) 1975. Soccer (goalkeeper) for Corinthian Casuals, Wimbledon, and Guildford City.

Lonsdale Ernest SKINNER (Hillcroft Comprehensive School, Tooting) B Plaisance, British Guiana 7/9/1950. RHB, WK. Joined staff 1969. Debut 1971. Played for Guyana in 1973–74, 1975–76 and 1976–77. Shell Shield Competitions. Cap 1975. Benson & Hedges Gold awards: 1. HS: 93 v Yorks (Oval) 1976. HSGC: 32 v Somerset (Taunton) 1974. HSJPL: 70 v Warwickshire (Birmingham) 1974. HSBH: 89 v Glos (Oval) 1975.

David James THOMAS (Licensed Victuallers School, Slough) B Solihull (Warwickshire) 30/6/1959. LHB, LM. Debut 1977. HS: 14 v Lancs (Oval) 1977.

Frederick John (Fred) TITMUS (The William Ellis School, Highgate. B St Pancras 24/11/1932. RHB, OB. Debut for Middlesex 1949 (aged 16). Cap 1953. Wisden 1962. Benefit (£6,833) in 1963. Appointed county captain in 1965, but resigned post during 1968 season. Appointed vice-captain in 1971. Second benefit (£6,196) in 1973. Played for Orange Free State in 1975–76 Currie Cup Competition. Retired after 1976 season. Awarded MBE in 1977 New Year Honours List. Joined Surrey as coach in 1977 and may play occasionally for county in 1978. Tests: 53 between 1955 and 1974–75. Tours: Pakistan 1955–56, Australia and New Zealand 1962–63, 1965–66 (Australia only), 1974–75, India 1963–64, South Africa 1964–65, West Indies 1967–68 (vice-captain), returning home early through loss of four toes in accident. 1,000 runs (8)—1,703 runs (av 37.02) in 1961 best. 100 wkts (16)—191 wkts (av 16.31) in 1955 best. Has taken more wickets (2,343) for Middlesex than any other bowler. Doubles (8): 1955 to 1957, 1959 to 1962, 1967. Missed double by 62 runs in 1963 and by 76 runs in 1968. Shared in 6th wkt partnership record for county, 227 with C. T. Radley v South Africans (Lord's) 1965. Hat-trick v Somerset (Weston-super-Mare) 1966. Took 4 wkts in 6 balls for England v New Zealand (Leeds) 1965. Gillette Man of Match awards: 3 (for Middlesex). HS: 137* MCC v South Australia (Adelaide) 1962–63. HSUK: 120* Middlesex v Sussex (Hove) 1961. HSTC: 84* v India (Bombay) 1963–64. HSGC: 41 v Sussex (Lord's) 1973. HSJPL: 28 Middlesex v Warwickshire (Lord's) 1973. HSBH: 17* Middlesex v Worcs (Lord's) 1974. BB: 9–52 Middlesex v Cambridge U (Cambridge) 1962 and 9–57 Middlesex v Lancs (Lord's) 1964. BBTC: 7–79 v Australia (Sydney) 1962–63. BBGC: 5–26 Middlesex v Derbyshire (Lord's) 1970. BBJPL: 5–25 Middlesex v Essex (Lord's)

1971. BBBH: 3–21 Middlesex v Northants (Lord's) 1976. Soccer (IL) for Watford and Hendon.

Mohammad YOUNIS AHMED (Moslem HS, Lahore) B Jullundur Pakistan 20/10/1947. LHB, LM/SLA. Younger step-brother of Saeed Ahmed, Pakistan Test cricketer, who has played for county 2nd XI. Debut 1961–62 for Pakistan Inter Board Schools XI v South Zone at age of 14 years 4 months. Debut for Surrey 1965. Cap 1969. Played for South Australia in 1972–73 Sheffield Shield competition. Tests: 2 for Pakistan v New Zealand 1969–70. 1,000 runs (7)—1,760 runs (av 47.56) in 1969 best. Benson & Hedges Gold awards: 1. HS: 183* v Worcs (Worcester) 1975. HSTC: 62 Pakistan v New Zealand (Karachi) 1969–70. HSGC: 87 v Middlesex (Oval) 1970. HSJPL: 113 v Warwickshire (Birmingham) 1976. HSBH: 101* v Kent (Canterbury) 1974. BB: 4–10 v Cambridge U (Cambridge) 1975.

NB The following players whose particulars appeared in the 1977 Annual have been omitted: A. J. Mack (not re-engaged) and D. M. Smith (not re-engaged). Their career records will be found elsewhere in this Annual.

COUNTY AVERAGES

Schweppes County Championship: Played 21, won 3, drawn 12, lost 6 abandoned 1
All first-class matches: Played 23, won 3, drawn 14, lost 6, abandoned 1

BATTING AND FIELDING

Cap		M	I	NO	Runs	HS	Avge	100	50	Ct	St
—	R. P. Baker	12	12	9	215	77*	71.66	—	1	3	—
1969	G. R. J. Roope	18	29	5	1359	115	56.62	5	7	21	—
1959	J. H. Edrich	15	26	4	1044	140	47.45	3	5	7	—
1970	R. D. Jackman	22	32	11	606	86*	28.85	—	2	15	—
1975	A. R. Butcher	21	35	1	890	112	26.17	1	5	4	—
1969	Younis Ahmed	20	34	3	786	61*	25.35	—	4	10	—
1974	G. P. Howarth	17	29	2	646	140	23.92	2	2	9	—
1975	L. E. Skinner	14	20	1	382	54	20.10	—	1	7	1
1976	G. G. Arnold	15	19	7	240	56	20.00	—	1	4	—
1969	Intikhab Alam	21	34	5	552	86	19.03	—	3	3	—
—	D. M. Smith	12	11	2	278	57	17.37	—	1	9	—
—	M. A. Lynch	5	10	0	170	44	17.00	—	—	—	—
—	T. M. G. Hansell	5	8	2	88	24*	14.66	—	—	1	—
—	C. J. Richards	12	15	4	137	33*	12.45	—	—	23	6
1967	P. I. Pocock	21	18	4	166	31	11.85	—	—	7	—
—	A. Needham	7	7	1	48	15*	8.00	—	—	2	—
—	I. R. Payne	7	9	1	63	29	7.87	—	—	2	—
—	A. J. Mack	7	5	0	34	16	6.80	—	—	—	—

Played in two matches: D. J. Thomas 14, 0*, 0.

BOWLING

	Type	O	M	R	W	Avge	Best	5 wI	10 wM
R. D. Jackman	RFM	585	102	1882	75	25.09	6–50	2	1
G. G. Arnold	RFM	314.1	85	781	30	26.03	6–24	2	—
R. P. Baker	RM	194.1	44	584	18	32.44	3–35	—	—
P. I. Pocock	OB	574.5	163	1521	38	40.02	6–80	1	—
A. R. Butcher	LM	134	22	512	12	42.66	3–72	—	—
Intikhab Alam	LBG	387.3	110	1214	28	43.35	4–21	—	—
A. Needham	OB	137.4	44	338	7	48.28	3–25	—	—
A. J. Mack	LM	135	11	539	5	107.80	2–50	—	—

Also bowled: J. H. Edrich 5–4–4–0; T. M. G. Hansell 4–4–0–0; G. P. Howarth 8–1–35–0; I. R. Payne 39–6–192–1; G. R. J. Roope 51.3–7–155–3; D. M. Smith 19–4–77–0; D. J. Thomas 37–10–101–1; Younis Ahmed 30–13–80–3.

County Records

First-class cricket

Highest innings totals:	For .....811 v Somerset (The Oval)	1899
	Agst.....705–8d by Sussex (Hastings)	1902
Lowest innings totals:	For ..... 16 v Nottinghamshire (The Oval)	1880
	Agst..... 15 by MCC (Lord's)	1839
Highest Individual innings:	For .....357* R. Abel v Somerset (The Oval)	1899
	Agst.....300*F.Watson for Lancashire (Manchester)	1928
	300 R. Subba Row for Northamptonshire (The Oval)	1958
Best bowling in an innings:	For .....10–43 T. Rushby v Somerset (Taunton)	1921
	Agst.....10–28 W. P. Howell for Australians (The Oval)	1899
Best bowling in a match:	For .....16–83 G. A. R. Lock v Kent (Blackheath)	1956
	Agst.....15–57 W. P. Howell for Australians (The Oval)	1899
Most runs in a season:	3246 (av 72.13) T. W. Hayward	1906
runs in a career:	43703 (av 49.77) J. B. Hobbs	1905–1934
100s in a season:	13 by T. W. Hayward	1906
	J. B. Hobbs	1925
100s in a career:	144 by J. B. Hobbs	1905–1934
wickets in a season:	250 (av 14.06) T. Richardson	1895
wickets in a career:	1775 (av 17.91) T. Richardson	1892–1905

RECORD WICKET STANDS

1st	428	J. B. Hobbs & A. Sandham v Oxford U (The Oval)	1926
2nd	371	J. B. Hobbs & E. G. Hayes v Hampshire (The Oval)	1909
3rd	353	A. Ducat & E. G. Hayes v Hampshire (Southampton)	1919
4th	448	R. Abel & T. W. Hayward v Yorkshire (The Oval)	1899
5th	308	J. N. Crawford & F. C. Holland v Somerset (The Oval)	1908
6th	298	A. Sandham & H. S. Harrison v Sussex (The Oval)	1913
7th	200	T. F. Shepherd & J. W. Hitch v Kent (Blackheath)	1921
8th	204	T. W. Hayward & L. C. Braund v Lancashire (The Oval)	1898
9th	168	E. R. T. Holmes & E. W. J. Brooks v Hampshire (The Oval)	1936
10th	173	A. Ducat & A. Sandham v Essex (Leyton)	1921

One-day cricket

Highest innings totals:	Gillette Cup	280–5 v Middlesex (Oval)	1970
	John Player League	248–2 v Gloucestershire (Oval)	1976
	Benson & Hedges Cup	264 v Kent (Oval)	1976
Lowest innings totals:	Gillette Cup	74 v Kent (Oval)	1967
	John Player League	82 v Lancashire (Manchester)	1971
	Benson & Hedges Cup	125 v Sussex (Hove)	1972
Highest individual innings:	Gillette Cup	101 M. J. Stewart v Durham (Chester-le-Street)	1972
	John Player League	122 G. P. Howarth v Gloucestershire (Oval)	1976
	Benson & Hedges Cup	115 G. R. J. Roope v Essex (Chelmsford)	1973
Best bowling figures:	Gillette Cup	7–33 R. D. Jackman v Yorkshire (Harrogate)	1970
	John Player League	6–25 Intikhab Alam v Derbyshire (Oval)	1974
	Benson & Hedges Cup	4–20 P. I. Pocock v Combined Universities (Cambridge)	1977

SUSSEX

Formation of present club: 1839, reorganised 1857.
Colours: Dark blue, light blue, and gold.
Badge: County Arms of six martlets (in shape of inverted pyramid).
Joint Champions: 1875.
County Championship runners-up (6): 1902, 1903, 1932, 1933, 1934, and 1953.
Gillette Cup winners (2): 1963 and 1964.
Gillette Cup finalists (3): 1968, 1970, and 1973.
John Player League runners-up: 1976.
Benson & Hedges Cup quarter-finalists (2): 1972 and 1977.
Gillette Man of the Match awards: 21.
Benson & Hedges Gold awards: 14.

Secretary: S. R. Allen, MBE, County Ground, Eaton Road, Hove, BN3 3AN.
Captain: A. Long.

Geoffrey Graham (Geoff) ARNOLD B Earlsfield (Surrey) 3/9/1944. RHB, RFM. Debut 1963. Cap 1967. *Wisden* 1971. Benefit (£15,000) in 1976. Played for Orange Free State in 1976–77 Currie Cup competition. Tests: 34 between 1967 and 1975. Tours: Pakistan 1966–67, India, Pakistan, and Sri Lanka 1972–73, West Indies 1973–74, Australia and New Zealand 1974–75. Took 109 wkts (av 18.22) in 1967. Hat-trick v Leics (Leicester) 1974. Gillette Man of Match awards: 2. HS: 73 MCC under-25 v Central Zone (Sahiwal) 1966–67. HSUK: 63 v Warwickshire (Birmingham) 1968. HSTC: 59 v Pakistan (Oval) 1967. HSGC: 15 v Sussex (Oval) 1970 and 15 v Worcs (Worcester) 1972. HSJPL: 24* v Notts (Nottingham) 1971. HSBH: 12* v Combined Universities (Oval) 1976. BB: 8–41 (13–128 match) v Glos (Oval) 1967. BBTC: 6–45 v India (Delhi) 1972–73. BBGC: 5–9 v Derbyshire (Oval) 1967. BBJPL: 5–11 v Glamorgan (Oval) 1969. BBBH: 3–19 v Yorks (Bradford) 1976. Soccer for Corinthian Casuals.

John Robert Troutbeck BARCLAY (Eton College) B Bonn, West Germany 22/1/1954. RHB, OB. Debut 1970 age 16½, whilst still at school. Was in XI at school from age of 14 and scored the record number of runs for school in a season in 1970. Played in MCC Schools matches at Lord's in 1969–71. Vice-captain of English Schools Cricket Association team to India 1970–71. Captain of England Young Cricketers team to West Indies 1972. Cap 1976. 1,000 runs (2)—1,090 runs (av 30.27) in 1977 best. Benson & Hedges Gold awards: 2. HS: 112 v Warwickshire (Hove) 1977. HSGC: 44 v Derbyshire (Hove) 1977. HSJPL: 48 v Derbyshire (Derby) 1974. HSBH: 93* v Surrey (Oval) 1976. BB: 6–94 v Lancs (Manchester) 1976. BBJPL: 3–27 v Northants (Northampton) 1975.

Michael Alan (Mike) BUSS B Brightling (Sussex) 24/1/1944. Younger brother of A. Buss. LBH, LM. Debut 1961. Developed into opening batsman in 1966, and changed bowling style from SLA to LM in 1967. Cap 1967. Played for Orange Free State from 1972–73 to 1974–75 in Currie Cup competition. Benefit £12,000) in 1976. Tour: Pakistan 1966–67, flown out as replacment for R. N. Abberley. 1,000 runs (4)—1,379 runs (av 37.27) in 1970 best. Gillette Man of Match awards: 2. Benson & Hedges Gold awards: 1. HS: 159 v Glamorgan (Swansea) 1967. HSGC: 72 v Essex (Chelmsford) 1970. HSJPL: 121 v Notts (Worksop) 1971. HSBH: 78 v Middlesex (Hove) 1972. BB: 7–58 v Hants (Bournemouth) 1970. BBGC: 4–14 v Glos (Hove) 1969. BBJPL: 6–14 v Lancs (Hove) 1973. BBBH: 3–17 v Yorks (Hove) 1976.

Robert Giles Lenthall CHEATLE (Stowe School) B London 31/7/1953. LHB, SLA. Debut 1974. HS: 34 v Kent (Hove) 1977. BB: 6–54 v Kent (Canterbury) 1976. BBJPL: 4–33 v Glamorgan (Eastbourne) 1977.

Peter John GRAVES (Hove Manor School) B Hove 19/5/1946. LHB, SLA. Close field. Debut 1965. Cap 1969. Is vice-captain of county. Benefit in 1978. Played for Orange Free State in 1969–70, 1970–71 (captain), 1973–74 to 1976–77 Currie Cup competitions whilst appointed as coach. 1,000 runs (5)—1,282 runs (av 38.84) in 1974 best. Scored two centuries in match (119 and 136*) for Orange Free State v Border (Bloemfontein) 1976–77. Gillette Man of Match awards: 1. Benson & Hedges Gold

136

awards: 1. HS: 145* v Glos (Gloucester) 1974. HSGC: 84* v Derbyshire (Chesterfield) 1973. HSJPL: 101* v Middlesex (Eastbourne) 1972. HSBH: 114* v Cambridge U (Hove) 1974. BB: 3–69 Orange Free State v Australians (Bloemfontein) 1969–70. BBUK: 3–75 v Glos (Cheltenham) 1965. Soccer player.

Anthony William (Tony) GREIG (Queen's College, Queenstown) B Queenstown, South Africa 6/10/1946. Very tall (6ft 7½in). RHB, RM/OB. Debut for Border in 1965–66 Currie Cup competition. Debut for Sussex 1966. Cap 1967. Elected Best Young Cricketer of the Year 1967 by the Cricket Writers' Club. Transferred to Eastern Province in 1970–71. Appointed county captain in 1973. *Wisden* 1974. Tests: 58 between 1972 and 1977, captaining England in 14 Tests between 1975 and 1977. Played in 3 matches against Rest of World in 1970 and 5 matches for Rest of World v Australia 1971–72. Tours: Rest of World to Australia 1971–72, India, Pakistan, and Sri Lanka 1972–73, West Indies 1973–74 (vice-captain), Australia and New Zealand 1974–75, India, Sri Lanka and Australia 1976–77 (captain). 1,000 runs (7)—1,699 runs (av 47.19) in 1975 best. Scored two centuries in match for L. C. Stevens' XI v Cambridge U (Eastbourne) 1966—a match not regarded as first-class. Hat-trick. Eastern Province v Natal (Port Elizabeth) 1971–72. Took 3 wkts in 4 balls v Hants (Hove) 1967. Gillette Man of Match awards: 5. HS: 226 v Warwickshire (Hastings) 1975. HSTC: 148 v India (Bombay) 1972–73 and 148 v West Indies (Bridgetown) 1973–74. HSGC: 62 v Notts (Nottingham) 1975, and 62 v Kent (Canterbury) 1976. HSJPL: 129 v Yorks (Scarborough) 1976. HSBH: 103 v Cambridge U (Hove) 1974. BB: 8–25 v Glos (Hove) 1967. BBTC: 8–86 (13–156 match) v West Indies (Port of Spain) 1973–74. BBGC: 5–42 v Kent (Canterbury) 1970. BBJPL: 6–28 v Middlesex (Hove) 1971. BBBH: 5–40 v Notts (Hove) 1977.

Jeremy Jonathan (Jerry) GROOME (Seaford College) B Bognor Regis 7/4/1955. RHB, RM. Debut 1974. Played in one Championship match only in 1977. HS: 86 v Middlesex (Lord's) 1975. HSJPL: 72 v Glos (Eastbourne) 1975. HSBH: 35 v Kent (Canterbury) 1974.

Timothy John (Tim) HEAD (Lancing College) B Hammersmith 22/9/1957. RHB, WK. Debut 1976. One match v Oxford U (Pagham) and one match v Cambridge U (Cambridge) 1977. Held 7 catches in his first match.

IMRAN KHAN NIAZI (Aitchison College and Cathedral School, Lahore, Worcester RGS and Oxford) B Lahore, Pakistan 25/11/1952. RHB, RF. Cousin of Majid Jahangir Khan. Debut for Lahore A 1969–70 and has played subsequently for various Lahore teams. Debut for Worcs 1971. Blue 1973–74–75 (capt in 1974). Cap 1976. Left Worcs in 1977 and joined Sussex by special registration. Tests: 15 for Pakistan between 1971 and 1976–77. Tours: Pakistan to England 1971 and 1974, Australia and West Indies 1976–77. 1,000 runs (2)—1,092 runs (av 40.44) in 1976 best. Scored two centuries in match (117* and 106), Oxford U v Notts (Oxford) 1974. Had match double of 111* and 13–99 (7–53 & 6–46) v Lancs (Worcester) 1976. Gillette Man of Match awards: 1. Benson & Hedges Gold awards: 2 (1 for Oxford and Cambridge Universities).

SUSSEX

HS: 170 Oxford U v Northants (Oxford) 1974. HSC: 59 v Glamorgan (Eastbourne) 1977. HSTC: 59 Pakistan v New Zealand (Karachi) 1976–77. HSGC: 55* Worcs v Essex (Worcester) 1975. HSJPL: 75 Worcs v Warwickshire (Worcester) 1976. HSBH: 72 Worcs v Warwickshire (Birmingham) 1976. BB: 7–53 Worcs v Lancs (Worcester) 1976. BBC: 5–51 v Hants (Hove) 1977. BBTC: 6–63 (12–165 match) Pakistan v Australia (Sydney) 1976–77. BBJPL: 5–29 Worcs v Leics (Leicester) 1973. BBBH: 4–4 Oxford and Cambridge Universities v Worcs (Cambridge) 1975.

JAVED MIANDAD KHAN B Karachi 12/6/1957. RHB, LBG. Debut 1973–74 for Karachi Whites in Patron Trophy tournament aged 16 years 5 months. Has subsequently played for various Karachi and Sind sides. Vice-captain of Pakistan Under–19 side in England 1974 and captain of Under–19 side in Sri Lanka 1974–75. Scored 227 for county 2nd XI v Hants (Hove) 1975 whilst qualifying for county. Debut for county 1976. Cap 1977. Tests: 7 for Pakistan in 1976–77. Tour: Pakistan to Australia and West Indies 1976–77. Scored 1,326 runs (av 40.18) in 1977. Scored 163 for Pakistan v New Zealand (Lahore) 1976–77 on Test debut and 206 v New Zealand (Karachi) in third Test becoming youngest double-century maker in Test cricket at age of 19 years 4 months. HS: 311 Karachi Whites v National Bank (Karachi) 1974–75. HSUK: 162 v Kent (Canterbury) 1976. HSTC: 206 Pakistan v New Zealand (Karachi) 1976–77. HSGC: 69 v Warwickshire (Hove) 1976. HSJPL: 47 v Lancs (Blackpool) 1976. HSBH: 76 v Surrey (Oval) 1977. BB: 6–93 Sind v Railways (Lahore) 1974–75. BBUK: 4–10 v Northants (Northampton) 1977. BBTC: 3–74 Pakistan v New Zealand (Hyderabad) 1976–77.

Arnold LONG (Wallington CGS) B Cheam 18/12/1940. LBH, WK. Debut for Surrey 1960. Cup 1962. Benefit (£10,353) in 1971. Appointed county vice-captain in 1973. Left staff after 1975 season and made debut for Sussex in 1976. Cap 1976. Dismissed 7 batsmen in innings and 11 in match (all ct) v Sussex (Hove) 1964, world record for most catches in match and only one short of record for most dismissals in match. Dismissed 89 batsmen (72 ct 17 st) in 1962. HS: 92 Surrey v Leics (Leicester) 1970. HSC: 60 v Hants (Basingstoke) 1976. HSGC: 42 Surrey v Sussex (Oval) 1970. HSJPL: 71 Surrey v Warwickshire (Birmingham) 1971. HSBH: 46 Surrey v Kent (Oval) 1973. Soccer for Corinthian Casuals.

Gehan Dixon MENDIS (St Thomas College, Colombo and Brighton, Hove and Sussex GS) B Colombo, Ceylon 20/4/1955. RHB, WK. Played for 2nd XI since 1971. Played in one John Player League match in 1973. Debut 1974. HS: 68* v Leics (Leicester) 1977. HSJPL: 16* v Kent (Canterbury) 1975.

Paul William Giles PARKER (Collyers' GS, Horsham and Cambridge) B Bulawayo, Rhodesia 15/1/1956. Son of John Parker (ITN Sports Editor). RHB, RM. Debut for both Cambridge U and county 1976. Blue 1976–77. University Secretary for 1977 and 1978. Scored 1,115 runs (av 28.58) in 1976. HS: 215 Cambridge U v Essex (Cambridge) 1976. HSC: 110* v Hants (Southampton) 1977. HSGC: 22* v Derbyshire (Hove) 1977. HSJPL: 26* v Glamorgan (Cardiff) 1976. HSBH: 36* Combined Universities v Sussex (Cambridge) 1976. Selected for University rugby match in 1977, but had to withdraw through injury.

138

Christopher Paul PHILLIPSON (Ardingly College) B Brindaban, India 10/2/1952. RHB, RM. Debut 1970. Benson & Hedges Gold awards: 1. HS: 52 v Northants (Hove) 1976. HSJPL: 13* v Worcs (Worcester) 1975. BB: 6–56 v Notts (Hove) 1972. BBJPL: 4–25 v Middlesex (Eastbourne) 1972. BBBH: 5–32 v Combined Universities (Oxford) 1977. Trained as a teacher at Loughborough College of Education.

John Augustine SNOW (Christ's Hospital, Horsham) B Peopleton (Worcs) 13/10/1941. RHB, RFM. Debut 1961. Cap 1964. *Wisden* 1972. Benefit (£18,000) in 1974. Tests: 49 between 1965 and 1976. Played in 5 matches v Rest of World 1970. Shared in 10th wkt partnership of 128 with K. Higgs v West Indies (Oval) 1966—2 runs short of then record 10th wkt partnership in Test cricket. Tours: West Indies 1967–68, Ceylon and Pakistan 1968–69, Australia 1970–71. 100 wkts (2)—126 wkts (av 19.09) in 1966 best. Gillette Man of Match awards: 1. Benson & Hedges Gold awards: 2. HS: 73 England v India (Lord's) 1971 and 73* v Worcs (Worcester) 1977. HSGC: 19 v Worcs (Hove) 1974. HSJPL: 57 v Lancs (Horsham) 1977. HSBH: 25 v Essex (Chelmsford) 1972. BB: 8–87 v Middlesex (Lord's) 1975. BBTC: 7–40 v Australia (Sydney) 1970–71. BBGC: 4–35 v Surrey (Oval) 1970. BBJPL: 5–15 v Surrey (Hove) 1972. BBBH: 5–30 v Kent (Canterbury) 1974.

John SPENCER (Brighton, Hove and Sussex GS, and Cambridge) B Brighton 6/10/1949. RHB, RM. Debut 1969. Cap 1973. Benson & Hedges Gold awards: 3. HS: 79 v Hants (Southampton) 1975. HSGC: 14 v Glos (Hove) 1971. HSJPL: 35 v Northants (Northampton) 1977. HSBH: 18 Cambridge U v Warwickshire (Birmingham) 1972. BB: 6–19 v Glos (Gloucester) 1974. BBGC: 4–25 v Derbyshire (Chesterfield) 1973. BBJPL: 4–16 v Somerset (Hove) 1973. BBBH: 4–19 v Minor Counties (Hove) 1975.

Christopher Edward (Chris) WALLER B Guildford 3/10/1948. RHB, SLA. Debut for Surrey 1967. Cap 1972. Left staff after 1973 season and made debut for Sussex in 1974. Cap 1976. HS: 47 Surrey v Pakistanis (Oval) 1971. HSC: 38 v Worcs (Worcester) 1975. HSGC: 14* v Notts (Nottingham) 1975. HSJPL: 18* v Glamorgan (Hove) 1975. HSBH: 11* v Essex (Chelmsford) 1975. BB: 7–64 Surrey v Sussex (Oval) 1971. BBC: 6–40 v Surrey (Hove) 1975. BBJPL: 4–28 v Essex (Hove) 1976. BBBH: 4–25 v Minor Counties (Hove) 1975.

Kepler Christoffel WESSELS (Greys College, Bloemfontein) B Bloemfontein, South Africa 14/9/1957. LHB, OB. Debut for Orange Free State 1973–74 in Currie Cup competition, aged 16 years 4 months. Debut for county 1976 in non-championship matches v West Indians and Oxford U. Cap 1977. Is unavailable until July 1979 through national service commitment in South Africa. Benson & Hedges Gold awards: 1. HS: 138* v Kent (Tunbridge Wells) 1977. HSJPL: 88 v Notts (Nottingham) 1977. HSBH: 106 v Notts (Hove) 1977.

NB The following players whose particulars appeared in the 1977 Annual have been omitted: S. J. Hoadley and S. J. Still.

COUNTY AVERAGES

Schweppes County Championship: Played 22, won 6, drawn 11, lost 5
All first-class matches: Played 24, won 7, drawn 12, lost 5

BATTING AND FIELDING

Cap		M	I	NO	Runs	HS	Avge	100	50	Ct	St
1977	K. C. Wessels	11	17	3	663	138*	47.35	4	2	—	—
1977	Javed Miandad	24	39	6	1326	111	40.18	3	7	27	—
—	P. W. G. Parker	10	13	1	400	110*	33.33	1	1	5	—
1976	J. R. T. Barclay	24	39	5	1084	112	31.88	2	5	19	—
1967	A. W. Greig	13	17	0	509	88	29.94	—	2	12	—
—	Imran Khan	9	13	2	277	59	25.18	—	1	2	—
—	G. D. Mendis	14	26	3	578	68*	25.13	—	3	5	—
1976	R. D. V. Knight	23	37	1	872	100*	24.22	1	3	13	—
1967	M. A. Buss	19	30	4	627	125	24.11	1	2	12	—
1964	J. A. Snow	22	30	7	541	73*	23.52	—	4	2	—
1969	P. J. Graves	20	31	5	597	75*	22.96	—	4	11	—
1976	A. Long	23	28	11	369	47	21.70	—	—	40	3
—	C. P. Phillipson	3	4	0	65	24	16.25	—	—	3	—
1973	J. Spencer	23	25	8	273	43*	16.05	—	—	7	—
—	R. G. L. Cheatle	11	7	2	54	34	10.80	—	—	8	—
1976	C. E. Waller	13	13	7	57	15	9.50	—	—	7	—

Played in one match: J. J. Groome 9, 8, (1 ct); T. J. Head 4* (1 ct).

BOWLING

	Type	O	M	R	W	Avge	Best	5 wI	10 wM
Imran Khan	RF	203	50	551	25	22.04	5–51	1	—
A. W. Greig	RM/OB	236.2	65	654	28	23.35	4–22	—	—
J. Spencer	RM	516.2	160	1231	51	24.13	6–40	3	—
M. A. Buss	LM	326.4	106	759	31	24.48	4–14	—	—
J. R. T. Barclay	OB	155.1	39	447	18	24.83	3–31	—	—
R. G. L. Cheatle	SLA	200.2	43	671	23	29.17	5–9	1	—
J. A. Snow	RFM	459.4	112	1287	44	29.25	6–70	1	—
R. D. V. Knight	RM	170	36	573	16	35.81	3–22	—	—
Javed Miandad	LBG	157	28	602	16	37.62	4–10	—	—
C. E. Waller	SLA	234.2	54	755	20	37.75	4–48	—	—
C. P. Phillipson	RM	67.3	14	196	5	39.20	2–48	—	—

Also bowled: A. Long 1–0–2–0.

County Records

First-class cricket

Highest innings totals:	For	705–8d v Surrey (Hastings)	1902
	Agst	726 by Nottinghamshire (Nottingham)	1895
Lowest innings totals:	For	19 v Surrey (Godalming)	1830
		19 v Nottinghamshire (Hove)	1873
	Agst	18 by Kent (Gravesend)	1867
Highest individual innings:	For	333 K. S. Duleepsinhji v Northants (Hove)	1930
	Agst	322 E. Paynter for Lancashire (Hove)	1937
Best bowling in an innings:	For	10–48 C. H. G. Bland v Kent (Tonbridge)	1899
	Agst	9–11 A. P. Freeman for Kent (Hove)	1922
Best bowling in a match:	For	17–106 G. R. Cox v Warwicks (Horsham)	1926
	Agst	17–67 A. P. Freeman for Kent (Hove)	1922

Most runs in a season:	2850 (av 64.77) John Langridge	1949
runs in a career:	34152 (av 37.69) John Langridge	1928–1955
100s in a season:	12 by John Langridge	1949
100s in a career:	76 by John Langridge	1928–1955
wickets in a season:	198 (av 13.45) M. W. Tate	1925
wickets in a career:	2223 (av 16.34) M. W. Tate	1912–1937

RECORD WICKET STANDS

1st	490	E. H. Bowley & John Langridge v Middlesex (Hove)	1933
2nd	385	E. H. Bowley & M. W. Tate v Northamptonshire (Hove)	1921
3rd	298	K. S. Ranjitsinhji & E. H. Killick v Lancashire (Hove)	1901
4th	326*	G. Cox & James Langridge v Yorkshire (Leeds)	1949
5th	297	J. H. Parks & H. W. Parks v Hampshire (Portsmouth)	1937
6th	255	K. S. Duleepsinhji & M. W. Tate v Northamptonshire (Hove)	1930
7th	344	K. S. Ranjitsinhji & W. Newham v Essex (Leyton)	1902
8th	229*	C. L. A. Smith & G. Brann v Kent (Hove)	1902
9th	178	H. W. Parks & A. F. Wensley v Derbyshire (Horsham)	1930
10th	156	G. R. Cox & H. R. Butt v Cambridge U (Cambridge)	1908

One-day cricket

Highest innings totals:	Gillette Cup	314–7 v Kent (Tunbridge Wells)	1963
	John Player League	288–6 v M'sex (Hove)	1969
	Benson & Hedges Cup	280–5 v Cambridge U (Hove)	1974
Lowest innings totals:	Gillette Cup	49 v Derbyshire (Chesterfield)	1969
	John Player League	63 v Derbyshire (Hove)	1969
	Benson & Hedges Cup	85 v Yorks (Bradford)	1972
		85 v Kent (Hove)	1976
Highest individual innings:	Gillette Cup	115 E. R. Dexter v Northants (Northampton)	1963
	John Player League	129 A. W. Greig v Yorks (Scarborough)	1976
	Benson & Hedges Cup	114* P. J. Graves v Cambridge U (Hove)	1974
Best bowling figures:	Gillette Cup	6–30 D. L. Bates v Glos (Hove)	1968
	John Player League	6–14 M. A. Buss v Lancashire (Hove)	1973
	Benson & Hedges Cup	5–30 J. A. Snow v Kent (Canterbury)	1974

WARWICKSHIRE

Formation of present club: 1884.
Colours: Blue, gold, and silver.
Badge: Bear and ragged staff.
County Champions (3): 1911, 1951, and 1972.
Gillette Cup winners (2): 1966 and 1968.
Gillette Cup finalists (2): 1964 and 1972.
Best final position in John Player League: 5th in 1970 and 1975.
Benson & Hedges Cup semi-finalists (3): 1972, 1975, and 1976.
Gillette Man of the Match awards: 20.
Benson & Hedges Gold awards: 17.

Secretary: A. C. Smith, County Ground, Edgbaston, Birmingham, B5 7QU.
Captain: J. Whitehouse.

Robert Neal ABBERLEY (Saltley GS) B Birmingham 22/4/1944. RHB, OB. Debut 1964. Cap 1966. Tour: Pakistan 1966–67 (returning home early owing to injury). 1,000 runs (3)—1,315 runs (av 28.58) in 1966 best. Benson & Hedges Gold awards: 1. HS: 117* v Essex (Birmingham) 1966. HSGC: 47 v Lincs (Birmingham) 1971. HSJPL: 76 v Glamorgan (Birmingham) 1974. HSBH: 113* v Hants (Bournemouth) 1976.

Dennis Leslie AMISS B Birmingham 7/4/1943. RHB, SLC. Joined county staff 1958. Debut 1960. Cap 1965. *Wisden* 1974. Benefit (£34,947) in 1975. Tests: 50 between 1966 and 1977. Played in one match v Rest of World in 1970. Tours: Pakistan 1966–67, India, Pakistan, and Sri Lanka 1972–73, West Indies 1973–74, Australia and New Zealand 1974–75, India, Sri Lanka and Australia 1976–77. 1,000 runs (13)—2,110 runs (av 65.93) in 1976 best. Also scored 1,120 runs (av 74.66) in West Indies 1973–74. Gillette Man of Match awards: 2. Benson & Hedges Gold awards: 2. HS: 262* England v West Indies (Kingston) 1973–74. HSUK: 203 England v West Indies (Oval) 1976. HSC: 195 v Middlesex (Birmingham) 1974. HSGC: 113 v Glamorgan (Swansea) 1966. HSJPL: 110 v Surrey (Birmingham) 1974. HSBH: 73* v Minor Counties (West) (Coventry) 1977. BB: 3–21 v Middlesex (Lord's) 1970.

David John (Dave) BROWN (Queen Mary GS, Walsall) B Walsall 30/1/1942. RHB, RFM. Tall (6ft 4in). Debut 1961. Cap 1964. Benefit (£21,109) in 1973. County captain from 1975 to 1977. Tests: 26 between 1965 and 1969. Played in 2 matches v Rest of World 1970. Tours: South Africa 1964–65, Australia and New Zealand 1965–66, Pakistan 1966–67 (vice-captain), West Indies 1967–68, Ceylon and Pakistan 1968–69. Gillette Man of Match awards: 1. HS: 79 v Derbyshire (Birmingham) 1972. HSTC: 44 v New Zealand (Christchurch) 1965–66 and 44* v Pakistan (Lahore) 1968–69. HSGC: 41 v Middlesex (Lord's) 1977. HSJPL: 38* v Worcs (Birmingham) 1972. HSBH: 20* v Northants (Coventry) 1973. BB: 8–60 v Middlesex (Lord's) 1975. BBTC: 5–42 v Australia (Lord's) 1968. BBGC: 5–18 v Glamorgan (Swansea) 1966. BBJPL: 5–13 v Worcs (Birmingham) 1970. BBBH: 3–23 v Minor Counties (West) (Coventry) 1977.

142

Richard John DAVIES (Marple Hall GS, Marple, Cheshire) B Selly
Oak, Birmingham 11/2/1954. RHB, RM. Debut 1976. One match v
Oxford U (Birmingham) 1976. Did not play in 1977. HS: 18 v Oxford U
(Birmingham) 1976.

Edward Ernest (Eddie) HEMMINGS (Campion School, Leamington
Spa) B Leamington Spa 20/2/1949. RHB, OB. Debut 1966. Cap 1974.
Hat-trick v Worcs (Birmingham) 1977. HS: 85 v Essex (Birmingham) 1977.
HSGC: 20 v Worcs (Birmingham) 1973. HSJPL: 44* v Kent (Birmingham)
1971. HSBH: 61* v Leics (Birmingham) 1974. BB: 7–33 (12–64 match)
v Cambridge U (Cambridge) 1975. BBJPL: 5–22 v Northants (Birmingham) 1974. BBBH: 3–18 v Oxford and Cambridge Universities (Coventry) 1975.

David Charles HOPKINS (Moseley GS) B Birmingham 11/2/1957.
RHB, RM. Very tall (6ft 6½ins). Played for 2nd XI since 1975. Debut 1977.
(two matches). HS: 13* v Somerset (Birmingham) 1977. BB: 3–40 v
Somerset (Birmingham) 1977.

Geoffrey William (Geoff) HUMPAGE (Golden Hillock Comprehensive
School, Birmingham) B Birmingham 24/4/1954. RHB, WK. Debut 1974.
Cap 1976. 1,000 runs (2)–1,329 runs (av 44.30) in 1976 best. HS: 125*
v Sussex (Birmingham) 1976. HSGC: 45* v Lancs (Birmingham) 1976.
HSJPL: 54 v Worcs (Worcester) 1976. HSBH: 46 v Derbyshire (Derby)
1977.

Alvin Isaac (Kalli) KALLICHARRAN B Port Mourant, Berbice,
Guyana 21/3/1949. LHB, LBG. 5ft 4in tall. Debut 1966–67 for Guyana
in Shell Shield competition. Debut for county 1971. Cap 1972. Played for
Queensland in 1977–78 Sheffield Shield competition. Tests: 40 for West
Indies between 1971–72 and 1976–77, scoring 100* and 101 in first two
innings in Tests v New Zealand. Tours: West Indies to England 1973
and 1976, India, Sri Lanka and Pakistan 1974–75, Australia 1975–76.
1,000 runs (4)–1,343 runs (av 41.96) in 1977 best. Also scored 1,249 runs
(av 56.77) on 1974–75 tour. Benson & Hedges Gold awards: 1. HS: 197
Guyana v Jamaica (Kingston) 1973–74. HSUK: 164 v Notts (Coventry)
1972. HSTC: 158 West Indies v England (Port of Spain) 1973–74. HSGC:
88 v Glamorgan (Birmingham) 1972. HSJPL: 101* v Derbyshire (Chesterfield) 1972. HSBH: 71* v Worcs (Worcester) 1975 and 71* v Essex
(Birmingham) 1975.

Rohan Babulal KANHAI B Port Mourant, Berbice, British Guiana
26/12/1935. RHB, RM. Former WK. Debut for British Guiana (now
Guyana) 1954–55. Played for Western Australia in Sheffield Shield competition in 1961–62. Played league cricket for Aberdeenshire, Blackpool,
and Ashington. Debut for county and cap 1968. Played for Tasmania
1969–70 whilst coaching there. Benefit in 1977. Tests: 79 for West Indies
between 1957 and 1973–74, 61 of them consecutive from 1st Test v England
1957 to 1968–69, sequence being broken by his returning to England at end
of Australian tour to undergo cartilage operation. Captained country in 13
Tests. Played in 5 matches for Rest of World against England 1970 and 3
against Australia 1971–72. Tours: West Indies to England 1957, 1963,
1966, and 1973 (captain), India and Pakistan 1958–59, Australia 1960–61,
India and Ceylon 1966–67, Australia 1968–69, Rest of World to Australia
1971–72. 1,000 runs (10)–1,894 runs (av 57.39) in 1970 best. Also scored
over 1,000 runs in India and Pakistan 1958–59 and in Australia 1960–61.

Scored two centuries in Test match (117 and 115) v Australia (Adelaide) 1960–61. Scored 8 centuries in 1972 to equal county record. Gillette Man of Match awards: 3. Benson & Hedges gold awards: 5. HS: 256 West Indies v India (Calcutta) 1958–59. HSUK: 253 v Notts (Nottingham) 1968 sharing in record partnership for county for 4th wkt, 402 with K. Ibadulla. Also shared in world record partnership for 2nd wkt—465* with J. A. Jameson v Glos (Birmingham) 1974. HSGC: 126 v Lincs (Birmingham) 1971. HSJPL: 120 v Leics (Birmingham) 1972. HSBH: 119* v Northants (Northampton) 1975.

Timothy Andrew (Andy) LLOYD (Oswestry Boys' HS) B Oswestry (Shropshire) 5/11/1956. LHB. Played for both Shropshire and county 2nd XI in 1975. Appeared in one John Player League match in 1976. v Yorks (Leeds). Debut 1977. HS: 70* v Somerset (Birmingham) 1977.

Philip Robert OLIVER B West Bromwich (Staffs) 9/5/1956. RHB, RM. Played for Shropshire 1972–74. Debut 1975. HS: 59 v Glamorgan (Swansea) 1975. HSGC: 12* v Glamorgan (Birmingham) 1976. HSJPL: 46* v Notts (Nottingham) 1977. HSBH: 39* v Worcs (Worcester) 1977. BBJPL: 3–36 v Middlesex (Lord's) 1977. Plays soccer for Telford in Southern League.

Stephen Peter (Steve) PERRYMAN (Sheldon Heath Comprehensive School) B Yardley, Birmingham 22/10/1955. RHB, RM. Debut 1974. Cap 1977. Benson & Hedges Gold awards: 1. HS: 43 v Somerset (Birmingham) 1977. HSJPL: 17* v Worcs (Birmingham) 1975. BB: 7–66 v Middlesex (Lord's) 1977. BBGC: 3–35 v Middlesex (Lord's) 1977. BBJPL: 4–19 v Surrey (Oval) 1975.

Stephen John (Mic) ROUSE (Moseley County School) B Merthyr Tydfil (Glamorgan) 20/1/1949. LHB, LM. Debut 1970. Cap 1974. Benson & Hedges Gold awards: 2. HS: 93 v Hants (Bournemouth) 1976. HSGC: 34 v Middlesex (Lord's) 1977. HSJPL: 23 v Notts (Birmingham) 1974. HSBH: 25 v Leics (Birmingham) 1974. BB: 6–34 v Leics (Leicester) 1976. BBGC: 4–27 v Sussex (Hove) 1976. BBJPL: 5–20 v Kent (Canterbury) 1976. BBBH: 5–21 v Worcs (Worcester) 1974.

Richard Le Quesne SAVAGE (Marlborough College and Oxford) B Waterloo, London 10/12/1955. RHB, RM/OB. Played for county 2nd XI since 1974. Debut for both county and University 1976. Blue 1976–77. HS: 22* Oxford U v Worcs (Oxford) 1977. HSC: 13* v Northants (Northampton) 1977. BB: 7–50 v Glamorgan (Nuneaton) 1977.

Kenneth David SMITH (Heaton GS) B Jesmond, Newcastle upon Tyne 9/7/1956. RHB. Son of Kenneth D. Smith, former Northumberland and Leics player. Played for 2nd XI 1972. Debut 1973. Scored 1,023 runs (av 37.88) in 1976. HS: 135 v Lancs (Manchester) 1977. HSJPL: 56 v Middlesex (Lord's) 1977. HSBH: 59* v Minor Counties (West) (Coventry) 1977.

John WHITEHOUSE (King Edward VI School, Nuneaton and Bristol University) B Nuneaton 8/4/1949. RHB, OB. Played for county against Scotland in 1970 a match no longer counted as first-class. Debut 1971, scoring 173 v Oxford U (Oxford) in first innings of debut match, in 167 minutes with 35 4's. Elected Best Young Cricketer of the Year in 1971 by Cricket Writers' Club. Cap 1973. Appointed county captain for 1978.

1,000 runs (3)—1,543 runs (av 42.86) in 1977 best. HS as above. HSGC: 109 v Glamorgan (Birmingham) 1976. HSJPL: 92 v Surrey (Birmingham) 1976. HSBH: 71* v Lancashire (Birmingham) 1976.

Robert George Dylan (Bob) WILLIS (Guildford RGS) B Sunderland 30/5/1949. RHB, RF. Debut for Surrey 1969. Left staff after 1971 season and made debut for Warwickshire in 1972. Cap 1972. Tests: 29 between 1970–71 and 1977. Tours: Australia and New Zealand 1970–71 (flown out as replacement for A. Ward) and 1974–75. West Indies 1973–74, India, Sri Lanka and Australia 1976–77. Pakistan and New Zealand 1977–78. Hat-tricks (2) v Derbyshire (Birmingham) 1972 and v West Indians (Birmingham) 1976. Also in John Player League v Yorks (Birmingham) 1973. Gillette Man of Match awards: 1 (for Surrey). Benson & Hedges Gold awards: 1. HS: 43 v Middlesex (Birmingham) 1976. HSTC: 24 v India (Manchester) 1974 and 24* v Australia (Oval) 1977. HSGC: 12* Surrey v Sussex (Oval) 1970. HSJPL: 52* v Derbyshire (Birmingham) 1975. HSBH: 25* v Northants (Northampton) 1977. BB: 8–32 v Glos (Bristol) 1977. BBTC: 7–78 v Australia (Lord's) 1977. BBGC: 6–49 Surrey v Middlesex (Oval) 1970. BBJPL: 4–12 v Middlesex (Lord's) 1973. BBBH: 5–27 v Lancs (Birmingham) 1976. Has played soccer (goalkeeper) for Guildford City.

NB The following players whose particulars appeared in the 1977 Annual have been omitted: W. A. Bourne (not re-engaged) and R. T. Tudor. The career record of Bourne will be found elsewhere in this Annual.

COUNTY AVERAGES

Schweppes County Championship: Played 22, won 4, drawn 10, lost 8
All first-class matches: Played 24, won 5, drawn 10, lost 9

BATTING AND FIELDING

Cap		M	I	NO	Runs	HS	Avge	100	50	Ct	St
1965	D. L. Amiss	17	30	4	1470	162*	56.53	6	3	7	—
1973	J. Whitehouse	24	41	5	1543	158*	42.86	6	6	21	—
1972	A. I. Kallicharran	22	36	4	1343	149*	41.96	1	10	15	—
1968	R. B. Kanhai	18	26	5	738	176	35.14	2	2	19	—
1976	G. W. Humpage	24	38	5	1145	104	34.69	1	8	65	2
1966	R. N. Abberley	21	35	1	969	92	28.55	—	7	8	—
—	P. R. Oliver	4	7	2	121	38*	24.40	—	—	5	—
—	K. D. Smith	16	27	2	594	135	23.76	1	2	6	—
1974	S. J. Rouse	19	22	6	353	33	22.06	—	—	5	—
1977	S. P. Perryman	24	24	10	233	43	16.64	—	—	10	—
1974	E. E. Hemmings	23	30	5	412	85	16.48	—	1	10	—
1964	D. J. Brown	17	17	4	182	70*	14.00	—	1	5	—
—	W. A. Bourne	11	13	2	105	25*	9.54	—	—	7	—
1972	R. G. D. Willis	11	9	1	75	29	9.37	—	—	3	—
—	R. L. Savage	9	9	2	20	13*	5.00	—	—	2	—

Played in two matches: D. C. Hopkins 13*, 10; T. A. Lloyd 0, 25, 70*, 27*.

145

BOWLING

	Type	O	M	R	W	Avge	Best	5 wI	10 wM
D. C. Hopkins	RM	53	11	124	6	20.66	3–40	—	—
R. G. D. Willis	RF	232.2	58	649	31	20.93	8–32	2	1
D. J. Brown	RFM	405.1	76	1209	57	21.21	5–43	2	—
S. P. Perryman	RM	738.3	198	1928	73	26.41	7–66	5	1
S. J. Rouse	LM	432	105	1325	49	27.04	5–22	2	—
R. L. Savage	RM/OB	261.3	49	873	30	29.10	7–50	1	—
W. A. Bourne	RFM	300.5	53	972	30	32.40	5–68	1	—
E. E. Hemmings	OB	576.1	155	1690	46	36.73	6–82	2	1

Also bowled: R. N. Abberley 2–0–20–0; A. I. Kallicharran 2–0–7–0; R. B. Kanhai 28–6–90–3; P. R. Oliver 37–7–101–0; J. Whitehouse 46.3–11–144–2.

County Records

First-class cricket

Highest innings totals:	For	657–6d v Hampshire (Birmingham)	1899
	Agst.	887 by Yorkshire (Birmingham)	1896
Lowest innings totals:	For	16 v Kent (Tonbridge)	1913
	Agst.	15 by Hampshire (Birmingham)	1922
Highest individual innings:	For	305* F. R. Foster v Worcestershire (Dudley)	1914
	Agst.	316 R. H. Moore for Hants (Bournemouth)	1937
Best bowling in an innings:	For	10–41 J. D. Bannister v Combined Services (Birmingham)	1959
	Agst.	10–36 H. Verity for Yorkshire (Leeds)	1931
Best bowling in a match:	For	15–76 S. Hargreave v Surrey (The Oval)	1903
	Agst.	17–92 A. P. Freeman for Kent (Folkestone)	1932
Most runs in a season:		2417 (av 60.42) M. J. K. Smith	1959
runs in a career:		34172 (av 35.31) W. G. Quaife	1894–1928
100s in a season:		8 by R. E. S. Wyatt	1937
		and R. B. Kanhai	1972
100s in a career:		71 by W. G. Quaife	1894–1928
wickets in a season:		180 (av 15.13) W. E. Hollies	1946
wickets in a career:		2201 (av 20.45) W. E. Hollies	1932–1957

RECORD WICKET STANDS

1st	377*	N. F. Horner & K. Ibadulla v Surrey (The Oval)	1960
2nd	465*	J. A. Jameson & R. B. Kanhai v Gloucestershire (Birmingham)	1974
3rd	327	S. P. Kinneir & W. G. Quaife v Lancashire (Birmingham)	1901
4th	402	R. B. Kanhai & K. Ibadulla v Notts (Nottingham)	1968
5th	268	W. Quaife & W. G. Quaife v Essex (Leyton)	1900
6th	220	H. E. Dollery & J. Buckingham v Derbyshire (Derby)	1938
7th	250	H. E. Dollery & J. S. Ord v Kent (Maidstone)	1953
8th	228	A. J. Croom & R. E. S. Wyatt v Worcestershire (Dudley)	1925
9th	154	G. W. Stephens & A. J. Croom v Derbyshire (Birmingham)	1925
10th	128	F. R. Santall & W. Sanders v Yorkshire (Birmingham)	1930

One-day cricket

Highest innings totals:	Gillette Cup	307–8 v Hampshire (Birmingham)	1964
	John Player League	261–8 v Nottinghamshire (Birmingham)	1976
	Benson & Hedges Cup	269–9 v Worcestershire (Birmingham)	1976
Lowest innings totals:	Gillette Cup	109 v Kent (Canterbury)	1971
	John Player League	85 v Glamorgan (Swansea)	1972
		85 v Gloucestershire (Cheltenham)	1973
	Benson & Hedges Cup	96 v Leics (Leicester)	1972
Highest individual innings:	Gillette Cup	126 R. B. Kanhai v Lincs (Birmingham)	1971
	John Player League	123* J. A. Jameson v Notts (Nottingham)	1973
	Benson & Hedges Cup	119* R. B. Kanhai v Northants (Northampton)	1975
Best bowling figures:	Gillette Cup	6–32 K. Ibadulla v Hants (Birmingham)	1965
	John Player League	5–13 D. J. Brown v Worcs (Birmingham)	1970
	Benson & Hedges Cup	5–21 S. J. Rouse v Worcestershire (Worcester)	1974

WORCESTERSHIRE

Formation of present club: 1865.
Colours: Dark green and black.
Badge: Shield, *Argent* bearing *Fess* between three *Pears Sable.*
County Champions (3): 1964, 1965, and 1974.
Gillette Cup finalists (2): 1963 and 1966.
John Player League Champions: 1971.
Benson & Hedges Cup finalists (2): 1973 and 1976.
Gillette Man of the Match awards: 16.
Benson & Hedges Gold awards: 16.

Secretary: M. D. Vockins, County Ground, New Road, Worcester WR2 4QQ.
Captain: N. Gifford.

Cedric Nigel BOYNS (Adams' GS, Newport, Shropshire and Cambridge) B Harrogate 14/8/1954. RHB, RM. Played for county 2nd XI since 1972 and also for Shropshire. Debut for county and University 1976. HS: 95 v Yorks (Scarborough) 1976. HSJPL: 29* v Sussex (Hove) 1976.

WORCESTERSHIRE

HSBH: 15 v Kent (Lord's) 1976. BB: 3–24 v Oxford U (Oxford) 1977. BBGC: 3–36 v Glamorgan (Worcester) 1977. Obtained degree at London University.

James (Jimmy) CUMBES (Didsbury Secondary Technical School) B East Didsbury (Lancs) 4/5/1944. RHB, RFM. Debut for Lancs 1963. Not re-engaged at end of 1967 season and made debut for Surrey in 1968. Not re-engaged after 1970 season and rejoined Lancs in 1971. Made debut for Worcs in 1972 by special registration. Hat-trick v Northants (Worcester) 1977. HS: 25* Surrey v West Indians (Oval) 1969. HSC: 22 v Middlesex (Lord's) 1977. BB: 6–24 v Yorks (Worcester) 1977. BBGC: 4–23 v Sussex (Hove) 1974. BBJPL: 3–18 Surrey v Lancs (Manchester) 1969. Soccer (goalkeeper) for Tranmere Rovers, West Bromwich Albion, and Aston Villa.

Basil Lewis D'OLIVEIRA B Cape Town 4/10/1931. RHB, RM/OB. Played for Middleton in Central Lancashire League from 1960 to 1963. Made first-class debut on Commonwealth tour of 1961–62 playing in two matches in Rhodesia. Took part in further tour of Rhodesia in 1962–63. Toured Pakistan with Commonwealth XI 1963–64. Joined Worcestershire in 1964, becoming eligible for Championship matches in 1965. Cap 1965. *Wisden* 1966. Played for Kidderminster in Birmingham League whilst qualifying. Awarded OBE in 1969 Birthday Honours list. Benefit (£27,000) in 1975. Tests: 44 between 1966 and 1972. Played in 4 matches against Rest of World 1970. Tours: West Indies 1967–68, Ceylon and Pakistan 1968–69, Australia and New Zealand 1970–71. 1,000 runs (9)—1,691 runs (av 43.35) in 1965 best. Gillette Man of Match awards: 6. Benson & Hedges Gold awards: 2. HS: 227 v Yorks (Hull) 1974. HSTC: 158 v Australia (Oval) 1968. HSGC: 102 v Sussex (Hove) 1974. HSJPL: 100 v Surrey (Byfleet) 1973. HSBH: 84 v Middlesex (Lord's) 1974. BB: 6–29 v Hants (Portsmouth) 1968. BBTC: 3–46 v Pakistan (Leeds) 1971. BBGC: 4–18 v Notts (Worcester) 1974. BBJPL: 5–26 v Glos (Lydney) 1972. BBBH: 4–23 v Oxford and Cambridge Universities (Cambridge) 1975.

Norman GIFFORD B Ulverston (Lancs) 30/3/1940. LHB, SLA. Joined staff 1958 and made debut 1960. Cap 1961. Appointed county captain in 1971 after being vice-captain since 1969. Benefit (£11,047) in 1974. *Wisden* 1974. Tests: 15 between 1964 and 1973. Played in one match for Rest of World v Australia 1971–72. Tours: Rest of World to Australia 1971–72, India, Pakistan and Sri Lanka 1972–73. 100 wkts (3)—133 wkts (av 19.66) in 1961 best. Hat-trick v Derbyshire (Chesterfield) 1965. Took 4 wkts in 6 balls v Cambridge U (Cambridge) 1972. Gillette Man of Match awards: 1. Benson & Hedges Gold awards: 2. HS: 89 v Oxford U (Oxford) 1963. HSTC: 25* v New Zealand (Nottingham) 1973. HSGC: 38 v Warwickshire (Lord's) 1966. HSJPL: 29 v Essex (Worcester) 1974. HSBH: 33 v Kent (Lord's) 1973. BB: 8–28 v Yorks (Sheffield) 1968. BBTC: 5–55 v Pakistan (Karachi) 1972–73. BBGC: 4–7 v Surrey (Worcester) 1972. BBJPL: 4–18 v Middlesex (Worcester) 1974. BBBH: 5–32 v Northants (Worcester) 1973.

Edward John Orton (Ted) HEMSLEY (Bridgnorth GS) B Norton, Stoke-on-Trent 1/9/1943. RHB, RM. Debut 1963. Cap 1969. Shared in 6th wkt partnership record for county, 227 with D. N. Patel v Oxford U (Oxford) 1976. Benson & Hedges Gold awards: 2. HS: 176* v Lancs (Worcester) 1977. HSGC: 73 v Sussex (Hove) 1972. HSJPL: 72 v Notts

148

(Nottingham) 1969. HSBH: 73 v Warwickshire (Birmingham) 1973. BB: 3–5 v Warwickshire (Worcester) 1971. BBJPL: 4–42 v Essex (Worcester) 1971. Soccer for Shrewsbury Town and Sheffield United.

Stephen Peter HENDERSON (Downside School) B Oxford 24/9/1958. Son of D. Henderson, former Oxford Blue. LHB, RM. Debut 1977. HS: 52 v Northants (Worcester) 1977. HSGC: 33 v Glamorgan (Worcester) 1977. HSJPL: 19 v Hants (Worcester) 1977. Is studying at Durham University.

Vanburn Alonza (Van) HOLDER B St Michael, Barbados 8/10/1945. RHB, RFM. Debut 1966–67 for Barbados in one match in Shell Shield tournament. Debut for county 1968. Cap 1970. Tests: 31 for West Indies between 1969 and 1976–77. Tours: West Indies to England 1969, 1973 and 1976. India, Sri Lanka, and Pakistan 1974–75, Australia 1975–76. HS: 122 Barbados v Trinidad (Bridgetown) 1973–74. HSUK: 52 v Glos (Dudley) 1970. HSTC: 42 West Indies v New Zealand (Port of Spain) 1971–72. HSGC: 25* v Notts (Worcester) 1974. HSJPL: 35* v Middlesex (Lord's) 1970. HSBH: 15* v Leics (Leicester) 1973. BB: 7–40 v Glamorgan (Cardiff) 1974. BBTC: 6–39 West Indies v India (Bombay) 1974–75 BBGC: 3–14 v Oxfordshire (Cowley) 1970. BBJPL: 6–33 v Middlesex (Lord's) 1972. BBBH: 5–12 v Northants (Northampton) 1974.

David John HUMPHRIES B Alveley (Shropshire) 6/8/1953. LHB, WK. Played for Shropshire 1971–73. Debut for Leics 1974. Left county after 1976 season and made debut for Worcs in 1977. HS: 62* Leics v Derbyshire (Leicester) 1975. HSC: 59 v Yorks (Worcester) 1977. HSGC: 58 v Glamorgan (Worcester) 1977. HSJPL: 62 v Notts (Dudley) 1977. HSBH: 22* v Minor Counties (West) (Worcester) 1977.

John Darling INCHMORE (Ashington GS) B Ashington (Northumberland) 22/2/1949. RHB, RFM. Played for Northumberland in 1970. Played for both Warwickshire and Worcs 2nd XIs in 1972 and for Stourbridge in Birmingham League. Debut 1973. Cap 1976. Played for Northern Transvaal in 1976–77 Currie Cup competition. Benson & Hedges Gold awards: 1. HS: 113 v Essex (Worcester) 1974. HSGC: 12 v Glos (Bristol) 1976. HSJPL: 30* v Essex (Dudley) 1976. HSBH: 49* v Somerset (Taunton) 1976. BB: 8–58 v Yorks (Worcester) 1977. BBGC: 3–11 v Essex (Worcester) 1975. BBJPL: 4–9 v Northants (Dudley) 1975.

Barry John Richardson JONES (Wrekin College) B Shrewsbury 2/11/1955. LHB, RM. Debut 1976. HS: 65 v Warwickshire (Birmingham) 1977. HSJPL: 23 v Essex (Chelmsford) 1977.

Philip Anthony (Phil) NEALE (Frederick Gough Comprehensive School, Bottesford and John Leggott Sixth Form College, Scunthorpe) B Scunthorpe (Lincs) 5/6/1954. RHB, RM. Played for Lincolnshire 1973–74. Debut 1975. HS: 143 v West Indians (Worcester) 1976. HSGC: 68 v Glos (Bristol) 1976. HSJPL: 79* v Somerset (Worcester) 1976. HSBH: 50 v Warwickshire (Worcester) 1977. Soccer for Lincoln City. Studied at Leeds University and obtained degree in Russian.

Joseph Alan ORMROD (Kirkcaldy HS) B Ramsbottom (Lancs) 22/12/1942. RHB, OB. Debut 1962. Cap 1966. Benefit in 1977. Tour:

Pakistan 1966–67. 1,000 runs (9)—1,507 runs (av 41.86) in 1976 best. Benson & Hedges Gold awards: 3. HS: 204* v Kent (Dartford) 1973. HSGC: 59 v Essex (Worcester) 1975. HSJPL: 110* v Kent (Canterbury) 1975. HSBH: 124* v Glos (Worcester) 1976. BB: 5–27 v Glos (Bristol) 1972. BBJPL: 3–51 v Hants (Worcester) 1972.

Dipak Narshibhai PATEL (George Salter Comprehensive School, West Bromwich) B Nairobi, Kenya 25/10/1958. Has lived in UK since 1967. RHB, OB. Debut 1976. Shared in 6th wkt partnership record for county, 227 with E. J. O. Hemsley v Oxford U (Oxford) 1976. HS: 107 v Surrey (Worcester) 1976. HSJPL: 22 v Glamorgan (Ebbw Vale) 1976. HSBH: 14 v Glamorgan (Swansea) 1977.

Alan Paul PRIDGEON B Wall Heath (Staffs) 22/2/1954. RHB, RM. 6ft 3ins tall. Joined staff 1971. Debut 1972. HS: 26 v Glamorgan (Worcester) 1977. HSJPL: 16* v Essex (Dudley) 1976. HSBH: 10 v Leics (Leicester) 1976. BB: 7–35 v Oxford U (Oxford) 1976. BBJPL: 4–17 v Essex (Worcester) 1974. BBBH: 3–57 v Warwickshire (Birmingham) 1976. Plays amateur soccer.

Glenn Maitland TURNER (Otago Boys' HS) B Dunedin (New Zealand) 26/5/1947. RHB, OB. Debut for Otago in Plunket Shield competition 1964–65 whilst still at school. Debut for county 1967. Cap 1968. *Wisden* 1970. Benefit in 1978. Tests: 39 for New Zealand between 1968–69 and 1976–77 captaining country in 10 Tests. Tours: New Zealand to England 1969 and 1973 (vice-captain), India and Pakistan 1969–70, Australia 1969–70 and 1973–74 (vice-captain), West Indies 1971–72, Pakistan and India 1976–77 (captain). 1,000 runs (10)—2,416 runs (av 67.11) in 1973 best, including 1,018 runs (av 78.30) by 31 May—the first occasion since 1938. Scored 1,284 runs (av 85.60) in West Indies and Bermuda 1971-72. Scored 1,244 runs (av 77.75) in 1975–76—record aggregate for New Zealand season. Scored 10 centuries in 1970, a county record. Scored two centuries in a match on four occasions (122 and 128*) v Warwickshire (Birmingham) 1972, (101 and 110*) New Zealand v Australia (Christchurch) 1973–74, (135 and 108) Otago v Northern Districts (Gisborne) 1974–75 and (105 and 186*) Otago v Central Districts (Dunedin) 1974–75. Scored 141* out of 169—83.4% of total—v Glamorgan (Swansea) 1977 —a record for first-class cricket. Benson & Hedges Gold awards: 2. HS: 259 twice in successive innings, New Zealanders v Guyana and New Zealand v West Indies (Georgetown) 1971–72. HSUK: 214* v Oxford U (Worcester) 1975. HSGC: 117* v Lancs (Worcester) 1971. HSJPL: 129* v Glamorgan (Worcester) 1973. HSBH: 143* v Warwickshire (Birmingham) 1976. BB: 3–18 v Pakistanis (Worcester) 1967. Has played hockey for Worcs and had trial for Midlands.

Gregory George (Greg) WATSON (Mudgee High School and University of New South Wales) B Mudgee, New South Wales, Australia 29/1/1955. RHB, RFM. Toured England with old collegians team in 1977 and has played for Smethwick in Birmingham League. Debut for New South Wales in 1977-78. Has joined Worcs for 1978.

Howard Gordon WILCOCK (Giggleswick School, Settle, Yorks) B New Malden (Surrey) 26/2/1950. RHB, WK. Joined staff 1969. Debut 1971. HS: 74 v Yorks (Worcester) 1977. HSGC: 16 v Glos (Bristol)

1976. HSJPL: 43* v Northants (Worcester) 1977. HSBH: 49* v Warwickshire) (Worcester) 1975.

NB The following players whose particulars appeared in the 1977 Annual have been omitted: I. A. Rutherford and R. Senghera.

In addition Imran Khan has joined Sussex and his particulars will be found under that county.

COUNTY AVERAGES

Schweppes County Championship: Played 22, won 5, drawn 7, lost 10
All first-class matches: Played 24, won 5, drawn 9, lost 10

BATTING AND FIELDING

Cap		M	I	NO	Runs	HS	Avge	100	50	Ct	St
1965	B. L. D'Oliveira	22	36	7	1257	156*	43.84	1	9	11	—
1968	G. M. Turner	22	38	5	1380	153	41.81	3	6	16	—
1966	J. A. Ormrod	16	26	1	708	103	28.32	1	4	5	—
1969	E. J. O. Hemsley	20	34	3	863	176*	27.83	1	5	10	—
—	P. A. Neale	15	26	2	596	112	24.83	1	1	11	—
—	H. G. Wilcock	9	15	2	242	74	18.61	—	1	4	—
—	A. P. Pridgeon	9	11	7	71	26	17.75	—	—	2	—
—	B. J. R. Jones	14	24	2	359	65	16.31	—	1	5	—
—	D. J. Humphries	22	32	5	440	59	16.29	—	2	30	5
—	S. P. Henderson	8	13	2	172	52	15.63	—	1	1	—
1976	J. D. Inchmore	11	15	3	143	33	11.91	—	—	3	—
—	C. N. Boyns	12	16	1	158	77*	10.53	—	1	12	—
—	D. N. Patel	16	24	0	215	27	8.95	—	—	7	—
1970	V. A. Holder	21	28	4	206	27	8.58	—	—	2	—
—	J. Cumbes	24	26	9	111	22	6.52	—	—	2	—
1961	N. Gifford	23	25	5	120	17*	6.00	—	—	11	—

BOWLING

	Type	O	M	R	W	Avge	Best	5 wI	10 wM
J. D. Inchmore	RFM	244.2	55	685	33	20.75	8–58	2	1
V. A. Holder	RFM	639.5	151	1653	69	23.95	7–117	5	—
N. Gifford	SLA	553.4	169	1288	45	28.62	5–64	1	—
B. L. D'Oliveira	RM/OB	272	78	617	21	29.38	5–50	1	—
J. Cumbes	RFM	554.4	103	1600	51	31.37	6–24	3	—
A. P. Pridgeon	RM	180.5	28	568	13	43.69	3–28	—	—
D. N. Patel	OB	75.4	13	236	5	47.20	2–73	—	—
C. N. Boyns	RM	235	51	710	14	50.71	3–24	—	—

Also bowled: E. J. O. Hemsley 39–4–118–2; S. P. Henderson 2–0–9–0; H. G. Wilcock 2–1–3–0.

County Records

First-class cricket

Highest innings	For	.....633 v Warwickshire (Worcester)	1906
totals:	Agst	....701–4d by Leicestershire (Worcester)	1906
Lowest innings	For	..... 24 v Yorkshire (Huddersfield)	1903
totals:	Agst	..... 30 by Hampshire (Worcester)	1903

WORCESTERSHIRE

Highest individual innings:	For .....276 F. L. Bowley v Hampshire (Dudley)	1914
	Agst....331*J.D. Robertson for Middx (Worcester)	1949
Best bowling in an innings:	For .....9–23 C. F. Root v Lancashire (Worcester)	1931
	Agst...10–51 J. Mercer for Glamorgan (Worcester)	1936
Best bowling in a match:	For .....15–87 A. J. Conway v Gloucestershire (Moreton-in-Marsh)	1914
	Agst....17–212 J. C. Clay for Glamorgan (Swansea)	1937
Most runs in a season:	2654 (av 52.03) H. H. I. H. Gibbons	1934
runs in a career:	34490 (av 34.04) D. Kenyon	1946–1967
100s in a season:	10 by G. M. Turner	1970
100s in a career:	70 by D. Kenyon	1946–1967
wickets in a season:	207 (av 17.52) C. F. Root	1925
wickets in a career:	2143 (av 23.73) R. T. D. Perks	1930–1955

RECORD WICKET STANDS

1st	309	F. L. Bowley & H. K. Foster v Derbyshire (Derby)	1901
2nd	274	H. H. I. H. Gibbons & Nawab of Pataudi v Kent (Worcester)	1933
		H. H. I. H. Gibbons & Nawab of Pataudi v Glamorgan (Worcester)	1934
3rd	314	M. J. Horton & T. W. Graveney v Somerset (Worcester)	1962
4th	277	H. H. I. H. Gibbons & B. W. Quaife v Middlesex (Worcester)	1931
5th	393	E.G. Arnold & W.B. Burns v Warwickshire (Birmingham)	1909
6th	227	E. J. O. Hemsley & D. N. Patel v Oxford U (Oxford)	1976
7th	197	H. H. I. H. Gibbons & R. Howorth v Surrey (The Oval)	1938
8th	145*	F. Chester & W. H. Taylor v Essex (Worcester)	1914
9th	181	J.A.Cuffe & R.O. Burrows v Gloucestershire (Worcester)	1907
10th	119	W. B. Burns & G. A. Wilson v Somerset (Worcester)	1906

One-day cricket

Highest innings totals:	Gillette Cup	261–7 v Essex (Worcester)	1975
	John Player League	307–4 v Derbyshire (Worcester)	1975
	Benson & Hedges Cup	281–4 v Warwickshire (Birmingham)	1976
Lowest innings totals:	Gillette Cup	98 v Durham (Chester-le-Street)	1968
	John Player League	86 v Yorkshire (Leeds)	1969
	Benson & Hedges Cup	92 v Oxford and Cambridge Universities (Cambridge)	1975
Highest individual innings:	Gillette Cup	117* G. M. Turner v Lancashire (Worcester)	1971
	John Player League	129* G. M. Turner v Glamorgan (Worcester)	1973
	Benson & Hedges Cup	143* G. M. Turner v Warwickshire (Birmingham)	1976
Best bowling figures:	Gillette Cup	6–14 J. A. Flavell v Lancs (Worcester)	1963
	John Player League	6–33 V. A. Holder v Middlesex (Lord's)	1972
	Benson & Hedges Cup	5–12 V. A. Holder v Northants (Northampton)	1974

YORKSHIRE

Formation of present club: 1863, reorganised 1891.
Colours: Oxford blue, Cambridge blue, and gold.
Badge: White rose.
County Champions (29): 1893, 1896, 1898, 1900,
1901, 1902, 1905, 1908, 1912, 1919, 1922,
1923, 1924, 1925, 1931, 1932, 1933, 1935,
1937, 1938, 1939, 1946, 1959, 1960, 1962
1963, 1966, 1967, and 1968.
Joint Champions (1): 1949.
Gillette Cup Winners (2): 1965 and 1969.
John Player League runners-up: 1973.
Benson & Hedges Cup finalists: 1972.
Fenner Trophy Winners (2): 1972 and 1974.
Gillette Man of the Match awards: 10.
Benson & Hedges Gold awards: 16.

Secretary: J. Lister, Headingley Cricket Ground, Leeds, LS6 3BU.
Captain: G. Boycott.

Charles William Jeffrey (Bill) ATHEY (Acklam Hall High School,
Middlesbrough) B Middlesbrough 27/9/1957. RHB, OB. Toured West
Indies with England Young Cricketers 1976. Debut 1976. HS: 131* v
Sussex (Leeds) 1976. HSGC: 10 v Glos (Leeds) 1976. HSJPL: 62 v
Glamorgan (Cardiff) 1977. HSBH: 31 v Minor Counties (East) (Jesmond)
1977.

David Leslie (Blue) BAIRSTOW (Hanson GS, Bradford) Bradford
1/9/1951. RHB, WK. Debut 1970 whilst still at school. Played for MCC
Schools at Lord's in 1970. Cap 1973. Played for Griqualand West in
1976–77 Currie Cup competition. Dismissed 70 batsmen (64 ct 6 st)
in 1971, including 9 in match and 6 in innings (all ct) v Lancs (Manchester).
Benson & Hedges Gold awards: 1. HS: 106 v Glamorgan (Middlesbrough)
1976 and 106 Griqualand West v Natal B (Pietermaritzburg) 1976–77.
HSGC: 21 v Warwickshire (Leeds) 1972. HSJPL: 76 v Sussex (Scarborough) 1976. HSBH: 31* v Derbyshire (Bradford) 1975. BB: 3–82
Griqualand West v Transvaal B (Johannesburg) 1976–77. Soccer for
Bradford City.

Michael Kenneth (Mike) BORE B Hull 2/6/1947. RHB, LM. Debut
1969. HS: 37* v Notts (Bradford) 1973. HSJPL: 15 v Kent (Dover) 1973.
BB: 7–63 v Derbyshire (Scarborough) 1977. BBGC: 3–35 v Kent (Canterbury) 1971. BBJPL: 4–21 v Sussex (Middlesbrough) 1970 and 4–21 v
Worcs (Worcester) 1970. BBBH: 3–29 v Minor Counties (Leeds) 1974,

Geoffrey (Geoff) BOYCOTT (Hemsworth GS) B Fitzwilliam (Yorks)
21/10/1940. RHB, RM. Plays in contact lenses. Debut 1962. Cap 1963.
Elected Best Young Cricketer of the Year in 1963 by the Cricket Writers'
Club. Wisden 1964. Appointed county captain in 1971. Played for
N. Transvaal in 1971–72. Benefit (£20,639) in 1974. Tests: 66 between 1964
and 1977. Played in 2 matches against Rest of World in 1970. Tours:
South Africa 1964–65, Australia and New Zealand 1965–66 and 1970–71

153

(returned home early through broken arm injury), West Indies 1967–68 and 1973–74. Pakistan and New Zealand 1977–78 (vice-captain). 1,000 runs (15)—2,503 runs (av 100.12) in 1971 best. Only English batsman ever to have an average of 100 for a season. Also scored 1,000 runs in South Africa 1964–65 (1,135 runs, av 56.75), West Indies 1967–68 (1,154 runs, av 82.42), Australia 1907–71 (1,535 runs av 95.93). Scored two centuries in match (103 and 105) v Notts (Sheffield) 1966 and (160* and 116) England v The Rest (Worcester) 1974. Completed 30,000 runs in 1977 and scored his 100th century in Leeds Test—only player to have done so in a Test match. Gillette Man of Match awards: 1. Benson & Hedges Gold awards: 6. HS: 261* MCC v President's XI (Bridgetown) 1973–74. HSUK: 260* v Essex (Colchester) 1970. HSTC: 246 v India (Leeds) 1967. HSGC: 146 v Surrey (Lord's) 1965. HSJPL: 108* v Northants (Huddersfield) 1974. HSBH: 102 v Northants (Middlesbrough) 1977. BB: 3–47 England v South Africa (Cape Town) 1964–65.

Philip (Phil) CARRICK B Armley, Leeds 16/7/1952. RHB, SLA. Debut 1970. Cap 1976. Played for Eastern Province in 1976–77 Currie Cup competition. HS: 87 v Derbyshire (Scarborough) 1975. HSGC: 18 v Durham (Harrogate) 1973. HSJPL: 16 v Hants (Bournemouth) 1976. HSBH: 10 v Middlesex (Lord's) 1977. BB: 8–33 v Cambridge U (Cambridge) 1973. BBJPL: 3–32 v Hants (Bournemouth) 1976.

Howard Pennett COOPER (Buttershaw Comprehensive School, Bradford) B Bradford 17/4/1949. LHB, RM. Debut 1971. Played for Northern Transvaal in 1973–74 Currie Cup competition. HS: 56 v Notts (Worksop) 1976. HSGC: 17 v Hants (Bournemouth) 1977. HSJPL: 29* v Hants (Bournemouth) 1976. HSBH: 20* v Minor Counties (East) (Jesmond) 1977. BB: 8–62 v Glamorgan (Cardiff) 1975. BBGC: 4–18 v Leics (Leeds) 1975. BBJPL: 6–14 v Worcs (Worcester) 1975. BBBH: 3–32 v Minor Counties (Leeds) 1974.

Geoffrey Alan (Geoff) COPE (Temple Moor School, Leeds) B Leeds 23/2/1947. RHB, OB. Wears glasses. Debut 1966. Cap 1970. Suspended from playing in second half of 1972 season by TCCB, owing to unsatisfactory bowling action. Action cleared in 1973 by TCCB subcommittee after watching film of him bowling. Tours: India, Sri Lanka and Australia 1976–77, Pakistan and New Zealand 1977–78. Hat-trick v Essex (Colchester) 1970. HS: 78 v Essex (Middlesbrough) 1977. HSJPL: 16* v Sussex (Bradford) 1974. HSBH: 18* v Surrey (Bradford) 1976. BB: 8–73 v Glos (Bristol) 1975. BBJPL: 3–24 v Northants (Bradford) 1969.

John Harry (Jackie) HAMPSHIRE (Oakwood Technical HS, Rotherham) B Thurnscoe (Yorks) 10/2/1941. RHB, LB. Debut 1961. Cap 1963. Played for Tasmania in 1967–68, 1968–69 and 1977–78. Benefit (£28,425) in 1976. Tests: 8 between 1969 and 1975. Scored 107 in his first Test v West Indies (Lord's) and is only English player to have scored a century on debut in Test cricket when this has occurred at Lord's. Tour: Australia and New Zealand 1970–71. 1,000 runs (12)—1,513 runs (av 32.19) in 1965 best. Gillette Man of Match awards: 3. HS: 183* v Sussex (Hove) 1971. HSTC: 107 v West Indies (Lord's) 1969. HSGC: 87* v Hants (Bradford) 1974. HSJPL: 119 v Leics (Hull) 1971. HSBH: 47 v Sussex (Hove) 1976. BB: 7–52 v Glamorgan (Cardiff) 1963.

Colin JOHNSON (Pocklington School) B Pocklington (Yorks) 5/9/1947. RHB, OB. Played in MCC Schools matches at Lord's 1966. Debut 1969.

Benson & Hedges Gold awards: 1. HS: 107 v Somerset (Sheffield) 1973. HSGC: 44 v Durham (Harrogate) 1973. HSJPL: 54 v Worcs (Bradford) 1974. HSBH: 73* v Middlesex 1 or 's) 1977.

Barrie LEADBEATER B Harehills, Leeds 14/8/1943. RHB, RM. Distant cousin of E. Leadbeater who played for county from 1949 to 1956 and subsequently for Warwickshire. Debut 1966. Cap 1969. Scored maiden century in 1976 in 208th innings in first-class cricket. Gillette Man of Match awards: 1 (in 1969 final). HS: 140* v Hants (Portsmouth) 1976. HSGC: 76 v Derbyshire (Lord's) 1969. HSJPL: 86* v Northants (Sheffield) 1972. HSBH: 90 v Lancs (Bradford) 1974.

James Derek LOVE B Leeds 22/4/1955. RHB, Debut 1975. HS: 163 v Notts (Bradford) 1976. HSJPL: 60 v Lancs (Leeds) 1977.

Richard Graham LUMB (Percy Jackson GS, Doncaster and Mexborough GS) B Doncaster 27/2/1950. RHB, RM. Played in MCC Schools matches at Lord's 1968. Debut 1970 after playing in one John Player League match in 1969. Cap 1974. 1,000 runs (2)—1,532 runs (av 41.40) in 1975 best. HS: 132 v Glos (Leeds) 1976. HSGC: 56 v Shropshire (Wellington) 1976. HSJPL: 101 v Notts (Scarborough) 1976. HSBH: 60* v Kent (Canterbury) 1976.

Christopher Middleton (Chris) OLD (Acklam Hall Secondary GS, Middlesbrough) B Middlesbrough 22/12/1948. LHB, RFM. Debut 1966. Cap 1969. Elected Best Young Cricketer of the Year in 1970 by the Cricket Writers' Club. Benefit in 1979. Tests: 33 between 1972–73 and 1977. Played in 2 matches against Rest of World 1970. Tours: India, Pakistan, and Sri Lanka 1972–73, West Indies 1973–74, Australia and New Zealand 1974–75, India, Sri Lanka and Australia 1976–77, Pakistan and New Zealand 1977–78. Scored century in 37 minutes v Warwickshire (Birmingham) 1977—second fastest ever in first-class cricket. Benson & Hedges Gold awards: 3. HS: 116 v Indians (Bradford) 1974. HSTC: 65 v Pakistan (Oval) 1974. HSGC: 29 v Lancs (Leeds) 1974. HSJPL: 82 v Somerset (Bath) 1974 and 82* v Somerset (Glastonbury) 1976. HSBH: 72 v Sussex (Hove) 1976. BB: 7–20 v Glos (Middlesbrough) 1969. BBTC: 5–21 v India (Lord's) 1974. BBGC: 4–32 v Lancs (Manchester) 1967. BBJPL: 5–53 v Sussex (Hove) 1971. BBBH: 4–17 v Derbyshire (Bradford) 1973.

Stephen (Steve) OLDHAM B High Green, Sheffield 26/7/1948. RHB, RFM. Debut 1974. Benson & Hedges Gold awards: 1. HS: 19 v Middlesex (Bradford) 1976. HSJPL: 38* v Glamorgan (Cardiff) 1977. BB: 5–47 v Somerset (Taunton) 1976. BBGC: 3–45 v Lancs (Leeds) 1974. BBJPL: 4–21 v Notts (Scarborough) 1974. BBBH: 5–32 v Minor Counties (Scunthorpe) 1975.

Alan RAMAGE (Warsett School, Brotton) B Guisborough 29/11/1957. LHB, RM. Has played in six John Player League matches and one Benson & Hedges Cup match between 1975 and 1977. Has yet to appear in first-class matches. HSBH: 17* v Combined Universities (Barnsley) 1976. BBJPL: 3–51 v Kent (Canterbury) 1977.

Arthur Leslie (Rocker) ROBINSON B Brompton (Yorks) 17/8/1946. LHB, LFM. Debut 1971. Cap 1976. Hat-trick v Notts (Worksop) 1974. HS: 30* v Glamorgan (Cardiff) 1977. HSGC: 18* v Lancs (Leeds) 1974.

HSJPL: 14 v Surrey (Oval) 1971. BB: 6–61 v Surrey (Oval) 1974. BBGC: 3–17 v Shropshire (Wellington) 1976. BBJPL: 4–25 v Surrey (Oval) 1974. BBBH: 3–20 v Notts (Nottingham) 1974.

Kevin SHARP (Abbey Grange C.E. High School, Leeds) B Leeds 6/4/1959. LHB, OB. Debut 1976. HS: 56 v Middlesex (Sheffield) 1977. HSJPL: 27 v Northants (Milton Keynes) 1977.

Arnold SIDEBOTTOM (Broadway GS, Barnsley) B Barnsley 1/4/1954. RHB, RFM. Played for 2nd XI since 1971 and in Schools matches at Lord's in that year. Debut 1973. HS: 124 v Glamorgan (Cardiff) 1977. HSGC: 45 v Hants (Bournemouth) 1977. HSJPL: 31 v Sussex (Hove) 1975. HSBH: 11 v Middlesex (Lord's) 1975. BB: 4–47 v Derbyshire (Chesterfield) 1975. BBGC: 4–36 v Hants (Bournemouth) 1977. BBJPL: 4–24 v Surrey (Scarborough) 1975. Soccer for Manchester United, and Huddersfield Town.

Stephen SILVESTER (Kelvin Hall Senior HS, Hull) B Hull 12/3/1951. RHB, RF. Debut 1976. HS: 14 v Worcs (Worcester) 1977. BB: 4–86 v Hants (Leeds) 1977. Trained as a teacher at St. John's College of Education, York.

Graham Barry STEVENSON (Minsthorpe GS) B Ackworth (Yorks) 16/12/1955. RHB, RM. Played for 2nd XI in 1972. Debut 1973. HS: 83 v Derbyshire (Chesterfield) 1976. HSGC: 27 v Glos (Leeds) 1976. HSJPL: 31 v Surrey (Oval) 1976. BB: 6–82 v Glamorgan (Cardiff) 1977. BBGC: 4–57 v Lancs (Leeds) 1974. BBJPL: 5–41 v Leics (Leicester) 1976. BBBH: 4–20 v Essex (Barnsley) 1977.

COUNTY AVERAGES

Schweppes County Championship: Played 21, won 6, drawn 10, lost 5, abandoned 1

All first-class matches: Played 23, won 7, drawn 11, lost 5, abandoned 1

BATTING AND FIELDING

Cap		M	I	NO	Runs	HS	Avge	100	50	Ct	St
1963	G. Boycott	17	25	3	1259	154	57.22	5	6	8	—
1963	J. H. Hampshire	18	23	5	779	100*	43.27	1	7	17	—
1969	C. M. Old	10	10	2	295	107	36.87	1	—	7	—
—	J. D. Love	17	29	5	739	129	30.79	1	5	8	—
1969	B. Leadbeater	10	18	1	472	73	27.76	—	3	8	—
—	A. Sidebottom	9	12	2	265	124	26.50	1	1	4	—
1974	R. G. Lumb	18	25	2	559	91	24.30	—	3	14	—
1973	D. L. Bairstow	23	31	7	566	81	23.58	—	5	49	2
—	C. Johnson	10	12	1	235	77	21.36	—	1	1	—
—	K. Sharp	9	18	2	303	56	18.93	—	1	6	—
1970	G. A. Cope	22	24	8	287	78	17.93	—	1	2	—
—	C. W. J. Athey	14	17	1	277	85*	17.31	—	1	11	1
—	G. B. Stevenson	14	24	3	303	52	14.42	—	1	6	—
1976	P. Carrick	14	11	2	126	30	14.00	—	—	3	—
—	H. P. Cooper	5	6	1	50	16*	10.00	—	—	4	—
—	S. Silvester	4	4	2	16	14	8.00	—	—	2	—
—	M. K. Bore	10	11	4	55	18	7.85	—	—	7	—
1976	A. L. Robinson	19	16	4	88	30*	7.33	—	—	10	—

Played in two matches: S. Oldham did not bat (1 ct).

BOWLING

	Type	O	M	R	W	Avge	Best	5 wI	10 wM
C. M. Old	RFM	203.4	55	481	25	19.24	6–36	1	—
G. A. Cope	OB	653.1	224	1357	56	24.23	6–29	4	1
H. P. Cooper	RM	135	37	295	12	24.58	3–5	—	—
A. L. Robinson	LFM	480.1	139	1115	44	25.34	5–28	2	—
G. B. Stevenson	RM	546.5	122	1772	69	25.68	6–82	2	1
S. Silvester	RF	65.4	8	240	9	26.66	4–86	—	—
M. K. Bore	LM	293.5	99	799	25	31.96	7–63	1	—
P. Carrick	SLA	296.4	96	770	24	32.08	6–37	2	—
A. Sidebottom	RFM	145	23	448	13	34.46	3–52	—	—

Also bowled: D. L. Bairstow 6–1–20–0; G. Boycott 10–4–16–1; J. H. Hampshire 2–0–17–0; S. Oldham 28.4–10–81–0; K. Sharp 4–1–21–0.

County Records

First-class cricket

Highest innings totals:	For ....887 v Warwickshire (Birmingham)	1896
	Agst....630 by Somerset (Leeds)	1901
Lowest innings totals:	For ....23 v Hampshire (Middlesbrough)	1965
	Agst....13 by Nottinghamshire (Nottingham)	1901
Highest individual innings:	For ....341 G. H. Hirst v Leicestershire (Leicester)	1905
	Agst....318* W. G. Grace for Glos (Cheltenham)	1876
Best bowling in an innings:	For ....10–10 H. Verity v Nottinghamshire (Leeds)	1932
	Agst....10–37 C. V. Grimmett for Australians (Sheffield)	1930
Best bowling in a match:	For ....17–91 H. Verity v Essex (Leyton)	1933
	Agst....17–91 H. Dean for Lancashire (Liverpool)	1913
Most runs in a season:	2883 (av 80.08) H. Sutcliffe	1932
runs in a career:	38561 (av 50.21) H. Sutcliffe	1919–1945
100s in a season:	12 by H. Sutcliffe	1932
100s in a career:	112 by H. Sutcliffe	1919–1945
wickets in a season:	240 (av 12.72) W. Rhodes	1900
wickets in a career:	3608 (av 16.00) W. Rhodes	1898–1930

RECORD WICKET STANDS

1st	555	P. Holmes & H. Sutcliffe v Essex (Leyton)	1932
2nd	346	W. Barber & M. Leyland v Middlesex (Sheffield)	1932
3rd	323*	H. Sutcliffe & M. Leyland v Glamorgan (Huddersfield)	1928
4th	312	G. H. Hirst & D. Denton v Hampshire (Southampton)	1914
5th	340	E. Wainwright & G. H. Hirst v Surrey (The Oval)	1899
6th	276	M. Leyland & E. Robinson v Glamorgan (Swansea)	1926
7th	254	D. C. F. Burton & W. Rhodes v Hampshire (Dewsbury)	1919
8th	292	Lord Hawke & R. Peel v Warwickshire (Birmingham)	1896
9th	192	G. H. Hirst & S. Haigh v Surrey (Bradford)	1898
10th	148	Lord Hawke & D. Hunter v Kent (Sheffield)	1898

One-day cricket

Highest innings totals:	Gillette Cup	317–4 v Surrey (Lord's)	1965
	John Player League	235–6 v Nottinghamshire (Sheffield)	1970
	Benson & Hedges Cup	218–3 v Minor Counties (North) (Scunthorpe)	1975
		218–9 v Minor Counties (East) (Jesmond)	1977
Lowest innings totals:	Gillette Cup	76 v Surrey (Harrogate)	1970
	John Player League	74 v Warwickshire (Birmingham)	1972
	Benson & Hedges Cup	125 v Lancashire (Manchester)	1973
Highest individual innings:	Gillette Cup	146 G. Boycott v Surrey (Lord's)	1965
	John Player League	119 J. H. Hampshire v Leicestershire (Hull)	1971
	Benson & Hedges Cup	102 G Boycott v Northamptonshire (Middlesbrough)	1977
Best bowling figures:	Gillette Cup	6–15 F. S. Trueman v Somerset (Taunton)	1965
	John Player League	7–15 R. A. Hutton v Worcestershire (Leeds)	1969
	Benson & Hedges Cup	6–27 A. G. Nicholson v Minor Counties (Middlesbrough)	1972

Young Cricketer of the Year

At the end of each season the members of the Cricket Writers' Club select by ballot the player they consider the best young cricketer of the season.

I. T. Botham (Somerset) was elected last year.

The selections to date are:

1950 R. Tattersall (Lancashire)
1951 P. B. H. May (Surrey)
1952 F. S. Trueman (Yorkshire)
1953 M. C. Cowdrey (Kent)
1954 P. J. Loader (Surrey)
1955 K. F. Barrington (Surrey)
1956 B. Taylor (Essex)
1957 M. J. Stewart (Surrey)
1958 A. C. D. Ingleby-
    Mackenzie (Hampshire)
1959 G. Pullar (Lancashire)
1960 D. A. Allen
    (Gloucestershire)
1961 P. H. Parfitt (Middlesex)
1962 P. J. Sharpe (Yorkshire)

1963 G. Boycott (Yorkshire)
1964 J. M. Brearley (Middlesex)
1965 A. P. E. Knott (Kent)
1966 D. L. Underwood (Kent)
1967 A. W. Greig (Sussex)
1968 R. M. H. Cottam
    (Hampshire)
1969 A. Ward (Derbyshire)
1970 C. M. Old (Yorkshire)
1971 J. Whitehouse (Warwickshire)
1972 D.R. Owen-Thomas (Surrey)
1973 M. Hendrick (Derbyshire)
1974 P. H. Edmonds (Middlesex)
1975 A. Kennedy (Lancashire)
1976 G. Miller (Derbyshire)
1977 I. T. Botham (Somerset)

THE FIRST-CLASS UMPIRES
FOR 1978

NB The abbreviations used below are identical with those given at the beginning of the section 'The Counties and their Players'.

William Edward (Bill) ALLEY B Sydney (Australia) 3/2/1919. LHB, RM. Played for New South Wales 1945–46 to 1947–48. Subsequently came to England to play League cricket and then for Somerset from 1957 to 1968. *Wisden* 1961. Testimonial (£2,700) in 1961. Tours: India and Pakistan 1949–50, Pakistan 1963–64 with Commonwealth team. Scored 3,019 runs (av 56.96) in 1961 including 2,761 runs and 10 centuries for county, both being records. Won Man of the Match award in Gillette Cup Competition on three occasions. HS: 221* v Warwickshire (Nuneaton) 1961. BB: 8–65 v Surrey (Oval) 1962. Career record: 19,612 runs (av 31.88), 31 centuries, 768 wkts (av 22.68). Appointed 1969. Umpired in 7 Tests between 1974 and 1977.

Ronald (Ron) ASPINALL B Almondbury (Yorks) 26/10/1918. RHB, RFM. Played for Yorkshire from 1946 to 1950 (retiring early through injury) and for Durham from 1951 to 1957. HS: 57* v Notts (Nottingham) 1948. BB: 8–42 v Northants (Rushden) 1949. Career record: 763 runs (av 19.07), 131 wkts (av 20.38). Appointed 1960.

Harold Denis BIRD B Barnsley 19/4/1933. RHB, RM. Played for Yorks from 1956 to 1959 and for Leics from 1960 to 1964. Has since been professional at Paignton CC. HS: 181* Yorks v Glamorgan (Bradford) 1959. Career record: 3,315 runs (av 20.71), 2 centuries. Appointed 1970. Umpired in 12 Tests between 1973 and 1977.

William Lloyd BUDD B Hawkley (Hants) 20/10/1913. RHB, RFM. Played for Hampshire from 1934 to 1946. HS: 77* v Surrey (Oval) 1937. BB: 4–22 v Essex (Southend) 1937. Career record: 941 runs (av 11.47). 64 wkts (av 39.15). Was on Minor Counties list for some years. Appointed 1969. Umpired in 3 Tests in 1976 and 1977.

David John CONSTANT B Bradford-on-Avon (Wilts) 9/11/1941. LHB, SLA. Played for Kent from 1961 to 1963 and for Leics from 1965 to 1968. HS: 80 v Glos (Bristol) 1966. Career record: 1,517 runs (av 19.20), 1 wkt (av 36.00). Appointed 1969. Umpired in 13 Tests between 1971 and 1977.

Cecil (Sam) COOK B Tetbury (Glos) 23/8/1921. RHB, SLA. Played for Gloucestershire from 1946 to 1964. Benefit (£3,067) in 1957. Took wicket with first ball in first-class cricket. Tests: 1 v SA 1947. HS: 35* v Sussex (Hove) 1957. BB: 9–42 v Yorks (Bristol) 1947. Career record: 1,964 runs (av 5.39), 1,782 wkts (av 20.52). Appointed 1971, after having withdrawn from appointment in 1966.

John Frederick (Jack) CRAPP B St Columb (Cornwall) 14/10/1912. LHB. Played for Gloucestershire from 1936 to 1956 captaining county in

159

1953 and 1954. Benefit (£3,611) in 1951. Tests: 7 in 1948 and 1948–49. Tours: South Africa 1948–49, India 1953–54 with Commonwealth Team. HS: 175 v Cambridge U (Cambridge) 1947. Career record: 23,615 runs (av 35.03), 38 centuries, 6 wkts (av 51.00). Appointed 1957. Umpired in 4 Tests in 1964 and 1965.

David Gwilliam Lloyd EVANS B Lambeth (London) 27/7/1933. RHB, WK. Played for Glamorgan from 1956 to 1969. Benefit (£3,500) in 1969. HS: 46* v Oxford U (Oxford) 1961. Career record: 2,875 runs (av 10.53), 558 dismissals (502 ct 56 st). Appointed 1971.

F. R. GOODALL Has not played first-class cricket. Became a first-class umpire in New Zealand in 1963–64. Umpired in 5 Tests in New Zealand between 1964–65 and 1976–77. Appointed for part of 1978 season.

David John HALFYARD B Winchmore Hill (Middlesex) 3/4/1931. RHB, RM. Played for Kent from 1956 to 1964 retiring through leg injury. Testimonial (£3,216) in 1965. Played for Notts from 1968 to 1970. Not re-engaged and has subsequently played in Minor Counties competition for Durham in 1971 and 1972, Northumberland in 1973 and Cornwall from 1974. HS: 79 Kent v Middlesex (Lord's) 1960. BB: 9–39 Kent v Glamorgan (Neath) 1957. Career record: 3,242 runs (av 10.91), 963 wkts (av 25.77). Appointed 1977, after having been on list in 1967.

Arthur JEPSON B Selston (Notts) 12/7/1915. RHB, RFM. Played for Notts from 1938 to 1959. Benefit (£2,000) in 1951. HS: 130 v Worcs (Nottingham) 1950. BB: 8–45 v Leics (Nottingham) 1958. Career record: 6,369 runs (av 14.31), 1 century, 1,051 wkts (av 29.08). Soccer (goalkeeper) for Port Vale, Stoke City and Lincoln City. Appointed 1960. Umpired in 4 Tests between 1966 and 1969.

Raymond (Ray) JULIAN B Cosby (Leics) 23/8/1936. RHB, WK. Played for Leicestershire from 1953 (debut at age of 16) to 1971, but lost regular place in side to R. W. Tolchard in 1966. HS: 51 v Worcs (Worcester) 1962. Career record: 2,581 runs (av 9.73), 421 dismissals (382 ct 39 st). Appointed 1972.

John George LANGRIDGE B Chailey (Sussex) 10/2/1910. Younger brother of late James Langridge. Opening RHB and outstanding slip field. Played for Sussex from 1928 to 1955. *Wisden* 1949. Shared joint benefit (£1,930) with H. W. Parks in 1948. Testimonial (£3,825) in 1953. Scored more runs and centuries in first-class cricket than any other player who never appeared in a Test match. Only F. E. Woolley, W. G. Grace, W. R. Hammond, G. A. R. Lock and D. B. Close have held more catches than his total of 786. HS: 250* v Glamorgan (Hove) 1933. Career record: 34,380 runs (av 37.45), 76 centuries, 44 wkts (av 42.00). Appointed 1956. Umpired in 7 Tests between 1960 and 1963.

Barrie John MEYER B Bournemouth 21/8/1932. RHB, WK. Played for Gloucestershire from 1957 to 1971. Benefit 1971. HS: 63 v Indians (Cheltenham) 1959, v Oxford U (Bristol) 1962 and v Sussex (Bristol) 1964. Career record: 5,367 runs (av 14.19) 826 dismissals (707 ct 119 st). Soccer for Bristol Rovers, Plymouth Argyle, Newport County and Bristol City. Appointed 1973.

Donald Osmund **OSLEAR** B Cleethorpes (Lincs) 3/3/1929. Has not played first-class cricket. Played soccer for Grimsby Town, Hull City, and Oldham Athletic. Also played ice hockey. Has umpired in county second XI matches since 1972. Appointed in 1975.

Kenneth Ernest (Ken) **PALMER** B Winchester 22/4/1937. RHB, RFM. Played for Somerset from 1955 to 1969. Testimonial (£4,000) in 1968. Tour: Pakistan with Commonwealth team 1963–64. Coached in Johannesburg 1964–65 and was called upon by MCC to play in final Test v South Africa owing to injuries to other bowlers. Tests (1): 1 v SA 1964–65. HS: 125* v Northants (Northampton) 1961. BB: 9–57 v Notts (Nottingham) 1963. Career record: 7,771 runs (av 20.66), 2 centuries, 866 wkts (av 21.34). Appointed 1972.

Cecil George (Cec) **PEPPER** B Forbes, New South Wales (Australia) 15/9/1918. RHB, LBG. Played for New South Wales 1938–39 to 1940–41, Australian Services 1945 and 1945–46. Returned to England to play in League cricket from 1947 and appeared in the Hastings Festivals in 1956 and 1957. Tours: India and Ceylon 1945–46 with Australian Services Team and India and Pakistan 1949–50 with Commonwealth Team. HS: 168 Australian Services v H. D. G. Leveson-Gower's XI (Scarborough) 1945. BB: 6–33 Commonwealth XI v Holkar Cricket Association (Indore) 1949–50. Career record: 1,927 runs (av 29.64), 1 century, 169 wkts (av 29.31). Appointed 1964.

William Edward (Eddie) **PHILLIPSON** B North Reddish (Lancs) 3/12/1910. RHB, RFM. Played for Lancashire from 1933 to 1948. Grant (£1,750) in 1948. Tour: New Zealand with Sir Julian Cahn's Team 1938–39. HS: 113 v Glamorgan (Preston) 1939. BB: 8–100 v Kent (Dover) 1934. Career record: 4,096 runs (av 25.76), 2 centuries, 555 wkts (av 24.72). Appointed 1956. Umpired in 12 Tests between 1958 and 1965.

B. Satyaji **RAO** B India 16/10/1930. Has not played first-class cricket. Umpired in 15 Tests in India between 1960–61 and 1976–77. Appointed for part of 1978 season.

Albert Ennion Growcott (Dusty) **RHODES** B Tintwistle (Cheshire) 10/10/1916. Father of H. J. Rhodes. RHB, LBG. Played for Derbyshire from 1937 to 1954. Testimonial (£2,096) in 1952. Tour: India 1951–52 returning home early owing to injury. Achieved 5 hat-tricks. HS: 127 v Somerset (Taunton) 1949. BB: 8–162 v Yorks (Scarborough) 1947. Career record: 7,363 runs (av 18.97), 3 centuries, 661 wkts (av 28.22). Appointed 1959. Has umpired in 8 Tests between 1963 and 1973. Also umpired in 2 matches between England and Rest of World 1970.

Thomas William (Tom) **SPENCER** B Deptford 22/3/1914. RHB, RM. Played for Kent from 1935 to 1946. HS: 96 v Sussex (Tunbridge Wells) 1946. Career record: 2,152 runs (av 20.11), 1 wkt (av 19.00). Appointed 1950 (longest serving umpire on list). Has umpired in 16 Tests between 1954 and 1977.

Jack **VAN GELOVEN** B Leeds 4/1/1934. RHB, RM. Played for Yorkshire in 1955 and for Leicestershire from 1956 to 1965. Subsequently played for Northumberland in Minor Counties competition from 1966 to 1973. HS: 157* v Somerset (Leicester) 1960. BB: 7–56 v Hants (Leicester) 1959. Career record: 7,522 runs (av 19.43), 5 centuries, 486 wkts (av 28.62). Appointed 1977.

Alan Geoffrey Thomas WHITEHEAD B Butleigh (Somerset) 28/10/1940. LHB, SLA. Played for Somerset from 1957 to 1961. HS: 15 v Hants (Southampton) 1959 and 15 v Leics (Leicester) 1960. BB: 6–74 v Sussex (Eastbourne) 1959. Career record: 137 runs (av 5.70), 67 wkts (av 34.41). Served on Minor Counties list in 1969. Appointed 1970.

Peter Bernard WIGHT B Georgetown (British Guiana) 25/6/1930. RHB, OB. Played for British Guiana in 1950–51 and for Somerset from 1953 to 1965. Benefit (£5,000) in 1963. HS: 222* v Kent (Taunton) 1959. BB: 6–29 v Derbyshire (Chesterfield) 1957. Career record: 17,773 runs (av 33.09), 28 centuries, 68 wkts (av 33.26). Appointed 1966.

Roderick Tudor WILSON B Rotherham (Yorks) 25/11/1931. Has not played first-class cricket. Has umpired in Minor Counties matches since 1967, and occasionally in first-class matches. Appointed 1978.

Thomas Guy WILSON B Chorley (Lancs) 5/11/1937. Has not played first-class cricket. Has umpired in Minor Counties matches since 1969, and occasionally in first-class matches. Appointed 1978.

NB The Test match panel for 1978 is H. D. Bird, W. L. Budd, D. J. Constant, B. J. Meyer, K. E. Palmer and T. W. Spencer.

SCORING OF POINTS IN THE SCHWEPPES CHAMPION-SHIP

The scheme is as follows:
  (a) For a win, 12 points, plus any points scored in the first innings.
  (b) In a tie, each side to score 5 points, plus any points scored in the first innings.
  (c) If the scores are equal in a drawn match, the side batting in the fourth innings to score 5 points, plus any points scored in the first innings.
  (d) First innings points (awarded only for performances in the first 100 overs of each innings and retained whatever the result of the match)
    (i) A maximum of 4 batting points to be available as follows: 150 to 199 runs—1 point; 200 to 249 runs—2 points; 250 to 299 runs—3 points; 300 runs or over—4 points.
    (ii) A maximum of 4 bowling points to be available as follows: 3–4 wickets taken—1 point; 5–6 wickets taken—2 points; 7–8 wickets taken—3 points; 9–10 wickets taken—4 points.
  (e) If play starts when less than eight hours playing time remains and a one innings match is played, no first innings points shall be scored. The side winning on the one innings to score 12 points.
  (f) The side which has the highest aggregate of points gained at the end of the season shall be the Champion County. Should any sides in the Schweppes Championship Table be equal on points, the side with most wins will have priority.

FIRST-CLASS AVERAGES 1977

The following averages include everyone who appeared in first-class cricket during the season. There were 223 first-class matches as follows: Test matches (5); Australian touring team (17); County Championship (181); Oxford and Cambridge Universities (18); MCC v Middlesex (1); Ireland v Scotland (1). 7 matches – Australian touring team (1), County Championship (6) – were abandoned without a ball being bowled, and are excluded.

† Indicates left-handed batsman.

BATTING AND FIELDING

	Cap	M	I	NO	Runs	HS	Avge	100	50	Ct	St
Abberley, R. N. (Wa)	1966	21	35	1	971	92	28.55	—	7	8	—
†Abrahams, J. (La)	—	22	28	5	652	101*	28.34	1	3	10	—
Acfield, D. L. (Ex)	1970	21	16	11	44	11*	8.80	—	—	6	—
Allbrook, M. E. (CU)	—	8	8	4	11	7*	2.75	—	—	5	—
Amiss, D. L. (E/Wa)	1965	19	34	5	1513	162*	52.17	6	3	9	—
Anderson, I. J. (Ire)	—	1	2	0	23	12	11.50	—	—	2	—
Arnold, G. G. (Sy)	1967	15	19	7	240	56	20.00	—	1	4	—
Arrowsmith, R. (La)	—	17	15	3	81	30*	6.75	—	—	5	—
Asif Iqbal (K)	1968	22	33	2	1224	116	39.48	1	7	14	—
Athey, C. W. J. (Y/MCC)	—	16	21	1	335	85*	16.75	—	1	13	1
Bainbridge, P. (Gs)	—	8	11	0	211	49	19.18	—	—	6	—
Bairstow, D. L. (Y/MCC)	1973	24	32	8	572	81	23.83	—	5	51	2
Baker, R. P. (Sy)	—	12	12	9	215	77*	71.66	—	1	3	—
Balderstone, J. C. (Le)	1973	25	38	8	1297	178*	43.23	2	8	17	—
Bannister, C. S. (CU)	—	5	7	1	55	45*	9.16	—	—	—	—
Barclay, J. R. T. (Sx/MCC)	1976	25	41	5	1090	112	30.27	2	5	20	—
Barlow, E. J. (D)	1976	21	33	4	886	88	30.55	—	7	34	—
†Barlow, G. D. (E/M/MCC)	1976	23	34	4	658	80	21.93	—	4	16	—
Beaumont, D. J. (CU)	—	7	10	0	168	44	16.80	—	—	5	—
Bedi, B. S. (No)	1972	19	22	7	172	38	11.46	—	—	5	—
Birch, J. D. (Nt)	—	16	27	2	484	86	19.36	—	3	10	—
†Birkenshaw, J. (Le)	1965	25	27	6	550	76	26.19	—	2	25	—
Booth, P. (Le)	1976	11	6	0	65	32	10.83	—	—	7	—
†Border, A. R. (Gs)	—	1	1	1	15	15*	—	—	—	—	—
Bore, M. K. (Y)	—	10	11	4	55	18	7.85	—	—	7	—
Borrington, A. J. (D)	1977	22	33	8	806	115	32.24	1	4	11	—
Botham, I. T. (E/So/MCC)	1976	17	27	3	738	114	30.75	1	5	15	—
Bourne, W. A. (Wa)	—	11	13	2	105	25*	9.54	—	—	7	—
Boyce, K. D. (Ex)	1967	7	7	1	139	69	23.16	—	1	5	—
Boycott, G. (E/Y)	1963	20	30	5	1701	191	68.04	7	7	8	—
Boyns, C. N. (Wo)	—	12	16	1	158	77*	10.53	—	1	12	—
Brain, B. M. (Gs)	1977	20	25	8	172	35	10.11	—	—	1	—
Brassington, A. J. (Gs)	—	6	6	3	56	14*	18.66	—	—	12	2
†Breakwell, D. (So)	1976	17	26	5	368	51	17.52	—	1	4	—
Brearley, J. M. (E/M/MCC)	1964	20	31	4	1251	152	46.33	3	5	15	—

163

	Cap	M	I	NO	Runs	HS	Avge	100	50	Ct	St
†Brettell, D. N. (OU)	—	7	10	2	110	39	13.75	—	—	2	—
Briers, N. E. (Le)	—	6	11	1	307	62	30.70	—	2	4	—
Bright, R. J. (Aus)	—	14	19	3	287	53*	26.09	—	1	5	—
Brown, A. (Sc)	—	1	2	0	34	25	17.00	—	—	—	—
Brown, D. J. (Wa)	1964	17	17	4	182	70*	14.00	—	1	9	—
Bugge, D. A. B. (OU)	—	1	—	—	—	—	—	—	—	—	—
Burgess, G. I. (So)	1968	13	15	2	163	32	12.53	—	—	7	—
†Buss, M. A. (Sx)	1967	19	30	4	627	125	24.11	1	2	12	—
†Butcher, A. R. (Sy)	1975	21	35	1	890	112	26.17	1	5	4	—
Butcher, R. O. (M)	—	8	15	0	298	42	19.86	—	—	6	—
Carrick, P. (Y)	1976	14	11	2	126	30	14.00	—	—	3	—
Cartwright, H. (D)	—	22	30	6	626	141*	26.08	1	1	5	—
Cartwright, T. W. (Gm)	—	7	11	2	76	22*	8.44	—	—	2	—
Chappell, G. S. (Aus)	—	16	25	5	1182	161*	59.10	5	2	18	—
†Cheatle, R. G. L. (Sx)	—	11	7	2	54	34	10.80	—	—	6	—
†Childs, J. H. (Gs)	1977	19	15	8	38	12	5.42	—	—	6	—
Clapp, R. J. (So)	—	1	—	—	—	—	—	—	—	—	—
Clark, J. (Sc)	—	1	2	1	10	7*	10.00	—	—	3	—
Claughton, J. A. (OU)	—	10	17	1	371	56	23.18	—	2	6	—
†Clements, S. M. (OU)	—	9	13	1	120	26*	10.00	—	—	9	—
Clift, P. B. (Le)	1976	15	17	2	243	64	16.20	—	1	5	—
†Clinton, G. S. (K)	—	18	28	1	828	88	30.66	—	7	6	—
Close, D. B. (So)	1971	16	25	2	438	87	19.04	—	2	19	—
Colhoun, O. D. (Ire)	—	1	2	0	8	4	4.00	—	—	3	—
Cook, G. (No)	1975	21	37	1	1201	126	33.36	2	5	30	—
†Cooper, H. P. (Y)	—	5	6	1	50	16*	10.00	—	—	4	—
†Cooper, K. (Nt)	—	8	9	1	48	18	6.00	—	—	1	—
†Cooper, N. H. C. (Gs)	—	2	3	0	51	25	17.00	—	—	1	—
†Coote, D. E. (Nt)	—	1	1	0	20	20	20.00	—	—	—	—
Cope, G. A. (Y)	1970	22	24	8	287	78	17.93	—	1	2	—
Cordle, A. E. (Gm)	1967	22	27	11	302	49	18.87	—	—	7	—
Corlett, S. C. (Ire)	—	1	2	0	61	60	30.50	—	1	2	—
Cosier, G. J. (Aus)	—	12	20	1	587	100	30.89	1	4	7	—
Coverdale, S. P. (CU)	—	9	14	1	334	58	25.69	—	2	4	3
Cowdrey, C. S. (K)	—	14	19	4	386	101*	25.73	1	1	8	—
Cowley, N. G. (H)	—	18	27	8	687	109*	36.15	1	6	8	—
Croft, C. E. H. (La)	—	19	16	4	200	46*	16.66	—	—	4	—
Crowther, P. G. (Gm)	—	5	7	0	138	99	19.71	—	1	2	—
Cumbes, J. (Wo)	—	24	26	9	111	22	6.52	—	—	2	—
Daniel, A. R. H. (CU)	—	2	2	0	85	75	42.50	—	1	—	—
Daniel, W. W. (M)	1977	23	19	9	106	28	10.60	—	—	4	—
†Davey, J. (Gs)	1971	1	2	2	55	53*	—	—	1	—	—
Davis, I. C. (Aus)	—	13	20	0	608	83	30.40	—	5	5	—
Davison, B. F. (Le)	1971	24	32	4	1075	141	38.39	2	7	21	—
Denness, M. H. (Ex)	1977	22	35	1	1343	195	39.50	3	7	13	—
†Denning, P. W. (So)	1973	17	29	3	1032	122	39.69	3	4	8	—
Dexter, R. E. (Nt)	—	3	5	0	102	48	20.40	—	—	1	—
†Dilley, G. R. (K)	—	1	2	0	31	16	15.50	—	—	—	—
D'Oliveira, B. L. (Wo)	1965	22	36	7	1257	156*	43.34	1	9	11	—
†Doshi, D. R. (Nt)	1977	25	29	3	150	18	5.76	—	—	5	—
Downton, P. R. (K)	—	7	7	3	87	31*	21.75	—	—	18	4
†Dredge, C. H. (So)	—	20	26	7	287	56*	15.10	—	1	11	—
Dudleston, B. (Le)	1969	11	15	4	306	93	27.81	—	2	15	5
Dye, J. C. J. (No)	1972	9	9	4	49	29	9.80	—	—	1	—
†Dymock, G. (Aus)	—	10	6	5	16	8*	16.00	—	—	2	—

164

	Cap	M	I	NO	Runs	HS	Avge	100	50	Ct	St
Ealham, A. G. E. (K)	1970	22	33	5	1116	99	39.85	—	10	16	—
East, R. E. (Ex)	1967	22	25	4	443	50*	21.09	—	1	11	—
Edmonds, P. H. (M/MCC)	1974	26	38	7	558	49	18.00	—	—	30	—
†Edrich, J. H. (Sy)	1959	15	26	4	1044	140	47.45	3	5	7	—
Elder, J. W. G. (Ire)	—	1	2	1	5	3*	5.00	—	—	—	—
Elms, R. B. (H)	—	14	14	4	148	30	14.80	—	—	7	—
Emburey, J. E. (M)	1977	18	23	8	228	48	15.20	—	—	22	—
Featherstone, N. G. (M)	1971	26	36	2	775	115	22.79	1	5	12	—
Finan, N. H. (Gs)	—	4	2	0	22	18	11.00	—	—	1	—
Fisher, P. B. (OU)	—	5	6	1	43	30	8.60	—	—	7	3
Fletcher, K. W. R. (Ex)	1963	22	37	6	1331	106*	42.93	3	7	27	—
Foat, J. C. (Gs)	—	14	23	3	282	44	14.10	—	—	4	—
†Fosh, M. K. (CU/Ex)	—	19	32	1	705	94	22.74	—	5	7	—
Francis, D. A. (Gm)	—	21	35	3	738	110	23.06	1	1	10	—
French, B. N. (Nt)	—	20	28	11	146	24	8.58	—	—	25	5
Gard, T. (So)	—	2	2	0	3	2	1.50	—	—	2	—
Garner, J. (So)	—	5	6	1	91	37	18.20	—	—	5	—
Gatting, M. W. (M)	1977	26	40	7	1095	82	33.18	—	11	24	—
†Gifford, N. (Wo/MCC)	1961	24	25	5	120	17*	6.00	—	—	11	—
†Gilliat, R. M. C. (H)	1969	11	15	4	310	90	28.18	—	1	10	—
Gooch, G. A. (Ex)	1975	23	37	6	837	105*	27.00	1	5	11	—
Gould, I. J. (M)	1977	21	30	5	330	41	13.20	—	—	42	8
†Gower, D. I. (Le/MCC)	1977	25	34	2	745	144*	23.28	1	3	8	—
Graham, J. N. (K)	1967	2	1	0	10	10	10.00	—	—	2	—
Graham-Brown, J. M. H. (D)	—	6	5	0	10	5	2.00	—	—	4	—
Graveney, D. A. (Gs)	1976	19	23	3	268	37	13.40	—	—	14	—
†Graves, P. J. (Sx)	1969	20	31	5	597	75*	22.96	—	4	11	—
Greenidge, C. G. (H)	1972	19	32	3	1771	208	61.06	6	6	18	—
Greig, A. W. (E/Sx)	1967	18	24	0	735	91	30.62	—	4	21	—
Greig, I. A. (CU)	—	9	14	1	394	96	30.30	—	3	3	—
Griffiths, B. J. (No)	—	10	11	6	3	2*	0.60	—	—	2	—
Groome, J. J. (Sx)	—	1	2	0	17	9	8.50	—	—	1	—
Gurr, D. R. (OU/So)	—	14	15	6	125	46*	13.88	—	—	5	—
Hacker, P. J. (Nt)	—	15	21	8	220	35	16.92	—	—	5	—
Hampshire, J. H. (Y)	1963	18	23	5	779	100*	43.27	1	7	17	—
†Hansell, T. M. G. (Sy)	—	5	8	2	88	24*	14.66	—	—	1	—
Hardie, B. R. (Ex)	1974	16	27	3	661	118*	27.54	1	3	12	—
Hare, W. H. (Nt)	—	1	2	0	15	13	7.50	—	—	—	—
Harris, M. J. (Nt)	1970	14	22	4	250	37	13.88	—	—	15	3
Harrison, J. (Ire)	—	1	2	1	103	100*	103.00	1	—	—	—
Harrison, S. C. (Gm)	—	1	2	0	4	4	2.00	—	—	—	—
Harvey-Walker, A. J. (D)	—	7	11	2	189	101*	21.00	1	—	2	—
Hassan, B. (Nt)	1970	23	42	4	1141	182*	30.02	2	2	14	—
Hayes, F. C. (La)	1972	20	26	3	1152	157*	50.08	3	4	7	—
Hayes, P. J. (CU)	—	6	9	4	104	56*	20.80	—	1	4	—
Head, T. J. (Sx)	—	1	1	1	4	4*	—	—	—	1	—
Hector, P. A. (Ex)	—	3	5	1	75	40	18.75	—	—	—	—
Hemmings, E. E. (Wa)	1974	23	30	5	412	85	16.48	—	1	10	—
Hemsley, E. J. O. (Wo)	1969	20	34	3	863	176*	27.83	1	5	10	—
†Henderson, S. P. (Wo)	—	8	13	2	172	52	15.63	—	1	1	—

	Cap	M	I	NO	Runs	HS	Avge	100	50	Ct	St
Hendrick, M. (E/D/MCC)	1972	21	16	6	66	17	6.60	—	—	17	—
Herbert, R. (Ex)	—	1	1	0	12	12	12.00	—	—	2	—
Herman, R. S. (H)	1972	1	1	0	0	0	0.00	—	—	—	—
†Higgs, K. (Le)	1972	23	16	11	186	98	37.20	—	1	19	—
Hignell, A. J. (CU/Gs)	1977	21	33	2	1010	149	32.58	1	9	20	—
Hill, A. (D)	1976	22	35	4	1014	90	32.70	—	9	4	—
Hills, R. W. (K)	1977	17	14	3	247	43	22.45	—	—	3	—
†Hodgson, A. (No)	1976	18	24	4	199	40	9.95	—	—	5	—
Hogg, W. (La)	—	6	4	1	19	17	6.33	—	—	2	—
Holder, V. A. (Wo)	1907	21	28	4	206	27	8.58	—	—	2	—
Hood, J. A. (OU)	—	2	3	0	9	7	3.00	—	—	1	—
†Hookes, D. W. (Aus)	—	17	26	1	804	108	32.16	1	6	4	—
Hopkins, D. C. (Wa)	—	2	2	1	23	13*	23.00	—	—	—	—
Hopkins, J. A. (Gm)	1977	24	43	1	1357	230	32.30	1	8	14	—
Howarth, G. P. (Sy)	1974	17	29	2	646	140	23.92	2	2	9	—
Howat, M. G. (CU)	—	8	8	2	15	5	2.50	—	—	1	—
Howgego, J. A. (K)	—	1	2	0	91	52	45.50	—	1	—	—
Hughes, D. P. (La)	1970	9	11	3	166	39*	20.75	—	—	7	—
Hughes, K. J. (Aus)	—	14	19	0	540	95	28.42	—	5	10	—
Humpage, G. W. (Wa)	1976	24	38	5	1145	104	34.69	1	8	65	2
†Humphries, D. J. (Wo)	—	22	32	5	440	59	16.29	—	2	30	5
Illingworth, R. (Le)	1969	25	24	3	506	119*	24.09	1	1	11	—
Imran Khan (Sx)	—	9	13	2	227	59	25.18	—	1	2	—
Inchmore, J. D. (Wo)	1976	11	15	3	143	33	11.91	—	—	3	—
Intikhab Alam (Sy)	1969	21	34	5	552	86	19.03	—	3	3	—
Jackman, R. D. (Sy)	1970	22	32	11	606	86*	28.85	—	2	15	—
Jarvis, K. B. S. (K)	1977	21	14	11	20	12*	6.66	—	—	5	—
Javed Miandad (Sx)	1977	24	39	6	1326	111	40.18	3	7	27	—
Jennings, K. F. (So)	—	8	12	2	42	14	4.20	—	—	8	—
Jesty, T. E. (H)	1971	21	34	3	1230	144	39.67	4	5	12	—
Johnson, C. (Y)	—	10	12	1	235	77	21.36	—	1	1	—
Johnson, G. W. (K)	1970	11	18	1	229	58*	13.47	—	1	11	—
Johnson, P. D. (Nt)	1975	18	32	4	719	106*	25.67	1	4	3	—
†Jones, A. (Gm)	1962	21	35	1	1272	115	37.41	2	7	6	—
Jones, A. A. (M/MCC)	1976	9	6	1	17	14	3.40	—	—	1	—
†Jones, A. L. (Gm)	—	3	3	1	63	46	31.50	—	—	—	—
†Jones, B. J. R. (Wo)	—	14	24	2	359	65	16.31	—	1	5	—
Jones, E. W. (Gm)	1967	24	31	5	481	51*	18.50	—	2	43	3
Julien, B. D. (K)	1972	16	21	3	451	55*	25.05	—	2	4	—
†Kallicharran, A. I. (Wa)	1972	22	36	4	1343	149*	41.96	1	10	15	—
Kanhai, R. B. (Wa)	1968	18	26	5	738	176	35.14	2	3	19	—
Kayum, D. A. (OU)	—	7	11	1	229	57	22.90	—	1	2	—
Kemp, N. J. (K)	—	3	3	0	16	14	5.33	—	—	1	—
†Kennedy, A. (La)	1975	7	9	0	166	37	18.44	—	—	7	—
Ker, J. E. (Sc)	—	1	2	0	6	6	3.00	—	—	—	—
King, C. L. (Gm)	—	16	27	1	811	78	31.19	—	6	13	—
†Kitchen, M. J. (So)	1966	20	33	1	1005	143*	31.40	3	2	16	—
†Knight, R. D. V. (Sx)	1976	23	37	1	872	100*	24.22	1	3	13	—
Knott, A. P. E. (E/K)	1965	16	20	2	771	135	42.83	2	4	47	3
†Laing, J. R. (Sc)	—	1	2	0	4	3	2.00	—	—	—	—
Lamb, T. M. (M)	—	4	4	1	19	8	6.33	—	—	1	—
Larkins, W. (No)	1976	21	34	2	793	110	24.78	2	—	11	—
Leadbeater, B. (Y)	1969	10	18	1	472	73	27.76	—	3	8	—

166

	Cap	M	I	NO	Runs	HS	Avge	100	50	Ct	St
Lee, P. G. (La/MCC)	1972	24	18	6	100	25	8.33	—	—	5	—
†L'Estrange, M. G. (OU)	—	10	16	2	211	45	15.07	—	—	4	—
Lever, J. K. (E/Ex)	1970	19	17	4	73	11	5.61	—	—	8	—
Littlewood, D. J. (CU)	—	1	—	—	—	—	—	—	—	2	1
†Llewellyn, M. J. (Gm)	1977	23	36	6	842	129*	28.06	1	4	12	—
Lloyd, B. J. (Gm)	—	7	7	6	54	13*	54.00	—	—	2	—
†Lloyd, C. H. (La)	1969	5	3	1	164	95	82.00	—	1	3	—
†Lloyd, D. (La)	1968	22	32	5	996	119*	36.88	1	6	29	—
†Lloyd, T. A. (Wa)	—	2	4	2	122	70*	61.00	—	1	—	—
†Long, A. (Sx)	1976	23	28	11	369	47	21.70	—	—	40	3
Love, J. D. (Y)	—	17	29	5	739	129	30.79	1	5	8	—
Lumb, R. G. (Y)	1974	18	25	2	559	91	24.30	—	3	14	—
Lynch, M. A. (Sy)	—	5	10	0	170	44	17.00	—	—	—	—
Lyon, J. (La/MCC)	1975	21	21	2	178	34	9.36	—	—	37	4
Lyons, K. J. (Gm)	—	6	7	1	126	65*	21.00	—	1	—	—
McCosker, R. B. (Aus)	—	18	32	1	737	107	23.77	1	4	20	—
McEvoy, M. S. A. (Ex)	—	2	3	1	73	67*	36.50	—	1	1	—
McEwan, K. S. (Ex)	1974	23	37	4	1702	218	51.57	8	4	14	—
†Mack, A. J. (Sy)	—	7	5	0	34	16	6.80	—	—	—	—
McKiddie, G. T. (Sc)	—	1	2	0	10	8	5.00	—	—	1	—
McPhail, A. W. (OU)	—	4	8	1	63	37	9.00	—	—	6	—
†McPherson, T. I. (Sc)	—	1	2	1	47	28	47.00	—	—	—	—
MacVicar, A. D. L. (CU)	—	1	—	—	—	—	—	—	—	—	—
Malone, M. F. (Aus)	—	10	10	3	95	46	13.57	—	—	4	—
Marks, V. J. (OU/So)	—	19	29	3	763	69	29.34	—	5	5	—
†Marsh, R. W. (Aus)	—	17	24	2	477	124	21.68	1	2	30	2
Matheson, J. A. (OU)	—	1	—	—	—	—	—	—	—	—	—
Mendis, G. D. (Sx)	—	14	26	3	578	68*	25.13	—	3	5	—
Miller, G. (E/D/MCC)	1976	21	30	3	730	86*	27.03	—	5	12	—
Monteith, J. D. (Ire)	—	1	2	0	19	17	9.50	—	—	—	—
Morris, A. (D)	—	7	8	1	53	16	7.57	—	—	3	—
Moseley, H. R. (So)	1972	14	13	10	45	10*	15.00	—	—	4	—
Moulding, R. P. (M)	—	1	1	0	26	26*	—	—	1	—	—
†Moylan, A. C. D. (CU)	—	4	7	0	132	26	18.85	—	—	1	—
Murtagh, A. J. (H)	—	5	7	2	91	41*	18.20	—	—	1	—
Mushtaq Mohammad (No)	1967	21	37	5	1469	147	45.90	5	7	9	—
Nanan, N. (Nt)	—	1	2	0	109	54	54.50	—	2	1	—
†Nash, M. A. (Gm)	1969	22	31	6	477	56	19.08	—	2	6	—
Neale, P. A. (Wo)	—	15	26	2	596	112	24.83	1	1	11	—
Needham, A. (Sy)	—	7	7	1	48	15*	8.00	—	—	2	—
†Nicholls, D. (K)	1969	7	8	2	142	48	23.66	—	—	17	1
O'Brien, B. A. (Ire)	—	1	2	0	0	0	0.00	—	—	3	—
O'Brien, G. P. (Ire)	—	1	2	0	14	11	7.00	—	—	—	—
O'Keeffe, K. J. (Aus)	—	13	19	12	355	48*	50.71	—	5	5	—
†Old, C. M. (E/Y)	1969	12	13	2	341	107	31.00	1	—	9	—
Oldham, S. (Y)	—	2	—	—	—	—	—	—	—	1	—
Olive, M. (So)	—	3	5	1	24	15	6.00	—	—	4	—
Oliver, P. R. (Wa)	—	4	7	2	122	38*	24.40	—	—	5	—
Ontong, R. C. (Gm)	—	20	33	2	587	62	18.93	—	2	10	—
O'Riordan, A. J. (Ire)	—	1	2	0	3	2	1.50	—	—	—	—
Ormrod, J. A. (Wo)	1966	16	26	1	708	103	28.32	1	4	5	—
Parker, P. W. G. (CU/Sx)	—	17	26	2	686	110*	28.58	1	3	8	—

	Cap	M	I	NO	Runs	HS	Avge	100	50	Ct	St
Partridge, B. J. M. (OU)	—	4	6	4	5	4	2.50	—	—	—	—
†Partridge, M. D. (Gs)	—	4	5	2	27	17*	9.00	—	—	2	—
Pascoe, L. S. (Aus)	—	11	9	3	44	20	7.33	—	—	—	—
Patel, D. N. (Wo)	—	16	24	0	215	27	8.95	—	—	7	—
Pathmanathan, G. (OU)	—	3	5	0	175	63	35.00	—	2	2	—
Payne, I. R. (Sy)	—	7	9	1	63	29	7.87	—	—	2	—
Perryman, S. P. (Wa)	1977	24	24	10	233	43	16.64	—	—	10	—
Phillipson, C. P. (Sx)	—	3	4	0	65	24	16.25	—	—	3	—
Pilling, H. (La)	1965	23	34	5	784	105*	27.03	1	3	7	—
Plumb, S. G. (Ex)	—	1	2	0	31	20	15.50	—	—	—	—
Pocock, N. E. J. (H)	—	7	13	2	265	46*	24.09	—	—	7	—
Pocock, P. I. (Sy)	1967	21	18	4	166	31	11.85	—	—	7	—
Pont, K. R. (Ex)	1976	18	26	5	455	101*	21.66	1	1	7	—
Popplewell, N. F. M. (CU)	—	7	9	3	38	19*	6.33	—	—	2	—
Pridgeon, A. P. (Wo)	—	9	11	7	71	26	17.75	—	—	2	—
Procter, M. J. (Gs)	1968	21	33	2	857	115	27.64	2	3	17	—
Racionzer, T. B. (Sc)	—	1	2	0	28	23	14.00	—	—	—	—
Radley, C. T. (M)	1967	26	40	5	1309	85	37.40	—	9	29	—
Randall, D. W. (E/Nt/MCC)	1973	19	33	3	709	79	23.63	—	6	12	—
Ratcliffe, R. M. (La)	1976	3	1	0	0	0	0.00	—	—	—	—
†Reidy, B. W. (La)	—	9	12	3	240	78	26.66	—	1	1	—
†Reith, M. S. (Ire)	—	1	2	0	8	4	4.00	—	—	—	—
Rice, C. E. B. (Nt)	1975	25	42	5	1300	114	35.13	1	9	19	—
Rice, J. M. (H)	1975	21	29	0	566	78	19.51	—	4	19	—
Richards, B. A. (H)	1968	16	25	3	927	115	42.13	2	5	19	—
Richards, C. J. (Sy)	—	12	15	4	137	33*	12.45	—	—	23	6
Richards, G. (Gm)	1976	24	37	5	621	74*	19.40	—	3	6	—
Richards, I. V. A. (So)	1974	20	35	2	2161	241*	65.48	7	9	16	—
Roberts, A. M. E. (H)	1974	14	13	2	102	19	9.27	—	—	4	—
Robertson, F. (Sc)	—	1	2	0	22	12	11.00	—	—	—	—
†Robinson, A. L. (Y)	1976	19	16	4	88	30*	7.35	—	—	10	—
†Robinson, P. J. (So)	1966	1	1	0	0	0*	—	—	—	1	—
Robinson, R. D. (Aus)	—	14	23	4	715	137*	37.63	1	4	31	3
Rock, D. J. (H)	—	11	19	0	454	114	23.89	2	1	5	—
Roebuck, P. M. (CU/So)	—	14	21	3	381	112	21.16	1	1	8	—
Roope, G. R. J. (E/Sy)	1969	20	31	5	1431	115	55.03	5	7	21	—
†Rose, B. C. (So/MCC)	1975	20	35	3	1193	205	37.28	3	6	11	—
Ross, N. P. D. (M)	—	10	13	1	238	53	19.83	—	2	7	—
†Rouse, S. J. (Wa)	1974	19	22	6	353	33	22.06	—	—	5	—
Rowe, C. J. C. (K)	1977	20	29	3	540	103	20.76	1	2	13	—
Russell, P. E. (D)	1975	1	2	1	21	12*	21.00	—	—	—	—
†Sadiq Mohammad (Gs)	1973	21	38	1	997	88	26.94	—	6	19	—
Sarfraz Nawaz (No)	1975	18	28	5	450	61	19.56	—	1	14	—
Savage, R. L. (OU/Wa)	—	19	21	7	98	22*	7.00	—	—	3	—
Schepens, M. (Le)	—	3	4	1	40	23*	13.33	—	—	—	—
†Scott, C. J. (La)	—	3	3	0	16	10	5.33	—	—	3	2
Selvey, M. W. W. (M)	1973	24	26	8	215	41*	11.94	—	—	10	—
Serjeant, C. S. (Aus)	—	15	22	2	663	159	33.15	1	6	2	—
Shackleton, J. H. (Gs)	—	19	23	6	260	41*	15.29	—	—	18	—
Sharp, G. (No)	1973	21	31	9	474	53*	21.54	—	1	37	10

	Cap	M	I	NO	Runs	HS	Avge	100	50	Ct	St
†Sharp, K. (Y)	—	9	18	2	303	56	18.93	—	1	6	—
Shepherd, D. R. (Gs)	1969	22	32	5	737	142*	27.29	1	4	7	—
Shepherd, J. N. (K)	1967	20	25	4	446	77	21.23	—	2	18	—
Short, J. F. (Ire)	—	1	2	0	0	0	0.00	—	—	—	—
Shuttleworth, K. (Le)	1977	13	15	4	154	30*	14.00	—	—	10	—
Sidebottom, A. (Y)	—	9	12	2	265	124	26.50	1	1	4	—
Silvester, S. (Y)	—	4	4	2	16	14	8.00	—	—	2	—
Simmons, J. (La)	1971	22	24	6	377	64*	20.94	—	1	17	—
Siviter, K. (OU)	—	1	2	2	3	2*	—	—	—	—	—
Skinner, L. E. (Sy)	1975	14	20	1	382	54	20.10	—	1	7	1
†Slack, W. N. (M)	—	3	5	0	65	30	13.00	—	—	—	—
Slocombe, P. A. (So)	—	12	19	3	437	55*	27.31	—	2	4	—
Smedley, M. J. (Nt)	1966	23	38	8	942	130*	31.40	1	4	9	—
†Smith, D. M. (Sy)	—	12	17	1	278	57	17.37	—	1	9	—
Smith, K. D. (Wa)	—	16	27	2	594	135	23.76	1	2	6	—
Smith, M. J. (Wa)	1967	25	42	2	1278	141	31.95	3	6	13	—
Smith, N. (Ex)	1975	23	23	3	178	23	8.90	—	—	41	11
Snow, J. A. (Sx)	1964	22	30	7	541	73*	23.52	—	4	2	—
Southern, J. W. (H)	—	22	19	10	94	31*	10.44	—	—	4	—
Spencer, J. (Sx)	1973	23	25	8	273	43*	16.05	—	—	7	—
Steele, A. (Sc)	—	1	2	0	27	23	13.50	—	—	4	1
Steele, D. S. (No)	1965	19	33	4	938	117*	32.34	2	3	21	—
Steele, J. F. (Le)	1971	24	39	7	961	124	30.03	1	4	15	—
Stephenson, G. R. (H)	1969	22	23	6	415	76	24.41	—	1	41	3
Stevenson, G. B. (Y)	—	22	25	4	303	52	14.42	—	1	6	—
Stevenson, K. (D)	—	8	5	2	25	9	8.33	—	—	5	—
Stewart, D. E. R. (Sc)	—	1	2	0	63	53	31.50	—	1	2	—
Stovold, A. W. (Gs)	1976	22	39	4	1223	196	34.94	1	6	32	6
Sullivan, J. P. (Gs)	—	2	4	0	26	21	6.50	—	—	2	—
†Swarbrook, F. W. (D)	1975	21	22	6	347	81	21.68	—	1	12	—
Swindell, R. S. (D)	—	1	2	0	1	1	0.50	—	—	—	—
Tavare, C. J. (OU/K)	—	13	24	4	584	124*	29.20	1	2	12	—
Taylor, D. J. S. (So)	1971	20	28	9	496	84*	26.10	—	2	51	5
Taylor, L. B. (Le)	—	2	2	2	2	1*	—	—	—	—	—
Taylor, M. N. S. (H)	1973	21	26	5	467	102	22.23	1	—	11	—
Taylor, R. W. (D)	1962	22	23	4	269	36	14.15	—	—	49	2
Taylor, W. (Nt)	1975	9	13	2	79	23	7.18	—	—	—	—
†Thomas, D. J. (Sy)	—	2	3	1	14	14	7.00	—	—	—	—
Thomson, J. R. (Aus)	—	16	17	1	130	25	8.12	—	—	3	—
Todd, P. A. (Nt)	1977	17	30	1	743	86	25.62	—	6	19	—
Tolchard, J. G. (Le)	—	7	10	2	229	78	28.62	—	3	7	—
Tolchard, R. W. (Le)	1966	17	22	6	524	76	32.75	—	4	20	4
Tomlins, K. P. (M)	—	3	3	0	1	1	0.33	—	—	1	—
Tremlett, T. M. (H)	—	1	2	1	15	14	15.00	—	—	1	—
Tunnicliffe, C. J. (D)	1977	22	20	5	204	82*	13.60	—	1	11	—
Tunnicliffe, H. T. (Nt)	—	4	8	1	133	64*	19.00	—	1	1	—
†Turner, D. R. (H)	1970	18	29	2	567	69	21.00	—	2	5	—
Turner, G. M. (Wo)	1968	22	38	5	1380	153	41.81	3	6	16	—
Turner, S. (Ex)	1970	22	28	5	504	73	21.91	—	1	14	—
Underwood, D. L. (E/K)	1964	17	19	6	91	20	7.00	—	—	7	—
Vernon, M. J. (Gs)	—	5	6	0	13	4	2.16	—	—	3	—
Verrinder, A. O. C. (K)	—	1	2	1	24	23	24.00	—	—	1	—
Virgin, R. T. (No)	1974	21	37	2	992	107	28.34	3	3	12	—
Walker, M. H. N. (Aus)	—	15	17	2	250	78*	16.66	—	1	2	—

169

	Cap	M	I	NO	Runs	HS	Avge	100	50	Ct	St
Waller, C. E. (Sx)	1976	13	13	7	57	15	9.50	—	—	7	—
†Walters, J. (D)	—	5	4	0	63	28	15.75	—	—	—	—
Walters, K. D. (Aus)	—	17	26	1	663	88	26.52	—	3	8	—
Ward, A. (Le)	1977	20	15	4	81	19	7.36	—	—	6	—
Weir, R. S. (Sc)	—	1	2	0	58	51	29.00	—	1	—	—
Wells, R. R. C. (OU)	—	7	11	1	158	85	15.80	—	1	3	—
†Wessels, K. C. (Sx)	1977	11	17	3	663	138*	47.35	2	4	2	—
†White, R. A. (Nt)	1966	25	34	5	642	90	22.13	—	2	6	—
Whitehouse, J. (Wa)	1973	24	41	5	1543	158*	42.86	6	6	21	—
Wilcock, H. G. (Wo)	—	9	15	2	242	74	18.61	—	1	4	—
Wilkins, A. H. (Gm)	—	18	21	6	157	70	10.46	—	1	5	—
Wilkinson, P. A. (Nt)	1974	14	19	4	216	40*	14.40	—	—	5	—
Willey, P. (No/MCC)	1971	21	37	2	646	73	18.45	—	1	6	—
Williams, R. G. (No)	—	7	13	2	135	43	12.27	—	—	2	—
Willis, R. G. D. (E/Wa)	1972	16	15	5	124	29	12.40	—	—	5	—
†Wilson, J. D. (OU)	—	1	2	0	19	18	9.50	—	—	—	—
†Wingfield Digby, A. R. (OU)	—	9	14	0	148	36	10.57	—	—	4	—
Wood, B. (La)	1968	23	34	6	1439	155*	51.39	3	7	21	—
Woolmer, R. A. (E/K)	1970	20	34	4	1238	137	47.61	6	4	10	—
†Wright, J. G. (D)	1977	22	36	3	1080	151	32.72	1	4	18	—
†Yardley, T. J. (No)	—	7	11	1	112	37	11.20	—	—	2	—
†Younis Ahmed (Sy)	1969	20	34	3	786	61*	25.35	—	4	10	—
Zaheer Abbas (Gs)	1975	20	36	6	1584	205*	52.80	5	9	16	—

NB *Players who have not bowled in first-class cricket are omitted from the following list.*

	Type	Overs	Mdns	Runs	Wkts	Avge	Best	5 wI	10 wM
Abberley, R. N. (Wa)	OB	2	0	20	0	—	—	—	—
Acfield, D. L. (Ex)	OB	669	174	1571	56	28.05	5-54	1	—
Allbrook, M. E. (CU)	OB	232.4	65	631	12	52.58	4-26	—	—
Anderson, I. J. (Ire)	OB	39	18	55	1	55.00	1-29	—	—
Arnold, G. G. (Sy)	RFM	314.1	85	781	30	26.03	6-24	2	—
Arrowsmith, R. (La)	SLA	480.2	170	1192	44	27.09	6-29	2	—
Asif Iqbal (K)	RM	72	22	192	4	48.00	2-12	—	—
Bairstow, D. L. (Y/MCC)	RM	6	1	20	0	—	—	—	—
Baker, R. P. (Sy)	RM	194.1	44	584	18	32.44	3-35	—	—
Balderstone, J. C. (Le)	SLA	373.3	112	933	38	24.55	4-33	—	—
Bannister, C. S. (CU)	RM	55.4	13	186	5	37.20	4-40	—	—
Barclay, J. R. T. (Sx/MCC)	OB	155.1	39	447	18	24.83	3-31	—	—
Barlow, E. J. (D)	RM	257.4	55	683	28	24.39	4-52	—	—
Bedi, B. S. (No)	SLA	667.1	195	1554	68	22.85	6-83	4	1
Birch, J. D. (Nt)	RM	115.5	17	410	13	31.53	3-42	—	—
Birkenshaw, J. (Le)	OB	641.1	188	1516	59	25.69	6-74	1	—
Booth, P. (Le)	RFM	179	37	494	25	19.76	4-39	—	—
Bore, M. K. (Y)	LM	293.5	99	799	25	31.96	7-63	1	—
Borrington, A. J. (D)	LB	0.4	0	4	0	—	—	—	—

	Type	Overs	Mds	Runs	Wkt	Avge	Best	5 wI	10 wM
Botham, I. T. (E/So/MCC)	RM	665.5	149	1983	88	22.53	6–50	6	1
Bourne, W. A. (Wa)	RFM	300.5	53	972	30	32.40	5–68	1	—
Boyce, K. D. (Ex)	RFM	189.4	45	496	23	21.56	4–48	—	—
Boycott, G. (E/Y)	RM	10	4	16	1	16.00	1–10	—	—
Boyns, C. N. (Wo)	RM	235	51	710	14	50.71	3–24	—	—
Brain, B. M. (Glos)	RFM	571.1	132	1637	77	21.25	7–51	4	—
Breakwell, D. (So)	SLA	355	110	890	29	30.68	4–44	—	—
Brettell, D. N. (OU)	SLA	1223.	37	329	10	32.90	3–49	—	—
Bright, R. J. (Aus)	SLA	333.5	114	794	39	20.35	5–67	2	—
Brown, D. J. (Wa)	RFM	405.1	76	1209	57	21.21	5–43	2	—
Bugge, D. A. B. (OU)	RM	7	2	22	0	—	—	—	—
Burgess, G. I. (So)	RM	367.1	101	1043	38	27.44	5–25	1	—
Buss, M. A. (Sx)	LM	326.4	106	759	31	24.48	4–14	—	—
Butcher, A. R. (Sy)	LM	134	22	512	12	42.66	3–72	—	—
Carrick, P. (Y)	SLA	296.4	96	770	24	32.08	6–37	2	—
Cartwright, H. (D)	RM	5	2	10	0	—	—	—	—
Cartwright, T. W. (Gm)	RM	131.3	52	258	10	25.80	4–46	—	—
Chappell, G. S. (Aus)	RM	106	28	304	6	50.66	3–45	—	—
Cheatle, R. G. L. (Sx)	SLA	200.2	43	671	23	29.17	5–9	1	—
Childs, J. H. (Gs)	SLA	468	119	1372	47	29.19	5–41	2	—
Clapp, R. J. (So)	RM	19.1	8	37	4	9.25	2–2	—	—
Clark, J. (Sc)	RM	36	15	55	5	11.00	4–10	—	—
Clements, S. M. (OU)	RM	8	1	28	0	—	—	—	—
Clift, P. B. (Le)	RM	379.5	100	949	44	21.56	5–19	4	—
Close, D. B. (So)	RM/OB	0.2	0	8	0	—	—	—	—
Cook, G. (No)	SLA	2	0	2	0	—	—	—	—
Cooper, H. P. (Y)	RM	135	37	295	12	24.58	3–5	—	—
Cooper, K. (Nt)	RFM	143	38	399	10	39.90	4–75	—	—
Cope, G. A. (Y)	OB	653.1	224	1357	56	24.23	6–29	4	1
Cordle, A. E. (Gm)	RFM	528	120	1612	55	29.30	6–13	3	—
Corlett, S. C. (Ire)	RM	45	16	85	6	14.16	5–62	1	—
Cosier, G. J. (Aus)	RM	16	3	36	0	—	—	—	—
Cowdrey, C. S. (K)	RM	10	0	54	1	54.00	1–30	—	—
Cowley, N. G. (H)	OB	400.3	92	1125	29	38.79	5–94	1	—
Croft, C. E. H. (La)	RFM	476	120	1335	47	28.40	7–54	1	—
Crowther, P. G. (Gm)	OB	7	1	22	1	22.00	1–22	—	—
Cumbes, J. (Wo)	RFM	554.4	103	1600	51	31.37	6–24	3	—
Daniel, W. W. (M)	RF	516.1	142	1233	75	16.44	6–33	6	2
Davey, J. (Gs)	LFM	17	5	48	0	—	—	—	—
Davison, B. F. (Le)	RM	10	1	42	1	42.00	1–38	—	—
Denness, M. H. (Ex)	RM/OB	1	1	0	0	—	—	—	—
Dilley, G. R. (K)	RM	6	0	23	0	—	—	—	—
D'Oliveira, B.L. (Wo)	RM/OB	272	78	617	21	29.38	5–50	1	—
Doshi, D. R. (Nt)	SLA	950.5	288	2442	82	29.78	6–97	2	—
Dredge, C. H. (So)	RM	464	98	1396	37	37.72	4–42	—	—
Dye, J. C. J. (No)	LFM	195	45	581	24	24.20	4–55	—	—
Dymock, G. (Aus)	LFM	192	54	468	15	31.20	3–30	—	—
East, R. E. (Ex)	SLA	658.4	197	1477	73	20.23	8–30	6	2
Edmonds, P. H. (M/MCC)	SLA	885.3	292	1899	81	23.44	8–132	3	1
Edrich, J. H. (Sy)	RM	5	4	4	0	—	—	—	—
Elder, J. W. G. (Ire)	RFM	22	13	18	2	9.00	1–7	—	—

171

	Type	Overs	Mds	Runs	Wkt	Avge	Best	5 wI	10 wM
Elms, R. B. (H)	LFM	287.4	64	926	26	35.61	4-83	—	—
Emburey, J. E. (M)	OB	686.1	205	1488	81	18.37	7-36	9	3
Featherstone, N. G. (M)	OB	275.4	62	801	26	30.80	5-65	1	—
Finan, N. H. (Gs)	RM	41	9	129	1	129.00	1-30	—	—
Fletcher, K. W. R. (Ex)	LBG	8	0	76	0	—	—	—	—
Foat, J. C. (Gs)	RM	1	0	6	0	—	—	—	—
Garner, J. (So)	RFM	215.1	60	539	27	19.96	8-31	1	—
Gatting, M. W. (M)	RM	148.2	36	426	14	30.42	2-1	—	—
Gifford, N. (Wo/MCC)	SLA	553.4	169	1288	45	28.62	5-64	1	—
Gooch, G. A. (Ex)	RM	109.3	26	345	8	43.12	4-60	—	—
Gower, D. I. (Le/MCC)	RM	14	2	59	3	19.66	3-47	—	—
Graham, J. N. (K)	RM	46	13	83	2	41.50	1-5	—	—
Graham-Brown, J. M. H. (D)	RM	27	3	119	2	59.50	1-29	—	—
Graveney, D. A. (Gs)	SLA	572.5	184	1536	63	24.38	6-70	3	—
Greenidge, C. G. (H)	RM	1	0	4	0	—	—	—	—
Greig, A. W. (E/Sx)	RM/OB	313.2	90	850	35	24.28	4-22	—	—
Greig, I. A. (CU)	RM	210	34	685	18	38.05	4-76	—	—
Griffiths, B. J. (No)	RM	169	44	488	17	28.70	5-69	1	—
Gurr, D. R. (OU/So)	RFM	331	70	912	36	25.33	5-42	2	—
Hacker, P. J. (Nt)	LFM	262.3	54	846	20	42.30	3-27	—	—
Hampshire, J. H. (Y)	LBG	2	0	17	0	—	—	—	—
Hansell, T.M.G. (Sy)	SLA	4	4	0	0	—	—	—	—
Hardie, B. R. (Ex)	RM	1	0	2	0	—	—	—	—
Harrison, S. C. (Gm)	RM	20	6	59	1	59.00	1-59	—	—
Harvey-Walker, A. J. (D)	OB	136.2	29	406	7	58.00	2-45	—	—
Hayes, P. J. (CU)	RM	210	54	527	19	27.73	4-53	—	—
Hector, P. A. (Ex)	RM	56	7	190	7	27.14	3-56	—	—
Hemmings, E.E. (Wa)	OB	576.1	155	1690	46	36.73	6-82	2	1
Hemsley, E.J.O. (Wo)	RM	39	4	118	2	59.00	2-65	—	—
Henderson, S.P. (Wo)	RM	2	0	9	0	—	—	—	—
Hendrick, M. (E/D/MCC)	RFM	562.3	189	1068	67	15.94	6-19	2	—
Herman, R. S. (H)	RFM	14	1	48	0	—	—	—	—
Higgs, K. (Le)	RFM	449.1	119	1001	38	26.34	5-45	2	—
Hignell, A.J.(CU/Gs)	RM	6.5	1	18	0	—	—	—	—
Hill, A. (D)	OB	3.2	0	14	0	—	—	—	—
Hills, R. W. (K)	RM	215.3	60	566	33	17.15	5-44	1	—
Hodgson, A. (No)	RFM	321.4	75	965	35	27.57	4-15	—	—
Hogg, W. (La)	RFM	93.2	20	303	7	43.28	3-48	—	—
Holder, V. A. (Wo)	RFM	639.5	151	1653	69	23.95	7-117	5	—
Hookes, D. W. (Aus)	SLA	4	0	18	1	18.00	1-17	—	—
Hopkins, D. C. (Wa)	RM	53	1†	124	6	20.66	3-40	—	—
Hopkins, J. A. (Gm)		2	1	2	0	—	—	—	—
Howarth, G. P. (Sy)	OB	8	1	35	0	—	—	—	—
Howat, M. G. (CU)	RM	135	24	395	8	49.37	3-39	—	—
Hughes, D. P. (La)	SLA	154	40	401	18	22.27	4-9	—	—
Illingworth, R. (Le)	OB	388.4	143	777	37	21.00	5-32	1	—
Imran Khan (Sx)	RF	203	50	551	25	22.04	5-51	1	—

172

	Type	Overs	Mds	Runs	Wkt	Avge	Best	5 wI	10 wM
Inchmore, J. D. (Wo)	RFM	244.2	55	685	33	20.75	8–58	2	1
Intikhab Alam (Sy)	LBG	387.3	110	1214	28	43.35	4–21	—	—
Jackman, R. D. (Sy)	RFM	585	102	1882	75	25.09	6–50	2	1
Jarvis, K. B. S. (K)	RFM	440.4	107	1304	55	23.70	7–58	3	—
Javed Miandad (Sx)	LBG	157	28	602	16	37.62	4–10	—	—
Jennings, K. F. (So)	RM	139.3	41	386	8	48.25	3–23	—	—
Jesty, T. E. (H)	RM	260	72	692	18	38.44	3–62	—	—
Johnson, G. W. (K)	OB	148	42	441	12	36.75	5–77	1	—
Johnson, P. D. (Nt)	LB	0.1	0	0	0	—	—	—	—
Jones, A. (Gm)	OB	2.4	2	4	0	—	—	—	—
Jones, A. A. (M/MCC)	RFM	139.4	32	421	21	20.04	4–27	—	—
Julien, B. D. (K)	LM	421.4	119	1076	37	29.08	4–42	—	—
Kallicharran, A. I. (Wa)	LB	2	0	7	0	—	—	—	—
Kanhai, R. B. (Wa)	RM	28	6	90	3	30.00	2–33	—	—
Kemp, N. J. (K)	RM	19	7	48	0	—	—	—	—
Ker, J. E. (Sc)	RM	18	7	17	1	17.00	1–17	—	—
King, C. L. (Gm)	RM	259.1	58	730	20	36.50	4–31	—	—
Knight, R. D. V. (Sx)	RM	170	36	573	16	35.81	3–22	—	—
Lamb, T. M. (M)	RM	62	15	151	3	50.33	1–12	—	—
Larkins, W. (No)	RM	40	10	135	1	135.00	1–51	—	—
Lee, P. G. (La/MCC)	RFM	607.5	125	1745	73	23.90	7–24	3	3
Lever, J. K. (E/Ex)	LFM	504.4	123	1303	58	22.46	6–34	4	—
Lloyd, B. J. (Gm)	OB	155	46	434	11	39.45	2–31	—	—
Lloyd, D. (La)	SLA	21	7	57	1	57.00	1–26	—	—
Long, A. (Sx)	RM	1	0	2	0	—	—	—	—
Lyons, K. J. (Gm)	RM	12.1	3	47	1	47.00	1–43	—	—
McCosker, R.B. (Aus)	RM	2	1	5	0	—	—	—	—
McEvoy, M.S.A. (Ex)	RM	3	1	4	0	—	—	—	—
McEwan, K. S. (Ex)	OB	3	1	8	0	—	—	—	—
Mack, A. J. (Sy)	LM	135	11	539	5	107.80	2–50	—	—
McKiddie, G. T. (Sc)	OB	13	3	41	2	20.50	1–3	—	—
McPherson, T. I. (Sc)	SLA	31.2	9	74	5	14.80	4–74	—	—
MacVicar, A. D. L. (CU)	RM	49	10	141	2	70.50	2–82	—	—
Malone, M. F. (Aus)	RFM	327	95	837	32	26.15	5–63	1	—
Marks, V. J. (OU/So)	OB	437	142	1170	32	36.56	5–50	1	—
Marsh, R. W. (Aus)	RM	1	0	6	0	—	—	—	—
Miller, G. (E/D/MCC)	OB	655.4	224	1551	87	17.82	7–54	4	1
Monteith, J. D. (Ire)	SLA	77	42	97	8	12.12	5–54	1	—
Morris, A. (D)	LB	5.3	0	43	0	—	—	—	—
Moseley, H. R. (So)	RFM	451.2	107	1089	42	25.92	4–50	—	—
Moylan, A.C.D. (CU)	SLA	3	0	3	0	—	—	—	—
Murtagh, A. J. (H)	RM	19	5	66	1	66.00	1–38	—	—
Mushtaq Mohammad (No)	LBG	286.4	71	870	27	32.22	6–63	1	—
Nash, M. A. (Gm)	LM	646.3	176	1970	81	24.32	6–102	4	—
Needham, A. (Sy)	OB	137.4	44	338	7	48.28	3–25	—	—
O'Keeffe, K. J. (Aus)	LBG	335.4	112	1035	36	28.75	4–21	—	—
Old, C. M. (E/Y)	RFM	280.4	69	680	30	22.66	6–36	1	—
Oldham, S. (Y)	RM	28.4	10	81	0	—	—	—	—
Oliver, P. R. (Wa)	RM	37	7	101	0	—	—	—	—
Ontong, R. C. (Gm)	RFM	248.1	47	851	25	34.04	5–71	1	—

	Type	Overs	Mds	Runs	Wkt	Avge	Best	5wI	10wM
O'Riordan, A. J. (Ire)	LM	28	8	54	2	27.00	2-50	—	—
Parker, P. W. G. (CU/Sy)	RM	1	0	2	0	—	—	—	—
Partridge, B. J. M. (OU)	RM	58	16	170	4	42.50	2-38	—	—
Partridge, M. D. (Gs)	RM	20.2	5	58	3	19.33	2-9	—	—
Pascoe, L. S. (Aus)	RF	323.4	79	893	41	21.78	6-68	1	—
Patel, D. N. (Wo)	OB	75.4	13	236	5	47.20	2-73	—	—
Payne, I. R. (Sy)	RM	39	6	192	1	192.00	1-11	—	—
Perryman, S. P. (Wa)	RM	738.3	198	1928	73	26.41	7-66	5	1
Phillipson, C.P. (Sx)	RM	67.3	14	196	5	39.20	2-48	—	—
Pocock, N. E. J. (H)	LM	6	3	7	0	—	—	—	—
Pocock, P. I. (Sy)	OB	574.5	163	1521	38	40.02	6-80	1	—
Pont, K. R. (Ex)	RM	186	27	599	20	29.95	4-100	—	—
Popplewell, N. F. M. (CU)	RM	104	27	336	4	84.00	2-64	—	—
Pridgeon, A. P. (Wo)	RM	180.5	28	568	13	43.69	3-28	—	—
Procter, M. J. (Gs)	RF/OB	777.3	226	1967	109	18.04	7-35	9	1
Randall, D. W. (E/Nt/MCC)	RM	1	0	1	0	—	—	—	—
Ratcliffe, R. M. (La)	RM	5	2	9	0	—	—	—	—
Rice, C. E. B. (Nt)	RFM	395.1	98	1113	50	22.26	6-16	3	—
Rice, J. M. (H)	RM	484	139	1294	44	29.40	7-48	2	—
Richards, B. A. (H)	OB	20	3	93	0	—	—	—	—
Richards, G. (Gm)	OB	288.2	52	927	10	92.70	2-18	—	—
Richards, I.V.A. (So)	OB	89.5	24	248	7	35.42	3-15	—	—
Roberts, A. M. E. (H)	RF	349.2	109	793	40	19.82	5-32	2	—
Robertson, F. (Sc)	RM	33.1	13	57	6	9.50	3-20	—	—
Robinson, A. L. (Y)	RFM	480.1	139	1115	44	25.34	5-28	2	—
Robinson, P. J. (So)	SLA	13	3	32	3	10.66	2-7	—	—
Rock, D. J. H.	RM	1	1	0	0	—	—	—	—
Roebuck, P. M. (CU/So)	OB	276.5	87	703	23	30.56	6-50	1	—
Roope, G.R.J (E/Sy)	RM	51.3	7	155	3	51.66	1-20	—	—
Rose, B. C. (Sc/MCC)	LM	10	1	52	0	—	—	—	—
Ross, N. P. D. (M)	RM	7	1	13	0	—	—	—	—
Rouse, S. J. (Wa)	LM	432	105	1325	49	27.04	5-22	2	—
Rowe, C.J. C. (K)	OB	192.5	49	545	15	36.33	5-85	1	—
Russell, P. E. (D)	RM/OB	18	8	15	1	15.00	1-15	—	—
Sadiq Mohammad (Gs)	LBG	84.4	22	288	4	72.00	2-14	—	—
Sarfraz Nawaz (No)	RFM	486.4	130	1246	73	17.06	7-37	4	—
Savage, R. L. (OU/Wa)	RM/OB	542.1	112	1686	59	28.57	7-50	3	—
Selvey, M.W.W. (M)	RFM	629.1	158	1540	78	19.74	5-19	3	—
Shackleton, J.H. (Gs)	RM	231	54	715	12	59.58	2-19	—	—
Sharp, K. (Y)	OB	4	1	21	0	—	—	—	—
Shepherd, D. R. (Gs)	RM	1	0	8	0	—	—	—	—
Shepherd, J. N. (K)	RM	738.4	216	1734	87	19.93	8-83	6	—
Shuttleworth, K. (Le)	RFM	293.4	57	825	40	20.62	6-17	3	—
Sidebottom, A. (Y)	RFM	145	23	448	13	34.46	3-52	—	—
Silvester, S. (Y)	RF	65.4	8	240	9	26.66	4-86	—	—
Simmons, J. (La)	OB	592.2	199	1313	61	21.52	6-74	3	—
Siviter, K. (OU)	RM	19.1	3	84	2	42.00	2-64	—	—

174

	Type	Overs	Mdns	Runs	Wkts	Avge	Best	5 wI	10 wM
Slocombe, P. A. (So)	OB	3	1	14	0	—	—	—	—
Smedley, M. J. (Nt)	OB	1	1	0	0	—	—	—	—
Smith, D. M. (Sy)	RM	19	4	77	0	—	—	—	—
Smith, M. J. (M)	SLA	2	0	2	0	—	—	—	—
Snow, J. A. (Sx)	RFM	459.4	112	1287	44	29.25	6–70	1	—
Southern, J. W. (H)	SLA	671.1	217	1660	53	31.32	6–81	2	—
Spencer, J. (Sx)	RM	516.2	160	1231	51	24.13	6–40	3	—
Steele, D. S. (No)	SLA	29.3	11	68	1	68.00	1–0	—	—
Steele, J. F. (Le)	SLA	195	67	446	12	37.16	3–19	—	—
Stevenson, G. B. (Y)	RM	546.5	122	1772	69	25.68	6–82	2	1
Stevenson, K. (D)	RFM	190.5	38	550	26	21.15	7–68	1	—
Stovold, A. W. (Gs)		3	0	15	0	—	—	—	—
Sullivan, J. P. (Gs)	RM	11	2	50	2	25.00	2–50	—	—
Swarbrook, F. W. (D)	SLA	548.5	214	1161	39	29.76	5–70	1	—
Swindell, R. S. (D)	OB	7	1	33	0	—	—	—	—
Taylor, L. B. (Le)	RM	61	18	140	3	46.66	2–39	—	—
Taylor, M.N.S. (H)	RM	394.5	114	1147	42	27.30	7–23	1	—
Taylor, W. (Nt)	RFM	106	22	331	8	41.37	3–43	—	—
Thomas, D. J. (Sy)	LM	37	10	101	1	101.00	1–88	—	—
Thomson, J. R.(Aus)	RF	383.2	84	1207	43	28.06	4–41	—	—
Tolchard, R. W. (Le)	RM	2	0	6	0	—	—	—	—
Tremlett, T. M. (H)	RM	7	3	13	1	13.00	1–0	—	—
Tunnicliffe, C. J. (D)	LFM	544.1	142	1360	57	23.85	4–22	—	—
Tunnicliffe, H. T. (Nt)	RM	17	3	79	0	—	—	—	—
Turner, D. R. (H)	RM	2	0	4	0	—	—	—	—
Turner, S. (Ex)	RFM	718.4	187	1784	77	23.16	6–26	6	—
Underwood, D. L. (E/K)	LM	436.2	164	896	46	19.47	7–43	3	—
Vernon, M. J. (Gs)	RFM	54.5	7	217	3	72.33	1–21	—	—
Verrinder, A.O.C. (K)	RFM	8	0	39	0	—	—	—	—
Virgin, R. T. (No)	LB	1.4	1	7	0	—	—	—	—
Walker, M.H.N. (Aus)	RFM	514	154	1184	53	22.33	7–19	3	—
Waller, C. E. (Sx)	SLA	234.2	54	755	20	37.75	4–48	—	—
Walters, J. (D)	RFM	24	4	99	1	99.00	1–37	—	—
Walters, K. D. (Aus)	RM	17	5	30	0	—	—	—	—
Ward, A. (Le)	RF	316.5	62	956	33	28.96	4–37	—	—
White, R. A. (Nt)	OB	660.4	179	1721	55	31.26	6–49	3	—
Whitehouse, J. (Wa)	OB	46.3	11	144	2	72.00	2–55	—	—
Wilcock, H. G. (Wo)		2	1	3	0	—	—	—	—
Wilkins, A. H. (Gm)	LM	356.1	73	1103	47	23.46	5–58	2	—
Wilkinson, P. A. (Nt)	RM	351	100	877	30	29.23	6–81	1	—
Willey, P. (No)	OB	523	142	1226	45	27.24	5–14	2	—
Williams, R. G. (No)	OB	10	3	49	0	—	—	—	—
Willis, R. G. D. (E/Wa)	RF	399	94	1183	58	20.39	8–32	5	1
Wilson, J. D. (OU)	LB	3	0	6	0	—	—	—	—
Wingfield Digby, A. R. (OU)	RM	200	55	582	16	36.37	5–86	1	—
Wood, B. (La)	RM	120.3	40	306	15	20.40	6–19	1	—
Woolmer, R. A. (E/K)	RM	134.1	50	289	19	15.21	3–7	—	—
Younis Ahmed (Sy)	LM	30	13	80	3	26.66	2–42	—	—
Zaheer Abbas (Gs)	OB	9	3	23	0	—	—	—	—

There was an all-rounder called Pete,
The cleverest man you could meet.
His strokes were so deft
Batting right, he bowled left,
And shaved with the soles of his
feet.

(Naturally, being so clever he used a Techmatic razor automatically winding on a new edge when it was needed).

CAREER FIGURES FOR THE LEADING PLAYERS

The following are the abbreviated figures of the leading batsmen and bowlers based on their career averages, and fielders and wicket-keepers based on the number of their catches and dismissals. The figures are complete to the end of the 1977 season and the full career records will be found in the main table on pages 178 to 193. The qualification for inclusion for batsmen and bowlers are 100 innings and 100 wickets respectively.

Only those players likely to play in first-class county cricket in 1978 have been included.

BATTING AND FIELDING

BATSMEN	Runs	Avge	100s	BOWLERS	Wkts	Avge
G. Boycott	31,590	57.22	100	W. W. Daniel	147	18.53
B. A. Richards	26,596	56.27	79	M. J. Procter	1,059	18.93
C. H. Lloyd	20,277	50.81	53	T. W. Cartwright	1,536	19.11
Zaheer Abbas	18,269	50.18	55	R. Illingworth	2,006	19.86
R. B. Kanhai	28,639	49.29	83	D. L. Underwood	1,624	19.90
I. V. A. Richards	11,394	48.69	33	A. M. E. Roberts	491	20.19
G. M. Turner	25,417	47.86	67	N. Gifford	1,433	21.30
J. H. Edrich	39,057	45.89	102	D. R. Doshi	389	21.44
D. L. Amiss	26,336	42.61	61	M. Hendrick	436	21.75
A. I. Kallicharran	13,219	42.50	29	G. G. Arnold	936	21.87
Javed Miandad	5,412	41.31	14	G. Miller	251	22.27
C. G. Greenidge	13,257	41.29	30	F. J. Titmus	2,811	22.30
B. L. D'Oliveira	17,897	39.68	41	C. M. Old	606	22.58
E. J. Barlow	15,565	39.50	38	J. A. Snow	1,174	22.72
K. W. R. Fletcher	26,388	38.46	47	D. S. Steele	235	22.77

FIELDERS	Ct	WICKET-KEEPERS	Total	Ct	St
F. J. Titmus	470	R. W. Taylor	1,173	1,044	129
K. W. R. Fletcher	440	A. P. E. Knott	1,032	928	104
R. Illingworth	427	A. Long	923	809	114
G. R. J. Roope	423	R. W. Tolchard	749	661	88
B. W. Luckhurst	392	E. W. Jones	684	612	72
M. H. Denness	385	G. R. Stephenson	551	488	63
D. S. Steele	383	D. L. Bairstow	473	408	65
B. A. Richards	346	D. J. S. Taylor	459	408	51
A. W. Greig	341	G. Sharp	353	294	59
J. H. Hampshire	337	D. Nicholls	339	326	13
C. T. Radley	337	N. Smith	265	231	34
T. W. Cartwright	332	M. J. Harris	260	246	14
G. M. Turner	323	H. G. Wilcock	190	173	17
R. B. Kanhai	315	G. W. Humpage	148	139	9
J. A. Ormrod	315	A. W. Stovold	138	116	22

CAREER RECORDS
Compiled by Michael Fordham

The following career records are for all players appearing in first-class cricket in the 1977 season. A few cricketers who did not reappear for their counties in this season, but who may do so in 1978, are also included as well as others who appeared only in John Player League matches.

BATTING AND FIELDING

	M	I	NO	Runs	HS	Avge	100s	Ct	St
Abberley, R. N.	240	405	23	9378	117*	24.54	3	162	
Abrahams, J.	64	93	15	1887	101*	24.19	1	38	
Acfield, D. L.	226	247	118	1185	42	9.18	—	79	
Allbrook, M. E.	30	41	13	244	39	8.71	—	14	
Amiss, D. L.	414	705	87	26336	262*	42.61	61	270	
Anderson, I. J.	13	24	6	668	147	37.11	2	7	
Arnold, G. G.	288	298	71	3206	73	14.12	—	101	
Arrowsmith, R.	22	23	4	117	30*	6.15	—	6	
Asif Iqbal	351	563	57	18607	196	36.77	33	261	
Athey, C. W. J.	26	38	3	752	131*	21.48	1	28	1
Bainbridge, P.	8	11	0	211	49	19.18	—	6	
Bairstow, D. L.	185	263	42	4454	106	20.15	2	408	65
Baker, R. P.	43	39	27	314	77*	26.16	—	20	
Balderstone, J. C.	185	227	30	7869	178*	31.85	12	92	
Bannister, C. S.	17	30	2	383	50	13.67	—	2	
Barclay, J. R. T.	90	157	9	3140	112	21.21	2	75	
Barlow, E. J.	238	415	21	15565	217	39.50	38	279	
Barlow, G. D.	87	141	18	3872	160*	31.47	6	47	
Beaumont, D. J.	7	10	0	168	44	16.80	—	2	
Bedi, B. S.	317	373	91	3125	61	11.08	—	147	
Birch, J. D.	36	55	7	717	86	14.93	—	22	
Birkenshaw, J.	435	601	105	11578	131	23.34	4	283	
Booth, P.	51	50	14	413	58*	11.47	—	19	
Border, A. R.	6	9	2	143	68	20.42	—	6	
Bore, M. K.	74	78	21	481	37*	8.43	—	27	
Borrington, A. J.	80	138	16	2905	115	23.81	2	45	
Botham, I. T.	77	127	15	2785	167*	24.86	2	64	
Bourne, W. A.	60	78	15	1325	107	21.03	1	39	
Boyce, K. D.	285	420	27	8800	147*	22.39	4	215	
Boycott, G.	393	651	99	31590	261*	57.22	100	165	
Boyns, C. N.	26	39	3	589	95	16.36	—	29	
Brain, B. M.	182	194	54	1069	57	7.63	—	38	
Brassington, A. J.	34	46	18	326	28	11.64	—	63	17
Breakwell, D.	165	222	44	3071	97	17.25	—	63	
Brearley, J. M.	334	577	71	18966	312*	37.48	29	306	12
Brettell, D. N.	10	15	4	126	39	11.45	—	3	
Briers, N. E.	16	30	3	653	87	24.18	—	4	
Bright, R. J.	58	81	18	1253	67	19.88	—	44	
Brown, A.	1	2	0	34	25	17.00	—	—	
Brown, D. J.	362	419	103	3829	79	12.11	—	148	
Bugge, D. A. B.	1	—	—	—	—	—	—	—	
Burgess, G. I.	235	389	32	6773	129	18.97	2	107	

	M	I	NO	Runs	HS	Avge	100s	Ct	St
Buss, M. A.	298	521	44	11540	159	24.19	11	218	—
Butcher, A. R.	88	135	11	2845	112	22.94	2	23	—
Butcher, R. O.	31	55	3	1235	74	23.75	—	28	—
Carrick, P.	99	122	17	1860	87	17.71	—	56	—
Cartwright, H.	56	89	12	1668	141*	21.66	1	23	—
Cartwright, T. W.	479	737	94	13710	210	21.32	7	332	—
Chappell, G. S.	248	425	58	18685	247*	50.91	54	278	—
Cheatle, R. G. L.	17	12	4	56	34	7.00	—	13	—
Childs, J. H.	40	38	23	70	12	4.66	—	17	—
Clapp, R. J.	15	16	5	49	32	4.45	—	1	—
Clark, J.	8	10	3	56	29	8.00	—	11	—
Claughton, J. A.	20	37	2	722	112	20.62	1	9	—
Clements, S. M.	18	28	2	440	91	16.92	—	16	—
Clift, P. B.	89	134	34	2080	75*	20.80	—	44	—
Clinton, G. S.	26	42	1	1029	88	25.09	—	8	—
Close, D. B.	780	1215	169	34824	198	33.29	52	808	1
Colhoun, O. D.	26	35	18	74	9*	4.35	—	43	1
Cook, G.	143	250	20	6048	126	26.29	5	160	—
Cooper, H. P.	69	87	23	879	56	13.73	—	46	—
Cooper, K.	20	23	5	89	18	4.94	—	6	—
Cooper, N. H. C.	11	19	1	342	106	19.00	1	3	—
Coote, D. E.	1	1	0	20	20	20.00	—	—	—
Cope, G. A.	195	218	72	2013	78	13.78	—	57	—
Cordle, A. E.	270	386	66	4745	81	14.82	—	120	—
Corlett, S. C.	22	35	6	440	60	15.17	—	18	—
Cosier, G. J.	50	87	3	2968	168	35.33	5	37	—
Coverdale, S. P.	40	72	6	1214	85	18.39	—	32	7
Cowdrey, C. S.	14	19	4	386	101*	25.73	1	8	—
Cowley, N. G.	44	66	13	1312	109*	24.75	1	17	—
Crawford, I. C.	3	4	0	15	12	3.75	—	5	—
Croft, C. E. H.	32	32	16	294	46*	18.37	—	10	—
Cross, G. F.	83	128	15	2079	78	18.39	—	61	—
Crowther, P. G.	5	7	0	138	99	19.71	—	2	—
Cumbes, J.	91	74	36	256	25*	6.73	—	20	—
Daniel, A. R. H.	4	5	0	96	75	19.20	—	—	—
Daniel, W. W.	44	34	13	194	30	9.23	—	9	—
Davey, J.	160	189	84	783	53*	7.45	—	28	—
Davies, R. J.	1	2	0	18	18	9.00	—	1	—
Davis, I. C.	64	109	6	3468	156	33.66	4	25	—
Davison, B. F.	241	396	38	13400	189	37.43	24	196	—
Denness, M. H.	438	735	57	23164	195	34.16	30	385	—
Denning, P. W.	138	237	20	5676	122	26.15	4	58	—
Dexter, R. E.	4	6	0	106	48	17.66	—	1	—
Dilley, G. R.	1	2	0	31	16	15.50	—	—	—
D'Oliveira, B. L.	337	533	82	17897	227	39.68	41	207	—
Doshi, D. R.	96	104	22	617	31*	7.52	—	27	—
Downton, P. R.	7	7	3	87	31*	21.75	—	18	4
Dredge, C. H.	27	39	14	395	56*	15.80	—	13	—
Dudleston, B.	223	377	42	11045	172	32.97	27	186	6
Dye, J. C. J.	266	247	125	778	29*	6.37	—	53	—
Dymock, G.	61	77	33	423	27	9.61	—	27	—
Ealham, A. G. E.	234	365	57	8391	134*	27.24	4	140	—

179

	M	I	NO	Runs	HS	Avge	100s	Ct	St
East, R. E.	280	361	87	4851	113	17.70	1	182	—
Edmonds, P. H.	151	224	34	3586	103*	18.87	1	158	—
Edrich, J. H.	546	950	99	39057	310*	45.89	102	302	—
Elder, J. W. G.	4	6	2	12	5	3.00	—	5	—
Elms, R. B.	69	71	23	510	31*	10.62	—	17	—
Emburey, J. E.	35	42	19	391	48	17.00	—	48	—
Featherstone, N. G.	240	391	39	10301	147	29.26	8	200	—
Finan, N. H.	5	3	1	22	18	11.00	—	1	—
Fisher, P. B.	31	51	5	396	42	8.60	—	52	6
Fletcher, K. W. R.	475	799	113	26388	228*	38.46	47	440	—
Flynn, V. A.	1	—	—	—	—	—	—	3	—
Foat, J. C.	62	104	9	1327	116	13.96	1	27	—
Fosh, M. K.	20	33	1	728	94	22.75	—	7	—
Francis, D. A.	60	107	15	1989	110	21.61	1	33	—
French, B. N.	21	28	11	146	24	8.58	—	28	5
Gard, T.	3	4	1	12	7	4.00	—	5	1
Garner, J.	18	22	5	337	44*	19.82	—	17	—
Gatting, M. W.	43	56	11	1632	94	29.14	1	42	—
Gifford, N.	471	564	168	5131	89	12.95	—	233	—
Gilliat, R. M. C.	253	414	37	11136	223*	29.53	18	208	—
Gooch, G. A.	84	139	13	3912	136	31.04	6	49	—
Gould, I. J.	33	47	9	577	47*	15.18	—	57	12
Gower, D. I.	35	52	6	1133	144*	24.63	2	14	—
Graham, J. N.	189	178	73	404	23	3.84	—	40	—
Graham-Brown, J. M. H.	19	20	5	159	29*	10.60	—	7	—
Graveney, D. A.	105	152	31	1760	62	14.54	—	48	—
Graves, P. J.	269	468	49	11312	145*	26.99	14	217	—
Greenidge, C. G.	196	342	21	13257	273*	41.29	30	191	—
Greig, A. W.	345	571	44	16538	226	31.38	26	341	—
Greig, I. A.	14	22	2	523	96	26.15	—	4	—
Griffiths, B. J.	17	20	9	9	6	0.81	—	4	—
Groome, J. J.	31	57	2	891	86	16.20	—	17	—
Gurr, D. R.	33	41	18	367	46*	15.95	—	8	—
Hacker, P. J.	26	34	13	283	35	13.47	—	6	—
Hampshire, J. H.	423	674	77	19404	183*	32.50	29	337	—
Hansell, T. M. G.	14	26	5	319	54	15.19	—	2	—
Hardie, B. R.	92	165	17	4391	162	29.66	5	74	—
Hare, W. H.	10	18	4	171	36	12.21	—	5	—
Harris, M. J.	278	474	42	15947	201*	36.91	36	246	14
Harrison, J.	8	15	1	309	100*	22.07	1	3	—
Harrison, S. C.	5	6	0	32	15	5.33	—	1	—
Harvey-Walker, A. J.	72	130	8	2956	117	24.22	3	27	—
Hassan, B.	224	377	35	10088	182*	29.49	13	200	1
Hayes, F. C.	173	272	37	8511	187	36.21	16	129	—
Hayes, P. J.	27	44	11	343	56*	10.39	—	19	—
Head, T. J.	2	3	1	13	9	6.50	—	8	—
Hector, P. A.	3	5	1	75	40	18.75	—	—	—
Hemmings, E. E.	165	239	55	4031	85	21.90	—	79	—
Hemsley, E. J. O.	142	237	34	5969	176*	29.40	5	101	—
Henderson, S. P.	8	13	2	172	52	15.63	—	1	—
Hendrick, M.	155	154	58	881	46	9.17	—	105	—
Herbert, R.	3	5	0	33	12	6.60	—	2	—

180

	M	I	NO	Runs	HS	Avge	100s	Ct	St
Herman, R. S.	189	189	49	1426	56	10.18	—	74	—
Higgs, K.	468	502	192	3535	98	11.40	—	277	—
Hignell, A. J.	62	109	7	2745	149	26.91	3	68	—
Hill, A.	101	183	15	4934	160*	29.36	6	37	—
Hills, R. W.	50	55	15	718	45	17.95	—	15	—
Hodgson, A.	84	101	18	848	41*	10.21	—	27	—
Hogg, W.	7	5	1	19	17	4.75	—	2	—
Holder, V. A.	266	300	70	2825	122	12.28	1	83	—
Hood, J. A.	2	3	0	9	7	3.00	—	1	—
Hookes, D. W.	33	51	2	2060	185	42.04	6	18	—
Hopkins, D. C.	2	2	1	23	13*	23.00	—	—	—
Hopkins, J. A.	67	117	9	2700	230	25.00	2	48	1
Howarth, G. P.	131	234	13	6353	159	28.74	9	84	—
Howat, M. G.	8	8	2	15	5	2.50	—	1	—
Howgego, J. A.	1	2	0	91	52	45.50	—	—	—
Hughes, D. P.	213	260	54	3832	101	18.60	1	124	—
Hughes, K. J.	32	51	2	1577	137*	32.18	3	24	—
Humpage, G. W.	57	90	13	2794	125*	36.28	3	139	9
Humphries, D. J.	27	41	8	587	62*	17.78	—	37	6
Illingworth, R.	736	1036	202	23768	162	28.49	22	427	—
Imran Khan	135	219	25	5726	170	29.51	10	54	—
Inchmore, J. D.	75	94	20	1006	113	13.59	1	27	—
Intikhab Alam	420	628	66	13024	182	23.01	9	207	—
Jackman, R. D.	281	335	111	3785	92*	16.89	—	124	—
Jarvis, K. B. S.	51	38	21	57	12*	3.35	—	18	—
Javed Miandad	84	147	16	5412	311	41.31	14	95	—
Jennings, K. F.	19	32	5	242	49	8.96	—	13	—
Jesty, T. E.	204	315	40	7486	159*	27.22	7	122	1
Johnson, C.	92	136	11	2670	107	21.36	2	45	—
Johnson, G. W.	208	349	22	8201	168	25.07	10	169	—
Johnson, P. D.	87	145	14	3273	106*	24.98	2	33	—
Jones, A.	508	927	58	28583	187*	32.89	43	253	—
Jones, A. A.	172	174	58	626	27	5.39	—	40	—
Jones, A. L.	23	41	1	774	57	19.35	—	3	—
Jones, B. J. R.	20	36	3	493	65	14.93	—	9	—
Jones, E. W.	287	434	94	6520	146*	19.17	2	612	72
Julien, B. D.	184	253	34	5552	127	25.35	3	111	—
Kallicharran, A. I.	209	341	30	13219	197	42.50	29	145	—
Kanhai, R. B.	413	663	82	28639	256	49.29	83	315	7
Kayum, D. A.	7	11	1	229	57	22.90	—	2	—
Kemp, N. J.	3	3	0	16	14	5.33	—	1	—
Kennedy, A.	67	109	11	2824	176*	28.81	3	53	—
Ker, J. E.	1	2	0	6	6	3.00	—	—	—
King, C. L.	59	99	16	3452	163	41.59	8	65	—
Kirsten, P. N.	33	60	4	2365	173*	42.23	8	25	—
Kirsten, P.N.	33	60	4	2365	173*	42.23	8	25	—
Kitchen, M. J.	334	582	30	14725	189	26.67	17	137	—
Knight, R. D. V.	224	403	27	11433	165*	30.40	16	168	—
Knott, A. P. E.	379	560	102	14000	156	30.56	16	928	104
Laing, J. R.	5	9	1	231	127*	28.87	1	4	—
Lamb, A.J.	19	34	8	1135	109	37.83	2	14	—

	M	I	NO	Runs	HS	Avge	100s	Ct	St
Lamb, T. M.	52	63	21	622	77	14.80	—	15	—
Larkins, W.	78	126	10	2395	167	20.64	5	37	—
Leadbeater, B.	141	230	27	5152	140*	25.37	1	79	—
Lee, P. G.	162	131	56	646	26	8.61	—	28	—
L'Estrange, M. G.	10	16	2	211	45	15.07	—	4	—
Lever, J. K.	253	277	122	1698	91	10.95	—	112	—
Littlewood, D. J.	1	—	—	—	—	—	—	2	1
Llewellyn, M. J.	82	137	16	2628	129*	21.71	2	61	—
Lloyd, B. J.	34	45	14	258	45*	8.32	—	21	—
Lloyd, C. H.	302	464	65	20277	242*	50.81	53	213	—
Lloyd, D.	290	465	55	13251	214*	32.31	21	260	—
Lloyd, T. A.	2	4	2	122	70*	61.00	—	—	—
Long, A.	399	477	109	6026	92	16.37	—	809	114
Love, J. D.	32	56	6	1409	163	28.18	2	19	—
Luckhurst, B. W.	388	660	76	22293	215	38.17	48	392	—
Lumb, R. G.	121	205	17	5553	132	29.53	9	77	—
Lynch, M. A.	5	10	0	170	44	17.00	—	—	—
Lyon, J.	44	44	7	436	60	11.78	—	80	7
Lyons, K. J.	62	99	14	1673	92	19.68	—	27	—
McCosker, R. B.	73	132	14	5100	164	43.22	15	71	—
McEvoy, M. S. A.	5	8	1	209	67*	29.85	—	5	—
McEwan, K. S.	133	233	19	7835	218	36.61	18	149	7
Mack, A. J.	10	9	0	42	16	4.66	—	—	—
McKiddie, G. T.	1	2	0	10	8	5.00	—	1	—
MacPhail, A. W.	4	8	1	63	37	9.00	—	6	—
McPherson, T. I.	1	2	1	47	28	47.00	—	—	—
MacVicar, A. D. L.	1	—	—	—	—	—	—	—	—
McVicker, N. M.	173	210	53	3108	83*	19.79	—	48	—
Malone, M. F.	30	32	11	406	46	19.33	—	16	—
Marks, V. J.	51	88	4	2358	105	28.07	1	22	—
Marsh, R. W.	171	266	28	7921	236	33.28	10	508	50
Matheson, J. A.	1	—	—	—	—	—	—	—	—
Mendis, G. D.	19	34	4	709	68*	23.63	—	9	1
Miller, G.	95	145	14	2909	86*	22.20	—	47	—
Monteith, J. D.	12	19	2	240	78	14.11	—	10	—
Morris, A.	42	70	4	1058	74	16.03	—	25	—
Moseley, H. R.	136	154	64	1116	67	12.40	—	50	—
Mottram, T. J.	35	35	18	95	15*	5.58	—	11	—
Moulding, R. P.	1	1	1	26	26*	—	—	—	—
Moylan, A. C. D.	5	9	0	176	29	19.55	—	1	—
Murtagh, A. J.	27	47	5	640	65	15.23	—	9	—
Mushtaq Mohammad	476	803	98	29896	303*	42.40	70	323	—
Nanan, N.	32	58	5	874	72	16.49	—	22	—
Nash, M. A.	242	347	53	5343	130	18.17	1	101	—
Neale, P. A.	34	63	3	1614	143	26.90	2	19	—
Needham, A.	7	7	1	48	15*	8.00	—	2	—
Nicholls, D.	202	342	24	7072	211	22.23	2	326	13
O'Brien, B. A.	6	10	0	155	45	15.50	—	3	—
O'Brien, G. P.	2	4	0	22	11	5.50	—	3	—
O'Keeffe, K. J.	167	231	73	4133	99*	26.15	—	111	—
Old, C. M.	218	281	53	5155	116	22.60	5	141	—
Oldham, S.	16	14	6	44	19	5.50	—	7	—

182

	M	I	NO	Runs	HS	Avge	100s	Ct	St
Olive, M.	3	5	1	24	15	6.00	—	4	—
Oliver, P. R.	19	30	6	494	59	20.58	—	10	—
Ontong, R. C.	44	74	4	1414	106	20.20	1	25	—
O'Riordan, A. J.	25	44	5	614	117	15.74	1	18	—
Ormrod, J. A.	356	600	70	15569	204*	29.37	17	315	—
Parker, P. W. G.	38	68	5	1801	215	28.58	4	19	—
Partridge, B. J. M.	4	6	4	5	4	2.50	—	—	—
Partridge, M. D.	5	7	2	66	23	13.20	—	2	—
Pascoe, L. S.	31	34	11	187	51*	8.13	—	9	—
Patel, D. N.	31	49	3	863	107	18.76	2	17	—
Pathmanathan, G.	29	53	2	1089	82	21.35	—	25	—
Payne, I. R.	7	9	1	63	29	7.87	—	2	—
Perryman, S. P.	60	64	29	466	43	13.31	—	20	—
Phillipson, C. P.	60	70	35	354	52	10.11	—	28	—
Pilling, H.	320	522	66	14974	149*	32.83	25	85	—
Plumb, S. G.	2	3	1	68	37*	34.00	—	1	—
Pocock, N. E. J.	10	18	3	374	68	24.93	—	2	—
Pocock, P. I.	367	412	96	3816	75*	12.07	—	128	—
Pont, K. R.	89	141	19	2958	113	24.24	4	48	—
Popplewell, N. F. M.	7	9	3	38	19*	6.33	—	2	—
Pridgeon, A. P.	49	47	23	184	26	7.66	—	13	—
Procter, M. J.	294	490	44	16298	254	36.54	39	254	—
Recionzer, T. B.	39	69	9	1270	91	21.16	—	33	—
Radley, C. T.	327	531	75	15803	171	34.65	24	337	—
Randall, D. W.	136	238	20	6699	204*	30.72	8	76	—
Ratcliffe, R. M.	41	42	12	381	47*	12.70	—	12	—
Reidy, B. W.	39	58	8	1240	80	24.80	—	25	—
Reith, M. S.	5	10	0	206	82	20.60	—	2	—
Rice, C. E. B.	132	224	29	6432	246	32.98	5	87	—
Rice, J. M.	83	120	10	1947	96*	17.70	—	83	—
Richards, B. A.	313	532	53	26956	356	56.27	79	346	—
Richards, C. J.	13	15	4	137	33*	12.45	—	25	6
Richards, G.	75	124	14	2447	102*	22.24	1	27	—
Richards, I. M.	5	6	2	101	50	25.25	—	2	—
Richards, I. V·A.	147	251	17	11394	291	48.69	33	133	—
Roberts, A. M. E.	120	144	39	1189	56*	11.32	—	25	14
Robertson, F.	6	9	0	60	12	6.66	—	1	—
Robinson, A. L.	84	69	31	365	30*	9.60	—	46	—
Robinson, P. J.	185	287	55	4936	140	21.27	3	171	—
Robinson, R. D.	73	115	25	3701	185	41.12	5	230	33
Rock, D. J.	14	25	0	523	114	20.92	2	5	—
Roebuck, P. M.	46	82	11	1936	158	27.26	3	22	—
Roope, G. R. J.	288	469	91	14100	171	37.30	20	423	1
Rose, B. C.	99	175	15	4820	205	30.12	9	42	—
Ross, N. P. D.	25	36	3	506	53	15.33	—	21	—
Rouse, S. J.	98	118	25	1445	93	15.53	—	48	—
Rowe, C. J. C.	59	86	21	1535	103	23.61	1	19	—
Russell, P. E.	147	191	42	1917	72	12.86	—	108	—
Sadiq Mahammad	225	395	22	13940	184*	37.37	29	187	—
Sarfraz Nawaz	171	231	45	3632	86	19.52	—	101	—
Savage, R. L.	32	36	15	118	22*	5.61	—	9	—
Schepens, M.	8	11	1	120	39	12.00	—	3	—

	M	I	NO	Runs	HS	Avge	100s	Ct	St
Scott, C. J.	3	3	0	16	10	5.33	—	3	2
Selvey, M. W. W.	143	141	60	774	42	9.55	—	37	—
Serjeant, C. S.	25	37	6	1393	159	44.93	3	16	—
Shackleton, J. H.	41	55	16	547	41*	14.02	—	31	—
Sharp, G.	150	217	45	3342	85	19.43	—	294	59
Sharp, K.	10	20	2	324	56	18.00	—	7	—
Shepherd, D. R.	258	442	37	10003	153	24.69	12	91	—
Shepherd, J. N.	281	413	63	8961	170	25.60	5	215	—
Short, J. F.	4	7	0	228	114	32.57	1	1	—
Shuttleworth, K.	211	214	74	2234	71	15.95	—	99	—
Sidebottom, A.	29	40	4	619	124	17.19	1	12	—
Silvester, S.	6	7	4	30	14	10.00	—	2	—
Simmons, J.	208	238	70	3446	112	20.51	1	156	—
Siviter, K.	16	28	9	138	26	7.26	—	3	—
Skinner, L. E.	79	127	17	2503	93	22.75	—	119	16
Slack, W. N.	3	5	0	65	30	13.00	—	—	—
Slocombe, P. A.	52	91	11	2231	132	27.88	2	29	—
Smedley, M. J.	325	557	71	15471	149	31.83	28	231	—
Smith, D. M.	39	57	14	934	102*	21.72	1	22	—
Smith, K. D.	40	70	5	1821	135	28.01	2	10	—
Smith, M. J.	374	629	73	17882	181	32.16	35	211	—
Smith, N.	109	149	31	2115	126	17.92	2	231	34
Snow, J. A.	346	451	110	4832	73*	14.17	—	125	—
Southern, J. W.	56	64	29	300	31*	8.57	—	15	—
Spencer, J.	173	239	65	2387	79	13.71	—	61	—
Stead, B.	232	253	77	2166	58	12.30	—	59	—
Steele, A.	9	18	0	447	97	24.83	—	6	1
Steele, D. S.	337	563	69	16193	140*	32.77	24	383	—
Steele, J. F.	194	324	35	8277	195	28.64	11	217	—
Stephenson, G. R.	209	271	53	3794	100*	17.40	1	488	63
Stevenson, G. B.	46	56	5	1011	83	19.82	—	25	—
Stevenson, K.	47	60	19	374	33	9.12	—	15	—
Stewart, D. E. R.	28	44	3	809	69	19.73	—	14	—
Stovold, A. W.	92	168	8	4512	196	28.20	4	116	22
Sullivan, J. P.	23	40	1	480	53	12.30	—	14	—
Swarbrook, F. W.	203	298	79	4456	90	20.34	—	128	—
Swindell, R. S.	23	32	11	242	38	11.52	—	11	—
Tavare, C. J.	50	87	11	2285	124*	30.06	3	44	—
Taylor, D. J. S.	198	291	59	5215	179	22.47	4	408	51
Taylor, L. B.	2	2	2	2	1*	—	—	—	—
Taylor, M. N. S.	322	444	102	6487	105	18.96	2	194	—
Taylor, R. W.	452	645	121	8891	97	16.96	—	1044	129
Taylor, W.	95	97	39	374	26*	6.44	—	14	—
Thomas, D. J.	2	3	1	14	14	7.00	—	—	—
Thomson, J. R.	65	74	15	801	61	13.57	—	24	—
Titmus, F. J.	783	1131	202	21530	137*	23.17	6	470	—
Todd, P. A.	61	109	5	2589	178	24.89	3	57	—
Tolchard, J. G.	77	108	16	1863	78	20.25	—	24	—
Tolchard, R. W.	341	470	133	10299	126*	30.56	8	661	88
Tomlins, K. P.	3	3	0	1	1	0.33	—	1	—
Tremlett, T. M.	2	3	1	19	14	9.50	—	1	—
Trim, G. E.	2	4	0	36	15	9.00	—	—	—
Tunnicliffe, C. J.	37	38	12	299	82*	11.50	—	16	—
Tunnicliffe, H. T.	24	42	9	789	87	23.90	—	8	—

	M	I	NO	Runs	HS	Avge	100s	Ct	St
Turner, D. R.	216	356	31	9269	181*	28.52	14	130	—
Turner, G. M.	351	612	81	25417	259	47.86	67	323	—
Turner, S.	219	323	60	5553	121	21.11	3	151	—
Underwood, D. L.	425	465	119	3121	80	9.02	—	184	—
Vernon, M. J.	22	27	5	146	27	6.63	—	5	—
Verrinder, A. O. C.	4	4	1	24	23	8.00	—	3	—
Virgin, R. T.	437	773	39	21930	179*	29.87	37	414	—
Walker, M. H. N.	111	145	37	1751	78*	16.21	—	37	—
Waller, C. E.	113	128	40	756	47	8.59	—	54	—
Walters, J.	5	4	0	63	28	15.75	—	—	—
Walters, K. D.	235	390	49	14802	253	43.40	43	136	—
Ward, A.	161	157	47	928	44	8.43	—	51	—
Watson, W. K.	19	25	13	93	18	7.75	—	4	—
Watts, P. J.	330	553	79	13721	145	28.94	10	254	—
Weir, R. S.	3	6	1	108	51	21.60	—	1	—
Wells, R. R. C.	7	11	1	158	85	15.80	—	3	—
Wessels, K. C.	34	59	10	2239	138*	45.69	3	17	—
White, R. A.	394	623	102	12222	116*	23.45	5	180	—
Whitehouse, J.	124	214	18	6600	173	33.67	13	98	—
Wilcock, H. G.	98	136	31	1697	74	16.16	—	173	17
Wilkins, A. H.	23	25	7	175	70	9.72	—	5	—
Wilkinson, P. A.	92	117	38	949	77	12.01	—	28	—
Willey, P.	217	357	47	7655	227	24.69	9	94	—
Williams, D. L.	151	146	73	403	37*	5.52	—	38	—
Williams, R. G.	25	43	4	567	64	14.53	—	10	—
Willis, R. G. D.	154	163	80	1246	43	15.01	—	75	—
Wilson, J. D.	1	2	0	19	18	9.50	—	—	—
Wingfield Digby, A. R.	39	62	4	720	69	12.41	—	20	—
Wood, B.	263	436	54	12889	198	33.74	21	209	—
Woolmer, R. A.	223	331	56	8783	149	31.93	17	146	—
Wright, J. G.	34	60	4	1785	151	31.87	1	24	—
Yardley, T. J.	172	262	43	5454	135	24.90	4	145	2
Younis Ahmed	292	502	66	15753	183*	36.13	23	165	—
Zaheer Abbas	240	409	45	18269	274	50.18	55	182	—

BOWLING

	Runs	Wkts	Avge	BB	5 wI	10 wM	100 wS
Abberley, R. N.	285	4	71.25	2–19	—	—	—
Abrahams, J.	28	0	—	—	—	—	—
Acfield, D. L.	15302	542	28.23	7–36	19	2	—
Allbrook, M. E.	2382	46	51.78	4–26	—	—	—
Amiss, D. L.	680	18	37.77	3–21	—	—	—
Anderson, I. J.	180	16	11.25	5–21	1	—	—

185

	Runs	Wkts	Avge	BB	5 wI	10 wM	100 wS
Arnold, G. G.	20471	936	21.87	8–41	40	3	1
Arrowsmith, R.	1591	62	25.66	6–29	4	—	—
Asif Iqbal	8231	278	29.60	6–45	5	—	—
Athey, C. W. J.	9	1	9.00	1–9	—	—	—
Bainbridge, P.	—	—	—	—	—	—	—
Bairstow, D. L.	102	3	34.00	3–82	—	—	—
Baker, R. P.	2369	87	27.22	6–29	1	—	—
Balderstone, J. C.	5091	207	24.59	6–84	3	—	—
Bannister, C. S.	813	19	42.78	5–50	1	—	—
Barclay, J. R. T.	2622	82	31.97	6–94	3	1	—
Barlow, E. J.	12222	488	25.04	7–24	14	2	—
Barlow, G. D.	13	1	13.00	1–6	—	—	—
Beaumont, D. J.	—	—	—	—	—	—	—
Bedi, B. S.	29286	1377	21.26	7–5	93	17	2
Birch, J. D.	1434	33	43.45	6–64	1	—	—
Birkenshaw, J.	27003	1008	26.78	8–94	44	4	2
Booth, P.	2758	104	26.51	4–18	—	—	—
Border, A. R.	124	5	24.80	2–26	—	—	—
Bore, M. K.	4866	162	30.03	7–63	4	—	—
Borrington, A. J.	19	0	—	—	—	—	—
Botham, I. T.	6306	246	25.63	6–16	12	2	—
Bourne, W. A.	4164	128	32.53	6–47	2	—	—
Boyce, K. D.	21324	852	25.02	9–61	35	7	—
Boycott, G.	993	23	43.17	3–47	—	—	—
Boyns, C. N.	1038	23	45.13	3–24	—	—	—
Brain, B. M.	15032	626	24.01	8–55	26	6	—
Brassington, A. J.	10	0	—	—	—	—	—
Breakwell, D.	8940	293	30.51	8–39	9	1	—
Brearley, J. M.	103	1	103.00	1–21	—	—	—
Brettell, D. N.	510	15	34.00	3–49	—	—	—
Briers, N. E.	—	—	—	—	—	—	—
Bright, R. J.	4146	162	25.59	6–61	8	—	—
Brown, A.	—	—	—	—	—	—	—
Brown, D. J.	26944	1100	24.49	8–60	43	5	—
Bugge, D. A. B.	22	0	—	—	—	—	—
Burgess, G. I.	12645	447	28.28	7–43	17	2	—
Buss, M. A.	14600	516	28.29	7–58	18	—	—
Butcher, A. R.	2661	76	35.01	6–48	1	—	—
Butcher, R. O.	30	0	—	—	—	—	—
Carrick, P.	7786	299	26.04	8–33	14	1	—
Cartwright, H.	10	0	—	—	—	—	—
Cartwright, T. W.	29357	1536	19.11	8–39	94	18	8
Chappell, G. S.	6974	239	29.17	7–40	5	—	—
Cheatle, R. G. L.	974	32	30.43	6–54	2	—	—
Childs, J. H.	2989	95	31.46	5–39	3	—	—
Clapp, R. J.	734	25	29.36	3–15	—	—	—
Clark, J.	509	22	23.13	4–10	—	—	—
Claughton, J. A.	4	0	—	—	—	—	—
Clements, S. M.	45	0	—	—	—	—	—
Clift, P. B.	6232	252	24.73	8–17	9	—	—
Clinton, G. S.	1	0	—	—	—	—	—
Close, D. B.	30805	1166	26.41	8–41	43	3	2

	Runs	Wkts	Avge	BB	5 wI	10 wM	100 wS
Colhoun, O. D.	—	—	—	—	—	—	—
Cook, G.	50	0	—	—	—	—	—
Cooper, H. P.	4520	174	25.97	8–62	3	1	—
Cooper, K.	1539	53	29.03	5–24	1	—	—
Cooper, N. H. C.	35	1	35.00	1–4	—	—	—
Coote, D. E.	—	—	—	—	—	—	—
Cope, G. A.	13661	585	23.35	8–73	34	6	—
Cordle, A. E.	16443	614	26.78	9–49	17	2	—
Corlett, S. C.	1507	38	39.65	5–62	1	—	—
Cosier, G. J.	1020	41	24.87	3–20	—	—	—
Coverdale, S. P.	0	1	0.00	1–0	—	—	—
Cowdrey, C. S.	54	1	54.00	1–30	—	—	—
Cowley, N. G.	1954	46	42.47	5–94	1	—	—
Crawford, I. C.	137	3	45.66	1–18	—	—	—
Croft, C. E. H.	2667	107	24.92	8–29	4	1	—
Cross, G. F.	2756	92	29.95	4–28	—	—	—
Crowther, P. G.	22	1	22.00	1–22	—	—	—
Cumbes, J.	6250	236	26.48	6–24	9	—	—
Daniel, A. R. H.	—	—	—	—	—	—	—
Daniel, W. W.	2725	147	18.53	6–21	9	3	—
Davey, J.	10820	381	28.39	6–95	9	—	—
Davies, R. J.	—	—	—	—	—	—	—
Davis, I. C.	—	—	—	—	—	—	—
Davison, B. F.	2497	81	30.82	5–52	1	—	—
Denness, M. H.	62	2	31.00	1–7	—	—	—
Denning, P. W.	45	1	45.00	1–4	—	—	—
Dexter, R. E.	—	—	—	—	—	—	—
Dilley, G. R.	23	0	—	—	—	—	—
D'Oliveira, B. L.	14251	521	27.35	6–29	16	2	—
Doshi, D. R.	8342	389	21.44	7–29	20	2	—
Downton, P. R.	—	—	—	—	—	—	—
Dredge, C. H.	1844	46	40.08	4–42	—	—	—
Dudleston, B.	749	22	34.04	4–6	—	—	—
Dye, J. C. J.	17287	725	23.84	7–45	22	2	—
Dymock, G.	5466	223	24.51	5–24	5	—	—
Ealham, A. G. E.	94	2	47.00	1–1	—	—	—
East, R. E.	17843	688	25.93	8–30	31	6	—
Edmonds, P. H.	13098	518	25.28	8–132	23	4	—
Edrich, J. H.	53	0	—	—	—	—	—
Elder, J. W. G.	131	7	18.71	3–56	—	—	—
Elms, R. B.	4517	115	39.27	5–38	4	—	—
Emburey, J. E.	2830	119	23.78	7–36	10	3	—
Featherstone, N. G.	3221	127	25.36	5–58	2	—	—
Finan, N. H.	252	4	63.00	2–57	—	—	—
Fisher, P. B.	—	—	—	—	—	—	—
Fletcher, K. W. R.	1510	32	47.18	4–50	—	—	—
Flynn, V. A.	—	—	—	—	—	—	—
Foat, J. C.	16	0	—	—	—	—	—
Fosh, M. K.	—	—	—	—	—	—	—
Francis, D. A.	6	0	—	—	—	—	—
French, B. N.	—	—	—	—	—	—	—

	Runs	Wkts	Avge	BB	5 wI	10 wM	100 wS
Gard, T.	—	—		—	—	—	—
Garner, J.	1899	89	21.33	8–31	3	—	—
Gatting, M. W.	735	24	30.62	3–15	—	—	—
Gifford, N.	30528	1433	21.30	8–28	71	11	3
Gilliat, R. M. C.	157	3	52.33	1–3	—	—	—
Gooch, G. A.	945	23	41.08	5–40	1	—	—
Gould, I. J.	—	—		—	—	—	—
Gower, D. I.	59	3	19.66	3–47	—	—	—
Graham, J. N.	13722	614	22.34	8–20	26	3	1
Graham-Brown, J.M.H.	358	5	71.60	1–4	—	—	—
Graveney, D. A.	7643	282	27.10	8–85	12	2	—
Graves, P. J.	797	15	53.13	3–69	—	—	—
Greenidge, C. G.	413	15	27.53	5–49	1	—	—
Greig, A. W.	24381	850	28.68	8–25	33	8	—
Greig, I. A.	827	21	39.38	4–76	—	—	—
Griffiths, B. J.	1018	30	33.93	5–69	1	—	—
Groome, J. J.	0	0		—	—	—	—
Gurr, D. R.	2594	97	26.74	6–82	5	—	—
Hacker, P. J.	1751	36	48.63	3–27	—	—	—
Hampshire, J. H.	1540	27	57.03	7–52	2	—	—
Hansell, T. M. G.	0	0		—	—	—	—
Hardie, B. R.	21	0		—	—	—	—
Hare, W. H.	18	0		—	—	—	—
Harris, M. J.	3211	75	42.81	4–16	—	—	—
Harrison, J.	—	—		—	—	—	—
Harrison, S. C.	314	7	44.85	3–55	—	—	—
Harvey-Walker, A. J.	742	17	43.64	2–8	—	—	—
Hassan, B.	355	6	59.16	3–33	—	—	—
Hayes, F. C.	15	0		—	—	—	—
Hayes, P. J.	1832	51	35.92	5–48	1	—	—
Head, T. J.	—	—		—	—	—	—
Hector, P. A.	190	7	27.14	3–56	—	—	—
Hemmings, E. E.	13055	417	31.30	7–33	19	5	—
Hemsley, E. J. O.	2202	67	32.86	3–5	—	—	—
Henderson, S. P.	9	0		—	—	—	—
Hendrick, M.	9486	436	21.75	8–45	16	3	—
Herbert, R.	—	—		—	—	—	—
Herman, R. S.	13348	506	26.37	8–42	14	—	—
Higgs, K.	34115	1436	23.75	7–19	44	5	5
Hignell, A. J.	36	0		—	—	—	—
Hill, A.	53	3	17.66	3–5	—	—	—
Hills, R. W.	2730	107	25.51	5–44	1	—	—
Hodgson, A.	4794	178	26.93	5–30	2	—	—
Hogg, W.	367	8	45.87	3–48	—	—	—
Holder, V. A.	19945	849	23.49	7–40	37	3	—
Hood, J. A.	—	—		—	—	—	—
Hookes, D. W.	105	3	35.00	1–8	—	—	—
Hopkins, D. C.	124	6	20.66	3–40	—	—	—
Hopkins, J. A.	17	0		—	—	—	—
Howarth, G. P.	1841	56	32.87	5–32	1	—	—
Howat, M. G.	395	8	49.37	3–39	—	—	—
Howgego, J. A.	—	—		—	—	—	—
Hughes, D. P.	14144	488	28.98	7–24	18	2	—

188

	Runs	Wkt-	Avge	BB	5 wI	10 wM	100 wS
Hughes, K. J.	—	—	—	—	—	—	—
Humpage, G. W.	—	—	—	—	—	—	—
Humphries, D. J.	—	—	—	—	—	—	—
Illingworth, R.	39850	2006	19.86	9–42	102	11	10
Imran Khan	11759	447	26.30	7–53	24	5	—
Inchmore, J. D.	5417	202	26.81	8–58	7	1	—
Intikhab Alam	38425	1386	27.72	8–54	78	13	1
Jackman, R. D.	22677	959	23.64	8–40	42	7	—
Jarvis, K. B. S.	3928	134	29.31	7–58	3	—	—
Javed Miandad	3838	122	31.45	6–93	4	—	—
Jennings, K. F.	1053	18	58.50	3–23	—	—	—
Jesty, T. E.	9775	348	28.08	7–75	11	—	—
Johnson, C.	260	4	65.00	2–22	—	—	—
Johnson, G. W.	8522	260	32.77	6–35	6	1	—
Johnson, P. D.	972	11	88.36	3–34	—	—	—
Jones, A.	319	13	106.33	1–24	—	—	—
Jones, A. A.	12087	454	26.62	9–51	20	3	—
Jones, A. L.	13	0	—	—	—	—	—
Jones, B. J. R.	—	—	—	—	—	—	—
Jones, E. W.	5	0	—	—	—	—	—
Julien, B. D.	13016	454	28.66	7–63	14	—	—
Kallicharran, A. I.	929	17	54.64	2–22	—	—	—
Kanhai, R. B.	992	18	55.11	2–5	—	—	—
Kayum, D. A.	—	—	—	—	—	—	—
Kemp, N. J.	48	0	—	—	—	—	—
Kennedy, A.	—	—	—	—	—	—	—
Ker, J. E.	17	1	17.00	1–17	—	—	—
King, C. L.	2557	84	30.44	5–91	1	—	—
Kirsten, P. N.	73	4	18·25	2.15	—	—	—
Kitchen, M. J.	109	2	54.50	1–4	—	—	—
Knight, R. D. V.	8082	217	37.24	6–44	2	—	—
Knott, A. P. E.	77	1	77.00	1–40	—	—	—
Laing, J. R.	—	—	—	—	—	—	—
Lamb, A. J.	—	—	—	—	—	—	—
Lamb, T. M.	3400	125	27.20	6–49	6	—	—
Larkins, W.	407	13	31.30	3–34	—	—	—
Leadbeater, B.	5	1	5.00	1–1	—	—	—
Lee, P. G.	12983	529	24.54	8–53	26	6	2
L'Estrange, M. G.	—	—	—	—	—	—	—
Lever, J. K.	17594	695	25.31	8–127	24	1	—
Littlewood, D. J.	—	—	—	—	—	—	—
Llewellyn, M. J.	615	23	26.73	4–35	—	—	—
Lloyd, B. J.	1968	41	48.00	4–49	—	—	—
Lloyd, C. H.	4103	114	35.99	4–48	—	—	—
Lloyd, D.	4695	160	29.34	7–38	2	1	—
Lloyd, T. A.	—	—	—	—	—	—	—
Long, A.	2	0	—	—	—	—	—
Love, J. D.	—	—	—	—	—	—	—
Luckhurst, B. W.	2744	64	42.87	4–32	—	—	—
Lumb, R. G.	—	—	—	—	—	—	—

	Runs	Wkts	Avge	BB	5 wI	10 wM	100 wS
Lynch, M. A.	—	—	—	—	—	—	—
Lyon, J.	—	—	—	—	—	—	—
Lyons, K. J.	252	2	126.00	1–36	—	—	—
McCosker, R. B.	5	0	—	—	—	—	—
McEvoy, M. S. A.	4	0	—	—	—	—	—
McEwan, K. S.	87	2	43.50	1–0	—	—	—
Mack, A. J.	760	7	108.57	2–50	—	—	—
McKiddie, G. T.	41	2	20.50	1–3	—	—	—
MacPhail, A. W.	—	—	—	—	—	—	—
McPherson, T. I.	74	5	14.80	4–74	—	—	—
MacVicar, A. D. L.	141	2	70.50	2–82	—	—	—
McVicker, N. M.	11567	453	25.53	7–29	19	—	—
Malone, M. F.	2654	124	21.40	6–33	7	—	—
Marks, V. J.	2855	74	38.58	5–50	2	—	—
Marsh, R. W.	19	0	—	—	—	—	—
Matheson, J. A.	—	—	—	—	—	—	—
Mendis, G. D.	—	—	—	—	—	—	—
Miller, G.	5591	251	22.27	7–54	13	4	—
Monteith, J. D.	756	46	16.43	7–38	4	1	—
Morris, A.	60	0	—	—	—	—	—
Moseley, H. R.	8891	361	24.62	6–34	9	—	—
Mottram, T. J.	2677	111	24.11	6–63	4	—	—
Moulding, R. P.	—	—	—	—	—	—	—
Moylan, A. C. D.	3	0	—	—	—	—	—
Murtagh, A. J.	489	6	81.50	2–46	—	—	—
Mushtaq Mohammad	21432	895	23.94	7–18	38	2	—
Nanan, N.	322	9	35.77	3–12	—	—	—
Nash, M. A.	18471	748	24.69	9–56	36	3	—
Neale, P. A.	15	1	15.00	1–15	—	—	—
Needham, A.	338	7	48.28	3–25	—	—	—
Nicholls, D.	23	2	11.50	1–0	—	—	—
O'Brien, B. A.	—	—	—	—	—	—	—
O'Brien, G. P.	—	—	—	—	—	—	—
O'Keeffe, K. J.	13155	471	27.92	7–38	24	5	—
Old, C. M.	13685	606	22.58	7–20	21	1	—
Oldham, S.	915	33	27.72	5–47	1	—	—
Olive, M.	—	—	—	—	—	—	—
Oliver, P. R.	468	4	117.00	1–4	—	—	—
Ontong, R. C.	2881	99	29.10	7–60	4	—	—
O'Riordan, A. J.	1604	75	21.38	6–35	2	—	—
Ormrod, J. A.	1075	25	43.00	5–27	1	—	—
Parker, P. W. G.	120	1	120.00	1–3	—	—	—
Partridge, B. J. M.	170	4	42.50	2–38	—	—	—
Partridge, M. D.	120	6	20.00	2–9	—	—	—
Pascoe, L. S.	2821	116	24.31	6–20	4	—	—
Patel, D. N.	342	8	42.75	2–73	—	—	—
Pathmanathan, G.	26	0	—	—	—	—	—
Payne, I. R.	192	1	192.00	1–11	—	—	—
Perryman, S. P.	4300	163	26.38	7–66	8	1	—
Phillipson, C. P.	3820	115	33.21	6–56	4	—	—

	Runs	Wkts	Avge	BB	5 wI	10 wM	100 wS
Pilling, H.	195	1	195.00	1–42	—	—	—
Plumb, S. G.	47	2	23.50	2–47	—	—	—
Pocock, N. E. J.	68	1	68.00	1–40	—	—	—
Pocock, P. I.	28971	1120	25.86	7–57	39	5	1
Pont, K. R.	1433	44	32.56	4–100	—	—	—
Popplewell, N. F. M.	336	4	84.00	2–64	—	—	—
Pridgeon, A. P.	3361	75	44.81	7–35	2	1	—
Procter, M. J.	20056	1059	18.93	9–71	51	10	2
Racionzer, T. B.	5	0	—	—	—	—	—
Radley, C. T.	24	2	12.00	1–7	—	—	—
Randall, D. W.	80	0	—	—	—	—	—
Ratcliffe, R. M.	2538	95	26.71	7–67	9	1	—
Reidy, B. W.	89	1	89.00	1–58	—	—	—
Reith, M. S.	20	0	—	—	—	—	—
Rice, C. E. B.	8004	332	24.10	7–62	9	1	—
Rice, J. M.	5471	166	32.95	7–48	2	—	—
Richards, B. A.	2878	77	37.37	7–63	1	—	—
Richards, C. J.	—	—	—	—	—	—	—
Richards, G.	1343	20	67.15	4–55	—	—	—
Richards, I. M.	22	0	—	—	—	—	—
Richards, I. V. A.	2029	49	41.40	3–15	—	—	—
Roberts, A. M. E.	9917	491	20.19	8–47	24	2	1
Robertson, F.	393	24	16.37	6–58	1	—	—
Robinson, A. L.	4927	196	25.13	6–61	7	—	—
Robinson, P. J.	8101	297	27.27	7–10	10	1	—
Robinson, R. D.	—	—	—	—	—	—	—
Rock, D. J.	0	0	—	—	—	—	—
Roebuck, P. M.	1463	34	43.02	6–50	1	—	—
Roope, G. R. J.	7819	210	37.23	5–14	4	—	—
Rose, B. C.	134	5	26.80	3–9	—	—	—
Ross, N. P. D.	13	0	—	—	—	—	—
Rouse, S. J.	6608	234	28.23	6–34	5	—	—
Rowe, C. J. C.	1719	46	37.36	6–46	3	1	—
Russell, P. E.	9350	308	30.35	7–46	5	—	—
Sadiq Mohammad	5431	179	30.34	5–29	5	—	—
Sarfraz Nawaz	15008	645	23.26	8–27	33	3	1
Savage, R. L.	2837	105	27.01	7–50	6	1	—
Schepens, M.	13	0	—	—	—	—	—
Scott, C. J.	—	—	—	—	—	—	—
Selvey, M. W. W.	11094	425	26.10	7–20	18	3	—
Serjeant, C. S.	—	—	—	—	—	—	—
Shackleton, J. H.	1967	45	43.71	4–38	—	—	—
Sharp, G.	2	0	—	—	—	—	—
Sharp, K.	21	0	—	—	—	—	—
Shepherd, D. R.	80	2	40.00	1–1	—	—	—
Shepherd, J. N.	20633	803	25.69	8–40	44	2	—
Short, J. F.	—	—	—	—	—	—	—
Shuttleworth, K.	13421	564	23.79	7–41	21	1	—
Sidebottom, A.	1135	38	29.86	4–47	—	—	—
Silvester, S.	313	12	26.08	4–86	—	—	—
Simmons, J.	12507	468	26.72	7–64	16	2	—
Siviter, K.	964	25	38.56	4–67	—	—	—

	Runs	Wkts	Avge	BB	5 wI	10 wM	100 wS
Skinner, L. E.	—	—	—	—	—	—	—
Slack, W. N.	—	—	—	—	—	—	—
Slocombe, P. A.	14	0	—	—	—	—	—
Smedley, M. J.	4	0	—	—	—	—	—
Smith, D. M.	1055	20	52.75	3–40	—	—	—
Smith, K. D.	3	0	—	—	—	—	—
Smith, M. J.	1844	57	32.35	4–13	—	—	—
Smith, N.	—	—	—	—	—	—	—
Snow, J. A.	26675	1174	22.72	8–87	56	9	2
Southern, J. W.	4737	154	30.75	6–46	5	—	—
Spencer, J.	12039	461	26.11	6–19	17	1	—
Stead, B.	18318	653	28.05	8–44	24	2	—
Steele, A.	—	—	—	—	—	—	—
Steele, D. S.	5351	235	22.77	8–29	3	—	—
Steele, J. F.	7413	279	26.56	7–29	6	—	—
Stephenson, G. R.	38	0	—	—	—	—	—
Stevenson, G. B.	3161	111	28.47	6–82	2	1	—
Stevenson, K.	2997	98	30.58	7–68	4	—	—
Stewart, D. E. R.	72	0	—	—	—	—	—
Stovold, A. W.	23	1	23.00	1–0	—	—	—
Sullivan, J. P.	50	2	25.00	2–50	—	—	—
Swarbrook, F. W.	13493	455	29.65	9–20	15	2	—
Swindell, R. S.	1665	50	33.30	6–79	4	—	—
Tavare, C. J.	28	0	—	—	—	—	—
Taylor, D. J. S.	14	0	—	—	—	—	—
Taylor, L. B.	140	3	46.66	2–39	—	—	—
Taylor, M. N. S.	20109	767	26.21	7–23	22	—	—
Taylor, R. W.	46	0	—	—	—	—	—
Taylor, W.	6291	211	29.81	6–42	6	1	—
Thomas, D. J.	101	1	101.00	1–88	—	—	—
Thomson, J. R.	6092	255	23.89	7–33	12	2	—
Titmus, F. J.	62696	2811	22.30	9–52	168	26	16
Todd, P. A.	3	0	—	—	—	—	—
Tolchard, J. G.	5	0	—	—	—	—	—
Tolchard, R. W.	20	1	20.00	1–4	—	—	—
Tomlins, K. P.	—	—	—	—	—	—	—
Tremlett, T. M.	46	2	23.00	1–0	—	—	—
Trim, G. E.	—	—	—	—	—	—	—
Tunnicliffe, C. J.	2325	73	31.84	4–22	—	—	—
Tunnicliffe, H. T.	599	13	46.07	3–48	—	—	—
Turner, D. R.	135	2	67.50	1–4	—	—	—
Turner, G. M.	189	5	37.80	3–18	—	—	—
Turner, S.	13524	532	25.42	6–26	19	—	—
Underwood, D. L.	32323	1624	19.90	9–28	103	30	7
Vernon, M. J.	1198	31	38.64	6–58	2	1	—
Verrinder, A. O. C.	144	4	36.00	2–42	—	—	—
Virgin, R. T.	340	4	85.00	1–6	—	—	—
Walker, M. H. N.	10707	411	26.05	8–143	16	—	—
Waller, C. E.	7902	277	28.52	7–64	12	1	—
Walters, J.	99	1	99.00	1–37	—	—	—

	Runs	Wkts	Avge	BB	5 wI	10 wM	100 wS
Walters, K. D.	6385	183	34.89	7–63	6	—	—
Ward, A.	10425	456	22.86	7–42	15	4	—
Watson, W. K.	1650	67	24.62	5–54	1	—	—
Watts, P. J.	8170	318	25.69	6–18	7	—	—
Weir, R. S.	—	—	—	—	—	—	—
Wells, R. R. C.	—	—	—	—	—	—	—
Wessels, K. C.	75	2	37.50	1–21	—	—	—
White, R. A.	19538	655	29.82	7–41	27	3	—
Whitehouse, J.	374	5	74.80	2–55	—	—	—
Wilcock, H. G.	3	0	—	—	—	—	—
Wilkins, A. H.	1400	56	25.00	5–58	2	—	—
Wilkinson, P. A.	6335	175	36.20	6–81	2	—	—
Willey, P.	7244	266	27.23	7–37	10	1	—
Williams, D. L.	9883	364	27.15	7–60	13	1	—
Williams, R. G.	158	4	39.50	2–19	—	—	—
Willis, R. G. D.	11476	468	24.52	8–32	19	1	—
Wilson, J. D.	6	0	—	—	—	—	—
Wingfield Digby, A. R.	3532	96	33.87	5–79	4	—	—
Wood, B.	6462	235	27.49	7–52	8	—	—
Woolmer, R. A.	9542	365	26.14	7–47	11	1	—
Wright, J. G.	—	—	—	—	—	—	—
Yardley, T. J.	18	0	—	—	—	—	—
Younis Ahmed	1057	27	39.14	4–10	—	—	—
Zaheer Abbas	615	20	30.75	5–15	1	—	—

Future Cricket Tours

TO ENGLAND
1979 India and World Cup Competition
1980 West Indies and S. Africa
1981 Australia

MCC TOURS OVERSEAS
1978–79 Australia
1979–80 No Tour
1980–81 West Indies

OTHER TOURS
1978–79 New Zealand to India
West Indies to India
Pakistan to New Zealand and Australia
1979–80 West Indies to Pakistan and New Zealand
Australia to Pakistan and India
India to West Indies
1980–81 New Zealand to Australia
Australia to New Zealand
1981–82 West Indies to Australia
New Zealand to West Indies
1982–83 Pakistan to West Indies
1983–84 Australia to West Indies
India to New Zealand

When the batting is torpid and boring,
Or when the score's suddenly soaring—
Whatever the rate
You need Papermate
To keep up with the *Tempo* of
  scoring.

FIRST-CLASS CRICKET RECORDS

COMPLETE TO 30 SEPTEMBER 1977

Highest Innings Totals

1107	Victoria v New South Wales (Melbourne)	1926–27
1059	Victoria v Tasmania (Melbourne)	1922–23
951–7d	Sind v Baluchistan (Karachi)	1973–74
918	New South Wales v South Australia (Sydney)	1900–01
912–8d	Holkar v Mysore (Indore)	1945–46
910–6d	Railways v Dera Ismail Khan (Lahore)	1964–65
903–7d	England v Australia (Oval)	1938
887	Yorkshire v Warwickshire (Birmingham)	1896
849	England v West Indies (Kingston)	1929–30

NB There are 22 instances of a side making 800 or more in an innings, the last occasion being 951-7 declared by Sind as above.

Lowest Innings Totals

12†	Oxford University v MCC and Ground (Oxford)	1877
12	Northamptonshire v Gloucestershire (Gloucester)	1907
13	Wellington v Nelson (Nelson)	1862–63
13	Auckland v Canterbury (Auckland)	1877–78
13	Nottinghamshire v Yorkshire (Nottingham)	1901
15	MCC v Surrey (Lord's)	1839
15†	Victoria v MCC (Melbourne)	1903–04
15†	Northamptonshire v Yorkshire (Northampton)	1908
15	Hampshire v Warwickshire (Birmingham)	1922
16	MCC and Ground v Surrey (Lord's)	1872
16	Derbyshire v Nottinghamshire (Nottingham)	1879
16	Surrey v Nottinghamshire (Oval)	1880
16	Warwickshire v Kent (Tonbridge)	1913
16	Trinidad v Barbados (Bridgetown)	1941–42
16	Border v Natal (East London)	1959–60

†Batted one man short

NB There are 26 instances of a side making less than 20 in an innings, the last occasion being 16 and 18 by Border v Natal at East London in 1959–60. The total of 34 is the lowest by one side in a match.

Highest Aggregates in a Match

2376	(38)	Bombay v Maharashtra (Poona)	1948–49
2078	(40)	Bombay v Holkar (Bombay)	1944–45
1981	(35)	England v South Africa (Durban)	1938–39
1929	(39)	New South Wales v South Australia (Sydney)	1925–26
1911	(34)	New South Wales v Victoria (Sydney)	1908–09
1905	(40)	Otago v Wellington (Dunedin)	1923–24

In England the highest are:

1723	(34)	England v Australia (Leeds) 5 day match	1948
1601	(29)	England v Australia (Lord's) 4 day match	1930
1507	(28)	England v West Indies (Oval) 5 day match	1976
1502	(28)	MCC v New Zealanders (Lord's)	1927
1499	(31)	T. N. Pearce's XI v Australians (Scarborough)	1961
1496	(24)	England v Australia (Nottingham) 4 day match	1938
1494	(37)	England v Australia (Oval) 4 day match	1934
1492	(33)	Worcestershire v Oxford U (Worcester)	1904
1477	(32)	Hampshire v Oxford U (Southampton)	1913

| 1477 | (33) | England v South Africa (Oval) 4 day match | 1947 |
| 1475 | (27) | Northamptonshire v Surrey (Northampton) | 1920 |

Lowest Aggregates in a Match

105	(31)	MCC v Australia (Lord's)	1878
134	(30)	England v The B's (Lord's)	1831
147	(40)	Kent v Sussex (Sevenoaks)	1828
149	(30)	England v Kent (Lord's)	1858
151	(30)	Canterbury v Otago (Christchurch)	1866–67
153	(37)	MCC v Sussex (Lord's)	1843
153	(31)	Otago v Canterbury (Dunedin)	1896–97
156	(30)	Nelson v Wellington (Nelson)	1885–86
158	(22)	Surrey v Worcestershire (Oval)	1954

Wickets that fell are given in parentheses.

Tie Matches

Due to the change of law made in 1948 for tie matches, a tie is now a rarity. The law states that only if the match is played out and the scores are equal is the result a tie.

The most recent tied matches are as follows:

Yorkshire (351–4d & 113) v Leicestershire (328 & 136) at
  Huddersfield   1954
Sussex (172 & 120) v Hampshire (153 & 139) at Eastbourne   1955
Victoria (244 & 197) v New South Wales (281 & 160) at
  Melbourne (St Kilda)   1956–57
    (The first tie in Sheffield Shield cricket)
T. N. Pearce's XI (313–7d & 258) v New Zealanders (268 & 303–
  8d) at Scarborough   1958
Essex (364–6d & 176–8d) v Gloucestershire (329 & 211) at Leyton   1959
Australia (505 & 232) v West Indies (453 & 284) at Brisbane   1960–61
    (The first tie in Test cricket)
Bahawalpur (123 & 282) v Lahore B (127 & 278) at Bahawalpur 1961–62
Middlesex (327–5d & 123–9d) v Hampshire (277 & 173) at Portsmouth
    1967
England XI (312–8d & 190–3d) v England Under-25 XI (320–9d &
  182) at Scarborough   1968
Yorkshire (106–9d & 207) v Middlesex (102 & 211) at Bradford   1973
Sussex (245 & 173–5d) v Essex (200–8d & 218) at Hove   1974

Highest Individual Scores

499	Hanif Mohammad, Karachi v Bahawalpur (Karachi)	1958–59
452*	D. G. Bradman, New South Wales v Queensland (Sydney)	1929–30
443*	B. B. Nimbalkar, Maharashtra v Kathiawar (Poona)	1948–49
437	W. H. Ponsford, Victoria v Queensland (Melbourne)	1927–28
429	W. H. Ponsford, Victoria v Tasmania (Melbourne)	1922–23
428	Aftab Baloch, Sind v Baluchistan (Karachi)	1973–74
424	A. C. MacLaren, Lancashire v Somerset (Taunton)	1895
385	B. Sutcliffe, Otago v Canterbury (Christchurch)	1952–53
383	C. W. Gregory, New South Wales v Queensland (Brisbane)	1906–07
369	D. G. Bradman, South Australia v Tasmania (Adelaide)	1935–36
365*	C. Hill, South Australia v New South Wales (Adelaide)	1900–01
365*	G. S. Sobers, West Indies v Pakistan (Kingston)	1957–58
364	L. Hutton, England v Australia (Oval)	1938
359*	V. M. Merchant, Bombay v Maharashtra (Bombay)	1943–44
359	R. B. Simpson, New South Wales v Queensland (Brisbane)	1963–64
357*	R. Abel, Surrey v Somerset (Oval)	1899
357	D. G. Bradman, South Australia v Victoria (Melbourne)	1935–36
356	B. A. Richards, South Australia v Western Australia (Perth)	1970–71

355 B. Sutcliffe, Otago v Auckland (Dunedin)   1949–50
352 W. H. Ponsford, Victoria v New South Wales(Melbourne) 1926–27
350 Rashid Israr, National Bank v Habib Bank (Lahore)   1976–77
   NB There are 91 instances of a batsman scoring 300 or more in an innings, the last occasion being 350 by Rashid Israr as above.

Most Centuries in a Season
18 D. C. S. Compton   1947
16 J. B. Hobbs   1925
15 W. R. Hammond   1938
14 H. Sutcliffe   1932

Most Centuries in an Innings
6 for Holkar v Mysore (Indore)   1945–46
5 for New South Wales v South Australia (Sydney)   1900–01
5 for Australia v West Indies (Kingston)   1954–55

Most Centuries in Successive Innings
6 C. B. Fry   1901
6 D. G. Bradman   1938–39
6 M. J. Procter   1970–71
5 E. D. Weekes   1955–56
   NB The feat of scoring 4 centuries in successive innings has been achieved on 30 occasions.

Most Centuries in Succession in Test Matches
5 E. D. Weekes, West Indies   1947–48 and 1948–49
4 J. H. Fingleton, Australia   1935–36 and 1936–37
4 A. Melville, South Africa   1938–39 and 1947

Two Double Centuries in a Match
A. E. Fagg, 244 and 202* for Kent v Essex (Colchester   1938

A Double Century and a Century in a Match
C. B. Fry, 125 and 229, Sussex v Surrey (Hove)   1900
W. W. Armstrong, 157* and 245, Victoria v South Australia
   (Melbourne)   1920–21
H. T. W. Hardinge, 207 and 102* for Kent v Surrey (Blackheath) 1921
C. P. Mead, 113 and 224, Hampshire v Sussex (Horsham)   1921
K. S. Duleepsinhji, 115 and 246, Sussex v Kent (Hastings)   1929
D. G. Bradman, 124 and 225, Woodfull's XI v Ryder's XI
   (Sydney)   1929–30
B. Sutcliffe, 243 and 100* New Zealanders v Essex (Southend) 1949
M. R. Hallam, 210* and 157, Leicestershire v Glamorgan (Leicester) 1959
M. R. Hallam, 203* and 143* Leicestershire v Sussex (Worthing) 1961
Hanumant Singh, 109 and 213*, Rajasthan v Bombay (Bombay) 1966–67
Salahuddin, 256 and 102*, Karachi v East Pakistan (Karachi) 1968–69
K. D. Walters, 242 and 103, Australia v West Indies (Sydney) 1968–69
S. M. Gavaskar, 124 and 220, India v West Indies (P. of Spain) 1970–71
L. G. Rowe, 214 and 100* West Indies v New Zealand (Kingston) 1971–72
G. S. Chappell, 247* and 133, Australia v New Zealand
   (Wellington)   1973–74
L. Baichan, 216* and 102, Berbice v Demerara (Georgetown)   1973–74
Zaheer Abbas, 216* and 156*, Gloucestershire v Surrey (Oval) 1976
Zaheer Abbas, 230* and 104*, Gloucestershire v Kent (Canterbury) 1976
Zaheer Abbas, 205* and 108*, Gloucestershire v Sussex (Cheltenham) 1977

197

Two Centuries in a Match on Most Occasions
7 W. R. Hammond   6 J. B. Hobbs   5 C. B. Fry

NB 12 batsmen have achieved the feat on four occasions, 20 batsmen on three occasions and 37 batsmen on two occasions.

Most Centuries
J. B. Hobbs, 197 (175 in England); E. H. Hendren 170 (151); W. R. Hammond, 167 (134); C. P. Mead 153 (145); H. Sutcliffe, 149 (135); F. E. Woolley, 145 (135); L. Hutton, 129 (105); W. G. Grace, 124 (123); D. C. S. Compton, 123 (92); T. W. Graveney, 122 (91); D. G. Bradman, 117 (41); M. C. Cowdrey, 107 (79); A. Sandham, 107 (87); T. W. Hayward, 104 (100); J. H. Edrich, 102 (89); L. E. G. Ames, 102 (89); E. Tyldesley, 102 (94); G. Boycott, 100 (81).

Highest Individual Batting Aggregate in a Season

Runs		Season	M	Innings	NO	HS	Avge	100s
3,816	D. C. S. Compton	1947	30	50	8	246	90.85	18
3,539	W. J. Edrich	1947	30	52	8	267*	80.43	12

NB The feat of scoring 3,000 runs in a season has been achieved on 28 occasions, the last instance being by W. E. Alley (3,019 runs, av. 59.96) in 1961.

Partnerships for First Wicket
561 Waheed Mirza and Mansood Akhtar, Karachi Whites v Quetta (Karachi)   1976–77
555 H. Sutcliffe and P. Holmes, Yorkshire v Essex (Leyton)   1932
554 J. T. Brown and J. Tunnicliffe, Yorkshire v Derbyshire (Chesterfield)   1898
490 E. H. Bowley and John Langridge, Sussex v Middlesex (Hove) 1933
456 W. H. Ponsford and E. R. Mayne, Victoria v Queensland (Melbourne)   1923–24
451* S. Desai and R. Binny, Karnataka v Kerala (Chikmagalur)   1977–78
428 J. B. Hobbs and A. Sandham, Surrey v Oxford U (Oval)   1926
424 J. F. W. Nicholson and I. J. Siedle, Natal v Orange Free State (Bloemfontein)   1926–27
413 V. Mankad and P. Roy, India v New Zealand (Madras)   1955–56
405 C. P. S. Chauban and M. Gupte, Maharashtra v Vidarbha (Poona)   1972–73

Partnerships for Second Wicket
465* J. A. Jameson and R. B. Kanhai, Warwickshire v Gloucestershire (Birmingham)   1974
455 K. V. Bhandarkar and B. B. Nimbalkar, Maharashtra v Kathiawar (Poona)   1948–49
451 D. G. Bradman and W. H. Ponsford, Australia v England (Oval)   1934
446 C. C. Hunte and G. S. Sobers, West Indies v Pakistan (Kingston)   1957–58
429* J. G. Dewes and G. H. G. Doggart, Cambridge U v Essex (Cambridge)   1949
398 W. Gunn and A. Shrewsbury, Nottinghamshire v Sussex (Nottingham)   1890

Partnerships for Third Wicket
456 Aslam Ali and Khalid Irtiza, United Bank v Multan (Karachi)   1975–76
445 P. E. Whitelaw and W. N. Carson, Auckland v Otago (Dunedin)   1936–37

198

434　J. B. Stollmeyer and G. E. Gomez, Trinidad v British
　　　Guiana (Port of Spain)　　　　　　　　　　　　　　　1946–47
424*　W. J. Edrich and D. C. S. Compton, Middlesex v Somerset
　　　(Lord's)　　　　　　　　　　　　　　　　　　　　　　1948
410　R. S. Modi and L. Amarnath, India v Rest (Calcutta)　1946–47
399　R. T. Simpson and D. C. S. Compton, MCC v NE
　　　Transvaal (Benoni)　　　　　　　　　　　　　　　　　1948–49

Partnerships for Fourth Wicket

577　Gul Mahomed and V. S. Hazare, Baroda v Holkar (Baroda) 1946–47
574*　C. L. Walcott and F. M. M. Worrell, Barbados v Trinidad
　　　(Port of Spain)　　　　　　　　　　　　　　　　　　1945–46
502*　F. M. M. Worrell and J. D. C. Goddard, Barbados v Trinidad
　　　(Bridgetown)　　　　　　　　　　　　　　　　　　　1943–44
448　R. Abel and T. W. Hayward, Surrey v Yorkshire (Oval)　1899
424　I. S. Lee and S. O. Quin, Victoria v Tasmania (Melbourne) 1933–34
411　P. B. H. May and M. C. Cowdrey, England v West Indies
　　　(Birmingham)　　　　　　　　　　　　　　　　　　　1957
410　G. Abraham and B. Pandit, Kerala v Andhra (Pulghat)　1959–60
402　W. Watson and T. W. Graveney, MCC v British Guiana
　　　(Georgetown)　　　　　　　　　　　　　　　　　　　1953–54
402　R. B. Kanhai and K. Ibadulla, Warwickshire v
　　　Nottinghamshire (Nottingham)　　　　　　　　　　　1968

Partnerships for Fifth Wicket

405　D. G. Bradman and S. G. Barnes, Australia v England
　　　(Sydney)　　　　　　　　　　　　　　　　　　　　　1946–47
397　W. Bardsley and C. Kellaway, New South Wales v South
　　　Australia (Sydney)　　　　　　　　　　　　　　　　1920–21
393　E. G. Arnold and W. B. Burns, Worcestershire v
　　　Warwickshire (Birmingham)　　　　　　　　　　　　1909
360　V. M. Merchant and M. N. Raiji, Bombay v Hyderabad
　　　(Bombay)　　　　　　　　　　　　　　　　　　　　　1947–48
347　D. Brookes and D. Barrick, Northamptonshire v Essex
　　　(Northampton)　　　　　　　　　　　　　　　　　　1952

Partnerships for Sixth Wicket

487*　G. A. Headley and C. C. Passailaigue, Jamaica v Lord
　　　Tennyson's XI (Kingston)　　　　　　　　　　　　　1931–32
428　W. W. Armstrong and M. A. Noble, Australians v Sussex
　　　(Hove)　　　　　　　　　　　　　　　　　　　　　　1902
411　R. M. Poore and E. G. Wynyard, Hampshire v Somerset
　　　(Taunton)　　　　　　　　　　　　　　　　　　　　1899
376　R. Subba Row and A. Lightfoot, Northamptonshire v
　　　Surrey (Oval)　　　　　　　　　　　　　　　　　　　1958
371　V. M. Merchant and R. S. Modi, Bombay v Maharashtra
　　　(Bombay)　　　　　　　　　　　　　　　　　　　　　1943–44

Partnerships for Seventh Wicket

347　D. Atkinson and C. C. Depeiza, West Indies v Australia
　　　(Bridgetown)　　　　　　　　　　　　　　　　　　　1954–55
344　K. S. Ranjitsinhi and W. Newham, Sussex v Essex (Leyton) 1902
340　K. J. Key and H. Philipson, Oxford U v Middlesex
　　　(Chiswick Park)　　　　　　　　　　　　　　　　　1887
336　F. C. W. Newman and C. R. Maxwell, Cahn's XI v
　　　Leicestershire (Nottingham)　　　　　　　　　　　　1935
335　C. W. Andrews and E. C. Bensted, Queensland v New
　　　South Wales (Sydney)　　　　　　　　　　　　　　　1934–35

Partnerships for Eighth Wicket

433	V. T. Trumper and A. Sims, Australians v Canterbury (Christchurch)	1913–14
292	R. Peel and Lord Hawke, Yorkshire v Warwickshire (Birmingham)	1896
270	V. T. Trumper and E. P. Barbour, New South Wales v Victoria (Sydney)	1912–13
263	D. R. Wilcox and R. M. Taylor, Essex v Warwickshire (Southend)	1946
255	E. A. V. Williams and E. A. Martindale, Barbados v Trinidad (Bridgetown)	1935–36

Partnerships for Ninth Wicket

283	A. R. Warren and J. Chapman, Derbyshire v Warwickshire (Blackwell)	1910
251	J. W. H. T. Douglas and S. N. Hare, Essex v Derbyshire (Leyton)	1921
245	V. S. Hazare and N. D. Nagarwalla, Maharashtra v Baroda (Poona)	1939–40
239	H. B. Cave and I. B. Leggat, Central Districts v Otago (Dunedin)	1952–53
232	C. Hill and E. Walkley, South Australia v New South Wales (Adelaide)	1900–01

Partnerships for Tenth Wicket

307	A. F. Kippax and J. E. H. Hooker, New South Wales v Victoria (Melbourne)	1928–29
249	C. T. Sarwate and S. N. Bannerjee, Indians v Surrey (Oval)	1946
235	F. E. Woolley and A. Fielder, Kent v Worcestershire (Stourbridge)	1909
230	R. W. Nicholls and W. Roche, Middlesex v Kent (Lord's)	1899
228	R. Illingworth and K. Higgs, Leicestershire v Northamptonshire (Leicester)	1977
218	F. H. Vigar and T. P. B. Smith, Essex v Derbyshire (Chesterfield)	1947

Most Wickets in a Season

W		Season	M	O	M	R	Avge
304	A. P. Freeman	1928	37	1,976.1	432	5,489	18.05
298	A. P. Freeman	1933	33	2,039	651	4,549	15.26

NB The feat of taking 250 wickets in a season has been achieved on 2 occasions, the last instance being by A. P. Freeman in 1933 as above. 200 or more wickets in a season have been taken on 59 occasions, the last instance being by G. A. R. Lock (212 wks, av 12.02) in 1957.

The most wickets taken in a season since the reduction of County Championship matches in 1969 are as follows:

W		Season	Matches	O	M	R	Avge
131	L. R. Gibbs	1971	23	1024.1	295	2475	18.89
119	A. M. E. Roberts	1974	21	727.4	198	1621	13.62
112	P. G. Lee	1975	21	799.5	199	2067	18.45

NB 100 wickets in a season have been taken on 21 occasions since 1969

All Ten Wickets in an Innings

The feat has been achieved on 69 occasions.
On three occasions: A. P. Freeman, 1929, 1930, and 1931.
On two occasions: J. C. Laker, 1956, H. Verity, 1931 and 1932, V. E. Walker 1959 and 1965.
Instances since the war:

W. E. Hollies, Warwickshire v Nottinghamshire (Birmingham) 1946;
J. M. Sims of Middlesex playing for East v West (Kingston) 1948; J. K.
Graveney, Gloucestershire v Derbyshire (Chesterfield) 1949; T. E. Bailey,
Essex v Lancashire (Clacton) 1949; R. Berry, Lancashire v Worcestershire
(Blackpool) 1953; S. P. Gupte, Bombay v Pakistan Services (Bombay),
1954–55; J. C. Laker, Surrey v Australians (Oval) 1956; J. C. Laker,
England v Australia (Manchester) 1956; G. A. R. Lock, Surrey v Kent,
(Blackheath) 1956; K. Smales, Nottinghamshire v Gloucestershire
(Stroud) 1956; P. Chatterjee, Bengal v Assam (Jorbat) 1956–57; J. D.
Bannister, Warwickshire v Combined Services (Birmingham) 1959; A. J.
G. Pearson, Cambridge U v Leicestershire (Loughborough) 1961; N. I.
Thomson, Sussex v Warwickshire (Worthing) 1964; P. Allan, Queensland
v Victoria (Melbourne) 1965–66; I. Brayshaw, Western Australia v
Victoria (Perth) 1967–68; Shahid Mahmood, Karachi Whites v Khairpur
(Karachi) 1969–70.

Nineteen Wickets in a Match

J. C. Laker 19–90 (9–37 and 10–53), England v Australia (Manchester)
1956.

Eighteen Wickets in a Match

H. A. Arkwright 18–96 (9–43 and 9–53), MCC v Gentlemen of Kent
(Canterbury) 1861, (twelve-a-side match).

Seventeen Wickets in a Match

The feat has been achieved on 18 occasions.
Instances between the two wars were: A. P. Freeman (for 67 runs),
Kent v Sussex (Brighton) 1922; F. C. L. Matthews (89 runs), Nottingham-
shire v Northamptonshire (Nottingham) 1923; C. W. L. Parker (56 runs)
Gloucestershire v Essex (Gloucester) 1925; G. R. Cox (106 runs), Sussex v
Warwickshire (Horsham) 1926; A. P. Freeman (92 runs), Kent v
Warwickshire (Folkestone) 1932; H. Verity (91 runs), Yorkshire v Essex
(Leyton) 1933; J. C. Clay (212 runs), Glamorgan v Worcestershire
(Swansea) 1937; T. W. Goddard (106 runs), Gloucestershire v Kent
(Bristol) 1939. There has been no instance since the last war.

Most Hat-tricks in a Career

7 D. V. P. Wright.
6 T. W. Goddard, C. W. L. Parker.
5 S. Haigh, V. W. C. Jupp, A. E. G. Rhodes, F. A. Tarrant.
   NB Eight bowlers have achieved the feat on four occasions and 25 bowlers
on three occasions.

The 'Double' Event

3,000 runs and 100 wickets: J. H. Parks, 1937.
2,000 runs and 200 wickets: G. H. Hirst, 1906.
2,000 runs and 100 wickets: F. E. Woolley (4), J. W. Hearne (3), G. H.
Hirst (2), W. Rhodes (2), T. E. Bailey, E. Davies, W. G. Grace, G. L.
Jessop, V. W. C. Jupp, James Langridge, F. A. Tarrant, C. L. Townsend,
L. F. Townsend.
1,000 runs and 200 wickets: M. W. Tate (3), A. E. Trott (2), A. S. Kennedy.
Most 'Doubles': W. Rhodes (16), G. H. Hirst (14), V. W. C. Jupp (10).
'Double' in first season: D. B. Close, 1949. At the age of 18, Close is the
youngest player ever to perform this feat.
*The feat of scoring 1,000 runs and taking 100 wickets has been achieved
on 302 occasions, the last instance being F. J. Titmus in 1967.*

FIELDING

Most catches in a season:	78 W. R. Hammond	1928
	77 M. J. Stewart	1957
Most catches in a match:	10 W. R. Hammond, Gloucestershire v Surrey (Cheltenham)	1928
Most catches in an innings:	7 M. J. Stewart, Surrey v Northamptonshire (Northampton)	1957
	7 A. S. Brown, Gloucestershire v Nottinghamshire (Nottingham)	1966

WICKET-KEEPING

Most Dismissals in a Season

127 (79 ct, 48 st), L. E. G. Ames   1929

NB The feat of making 100 dismissals in a season has been achieved on 12 occasions, the last instance being by R. Booth (100 dismissals—91 ct 9 st) in 1964.

Most dismissals in a match:	12 E. Pooley (8 ct 4 st) Surrey v Sussex (Oval)	1868
	12 D. Tallon (9 ct 3 st), Queensland v New South Wales (Sydney)	1938–39
	12 H. B. Taber (9 ct 3 st), New South Wales v South Australia (Adelaide)	1968–69
Most catches in a match:	11 A. Long, Surrey v Sussex (Hove) 1964	
	11 R. W. Marsh, Western Australia v Victoria (Perth)	1975–76
Most dismissals in an innings:	8 A. T. W. Grout (8 ct) Queensland v W. Australia (Brisbane)	1959–60

A more gruesome aspect of the game is shown as early as 1622, when certain parishioners of Boxgrove, on the edge of the Goodwood estate, were arraigned for playing in the churchyard on a Sunday in May and moreover, playing in such a violent manner that 'they used to breake the church windows with the ball; and that a little childe had like to have her braynes beaten out with a cricket batte.'

Cricket's first overseas tour was in 1859 when a strong team collected together by George Parr sailed from Liverpool for Quebec on 7th September. In the first match the team defeated XXII of Lower Canada at Montreal by 8 wickets.

The County Cricket Championship is the oldest cricket competition in the world. This summer it is to lose the prefix 'County', and now, at the request of the sponsors, is to be known as The Schweppes Championship.

LATE ADDITION TO ESSEX 1978
Norbert **PHILLIP** B in Dominica 22/6/1949. RHB, RFM. Debut 1969–70 for Windward Islands v Glamorgan and has played subsequently for Combined Islands in Shell Shield Competition. Has joined Essex for 1978. HS: 99 Combined Islands v Guyana (Skeldon) 1971–72. BB: 5–43 Combined Islands v Guyana (Plymouth, Montserrat) 1976–77.

TEST CRICKET RECORDS

COMPLETE TO 30 SEPTEMBER 1977

Matches between England and Rest of the World 1970 and between
Australia and Rest of the World 1971–72 are excluded

HIGHEST INNINGS TOTALS

903—7d	England v Australia (Oval)	1938
849	England v West Indies (Kingston)	1929–30
790—3d	West Indies v Pakistan (Kingston)	1957–58
758—8d	Australia v West Indies (Kingston)	1954–55
729—6d	Australia v England (Lord's)	1930
701	Australia v England (Oval)	1934
695	Australia v England (Oval)	1930
687—8d	West Indies v England (Oval)	1976
681—8d	West Indies v England (Port of Spain)	1953–54
674	Australia v India (Adelaide)	1947–48
668	Australia v West Indies (Bridgetown)	1954–55
659—8d	Australia v England (Sydney)	1946–47
658—8d	England v Australia (Nottingham)	1938
657—8d	Pakistan v West Indies (Bridgetown)	1957–58
656—8d	Australia v England (Manchester)	1964
654—5	England v South Africa (Durban)	1938–39
652—8d	West Indies v England (Lord's)	1973
650—6d	Australia v West Indies (Bridgetown)	1964–65

The highest innings for the countries not mentioned above are:

622—9d	South Africa v Australia (Durban)	1969–70
551—9d	New Zealand v England (Lord's)	1973
539—9d	India v Pakistan (Madras)	1960–61

*NB There are 41 instances of a side making 600 or more in an innings
in a Test Match.*

LOWEST INNINGS TOTALS

26	New Zealand v England (Auckland)	1954–55
30	South Africa v England (Port Elizabeth)	1895–96
30	South Africa v England (Birmingham)	1924
35	South Africa v England (Cape Town)	1898–99
36	Australia v England (Birmingham)	1902
36	South Africa v Australia (Melbourne)	1931–32
42	Australia v England (Sydney)	1887–88
42	New Zealand v Australia (Wellington)	1945–46
42†	India v England (Lord's)	1974
43	South Africa v England (Cape Town)	1888–89
44	Australia v England (Oval)	1896
45	England v Australia (Sydney)	1886–87
45	South Africa v Australia (Melbourne)	1931–32
47	South Africa v England (Cape Town)	1888–89
47	New Zealand v England (Lord's)	1958

†Batted one man short.

The lowest innings for the countries not mentioned above are:

76	West Indies v Pakistan (Dacca)	1958–59
87	Pakistan v England (Lord's)	1954

HIGHEST INDIVIDUAL INNINGS

365*	G. S. Sobers: West Indies v Pakistan (Kingston)	1957–58
364	L. Hutton: England v Australia (Oval)	1938
337	Hanif Mohammad: Pakistan v West Indies (Bridgetown)	1957–58
336*	W. R. Hammond: England v New Zealand (Auckland)	1932–33
334	D. G. Bradman: Australia v England (Leeds)	1930
325	A. Sandham: England v West Indies (Kingston)	1929–30
311	R. B. Simpson: Australia v England (Manchester)	1964
310*	J. H. Edrich: England v New Zealand (Leeds)	1965
307	R. M. Cowper: Australia v England (Melbourne)	1965–66
304	D. G. Bradman: Australia v England (Leeds)	1934
302	L. G. Rowe: West Indies v England (Bridgetown)	1973–74
299*	D. G. Bradman: Australia v South Africa (Adelaide)	1931–32
291	I. V. A. Richards: West Indies v England (Oval)	1976
287	R. E. Foster: England v Australia (Sydney)	1903–04
285*	P. B. H. May: England v West Indies (Birmingham)	1957
278	D. C. S. Compton: England v Pakistan (Nottingham)	1954
274	R. G. Pollock: South Africa v Australia (Durban)	1969–70
274	Zaheer Abbas: Pakistan v England (Birmingham)	1971
270*	G. A. Headley: West Indies v England (Kingston)	1934–35
270	D. G. Bradman: Australia v England (Melbourne)	1936–37
266	W. H. Ponsford: Australia v England (Oval)	1934
262*	D. L. Amiss: England v West Indies (Kingston)	1973–74
261	F. M. M. Worrell: West Indies v England (Nottingham)	1950
260	C. C. Hunte: West Indies v Pakistan (Kingston)	1957–58
259	G. M. Turner: New Zealand v West Indies (Georgetown)	1971–72
258	T. W. Graveney: England v West Indies (Nottingham)	1957
258	S. M. Nurse: West Indies v New Zealand (Christchurch)	1968–69
256	R. B. Kanhai: West Indies v India (Calcutta)	1958–59
256	K. F. Barrington: England v Australia (Manchester)	1964
255*	D. J. McGlew: South Africa v New Zealand (Wellington)	1952–53
254	D. G. Bradman: Australia v England (Lord's)	1930
251	W. R. Hammond: England v Australia (Sydney)	1928–29
250	K. D. Walters, Australia v New Zealand (Christchurch)	1976–77

The highest individual innings for India is:

231	V. Mankad: India v New Zealand (Madras)	1955–56

NB There are 111 instances of a double-century being scored in a Test Match.

HIGHEST RUN AGGREGATES IN A TEST RUBBER

R		Season	T	I	NO	HS	Avge	100s	50s
974	D. G. Bradman (A v E)	1930	5	7	0	334	139.14	4	—
905	W. R. Hammond (E v A)	1928–29	5	9	1	251	113.12	4	—
834	R. N. Harvey (A v SA)	1952–53	5	9	0	205	92.66	4	3
829	I. V. A. Richards (WI v E)	1976	4	7	0	291	118.42	3	2
827	C. L. Walcott (WI v A)	1954–55	5	10	0	155	82.70	5	2
824	G. S. Sobers (WI v P)	1957–58	5	8	2	365*	137.33	3	3
810	D. G. Bradman (A v E)	1936–37	5	9	0	270	90.00	3	1
806	D. G. Bradman (A v SA)	1931–32	5	5	1	299*	201.50	4	—
779	E. D. Weekes (WI v I)	1948–49	5	7	0	194	111.28	4	2
774	S. M. Gavaskar (I v WI)	1970–71	4	8	3	220	154.80	4	3
758	D. G. Bradman (A v E)	1934	5	8	0	304	94.75	2	1
753	D. C. S. Compton (E v SA)	1947	5	8	0	208	94.12	4	2

RECORD WICKET PARTNERSHIPS—ALL TEST CRICKET

1st	413	V. Mankad & P. Roy: I v NZ (Madras)	1955–56
2nd	451	W. H. Ponsford & D. G. Bradman: A v E (Oval)	1934
3rd	370	W. J. Edrich & D. C. S. Compton: E v SA (Lord's)	1947
4th	411	P. B. H. May & M. C. Cowdrey: E v WI (Birm'ham)	1957
5th	405	S. G. Barnes & D. G. Bradman: A v E (Sydney)	1946–47
6th	346	J. H. Fingleton & D. G. Bradman: A v E (Melbourne)	1936–37
7th	347	D. Atkinson & C. C. Depeiza: WI v A (Bridgetown)	1954–55
8th	246	L. E. G. Ames & G. O. Allen: E v NZ (Lord's)	1931
9th	190	Asif Iqbal & Intikhab Alam: P v E (Oval)	1967
10th	151	B. F. Hastings & R. O. Collinge: NZ v P (Auckland)	1972–73

WICKET PARTNERSHIPS OF OVER 300

451	2nd	W. H. Ponsford & D. G. Bradman: A v E (Oval)	1934
446	2nd	C. C. Hunte & G. S. Sobers: WI v P (Kingston)	1957–58
413	1st	V. Mankad & P. Roy: I v NZ (Madras)	1955–56
411	4th	P. B. H. May & M. C. Cowdrey: E v WI (Birm'ham)	1957
405	5th	S. G. Barnes & D. G. Bradman: A v E (Sydney)	1946–47
399	4th	G. S. Sobers & F. M. M. Worrell: WI v E (Bridgetown)	1959–60
388	4th	W. H. Ponsford & D. G. Bradman: A v E (Leeds)	1934
387	1st	G. M. Turner & T. W. Jarvis: NZ v WI (Georgetown)	1971–72
382	2nd	L. Hutton & M. Leyland: E v A (Oval)	1938
382	1st	W. M. Lawry & R. B. Simpson: A v WI (Bridgetown)	1964–65
370	3rd	W. J. Edrich & D. C. S. Compton: E v SA (Lord's)	1947
369	2nd	J. H. Edrich and K. F. Barrington: E v NZ (Leeds)	1965
359	1st	L. Hutton & C. Washbrook: E v SA (Johannesburg)	1948–49
350	4th	Mushtaq Mohammad & Asif Iqbal: P v NZ (Dunedin)	1972–73
347	7th	D. Atkinson & C. C. Depeiza: WI v A (Bridgetown)	1954–55
346	6th	J. H. Fingleton & D. G. Bradman: A v E (Melbourne)	1936–37
341	3rd	E. J. Barlow & R. G. Pollock: SA v A (Adelaide)	1963–64
338	3rd	E. D. Weekes & F. M. M. Worrell: WI v E (P. of Spain)	1953–54
336	4th	W. M. Lawry & K. D. Walters: A v WI (Sydney)	1968–69
323	1st	J. B. Hobbs & W. Rhodes: E v A (Melbourne)	1911–12
319	3rd	A. Melville & A. D. Nourse, Jun: SA v E (Nottingham)	1947
308	7th	Waqar Hasan & Imtiaz Ahmed: P v NZ (Lahore)	1955–56
303	1st	V. A. Richards & A. I. Kallicharran, WI v E (Nottingham)	1976
301	2nd	A. R. Morris & D. G. Bradman: A v E (Leeds)	1948

HAT-TRICKS

F. R. Spofforth	Australia v England (Melbourne)	1878–79
W. Bates	England v Australia (Melbourne)	1882–83
J. Briggs	England v Australia (Sydney)	1891–92
G. A. Lohmann	England v South Africa (Port Elizabeth)	1895–96
J. T. Hearne	England v Australia (Leeds)	1899
H. Trumble	Australia v England (Melbourne)	1901–02
H. Trumble	Australia v England (Melbourne)	1903–04
T. J. Matthews (2)†	Australia v South Africa (Manchester)	1912
M. J. C. Allom‡	England v New Zealand (Christchurch)	1929–30
T. W. Goddard	England v South Africa (Johannesburg)	1938–39
P. J. Loader	England v West Indies (Leeds)	1957
L. F. Kline	Australia v South Africa (Cape Town)	1957–58
W. W. Hall	West Indies v Pakistan (Lahore)	1958–59
G. M. Griffin	South Africa v England (Lord's)	1960

L. R. Gibbs   West Indies v Australia (Adelaide)   1960–61
P. J. Petherick   New Zealand v Pakistan (Lahore)   1976–77
† Matthews achieved the hat-trick in each innings.
‡ Allom took four wickets with five consecutive balls.

NINE OR TEN WICKETS IN AN INNINGS

10—53 J. C. Laker: England v Australia (Manchester)   1956
9—28 G. A. Lohmann: England v South Africa (Johannesb'g) 1895–96
9—37 J. C. Laker: England v Australia (Manchester)   1956
9—69 J. M. Patel: India v Australia (Kanpur)   1959–60
9—95 J. M. Noreiga: West Indies v India (Port of Spain)   1970–71
9—102 S. P. Gupte: India v West Indies (Kanpur)   1958–59
9—103 S. F. Barnes: England v South Africa (Johannesburg)   1913–14
9—113 H. J. Tayfield: South Africa v England (Johannesburg) 1956–57
9—121 A. A. Mailey: Australia v England (Melbourne)   1920–21
   NB   There are 35 instances of a bowler taking 8 wickets in an innings in
   Test Match.

FIFTEEN OR MORE WICKETS IN A MATCH

19—90 J. C. Laker: England v Australia (Manchester)   1956
17—159 S. F. Barnes: England v South Africa (Johannesburg) 1913–14
16—137 R. A. L. Massie: Australia v England (Lord's)   1972
15—28 J. Briggs: England v South Africa (Cape Town)   1888–89
15—45 G. A. Lohmann: England v South Africa (Pt. Elizabeth) 1895–96
15—99 C. Blythe: England v South Africa (Leeds)   1907
15—104 H. Verity: England v Australia (Lord's)   1934
15—124 W. Rhodes: England v Australia (Melbourne)   1903–04
   NB   There are 7 instances of a bowler taking 14 wickets in a Test Match.

HIGHEST WICKET AGGREGATES IN A TEST RUBBER

W.		Season	Tests	Balls	Mdns	Runs	Avge	5 wI	10 M
49	S. F. Barnes (E v SA)	1913–14	4	1356	56	536	10.93	7	3
46	J. C. Laker (E v A)	1956	5	1703	127	442	9.60	4	2
44	C. V. Grimmett (A v SA)	1935–36	5	2077	140	642	14.59	5	3
39	A. V. Bedser (E v A)	1953	5	1591	48	682	17.48	5	1
38	M. W. Tate (E v A)	1924–25	5	2528	62	881	23.18	5	1
37	J. J. Whitty (A v SA)	1910–11	5	1395	55	632	17.08	2	—
37	H. J. Tayfield (SA v E)	1956–57	5	2280	105	636	17.18	4	1
36	A. E. E. Vogler (SA v E)	1909–10	5	1349	33	783	21.75	4	1
36	A. A. Mailey (A v E)	1920–21	5	1463	27	946	26.27	4	2
35	G. A. Lohmann (E v SA)	1895–96	3	520	38	203	5.80	4	2
35	B. S. Chandrasekhar (I v E)	1972–73	5	1747	83	662	18.91	4	—

MOST WICKET-KEEPING DISMISSALS IN AN INNINGS

6 (6ct) A. T. W. Grout, Australia v South Africa (Johannesburg) 1957–58
6 (6ct) D. Lindsay, South Africa v Australia (Johannesburg)   1966–67
6 (6ct) J. T. Murray, England v India (Lord's)   1967
6 (5ct 1st) S. M. H. Kirmani, India v New Zealand (Christchurch) 1975–76

MOST WICKET KEEPING DISMISSALS IN A MATCH

9 (8ct 1st) G. R. A. Langley, Australia v England (Lord's)   1956

MOST WICKET-KEEPING DISMISSALS IN A SERIES

26 (23ct, 3st) J. H. B. Waite, South Africa v New Zealand   1961–62
26 (26ct) R. W. Marsh, Australia v West Indies   1975–76
24 (22ct, 2st) D. L. Murray, West Indies v England   1963
24 (24ct) D. Lindsay, South Africa v Australia   1966–67
24 (21ct, 3st) A. P. E. Knott, England v Australia   1970–71

HIGHEST WICKET-KEEPING DISMISSAL AGGREGATES

Total		Tests	Ct	St
252	A. P. E. Knott (E)	89	233	19
219	T. G. Evans (E)	91	173	46
198	R. W. Marsh (A)	52	190	8
187	A. T. W. Grout (A)	51	163	24
150	D. L. Murray (WI)	49	142	8
141	J. H. B. Waite (SA)	50	124	17
130	W. A. Oldfield (A)	54	78	52
114	J. M. Parks (E)	46	103	11
101	Wasim Bari (P)	36	86	15

NB Parks' figures include 2 catches as a fielder.

HIGHEST RUN AGGREGATES

Runs			Tests	Inns	NO	HS	Avge	100s	50s
8032	G. S. Sobers	(WI)	93	160	21	365*	57.78	26	30
7624	M. C. Cowdrey	(E)	114	188	15	182	44.06	22	38
7249	W. R. Hammond	(E)	85	140	16	336*	58.45	22	24
6996	D. G. Bradman	(A)	52	80	10	334	99.94	29	13
6971	L. Hutton	(E)	79	138	15	364	56.67	19	33
6806	K. F. Barrington	(E)	82	131	15	256	58.67	20	35
6227	R. B. Kanhai	(WI)	79	137	6	256	47.53	15	28
6149	R. N. Harvey	(A)	79	137	10	205	48.41	21	24
5807	D. C. S. Compton	(E)	78	131	15	278	50.06	17	28
5410	J. B. Hobbs	(E)	61	102	7	211	56.94	15	28
5234	W. M. Lawry	(A)	67	123	12	210	47.15	13	27
5187	I. M. Chappell	(A)	72	130	9	196	42.86	14	25
5138	J. H. Edrich	(E)	77	127	9	310*	43.54	12	24
5021	G. Boycott	(E)	66	115	16	246*	50.71	14	27
4960	K. D. Walters	(A)	68	116	12	250	47.69	14	30
4882	T. W. Graveney	(E)	79	123	13	258	44.38	11	20
4737	I. R. Redpath	(A)	66	120	11	171	43.45	8	31
4555	H. Sutcliffe	(E)	54	84	9	194	60.73	16	23
4537	P. B. H. May	(E)	66	106	9	285*	46.77	13	22
4502	E. R. Dexter	(E)	62	102	8	205	47.89	9	27
4466	C. H. Lloyd	(WI)	63	111	8	242*	43.35	11	21
4455	E. D. Weekes	(WI)	48	81	5	207	58.61	15	19
4334	R. C. Fredericks	(WI)	59	109	7	169	42.49	8	26
4175	A. P. E. Knott	(E)	89	138	14	135	33.66	5	28
4131	R. B. Simpson	(A)	52	92	7	311	48.60	8	24
4097	G. S. Chappell	(A)	51	90	13	247*	53.20	14	20
3915	Hanif Mohammad	(P)	55	97	8	337	43.98	12	15
3860	F. M. M. Worrell	(WI)	51	87	9	261	49.48	9	22
3798	C. L. Walcott	(WI)	44	74	7	220	56.68	15	14
3631	P. R. Umrigar	(I)	59	94	8	223	42.22	12	14
3612	D. L. Amiss	(E)	50	88	10	262*	46.30	11	11
3599	A. W. Greig	(E)	58	93	4	148	40.43	8	20
3533	A. R. Morris	(A)	46	79	3	206	46.48	12	12

Runs			Tests	Inns	NO	HS	Avge	100s	50s
3525	E. H. Hendren	(E)	51	83	9	205*	47.63	7	21
3471	B. Mitchell	(SA)	42	80	9	189*	48.88	8	21
3428	J. R. Reid	(NZ)	58	108	5	142	33.28	6	22
3412	C. Hill	(A)	49	89	2	191	39.21	7	19
3285	B. E. Congdon	(NZ)	55	102	7	176	34.57	7	19
3283	Mushtaq Mohammad	(P)	49	88	7	201	40.53	10	17
3283	F. E. Woolley	(E)	64	98	7	154	36.07	5	23
3245	C. C. Hunte	(WI)	44	78	6	260	45.06	8	13
3208	V. L. Manjrekar	(I)	55	92	10	189*	39.12	7	15
3163	V. T. Trumper	(A)	48	89	8	214*	39.04	8	13
3106	C. C. McDonald	(A)	47	83	4	170	39.31	5	17
3104	B. F. Butcher	(WI)	44	78	6	209*	43.11	7	16
3073	A. L. Hassett	(A)	43	69	3	198*	46.56	10	11
3061	C. G. Borde	(I)	55	97	11	177*	35.59	5	18

HIGHEST WICKET AGGREGATES

Wkts			Tests	Balls	Mdns	Runs	Avge	5 wI	10 wM
309	L. R. Gibbs	(WI)	79	27115	1313	8989	29.09	18	2
307	F. S. Trueman	(E)	67	15178	522	6625	21.57	17	3
265	D. L. Underwood	(E)	74	18979	1063	6600	24.90	16	6
252	J. B. Statham	(E)	70	16056	595	6261	24.84	9	1
248	R. Benaud	(A)	63	19090	805	6704	27.03	16	1
246	G. D. McKenzie	(A)	60	17681	547	7238	29.78	16	3
236	A. V. Bedser	(E)	51	15923	572	5876	24.89	15	5
235	G. S. Sobers	(WI)	93	21599	995	7999	34.03	6	—
228	R. R. Lindwall	(A)	61	13666	418	5257	23.05	12	—
216	C. V. Grimmett	(A)	37	14513	735	5231	24.21	21	7
215	B. S. Bedi	(I)	53	17376	970	5875	27.32	11	—
202	J. A. Snow	(E)	49	12021	415	5387	26.66	8	1
194	B. S. Chandrasekhar	(I)	45	12674	513	5566	28.69	12	1
193	J. C. Laker	(E)	46	12009	673	4099	21.23	9	3
192	W. W. Hall	(WI)	48	10415	312	5066	26.38	9	1
189	S. F. Barnes	(E)	27	7873	356	3106	16.43	24	7
186	A. K. Davidson	(A)	44	11665	432	3838	20.58	14	2
181	E. A. S. Prasanna	(I)	43	12887	553	5212	28.79	10	2
174	G. A. R. Lock	(E)	49	13147	819	4451	25.58	9	3
171	D. K. Lillee	(A)	32	8791	266	4017	23.49	12	4
170	K. R. Miller	(A)	55	10474	338	3905	22.97	7	1
170	H. J. Tayfield	(SA)	37	13568	602	4405	25.91	14	2
162	V. Mankad	(I)	44	14686	777	5235	32.31	8	2
160	W. A. Johnston	(A)	40	11048	370	3825	23.90	7	—
158	S. Ramadhin	(WI)	43	13939	813	4579	28.98	10	1
155	M. W. Tate	(E)	39	12523	581	4055	26.16	7	1
153	F. J. Titmus	(E)	53	15118	777	4931	32.22	7	—

MOST TEST APPEARANCES FOR EACH COUNTRY

NB *The abandoned match at Melbourne in 1970–71 is excluded from these figures.*

England		Australia	
M. C. Cowdrey	114	R. N. Harvey	79
T. G. Evans	91	I. M. Chappell	72
A. P. E. Knott	89	K. D. Walters	68
W. R. Hammond	85	W. M. Lawry	67

K. F. Barrington	82	I. R. Redpath	66
T. W. Graveney	79	R. Benaud	63
L. Hutton	79	R. R. Lindwall	61
D. C. S. Compton	78	G. D. McKenzie	60
J. H. Edrich	77	S. E. Gregory	58
D. L. Underwood	74	K. R. Miller	55
J. B. Statham	70	W. A. S. Oldfield	54
F. S. Trueman	67	D. G. Bradman	52
G. Boycott	66	R. W. Marsh	52
P. B. H. May	66	R. B. Simpson	52
F. E. Woolley	64	G. S. Chappell	51
E. R. Dexter	62	A. T. W. Grout	51

	South Africa		**West Indies**	
J. H. B. Waite	50	G. S. Sobers	93
A. W. Nourse	45	L. R. Gibbs	79
B. Mitchell	42	R. B. Kanhai	79
H. W. Taylor	42	C. H. Lloyd	63
T. L. Goddard	41	R. C. Fredericks	59
R. A. McLean	40	F. M. M. Worrell	51
H. J. Tayfield	37	D. L. Murray	49
D. J. McGlew	34	W. W. Hall	48
A. D. Nourse	34	E. D. Weekes	48
E. J. Barlow	30	B. F. Butcher	44
W. R. Endean	28	C. C. Hunte	44
P. M. Pollock	28	C. L. Walcott	44
K. G. Viljoen	27	S. Ramadhin	43
		A. I. Kallicharran	40

New Zealand

J. R. Reid	58
B. E. Congdon	55
B. Sutcliffe	42
G. T. Dowling	39
G. M. Turner	39
M. G. Burgess	38
K. J. Wadsworth	33
R. C. Motz	32
V. Pollard	32
R. O. Collinge	31
B. F. Hastings	31
H. J. Howarth	30
B. R. Taylor	30

	India		**Pakistan**	
P. R. Umrigar	59	Hanif Mohammad	55
C. G. Borde	55	Mushtaq Mohammad	49
V. L. Manjrekar	55	Intikhab Alam	47
B. S. Bedi	53	Asif Iqbal	45
F. M. Engineer	46	Imtiaz Ahmed	41
M. A. K. Pataudi	46	Saeed Ahmed	41
B. S. Chandrasekhar	45	Majid Khan	37
V. Mankad	44	Wasim Bari	36
E. A. S. Prasanna	43	Fazal Mahmood	34
P. Roy	43	Nasim-ul-Ghani	29
R. G. Nadkarni	41	Sadiq Mohammad	29

ENGLAND

BATTING AND FIELDING

	M	I	NO	Runs	HS	Avge	100	50	Ct	St
D. L. Amiss	50	88	10	3612	262*	46.30	11	11	24	—
G. G. Arnold	34	46	11	421	59	12.02	—	1	9	—
J. C. Balderstone	2	4	0	39	35	9.75	—	—	1	—
G. D. Barlow	3	5	1	17	7*	4.25	—	—	—	—
J. Birkenshaw	5	7	0	148	64	21.14	—	1	3	—
I. T. Botham	2	2	0	25	25	12.50	—	—	1	—
G. Boycott	66	115	16	5021	246*	50.71	14	27	20	—
J. M. Brearley	13	23	0	587	91	25.52	—	3	18	—
D. J. Brown	26	34	5	342	44*	11.79	—	—	7	—
M. H. Denness	28	45	3	1667	188	39.69	4	7	28	—
B. L. D'Oliveira	44	70	8	2484	158	40.06	5	15	29	—
P. H. Edmonds	2	4	1	32	13*	10.66	—	—	—	—
J. H. Edrich	77	127	9	5138	310*	43.54	12	24	43	—
K. W. R. Fletcher	52	85	11	2975	216	40.20	7	16	46	—
N. Gifford	15	20	9	179	25*	16.27	—	—	8	—
G. A. Gooch	2	4	0	37	31	9.25	—	—	2	—
A. W. Greig	58	93	4	3599	148	40.43	8	20	87	—
J. H. Hampshire	8	16	1	403	107	26.86	1	2	9	—
F. C. Hayes	9	17	1	244	106*	15.25	1	—	7	—
M. Hendrick	13	13	5	45	15	5.62	—	—	16	—
K. Higgs	15	19	3	185	63	11.56	—	1	4	—
R. Illingworth	61	90	11	1836	113	23.24	2	5	45	—
A. P. E. Knott	89	138	14	4175	135	33.66	5	28	233	19
J. K. Lever	9	14	1	161	53	12.38	—	1	7	—
D. Lloyd	9	15	2	552	214*	42.46	1	—	11	—
G. Miller	3	4	0	79	36	19.75	—	—	—	—
C. M. Old	33	49	6	671	65	15.60	—	2	21	—
P. I. Pocock	17	27	2	165	33	6.60	—	—	13	—
D. W. Randall	10	17	2	471	174	31.40	1	2	7	—
G. R. J. Roope	11	18	1	451	77	26.52	—	3	18	—
M. W. W. Selvey	3	5	3	15	5*	7.50	—	—	1	—
K. Shuttleworth	5	6	0	46	21	7.66	—	—	1	—
J. A. Snow	49	71	14	772	73	13.54	—	2	16	—
D. S. Steele	8	16	0	673	106	42.06	1	5	7	—
R. W. Taylor	1	1	0	4	4	4.00	—	—	2	1
R. W. Tolchard	4	7	2	129	67	25.80	—	1	5	—
D. L. Underwood	74	100	31	824	45*	11.94	—	—	39	—
A. Ward	5	6	1	40	21	8.00	—	—	3	—
P. Willey	2	4	0	115	45	28.75	—	—	—	—
R. G. D. Willis	29	45	24	257	24*	12.23	—	—	17	—
B. Wood	11	20	0	440	90	22.00	—	2	6	—
R. A. Woolmer	15	26	1	920	149	36.80	3	2	8	—

BOWLING

	Balls	Runs	Wkts	Avge	Best	5 wI	10 wM
G. G. Arnold	7650	3254	115	28.29	6–45	6	—
J. C. Balderstone	96	80	1	80.00	1–80	—	—
J. Birkenshaw	1017	469	13	36.07	5–57	1	—
I. T. Botham	438	202	10	20.20	5–21	2	—
G. Boycott	792	346	7	49.42	3–47	—	—
D. J. Brown	5098	2237	79	28.31	5–42	2	—
B. L. D'Oliveira	5706	1859	47	39.55	3–46	—	—
P. H. Edmonds	487	224	6	37.33	5–28	1	—
J. H. Edrich	30	23	0	—	—	—	—
K. W. R. Fletcher	249	173	1	173.00	1–48	—	—
N. Gifford	3084	1026	33	31.09	5–55	1	—
A. W. Greig	9802	4541	141	32.20	8–86	6	2
M. Hendrick	2542	1100	42	26.19	4–28	—	—
K. Higgs	4112	1473	71	20.74	6–91	2	—
R. Illingworth	11934	3807	122	31.20	6–29	3	—
J. K. Lever	1612	708	35	20.22	7–46	2	1
D. Lloyd	24	17	0	—	—	—	—
G. Miller	306	153	4	38.25	2–18	—	—
C. M. Old	6024	3032	102	29.72	5–21	2	—
P. I. Pocock	4482	2023	47	43.04	6–79	3	—
G. R. J. Roope	156	72	0	—	—	—	—
M. W. W. Selvey	492	343	6	57.16	4–41	—	—
K. Shuttleworth	1071	427	12	35.58	5–47	1	—
J. A. Snow	12021	5387	202	26.66	7–40	8	1
D. S. Steele	88	39	2	19.50	1–1	—	—
D. L. Underwoo	18979	6600	265	24.90	8–51	16	6
A. Ward	761	453	14	32.35	4–61	—	—
P. Willey	24	15	0	—	—	—	—
R. G. D. Willis	5457	2746	105	26.15	7–78	7	—
B. Wood	80	48	0	—	—	—	—
R. A. Woolmer	546	299	4	74.75	1–8	—	—

AUSTRALIA

BATTING AND FIELDING

	M	I	NO	Runs	HS	Avge	100	50	Ct	St
R. J. Bright	3	1	1	42	16	10.50	—	—	2	—
G. S. Chappell	51	90	13	4097	247*	53.20	14	20	73	—
D. J. Colley	3	4	0	84	54	21.00	—	1	1	—
B. J. Cosier	9	14	1	522	168	40.15	2	1	5	—
I. C. Davis	15	27	1	692	105	26.61	1	4	9	—
G. Dymock	4	5	1	13	13	3.25	—	—	—	—
G. J. Gilmour	15	22	1	483	101	23.00	1	3	8	—
J. R. Hammond	5	5	2	28	19	9.33	—	—	2	—
D. W. Hookes	6	11	0	356	85	32.36	—	3	2	—
K. J. Hughes	1	1	0	1	1	1.00	—	—	—	—
A. G. Hurst	1	1	0	16	16	16.00	—	—	—	—
T. J. Jenner	9	14	5	208	74	23.11	—	1	5	—
D. K. Lillee	32	40	14	448	73*	17.23	—	1	9	—
R. B. McCosker	22	40	5	1498	127	42.80	4	9	18	—
A. A. Mallett	35	47	13	393	43*	11.55	—	—	29	—

	M	I	NO	Runs	HS	Avge	100	50	Ct	St
M. F. Malone	1	1	0	46	46	46.00	—	—	—	8
R. W. Marsh	52	82	9	2396	132	32.82	3	12	190	8
K. J. O'Keeffe	24	34	9	644	85	25.76	—	1	15	—
L. S. Pascoe	3	5	2	23	20	7.66	—	—	—	—
R. D. Robinson	3	6	0	100	34	16.66	—	—	4	—
C. S. Serjeant	3	5	0	106	81	21.20	—	1	1	—
R. B. Simpson	52	92	7	4131	311	48.60	8	24	99	—
J. R. Thomson	22	25	4	288	49	13.71	—	—	9	—
A. Turner	14	27	1	768	136	29.53	1	3	15	—
M. H. N. Walker	34	43	13	586	78*	19.53	—	1	12	—
K. D. Walters	68	116	12	4960	250	47.69	14	30	38	—
G. D. Watson	5	9	0	97	50	10.77	—	1	1	—
A. J. Woodcock	1	1	0	27	27	27.00	—	—	1	—
G. N. Yallop	3	5	1	179	57	44.75	—	1	1	—

BOWLING

	Balls	Runs	Wkts	Avge	Best	5 wI	10 wM
R. J. Bright	433	147	5	29.40	3–69	—	—
G. S. Chappell	3752	1399	32	43.71	5–61	1	—
D. J. Colley	729	312	6	52.00	3–83	—	—
G. J. Cosier	152	72	0	—	—	—	—
G. Dymock	1352	452	14	32.28	5–58	1	—
G. J. Gilmour	2661	1406	54	26.03	6–85	3	—
J. R. Hammond	1031	488	15	32.53	4–38	—	—
A. G. Hurst	232	73	1	73.00	1–56	—	—
T. J. Jenner	1881	749	24	31.20	5–90	1	—
D. K. Lillee	8791	4017	171	23.49	6–26	12	4
A. A. Mallett	9136	3494	125	27.95	8–59	6	1
M. F. Malone	342	77	6	12.83	5–63	1	—
K. J. O'Keeffe	5384	2018	53	38.07	5–101	1	—
L. S. Pascoe	826	363	13	27.92	4–80	—	—
R. B. Simpson	5757	2352	60	39.20	5–57	2	—
J. R. Thomson	5083	2607	103	25.31	6–46	5	—
M. H. N. Walker	10094	3792	138	27.47	8–143	6	—
K. D. Walters	3211	1378	49	28.12	5–66	1	—
G. D. Watson	552	254	6	42.33	2–67	—	—

WEST INDIES

BATTING AND FIELDING

	M	I	NO	Runs	HS	Avge	100	50	Ct	St
Imtiaz Ali	1	1	1	1	1*	—	—	—	—	—
Inshan Ali	12	18	2	172	25	10.75	—	—	7	—
L. Baichan	3	6	2	184	105*	46.00	1	—	2	—
A. G. Barrett	6	7	1	40	19	6.66	—	—	2	—
C. E. H. Croft	5	8	7	53	23*	53.00	—	—	6	—
W. W. Daniel	5	5	2	29	11	9.66	—	—	2	—
C. A. Davis	15	29	5	1301	183	54.20	4	4	4	—
U. G. Dowe	4	3	2	8	5*	8.00	—	—	3	—
T. M. Findlay	10	16	3	212	44*	16.30	—	—	19	2
M. L. C. Foster	13	22	5	567	125	33.35	1	1	2	—
R. C. Fredericks	59	109	7	4334	169	42.49	8	26	62	—
J. Garner	5	8	0	92	43	11.50	—	—	6	—

212

H. A. Gomes	2	3	0	11	11	3.66	—	—	1	—
C. G. Greenidge	17	33	1	1510	134	47.18	5	8	21	—
G. A. Greenidge	5	9	2	209	50	29.85	—	1	3	—
V. A. Holder	31	45	9	534	42	14.83	—	—	14	—
M. A. Holding	13	20	1	213	55	11.21	—	1	3	—
D. A. J. Holford	24	39	5	768	105*	22.58	1	3	18	—
A. B. Howard	1	—	—	—	—	—	—	—	—	—
B. D. Julien	24	34	6	866	121	30.92	2	3	14	—
R. R. Jumadeen	8	8	5	20	11*	6.66	—	—	3	—
A. I. Kallicharran	40	68	7	2923	158	47.91	8	16	34	—
R. B. Kanhai	79	137	6	6227	256	47.53	15	28	50	—
C. L. King	4	7	1	211	63	35.16	—	2	3	—
D. M. Lewis	3	5	2	259	88	86.33	—	3	8	—
C. H. Lloyd	63	111	8	4466	242*	43.35	11	21	41	—
D. L. Murray	49	78	8	1624	91	23.20	—	9	142	8
A. L. Padmore	2	2	1	8	8*	8.00	—	—	—	—
I. V. A. Richards	26	45	2	2438	291	56.69	8	8	23	—
A. M. E. Roberts	25	34	5	218	35	7.51	—	—	5	—
L. G. Rowe	24	38	2	1706	302	47.38	6	5	13	—
G. C. Shillingford	7	8	1	57	25	8.14	—	—	2	—
I. T. Shillingford	3	5	0	199	120	39.80	1	—	1	—
E. T. Willett	5	8	3	74	26	14.80	—	—	—	—

BOWLING

	Balls	Runs	Wkts	Avge	Best	5 wI	10 wM
Imtiaz Ali	204	89	2	44.50	2–37	—	—
Inshan Ali	3718	1621	34	47.67	5–59	1	—
A. G. Barrett	1612	603	13	46.38	3–43	—	—
C. E. H. Croft	1307	676	33	20.48	8–29	1	—
W. W. Daniel	788	381	15	25.40	4–53	—	—
C. A. Davis	894	330	2	165.00	1–27	—	—
U. G. Dowe	1014	534	12	44.50	4–69	—	—
M. L. C. Foster	1542	510	8	63.75	2–41	—	—
R. C. Fredericks	1187	548	7	78.28	1–12	—	—
J. Garner	1317	688	25	27.52	4–48	—	—
H. A. Gomes	78	26	0	—	—	—	—
C. G. Greenidge	8	0	0	—	—	—	—
G. A. Greenidge	156	75	0	—	—	—	—
V. A. Holder	7217	2831	90	31.44	6–39	2	—
M. A. Holding	2910	1348	57	23.64	8–92	4	1
D. A. J. Holford	4816	2009	51	39.39	5–23	1	—
A. B. Howard	372	140	2	70.00	2–140	—	—
B. D. Julien	4542	1868	50	37.36	5–57	1	—
R. R. Jumadeen	2034	654	15	43.60	3–57	—	—
A. I. Kallicharran	151	73	1	73.00	1–7	—	—
R. B. Kanhai	183	85	0	—	—	—	—
C. L. King	276	113	2	56.50	1–30	—	—
C. H. Lloyd	1710	621	10	62.10	2–13	—	—
A. L. Padmore	464	135	1	135.00	1–36	—	—
I. V. A. Richards	644	235	4	58.75	2–34	—	—
A. M. E. Roberts	6472	3087	122	25.30	7–54	8	2
L. G. Rowe	56	40	0	—	—	—	—
G. C. Shillingford	1181	537	15	35.80	3–63	—	—
E. T. Willett	1326	482	11	43.81	3–33	—	—

NEW ZEALAND

BATTING AND FIELDING

	M	I	NO	Runs	HS	Avge	100	50	Ct	St
R. W. Anderson	3	6	0	178	92	29.66	—	1	—	—
G. P. Bilby	2	4	0	55	28	13.75	—	—	3	—
M. G. Burgess	38	69	4	2173	119*	33.43	5	11	26	—
B. L. Cairns	8	14	4	207	52*	20.70	—	1	3	—
E. J. Chatfield	3	5	3	22	13*	11.00	—	—	—	—
R. O. Collinge	31	42	11	458	68*	14.77	—	2	9	—
J. V. Coney	4	7	0	123	45	17.57	—	—	6	—
B. E. Congdon	55	102	7	3285	176	34.57	7	19	40	—
R. S. Cunis	20	31	8	295	51	12.82	—	1	1	—
G. N. Edwards	2	4	0	100	51	25.00	—	1	2	—
D. R. Hadlee	25	40	5	527	56	15.05	—	1	8	—
R. J. Hadlee	17	30	3	617	87	22.85	—	2	10	—
B. F. Hastings	31	56	6	1510	117*	30.20	4	7	23	—
G. P. Howarth	8	15	1	305	59	21.78	—	2	2	—
H. J. Howarth	30	42	18	291	61	12.12	—	1	33	—
T. W. Jarvis	13	22	1	625	182	29.76	1	2	3	—
W. K. Lees	7	14	1	440	152	33.84	1	—	8	7
R. W. Morgan	20	34	1	734	97	22.24	—	5	12	—
J. F. M. Morrison	14	24	0	610	117	25.41	1	3	9	—
D. R. O'Sullivan	11	21	4	158	23*	9.29	—	—	2	—
J. M. Parker	23	39	0	1073	121	27.51	3	2	21	—
N. M. Parker	3	6	0	89	40	14.83	—	—	2	—
P. J. Petherick	6	11	4	34	13	4.85	—	—	4	—
A. D. G. Roberts	7	12	1	254	84*	23.09	—	1	4	—
M. J. F. Shrimpton	10	19	0	265	46	13.94	—	—	2	—
G. B. Troup	1	1	0	0	0	0.00	—	—	1	—
G. M. Turner	39	70	6	2920	259	45.62	7	14	40	—
G. E. Vivian	5	6	0	110	43	18.33	—	—	3	—

BOWLING

	Balls	Runs	Wkts	Avge	Best	5 wI	10 wM
M. G. Burgess	498	212	6	35.33	3–23	—	—
B. L. Cairns	1626	675	16	42.18	5–55	1	—
E. J. Chatfield	718	369	7	52.71	4–100	—	—
R. O. Collinge	6636	3016	99	30.46	6–63	3	—
J. V. Coney	16	13	0	—	—	—	—
J. E. Congdon	4710	1914	57	33.57	5–65	1	—
R. S. Cunis	4250	1887	51	37.00	6–76	1	—
D. R. Hadlee	4707	2342	71	32.98	4–30	—	—
R. J. Hadlee	3736	2170	61	35.57	7–23	2	1
B. F. Hastings	22	9	0	—	—	—	—
G. P. Howarth	240	109	2	54.50	1–13	—	—
H. J. Howarth	8833	3178	86	36.95	5–34	2	—
T. W. Jarvis	12	3	0	—	—	—	—
W. K. Lees	5	4	0	—	—	—	—
R. W. Morgan	1114	609	5	121.80	1–16	—	—
J. F. M. Morrison	24	9	0	—	—	—	—
D. R. O'Sullivan	2739	1219	18	67.72	5–148	1	—
J. M. Parker	40	24	1	24.00	1–24	—	—

P. J. Petherick	1305	687	16	42.93	3–90	—	—
A. D. G. Roberts	440	182	4	45.50	1–12	—	—
M. J. F. Shrimpton	257	158	5	31.60	3–35	—	—
G. B. Troup	180	116	1	116.00	1–69	—	—
G. M. Turner	12	5	0			—	—
G. E. Vivian	198	107	1	107.00	1–14	—	—

INDIA

BATTING AND FIELDING

	M	I	NO	Runs	HS	Avge	100	50	Ct	St
M. Amarnath	13	24	1	738	85	32.08	—	5	14	—
S. Amarnath	7	13	0	403	124	31.00	1	2	4	—
B. S. Bedi	53	82	20	553	50*	8.91	—	1	22	—
B.S. Chandrasekhar	45	64	33	158	22	5.09	—	—	21	—
C. P. S. Chauhan	5	10	0	139	34	13.90	—	—	9	—
A. D. Gaekwad	13	24	2	703	81*	31.95	—	4	5	—
S. M. Gavaskar	32	62	5	2776	220	48.70	10	14	27	—
K. D. Ghavri	8	14	3	231	37	21.00	—	—	3	—
S. M. H. Kirmani	15	23	4	490	88	25.78	—	3	27	11
S. Madan Lal	14	26	6	376	55*	18.80	—	1	7	—
A. V. Mankad	19	37	3	872	97	25.64	—	6	11	—
B. P. Patel	19	34	5	926	115*	31.93	1	5	14	—
E. A. S. Prasanna	43	74	15	628	37	10.64	—	—	16	—
P. Sharma	5	10	0	187	54	18.70	—	1	1	—
E. D. Solkar	27	48	6	1068	102	25.42	1	6	53	—
D. B. Vengsarkar	6	11	1	152	39	15.20	—	—	4	—
S.Venkataraghavan	36	53	8	609	64	13.53	—	2	32	—
G. R. Viswanath	38	73	7	2681	139	40.62	5	16	28	—
Yajurvindra Singh	2	4	0	50	21	12.50	—	—	8	—

BOWLING

	Balls	Runs	Wkts	Avge	Best	5 wI	10 wM
M. Amarnath	1235	498	10	49.80	4–63	—	—
B. S. Bedi	17376	5875	215	27.32	7–98	11	—
B. S. Chandrasekhar	12674	5566	194	28.69	8–79	12	1
A. D. Gaekwad	36	16	0	—	—	—	—
S. M. Gavaskar	156	65	0	—	—	—	—
K. D. Ghavri	1026	562	19	29.57	5–33	1	—
S. Madan Lal	2017	780	20	39.00	5–134	1	—
A. V. Mankad	41	43	0	—	—	—	—
E. A. S. Prasanna	12887	5212	181	28.79	8–76	10	2
P. Sharma	24	8	0	—	—	—	—
E. D. Solkar	2265	1070	18	59.44	3–28	—	—
D. B. Vengsarkar	5	7	0	—	—	—	—
S.Venkataraghavan	9893	3655	111	32.92	8–72	3	1
G. R. Viswanath	24	18	0	—	—	—	—
Yajurvindra Singh	6	2	0	—	—	—	—

PAKISTAN

BATTING AND FIELDING

	M	I	NO	Runs	HS	Avge	100	50	Ct	St
Asif Iqbal	45	77	4	2748	175	37.64	8	10	29	—
Asif Masood	16	19	10	93	30*	10.33	—	—	5	—
Farukh Zaman	1	—	—	—	—	—	—	—	—	—
Haroon Rashid	6	11	0	357	72	32.45	—	3	5	—
Imran Khan	15	26	2	503	59	20.95	—	1	8	—
Intikhab Alam	47	77	10	1493	138	22.28	1	8	20	—
Iqbal Qasim	5	8	3	13	4	2.60	—	—	5	—
Javed Miandad	7	12	1	655	206	59.54	2	3	6	—
Majid Khan	37	64	2	2651	167	42.75	5	13	47	—
Mudassar Nazar	1	2	0	35	22	17.50	—	—	—	—
Mushtaq Mohammad	49	88	7	3283	201	40.53	10	17	33	—
Sadiq Mohammad	29	53	2	2070	166	40.58	5	8	22	—
Salim Altaf	20	31	12	276	53*	14.52	—	1	3	—
Sarfraz Nawaz	22	32	5	401	53	14.85	—	2	15	—
Shahid Israr	1	1	1	7	7*	—	—	—	2	—
Sikander Bakht	2	2	2	1	1*	—	—	—	1	—
Wasim Bari	36	56	15	703	72	17.14	—	4	86	15
Wasim Raja	14	26	5	946	117*	45.04	2	6	4	—
Zaheer Abbas	26	47	1	1583	274	34.41	3	6	18	—

BOWLING

	Balls	Runs	Wkts	Avge	Best	5 wI	10 wM
Asif Iqbal	3574	1401	50	28.02	5–48	2	—
Asif Masood	3038	1568	38	41.26	5–111	1	—
Farukh Zaman	80	15	0	—	—	—	—
Imran Khan	4129	2045	62	32.98	6–63	4	1
Intikhab Alam	10475	4492	125	35.93	7–52	5	2
Iqbal Qasim	1104	506	13	38.92	4–84	—	—
Javed Miandad	1056	460	14	32.85	3–74	—	—
Majid Khan	2668	1066	24	44.41	4–45	—	—
Mushtaq Mohammad	4063	1770	62	28.54	5–28	2	—
Sadiq Mohammad	170	78	0	—	—	—	—
Salim Altaf	3827	1640	45	36.44	4–11	—	—
Sarfraz Nawaz	5422	2422	72	33.63	6–89	1	—
Sikander Bakht	360	232	8	29.00	3–55	—	—
Wasim Raja	890	449	13	34.53	3–22	—	—
Zaheer Abbas	20	2	0	—	—	—	—

The earliest known laws of cricket were framed in 1774, but although there must have been something in existence before this date, they have never been to come to light.

The establishment of MCC in 1787 was inexorably linked with the name Thomas Lord – hence the name Lord's. It has no connection with the peerage! Lord was born at Thirsk in Yorkshire. Lord's first ground on what is now Dorset Square was opened in 1787. The first match played there was between Middlesex and Essex – for two hundred guineas.

PRINCIPAL FIXTURES 1978

Including play on Sunday

Wednesday 19 April
Lord's: MCC v Middlesex
Cambridge: Cambridge U v Essex
Oxford: Oxford U v Somerset

Saturday 22 April
Benson & Hedges Cup
Ilkeston: Derbys v Warwicks
Chelmsford: Essex v Surrey
Cardiff: Glam v Somerset
Canterbury: Kent v Yorks
Leicester: Leics v Sussex
Ipswich: M Counties (E) v Middx
Chippenham: M Counties (W) v
   Glos
Cambridge: Oxford U and
   Cambridge U v Hants

Wednesday 26 April
Worcester: Worcs v Pakistan
Oxford: Oxford U v Warwicks
Cambridge: Cambridge U v Middx

Saturday 29 April
Leicester: Leics v Pakistan
Cambridge: Cambridge U v Glos
Oxford: Oxford U v Kent
Benson & Hedges Cup
Southampton: Hants v Somerset
Old Trafford: Lancs v Derbys
Lord's: Middx v Northants
The Oval: Surrey v Notts
Eastbourne: Sussex v M Counties
   (E)
Edgbaston: Warwicks v M Counties
   (W)
Worcester: Worcs v Glam
Harrogate: Yorks v Essex

Sunday 30 April
John Player League
Derby: Derbys v Glos
Bournemouth: Hants v Somerset
Old Trafford: Lancs v Kent
Leicester: Leics v Warwicks
Lord's: Middx v Northants
Hove: Sussex v Notts
Worcester: Worcs v Glam
Bradford: Yorks v Essex

Wednesday 3 May
Burton-on-Trent: Derbys v
   Somerset
Cardiff: Glam v Worcs
Bristol: Glos v Northants
Old Trafford: Lancs v Sussex
Leicester: Leics v Essex
Lord's: Middx v Hants
Trent Bridge: Notts v Pakistan
Edgbaston: Warwicks v Surrey
Headingley: Yorks v Kent
Cambridge: Cambridge U v MCC

Saturday 6 May
Bradford: *Yorks v Pakistan
Benson & Hedges Cup
Chelmsford: Essex v Notts
Swansea: Glam v Hants
Bristol: Glos v Derbys
Northampton: Northants v Sussex
The Oval: Surrey v Kent
Worcester: Worcs v Oxford U and
   Cambridge U
Amersham: M Counties (E) v
   Leics

Sunday 7 May
John Player League
Derby: Derbys v Sussex
Chelmsford: Essex v Notts
Bristol: Glos v Middx
Maidstone: Kent v Somerset
Northampton: Northants v Lancs
The Oval: Surrey v Leics

Monday 8 May
Benson & Hedges Cup
Coventry (Courtaulds): Warwicks v
   Lancs

Wednesday 10 May
Chelmsford: Essex v Middx
Canterbury: Kent v Hants
Old Trafford: Lancs v Derbys
Northampton: Northants v
   Pakistan
Taunton: Somerset v Glam
The Oval: Surrey v Sussex
Edgbaston: Warwicks v Yorks

217

Worcester: Worcs v Notts
Cambridge: Cambridge U v Leics
Oxford: Oxford U v Glos

Saturday 13 May
Chelmsford: Essex v Pakistan
Benson & Hedges Cup
Derby: Derbys v M Counties (W)
Liverpool: Lancs v Glos
Leicester: Leics v Northants
Trent Bridge: Notts v Kent
Taunton: Somerset v Worcs
Hove: Sussex v Middx
Barnsley: Yorks v Surrey
Oxford: Oxford U and Cambridge
   U v Glam

Sunday 14 May
John Player League
Chelmsford: Essex v Glam
Old Trafford: Lancs v Glos
Taunton: Somerset v Worcs
Hove: Sussex v Hants
Edgbaston: Warwicks v Kent
Huddersfield: Yorks v Derbys

Wednesday 17 May
Old Trafford: Lancs v Scotland
Lord's: MCC v Pakistan
Cambridge: Cambridge U v Surrey
Oxford: Oxford U v Yorks

Saturday 20 May
Chesterfield: Derbys v Pakistan
Benson & Hedges Cup
Bristol: Glos v Warwicks
Bournemouth: Hants v Worcs
Dartford: Kent v Essex
Lord's: Middx v Leics
Northampton: Northants v M
   Counties (E)
Trent Bridge: Notts v Yorks
Taunton: Somerset v Oxford U and
   Cambridge U
Watford (Town Gd.): M Counties
   (W) v Lancs

Sunday 21 May
John Player League
Ebbw Vale: Glam v Yorks
Southampton: Hants v Warwicks
Canterbury: Kent v Essex
Lord's: Middx v Lancs
Northampton: Northants v Sussex

Trent Bridge: Notts v Leics
Yeovil: Somerset v Surrey

Wednesday 24 May
Bristol: Glos v Worcs
Portsmouth: Hants v Surrey
Leicester: Leics v Warwicks
Lord's: Middx v Lancs
Northampton: Northants v Notts
Taunton: Somerset v Kent
Sheffield: Yorks v Derbys
Oxford: Oxford U v Sussex

Wednesday 24 May
Old Trafford: PRUDENTIAL
   TROPHY: England v Pakistan
   (First One Day International
   Match)

Friday 26 May
The Oval: PRUDENTIAL
   TROPHY: England v Pakistan
   (Second One Day International
   Match)

Saturday 27 May
Swansea: Glam v Hants
Canterbury: Kent v Pakistan
Lord's: Middx v Sussex
Northampton: Northants v Leics
Trent Bridge: Notts v Derbys
Taunton: Somerset v Glos
The Oval: Surrey v Essex
Worcester: Worcs v Warwicks
Headingley: *Yorks v Lancs
Oxford: Oxford U v Free Foresters

Sunday 28 May
John Player League
Swansea: Glam v Hants
Bristol: Glos v Northants
Leicester: Leics v Middx
Trent Bridge: Notts v Derbys
The Oval: Surrey v Sussex
Worcester: Worcs v Warwicks

Wednesday 31 May
Derby: Derbys v Leics
Ilford: Essex v Kent
Old Trafford: Lancs v Worcs
Lord's: Middx v Northants
Worksop: Notts v Yorks
The Oval: Surrey v Somerset
Hove: Sussex v Glos
Oxford: Oxford U v Glam

Thursday 1 June
Cornhill Insurance Test Series
**EDGBASTON: ENGLAND v
PAKISTAN (first test match)**

Saturday 3 June
Ilkeston: Derbys v Surrey
Ilford: Essex v Northants
Swansea: Glam v Leics
Bournemouth: Hants v Lancs
Lord's: Middx v Kent
Trent Bridge: Notts v Warwicks
Hove: Sussex v Somerset
Middlesbrough: Yorks v Worcs
Oxford: Oxford U v MCC

Sunday 4 June
John Player League
Long Eaton (Trent College): Derbys
    v Surrey
Ilford: Essex v Northants
Swansea: Glam v Leics
Portsmouth: Hants v Lancs
Lord's: Middx v Kent
Horsham: Sussex v Somerset
Middlesbrough: Yorks v Worcs

Wednesday 7 June
Benson & Hedges Cup
(quarter-finals)
Cambridge: Cambridge U v Lancs
Oxford: Oxford U v Combined
    Services

Saturday 10 June
Chesterfield: Derbys v Glam
Gloucester: Glos v Essex
Southampton: Hants v Pakistan
Tunbridge Wells: Kent v Sussex
Leicester: Leics v Yorks
Northampton: Northants v Worcs
Bath: Somerset v Lancs
The Oval: Surrey v Notts
Edgbaston: Warwicks v Middx

Sunday 11 June
John Player League
Gloucester: Glos v Essex
Canterbury: Kent v Sussex
Leicester: Leics v Yorks
Milton Keynes: Northants v Worcs
Bath: Somerset v Lancs
Byfleet (BAC): Surrey v Notts
Edbaston: Warwicks v Middx

Wednesday 14 June
Cardiff: Glam v Essex
Gloucester: Glos v Derbys
Tunbridge Wells: Kent v Surrey
Northampton: Northants v
    Warwicks
Bath: Somerset v Sussex
Worcester: Worcs v Leics
Bradford: Yorks v Middx
Cambridge: Cambridge U v Notts
Oxford: Oxford U v Hants

Thursday 15 June
Cornhill Insurance Test Series
**LORD'S: ENGLAND v PAKISTAN
(second Test match)**

Saturday 17 June
Cardiff: Glam v Glos
Canterbury: Kent v Middx
Old Trafford: Lancs v Warwicks
Trent Bridge: Notts v Somerset
Hove: Sussex v Hants
Harrogate: Yorks v Northants
Cambridge: Cambridge U v
    Derbys
Eastbourne: D. H. Robins' XI v
    Oxford U

Sunday 18 June
John Player League
Cardiff: Glam v Glos
Bournemouth: Hants v Derbys
Old Trafford: Lancs v Warwicks
Trent Bridge: Notts v Somerset
The Oval: Surrey v Kent
Hove: Sussex v Essex
Worcester: Worcs v Leics
Scarborough: Yorks v Northants

Wednesday 21 June
Benson & Hedges Cup (semi-finals)
Cambridge: Oxford U and
    Cambridge U v Pakistan

Thursday 22 June
Downpatrick: Ireland v MCC
    (Three days)

Saturday 24 June
Chelmsford: Essex v Hants
Dartford: Kent v Northants
Liverpool: Lancs v Glam
Leicester: Leics v Derbys

219

Lord's: Middx v Notts
Taunton: Somerset v Yorks
The Oval: Surrey v Pakistan
Hove: Sussex v New Zealand
Edgbaston: Warwicks v Glos
Worcester: Worcs v Oxford U
Eastbourne: Derrick Robins' XI
v Cambridge U

Sunday 25 June
John Player League
Chelmsford: Essex v Hants
Moreton in Marsh: Glos v Worcs
Old Trafford: Lancs v Glam
Lord's: Middx v Notts
Bristol (Imperial): Somerset v
Yorks
Edgbaston: Warwicks v Surrey

Wednesday 28 June
Bristol: Glos v New Zealand
Southampton: Hants v Leics
Northampton: Northants v Derbys
The Oval: Surrey v Kent
Hove: Sussex v Notts
Nuneaton (Griff & Coton):
Warwicks v Somerset
Worcester: Worcs v Glam
Lord's: Oxford v Cambridge

Thursday 29 June
Cornhill Insurance Test Series
HEADINGLEY: ENGLAND v
PAKISTAN (third Test match)

Saturday 1 July
Chesterfield: Derbys v Sussex
Chelmsford: Essex v Yorks
Leicester: Leics v Glam
Trent Bridge: Notts v Hants
Taunton: Somerset v New Zealand
Guildford: Surrey v Glos
Edgbaston: Warwicks v Northants
Worcester: Worcs v Middx

Sunday 2 July
John Player League
Chesterfield: Derbys v Glam
Canterbury: Kent v Yorks
Old Trafford: Lancs v Sussex
Trent Bridge: Notts v Hants
Guildford: Surrey v Glos
Edgbaston: Warwicks v Northants
Worcester: Worcs v Middx

Wednesday 5 July
Swansea: Glam v New Zealand
Basingstoke: Hants v Glos
Old Trafford: Lancs v Kent
Lord's: Middx v Essex
Gillette Cup 1st round
Torquay: Devon v Staffs
Hove: Sussex v Suffolk
Middlesbrough: Yorks v Durham
Worcester: Worcs v Derbys
Taunton: Somerset v Warwicks
Wellington (Telford): Shropshire v
Surrey

Saturday 8 July
Cardiff: Glam v Somerset
Portsmouth: Hants v Worcs
Maidstone: Kent v Derbys
Old Trafford: Lancs v Notts
Leicester: Leics v Glos
Lord's: Middx v New Zealand
Northampton: Northants v Surrey
Hove: Sussex v Essex
Bradford: Yorks v Warwicks

Sunday 9 July
John Player League
Cardiff: Glam v Somerset
Basingstoke: Hants v Worcs
Maidstone: Kent v Derbys
Leicester: Leics v Glos
Lord's: Middx v Essex
Tring: Northants v Surrey
Headingley: Yorks v Warwicks

Wednesday 12 July
Ilkeston: Derbys v Northants
Colchester: Essex v Somerset
Bristol: Glos v Lancs
Portsmouth: Hants v Sussex
Maidstone: Kent v Glam
Lord's: Middx v Leics
Newark (R.H.P.): Notts v Worcs
The Oval: Surrey v Yorks
Edgbaston: Warwicks v
New Zealand

Saturday 15 July
Scarborough: PRUDENTIAL
TROPHY: England v New Zealand
(First One Day International
Match)
Colchester: Essex v Warwicks
Swansea: Glam v Middx

220

Bristol: Glos v Sussex
Northampton: Northants v Yorks
Trent Bridge: Notts v Lancs
Taunton: Somerset v Leics
The Oval: Surrey v Hants
Worcester: Worcs v Derbys

Sunday 16 July
John Player League
Colchester: Essex v Warwicks
Swansea: Glam v Middx
Bristol: Glos v Sussex
Trent Bridge: Notts v Lancs
Glastonbury: Somerset v Leics
The Oval: Surrey v Hants
Dudley: Worcs v Derbys

Monday 17 July
Old Trafford: PRUDENTIAL
TROPHY: England v New Zealand
(Second One Day International
Match)

Wednesday 19 July
Gillette Cup 2nd round
Torquay or Stone: Devon
or Staffs v Sussex or Suffolk
Northampton: Northants v Kent
Leicester: Leics v Hants
Bradford or Sunderland: Yorks or
Durham v Notts
Old Trafford: Lancs v Glos
Cardiff: Glam v Somerset or
Warwicks
Colchester: Essex v Shrops or
Surrey
Worcester: Worcs or Derbys v
Middx

Saturday 22 July
Lord's: Benson & Hedges Cup Final
Headingley (or Derby): Yorks v
New Zealand (or Derbys v New
Zealand if Yorks in B&H final)

Sunday 23 July
John Player League
Ilkeston: Derbys v Somerset
Chelmsford: Essex v Worcs
Leicester: Leics v Hants
Luton: Northants v Kent
Hove: Sussex v Glam
Edgbaston: Warwicks v Notts
Hull: Yorks v Glos

Wednesday 26 July
Derby: Derbys v Hants
Leicester: Leics v Kent
Northampton: Northants v Essex
Trent Bridge: Notts v Middx
Taunton: Somerset v Worcs
Hove: Sussex v Surrey
Edgbaston: Warwicks v Lancs
Sheffield: Yorks v Glam

Thursday 27 July
Cornhill Insurance Test series
THE OVAL: ENGLAND v
NEW ZEALAND (first Test match)

Saturday 29 July
Chesterfield: Derbys v Yorks
Bournemouth: Hants v Somerset
Southport: Lancs v Essex
Northampton: Northants v Glos
Trent Bridge: Notts v Kent
Hove: Sussex v Leics
Edgbaston: Warwicks v Glam
Worcester: Worcs v Surrey

Sunday 30 July
John Player League
Old Trafford: Lancs v Essex
Lord's: Middx v Yorks
Northampton: Northants v Derbys
Trent Bridge: Notts v Kent
Hove: Sussex v Leics
Edgbaston: Warwicks v Glam
Worcester: Worcs v Surrey

Wednesday 2 August
Gillette Cup (quarter-finals)
Torquay: MCCA v New
Zealand (two days)

Saturday 5 August
Cardiff: Glam v Northants
Cheltenham: Glos v Notts
Southampton: Hants v Yorks
Canterbury: Kent v Leics
Old Trafford: Lancs v New Zealand
Lord's: Middx v Surrey
Weston-super-Mare: Somerset v
Warwicks
Eastbourne: Sussex v Worcs

Sunday 6 August
John Player League
Chesterfield: Derbys v Lancs
Cardiff: Glam v Northants

Cheltenham: Glos v Notts
Portsmouth: Hants v Yorks
Folkestone: Kent v Leics
Lord's: Middx v Surrey
Weston-super-Mare: Somerset v
  Warwicks
Eastbourne: Sussex v Worcs

Wednesday 9 August
Chesterfield: Derbys v Lancs
Chelmsford: Essex v Worcs
Cheltenham: Glos v Glam
Canterbury: Kent v Warwicks
Leicester: Leics v Surrey
Lord's: Middx v Yorks
Weston-super-Mare: Somerset v
  Hants
Eastbourne: Sussex v Northants

Thursday 10 August
Cornhill Insurance Test Series
TRENT BRIDGE: ENGLAND v
NEW ZEALAND (second Test match)

Saturday 12 August
Chelmsford: Essex v Leics
Swansea: Glam v Notts
Cheltenham: Glos v Hants
Blackpool: Lancs v Surrey
Lords: Middx v Derbys
Wellingborough: Northants v
  Somerset
Worcester: Worcs v Kent
Headingley: Yorks v Sussex

Sunday 13 August
John Player League
Chelmsford: Essex v Leics
Swansea: Glam v Northants
Cheltenham: Glos v Hants
Old Trafford: Lancs v Surrey
Lord's: Middx v Derbys
Wellingborough: Northants v
  Somerset
Worcester: Worcs v Kent
Bradford: Yorks v Sussex

Wednesday 16 August
Gillette Cup (semi-finals)
*Leicester (or Edgbaston): Young
  England v New Zealand

Saturday 19 August
Derby: Derbys v Essex
Folkestone: Kent v Glos
Leicester: Leics v Lancs
Northampton: Northants v Hants
Taunton: Somerset v Middx
The Oval: Surrey v Glam
Edgbaston: Warwicks v Sussex
Worcester: Worcs v New Zealand
Scarborough: Yorks v Notts

Sunday 20 August
John Player League
Derby: Derbys v Essex
Canterbury: Kent v Glos
Leicester: Leics v Lancs
Northampton: Northants v Hants
Taunton: Somerset v Middx
The Oval: Surrey v Glam
Edgbaston: Warwicks v Sussex
Scarborough: Yorks v Notts

Wednesday 23 August
Swansea: Glam v Sussex
Bristol: Glos v Middx
Bournemouth: Hants v Warwicks
Folkestone: Kent v Essex
Trent Bridge: Notts v Leics
Worcester: Worcs v Lancs

Thursday 24 August
Cornhill Insurance Test Series
LORDS: ENGLAND v
NEW ZEALAND (third Test match)

Saturday 26 August
Ilkeston: Derbys v Notts
Southend: Essex v Surrey
Bristol: Glos v Somerset
Bournemouth: Hants v Kent
Old Trafford: Lancs v Yorks
Leicester: Leics v Northants
Hove: Sussex v Middx
Edgbaston: Warwicks v Worcs

Sunday 27 August
John Player League
Chesterfield: Derbys v Warwicks
Southend: Essex v Surrey
Bristol: Glos v Somerset
Southampton: Hants v Kent
Old Trafford: Lancs v Yorks
Leicester: Leics v Northants
Trent Bridge: Notts v Worcs
Hove: Sussex v Middx

CRICKET BOOKS OF 1977

The number of cricket books and publications produced during 1977 sets a new record, if not in volume, in overall price and possibly, both. £200 would just about have bought the lot, which ranged from the world's largest seller – *The Playfair Cricket Annual* at 60p – to *A Bibliography of Cricket* at £32. The *Bibliography* is a monumental work of immense value to collectors but would be beyond the aims and price of the average cricket enthusiast for whom even £12.50 would be stretching it a bit, but it would be worth stretching in the case of David Frith's book *England Versus Australia* which is also a work of painstaking research and very considerable range. It is a pictorial history of the Test matches between England and Australia since 1877 with forewords by Sir Donald Bradman and Sir Leonard Hutton. Many of the photographs are being reproduced for the first time and the whole subject is beautifully presented; it is, unquestionably, an exceptional book, and it could be an even more valuable asset than some three of the others.

A reviewer's brief is to state fact and not to allow personal likes and dislikes to enter into his mind, but I think I can incorporate both aspects in the case of *Arlott and Trueman on Cricket*, a splendid book edited by Gilbert Phelps, a novelist, literary critic, historian, and at one time a BBC producer. Arlott and Trueman have formed a fascinating combination on radio – their voices are known to millions –

and in a subsequent television series. The book is divided into three parts: a historical review of the game by John Arlott; an anthology edited by Gilbert Phelps, and 'Players of My Time' by Fred Trueman. There is enough of absorbing interest to satisfy the most avid collector of what is best in cricket. It is profusely illustrated both with black and white and colour.

Lovers of the writings of Neville Cardus will relish *Cardus on Cricket*, a selection from the cricket writings of Sir Neville Cardus, chosen and introduced by Sir Rupert Hart-Davis, which was first published in 1949. Cardus was unique; we shall never see his like again, and his was the sort of writing that you could read and re-read just as you would never tire of seeing a Gilbert and Sullivan operetta time and time again.

Arlott & Trueman on Cricket Edited by *Gilbert Phelps* (BBC) £4.75

Ashes 77 *Greg Chappell & David Frith* (Angus & Robertson) £4.95

Bats In The Pavilion *Michael Parkinson* (Stanley Paul) £3.25

Bibliography of Cricket Compiled by *E. W. Padwick* (The Library Association) £32.00

Cardus on Cricket *Neville Cardus* (Souvenir Press) specially bound limited edition £20.00, ordinary edition £5.50.

Come In No. 3 *David Steele* (Pelham) £4.50

Cricket Addict's Archive Edited by *Benny Green* (Elm Tree Books) £5.50

Cricket In Our Blood *Ian Chappell* (Stanley Paul) £3.95

Cricket's Great Characters *Gordon Ross* (limited edition of 300 copies, each numbered and signed. Gordon Ross at The Cricketer. Price includes postage & packing) £6.40

Encyclopedia of Cricket, 6th Edition *Maurice Golesworthy* (Robert Hale) £4.95

England Versus Australia *David Frith* (Lutterworth Press) £12.50

Follow On *E. W. Swanton* (Collins) £6.25

Great Collectors of the Past *Irving Rosenwater* (limited edition of 200 copies each numbered and signed.) The Cricketer. Price includes postage and packing) £10.30

100 Years of Test Cricket *David Foster & Peter Arnold* (Hamlyn) £2.50

I Declare *Mike Denness* (Arthur Barker) £4.50

MCC in India 1976–77 *Christopher Martin-Jenkins* (Macdonald & Jane's) £4.95

My Dear Victorious Stod *David Frith* (Lutterworth Press) £4.50

One Day Cricket *Jim Laker* (Batsford) £3.95

Spinner's Yarn *Ian Peebles* (Collins) £4.95

Test Match Cricket *Tony Greig* (Hamlyn) £3.95

Village Cricket Match *John Parker* (Weidenfeld & Nicholson) £3.65

This list is not intended as being fully comprehensive of every cricket title published in 1977, and, in any event, includes only hard-bound books.